P9-AGC-724

Qualitative Communication Research Methods

SECOND EDITION

Qualitative Communication Research Methods

SECOND EDITION

Thomas R. Lindlof
University of Kentucky

Bryan C. Taylor
University of Colorado, Boulder

SAGE Publications
International Educational and Professional Publisher
Thousand Oaks ▪ London ▪ New Delhi

For information:

Sage Publications, Inc.
2455 Teller Road
Thousand Oaks, California 91320
E-mail: order@sagepub.com

Sage Publications Ltd.
6 Bonhill Street
London EC2A 4PU
United Kingdom

Sage Publications India Pvt. Ltd.
M-32 Market
Greater Kailash I
New Delhi 110 048 India

Printed in the United States of America

Library of Congress Cataloging-in-Publication Data

Lindlof, Thomas R.
  Qualitative communication research methods.— 2nd ed. /
Thomas R.Lindlof and Bryan C. Taylor.
     p. cm.
  Rev. ed. of: Qualitative communication research methods /
Thomas R. Lindlof. c1995.
  Includes bibliographical references and index.
  ISBN 0-7619-2493-0 (c) — ISBN 0-7619-2494-9 (p)
   1. Communication—Research—Methodology. I. Taylor, Bryan C.
II. Title.
  P91.3 .L56 2002
  302.2´072—dc21

                        2002005205

06 07 08 09 10 9 8 7 6 5

Acquiring Editor:	Margaret H. Seawell
Editorial Assistant:	Alicia Carter
Production Editor:	Claudia A. Hoffman
Copy Editor:	Jamie Robinson

Contents

Preface

The first edition of this book was written at a time when qualitative communication research was evolving out of a vigorous adolescence. The "interpretive turn" of the 1980s and early 1990s opened up the study of cultures, meanings, symbolic performances, and social practices. Many of us were both excited with the new possibilities and unsure about who we would become in the profession. The lack of methodology texts written for our discipline was one reason for this quest for identity. Nearly all of the books we read in order to learn about qualitative research were written by sociologists and anthropologists. There was nothing in particular wrong with these texts. In fact, most were good at answering the questions we had about doing research. However, many of us continued to wonder how these volumes related to—or could be translated into—issues of research practice specific to *communication*. *Qualitative Communication Research Methods* originated in that question.

This second edition reflects a more confident community of scholars. As discussed in Chapter 1, Communication (hereafter capitalized when it refers to the discipline) has become large and diverse, and qualitative inquiry is a very important part of this pluralism. This does not mean that all questions about qualitative research and its role in the discipline have been resolved— far from it. In nearly every chapter of this book, you will see that aspects of what and how qualitative researchers study are still unsettled, and some-times even controversial. Yet even in the midst of differences of opinion, there remains solid consensus about our interest area: how people engage in symbolic performances to create the meaningful worlds in which they live.

In the rest of this volume, we build systematically on this foundation. Our logic is to chart the journey undertaken by the qualitative researcher from conceptualizing to completing a study. In this process, we have made some strategic choices, partly out of necessity, partly out of preference. One choice involves a bias toward field methods. We have chosen not to treat the specific methodologies associated with discourse analysis, because of their complexity. We refer the reader instead to the many excellent discussions available elsewhere (Cameron, 2001; Titscher, Meyer, Wodak, & Vetter, 2000). The qualitative researcher developed here is one who employs a full range of methods and techniques. Chief among the methods explored in this volume are participant observation and interviewing, but visual media, document analysis, research diaries, and other tools are also treated here. We know that some readers ultimately wish to use only some of these methods, based on their situational needs. Advanced readers may, as a result, wish to read in this book selectively, but we believe that novices will benefit from reading the entire book. When the moment of necessity arises, it's better to have too many resources than not enough.

Let us introduce you to the changes and new features in this second edition of *Qualitative Communication Research Methods*. We begin with a brief discussion of changes to the book as a whole, and then we explain how each chapter has been revised and updated.

The new edition is characterized by a more *accessible writing style*. We strived to make the book clear in its discussion of concepts and methods, as well as engaging and reader-friendly in tone. At the same time, its intellectual integrity remains strong. You will encounter the complex issues—methodological, conceptual, ethical, and political—that researchers face when they practice qualitative research. In short, we believe that you will find the second edition to be challenging, informative, and interesting to read.

The second edition incorporates *fresh and expanded examples* of research design, method, field relations, data analysis, textual strategy, and so forth. We have drawn upon dozens of examples from the most recent work of scholars across the subfields of Communication and allied disciplines. (Despite our emphasis on Communication scholarship, we do not ignore contributions from other disciplines when they have something of value to say about research practice.) We include as well some examples from graduate students whose work we've supervised or otherwise encountered. These student examples may help novices see how others have dealt with common dilemmas or problems in conducting field studies. We also include new examples of original research materials—for example, research proposals, informed consent forms, fieldnotes, interview guides, focus group scripts, interview transcriptions, texts from data coding, and so on. These materials exemplify good research practice and can be instructive about how to make better choices.

Placed at the end of several chapters are *exercises* designed for applying or "trying out" what you have learned. We have, for the most part, added exercises to those chapters that are dedicated to the practical matters of performing qualitative research. Thus, you will find exercises related to initial

(Chapter 3) and advanced (Chapter 4) tasks in designing a study, using participant observation and writing fieldnotes (Chapter 5), interviewing and using transcriptions (Chapter 6), data analysis (Chapter 7), and writing (Chapter 9). Because it is a relatively new field, however, and readers may benefit from a warm-up before diving in, we have also provided exercises in the new Chapter 8 that are related to the study of computer-mediated communication. And because Chapters 1 and 2 primarily contain epistemological orientation and theoretical surveys, they do not contain exercises.

Now we turn to changes in the individual chapters. The most obvious change to those familiar with the first edition is the new Chapter 8, Qualitative Research and Computer-Mediated Communication. Cyberspace communication has become a site of burgeoning research activity. This new chapter is justified on the basis of the many issues involved in moving qualitative inquiry into virtual settings. We first unpack some assumptions about the differences between virtual-based social action and personal presence, and discuss the cultural and historical backgrounds of the Internet and other technologies of distributed intelligence. We then introduce new uses for familiar methods (e.g., participant observation, interviewing) in computer-mediated scenes. The issues of data analysis, research ethics, and the growth of knowledge, we will argue, all take on new accents and challenges in the virtual environment.

Chapter 1, Introduction to Qualitative Communication Research, updates the first edition's survey of qualitative study in Communication. This survey now includes a useful set of distinctions between positivist, post-positivist, and interpretivist paradigms of research. This chapter's most important new feature is its overview of how qualitative research is conducted in nine subfields in Communication: interpersonal communication, language and social interaction, group communication, organizational communication, intercultural communication, media and cultural studies, performance studies, applied communication, and health communication. You will learn about the theories, topics, and methods that researchers in each subfield tend to gravitate toward.

Chapter 2, Theoretical Traditions and Qualitative Communication Research, explores the theoretical traditions that energize qualitative communication research. New to this edition are in-depth treatments of approaches that have become very important in the last two decades: critical theory, postmodernism, feminism, and cultural studies. The sections on the traditions of phenomenology, ethnomethodology, symbolic interactionism, and ethnography of communication have been fully updated as well. In this chapter, you will see how communication can be viewed through different theoretical lenses and how this makes a difference in the research questions one asks.

Chapter 3, Design I: Planning, introduces the first steps of carrying out a research project: developing an idea for a study, studying possible research sites, and writing a research proposal. For the second edition, we moved the section on the protection of human subjects into this chapter because such considerations are often worked out in tandem with the research proposal. Other major improvements in this edition include more detailed discussions of the growth of research ideas; the concepts of field, site, and scene; and the construction of research proposals.

Chapter 4, Design II: Getting Started, moves the reader into the action frame of a study. The basic framework of this chapter has stayed the same: It includes negotiating access, negotiating relationships with participants in the field, developing a research perspective, utilizing exploratory methods, and sampling. The presentation is now better organized, and new, updated examples show you many of the key options and strategies for getting started in field settings.

Chapter 5, Observing, Learning, and Reporting, focuses on the role of participant observation over the course of a study. Much of the structure from the first edition remains, but it has been enriched with new examples and alternate schemes. By bringing the discussion of writing fieldnotes and journals into this chapter, we create an integrated view of how participant-observers observe, learn, and report. The second edition also expands on ethnicity and gender as resources for entering and operating in a scene. This chapter will help you understand what it means to live as an intuitive, spontaneous, fallible, learning technology.

Chapter 6, Asking, Listening, and Telling, discusses the different forms and practices of qualitative interviewing. Among the changes to this chapter are the addition of more detailed treatments of the five major interview types—especially focus group and narrative interviews—and a fully revised section showing how questions are designed and used in the dynamic context of an interview. New sections on the use of tape recorders and doing interviews by telephone have been added. We also moved interview transcription into this chapter, so as to bundle interviewing practice with the techniques and issues of transcribing. In all, this chapter demonstrates how you can use interviews flexibly in nearly any type of field study.

Chapter 7, Qualitative Analysis and Interpretation, speaks to researchers who have compiled sufficient data and who are ready to progress to coding, analysis, and interpretation. There are two key changes to this chapter: First, we give more attention to the coding of data and show how this process unfolds through several examples. Second, we examine the tools of analysis. A significant addition to this volume is the discussion of computer-assisted, as well as manual, strategies for data analysis. With respect to data analysis software, we point out both its primary advantages and some issues that have been raised about its use. We also review the forms and standards of validation that guide the evaluation of qualitative research.

Chapter 9, Authoring and Writing, concludes the volume by discussing one of the most controversial realms of qualitative research: writing research narratives. We treat practical matters such as organization, style, and voice, and return to the opening discussion of epistemology by examining a passionate debate about the role of representation in creating knowledge about communication. We also look deeply inside the rhetorical machinery of qualitative writing through two exemplars—one that is relatively traditional in style, organization, and voice and one that is more experimental. In the final pages, we offer our thoughts about the state of the Communication discipline and the future of qualitative inquiry.

The changes for this edition were prompted by comments and ideas that came to us from several sources. We would like to acknowledge the help of several anonymous reviewers who provided reactions to the first edition and suggestions for improvement. We have benefited over the years from what our graduate students have said (or written) about the book as a teaching text. Tom Lindlof would especially like to thank the students in his Spring 1998 seminar on qualitative research, whose feedback to Sage Publications provided us with a detailed students'-eye view of the first edition. Bryan Taylor wishes to thank Jim Anderson and Maureen Mathison of the Department of Communication, University of Utah, for several helpful conversations during the Fall 2001 semester. We thank Jennifer Thackaberry of the Department of Communication, Purdue University, for her suggestions and comments about computer-aided data analysis in Chapter 7, several of which were used in that section. We also heard from many of our colleagues who have used the book in their classes. Maybe we heard a suspiciously disproportionate share of kudos and compliments from them, but we also received some good, honest advice. Finally, we want to acknowledge ourselves. As the first edition's sole author, Lindlof was aware of many of its imperfections and looked forward to the opportunity to create a better book. As one who joined this second edition venture as coauthor, Taylor contributed his own ideas about what would make the book more useful to the discipline. It did not take us long to realize that our visions for the book coincided to a remarkable degree, and we hope that we have anticipated many of your needs.

Throughout this process, Margaret Seawell, Executive Editor of Sage Publications, was a wonderful advocate for us and the project. Our work was eased greatly by her wise counsel about matters large and small, and by the support provided by Sage for our research. Specifically, we thank Jamie Robinson for her smart and sharp-eyed copyediting.

A final word about tone. As a matter of preference, qualitative researchers seek immediacy over detachment, and dialogue over assertion. Those goals, of course, cannot be fully realized in a book format. Nonetheless, we will try to liven up your journey by sharing some of our experiences as qualitative researchers. These comments will be brief and occasional, and they are intended to show how those experiences have helped us to arrive at the arguments we make.

By way of introduction, then, Taylor (hereafter, Bryan) is the proverbial young man who went west (from New England), stayed (mostly), and now has the privilege of working in Boulder, Colorado, where the sun shines 300 days a year and you cannot throw a rock without hitting an SUV, a therapist, or a double-latte. His primary qualitative research site, however, involves the shadowy realm of communication in—and about—nuclear weapons organizations. When possible, he escapes this grim—but compelling—topic by drinking excessive amounts of coffee, riding a bicycle up and down mountains, listening to jazz music, and reading crime fiction. He is, for better and worse, an academic lifer.

Lindlof (hereafter, Tom) is an émigré from Texas who now has the distinct honor of working in Lexington, Kentucky, one of the test-market capitals of the American heartland. He is passionate, among other things, about music (listening to it, that is), the First Amendment, yard sales, his wife and best friend Joanne, and long, long road trips. He would be willing to ride a bicycle up and down a mountain with Bryan as long as the gradient is no greater than 2˚. He will read anything written by Don DeLillo or Nick Tosches, and he counts himself among the die-hard fans of Lotion, Miles Davis, and Professor Irwin Corey. He is not yet an academic lifer.

For those of you who like to stay in your seats after the movie is over and read the credits—Bryan was responsible for revising the material from the first edition that corresponds with the current Chapters 1, 2, 5, and 9. He also wrote the new Chapter 8. Tom was responsible for revising Chapters 3, 4, 6, and 7 from the first edition. Rest assured that Tom and Bryan read each other's chapters, consulted closely throughout the process of writing, and each contributed material to the other's chapters. All in all, it was a splendid partnership.

Welcome to the second edition of *Qualitative Communication Research Methods*. We're glad you're coming along for the ride.

1

Introduction to Qualitative Communication Research

Two Researchers, Two Scenes of Research

READING COMMUNITY IN A POST OFFICE

The people of Burgin, Kentucky, and surrounding countryside pick up their mail, buy their stamps, and send off their parcels at the Burgin post office. But much more goes on there than just post office business. When something unusual or important happens around Burgin, discussion of it usually surfaces there. While Joel was finishing the last three weeks of his study, rumors were flying about a "satanic cult" in the area. A lot of high school students were convinced that some young person in the county was about to be murdered by this group, and many adults thought it was more than just a hoax. Almost every person who came to the post office had something to say about the story. These conversations would overlap as one person left and another came in.

At one point, two of the regular patrons were talking about this "stuff" when Bill arrived. Without telling him what they were talking about, they asked Bill what he knew. He proceeded to tell them about police officers, equipped with K-9s, who had been searching the railroad tracks in front of his house on the previous evening. They were looking for evidence of the cult, Bill reported, but "didn't find a thing." On a previous night, however, some satanic paraphernalia had evidently been discovered in a railroad underpass just outside Burgin.

In his final visits to the post office, Joel didn't hear whether or not this alleged find was ever confirmed; in fact, the cult speculations tailed off altogether. For a while, post office conversation returned to the usual concerns—the weather, tobacco farming, and the national news. Then one day a woman came in and announced that a member of her family had returned from fighting one of the regional forest fires that were raging that fall. A discussion ensued about marijuana growers being responsible for setting the fires.

THE (DIS-)ORGANIZED UNIVERSITY

The state had just enacted sweeping reform of its public school system, and a massive tax increase had been legislated to pay for it. There was much excitement, and expectations were running high. Educators recognized that these new reforms would be watched closely, both by political insiders who had staked their reputations on success and by those outside the state who had hailed the reforms as a model. It was now up to the educational establishment to make the reforms work, and nowhere was this felt more keenly than at the College of Education at the state's leading research university.

Recently, Monica had been hired by the college to improve its public relations. She saw this situation as an opportunity to study how it "tells its story" of research and training activities to its external stakeholders. In search of data, she began to scrutinize the flow of information that passed through her work life. Fund-raising materials, video features, bulletins, pamphlets, press releases, and newsletters all became pieces of an organizational puzzle. In trying to assemble these pieces, however, Monica increasingly found the meetings and other events she attended to be unsettling. Officially, she was there as a publicity writer, but she was also trying to understand the ambiguous actions of ambivalent people who sometimes failed, and only occasionally succeeded, in their roles.

One such scene involved the college's relationship with the media. The university's public relations officials seemed to define "news" as whatever was timely, or could be made to appear so. They often complained that they didn't hear from the college about potential stories "in time to do anything about them." They also seemed to prefer receiving announcements or reporting on media events—the splashier the better. At a small gala hosted by the college, for example, one PR official said to a college faculty member, "Now this is worth more than all those little stories you keep sending us." On another occasion, a faculty member spoke ruefully about typical coverage of college events: "You have to wait until the provost or the president of the university shows up, and then they'll get the credit, as usual. You never hear about the people who really do the work." And later, the education reporter for the local newspaper told Monica that academics used excessive "inside jargon" that he thought muddied issues instead of clarifying them.

Monica found the people she worked with in the college to be remarkable achievers. She concluded in her report that educators and media professionals could collaborate more effectively if they better understood each other's missions. Still, at the end of the study she found it hard not to be a little saddened by it all.

These are glimpses of qualitative communication researchers at work. Joel and Monica were in fact graduate students learning the craft of a particular methodology known as *ethnography*. Their stories reveal much about how research questions develop, how researchers decide what is significant to observe and report, and how they become implicated in the process of investigation. Both Joel and Monica saw something in their immediate surroundings as an opportunity for study.

Joel resided with his family in Burgin, and noticed that most of the community's citizens participated in informal interactions at a particular site, the local post office. His previous experiences living in villages overseas, and in American towns, had sensitized him to the significance of these performances. This familiarity helped him to understand pretty quickly what was happening: In exploring mysteries in and potential threats to their community, residents indirectly reaffirmed their common beliefs (e.g., in the range of acceptable religious practices) and commitments (e.g., to share information). At the same time, Joel had to develop a level of detachment that balanced this familiarity and allowed him to treat the interactions he witnessed as evidence of particular communication practices. As the study progressed, Joel developed analytic themes about community building, the mediation of news, and the functions of "entertainment" and "being neighborly" in a small town.

Monica had worked as a professional writer before she took the public relations job with the College of Education. She knew firsthand the tensions that can exist between creative workers and the corporate managers and clients who use (and abuse) their work. Like Joel, Monica experienced déjà vu at her research site. She recognized, and probably empathized with, problems faced by the college's administrators, faculty, and staff. As she developed her study, the routine elements of her job became evidence of something more abstract—an organizational culture. As the ending of the passage above indicates, this transformation had some emotional cost: Having conceptualized the problem, Monica confronted her own limitations in solving it.

What about the methods chosen by these researchers? Joel and Monica both struggled to reconcile the competing demands of participation and detachment in their sites, but there are also important differences between their cases. Joel's primary approach to data collection involved *participant observation*. As the term implies, researchers using this method become participating members of an existing culture, group, or setting, and typically adopt roles that other members recognize as appropriate and non-threatening. By participating in the activities of the group, researchers gain insight into the obligations, constraints, motivations, and emotions that members experience as they complete everyday actions. Effective participation—in the sense of being able to act, think, and feel as a true participant would—is thought by many qualitative researchers to be a prerequisite to making effective claims about communication. Stated a little differently, observing without participating may inhibit researchers' ability to adequately understand the complex, lived experience of human beings. Such understanding is one of the defining goals of qualitative research.

In practical terms, the depth and quality of participation can vary widely. As we will explore in Chapter 5, the degree to which an individual is known as a researcher to group members can differ from setting to setting. In Joel's case, his participant status derived from being a resident (but not a native) of Burgin, the pastor of a Burgin church, a post office patron, and a graduate student taken to "hanging around" that post office in order to do a study. Even in this small community, it is unlikely that all of the people with whom Joel interacted were aware of all these levels of his participation, particularly the last one. As an umbrella term covering several activities that are uniquely combined to meet situational needs, then, *participant observation* is not a single method (Gans, 1999). Instead, it is a strategy of reflexive learning. Its success is dependent on researchers using—and reflecting on—their cognitive and emotional responses to other human beings (Gans, 1982). Only by living an experience—and then describing and interpreting its significance—can a qualitative researcher make that experience useful to a reader.

In addition to observing others in her work as a staff member, Monica conducted *interviews*. When used in qualitative research, interviews go by several names, each with a slightly different shade of meaning: There are *in-depth, unstructured, semi-structured, intensive, collaborative*, and *ethnographic* interviews. Generally, these interviews resemble conversations between equals who systematically explore topics of mutual interest. Most of what is said and meant emerges through collaborative interaction. Although the researcher often goes into the interview wanting to cover certain areas, relatively little structure is imposed (e.g., questions are usually open-ended). Qualitative researchers interview people to understand their perspectives on a scene, to retrieve their experiences from the past, to gain expert insight or information, to obtain descriptions of events that are normally unavailable for observation, to foster trust, to understand sensitive relationships, and to create a record of discourse that can subsequently be analyzed. As we explore in Chapter 6, more specialized forms of interviewing such as the *life history* and *focus group* are also available to fit particular needs.

In completing her study, Monica also collected and analyzed *documents* and other *artifacts*. This was because her study examined stories about the college disseminated by the mass media, as well as materials circulated inside the college (e.g., announcements, memoranda, policy statements, minutes of meetings, research reports, and so on). This kind of analysis of artifacts (Webb, Campbell, Schwartz, & Sechrest, 1966) is typically used in qualitative research to support interviewing and participant observation. In recent years, however, communication scholars have argued that material culture (clothing, architecture, personal memorabilia, and the like) can function as a primary means of symbolic expression and should be "read" accordingly (Goodall, 1991). Moreover, visual media—photographs or video shot by the researcher or group members—can be used to document behavior or capture members' perspectives on action (LeBaron & Streeck, 1997).

These techniques of participant observation, interviewing, and document and artifact analysis are central concerns in this volume because they permit the kind of flexibility that is necessary for successful qualitative research. While we seek to provide thorough treatment and good advice in these matters, it is ultimately the researcher who decides how and when to utilize these methods. Qualitative inquiry is a uniquely personal and involved activity. If we hope to understand how people choose to express themselves in everyday life, we must come to terms with our own reasons for studying them and with the intellectual traditions that are embedded in these methods. Understanding these elements ensures better decisions.

These snapshots of Monica's and Joel's experiences "in the field" convey a sense of the fundamental questions that animate qualitative inquiry: What is going on here? What is the communicative action that is being performed? How do they do it? How does it change over time? Who are "they" (to themselves, and to each other)? Who are "we" to them? How do they evaluate what they do? What does it mean to them? How do they interpret what it means to others? How should we describe and interpret how they act, what they tell us they know, and how they justify their actions? How is this knowledge useful to our agendas as communication scholars and professionals?

For the qualitative researcher, humans infuse their actions—and the worlds that result—with meaning. We are, at root, trying to make sense and get by. In this view, meaning is not a mere accessory to behavior.

Rather, it saturates the performance of social action—from our imagination of possibilities to our reflection on accomplishments. In a world without meaning we would not make choices, because the very concept of choice would not be available to us. Our perceived choices are influenced—but not determined—by a variety of intersecting genetic, biological, and material conditions (Anderson, 1991). We can choose, in other words, but we cannot choose our choices. Out of this mix of influences, cultures develop unique rules and resources that guide members in how to act. Cultures embed that knowledge in their members through the formal and informal practices of socialization that begin in childhood and continue well on through adulthood. In using this knowledge, we construct the self and the other in ways that are culturally patterned. But this does not mean that our actions are uniform. Even the most rigid social structures contain pockets of ambiguity and opportunity in which members improvise and innovate, responding to changing conditions, leveraging the new from the old. In this process, humans conceptualize their actions at different levels of abstraction (e.g., as "common knowledge" vs. "theory").

These, then, are some of the assumptions that unite an often bewildering variety of research styles organized under the banner of qualitative research. They express what is arguably the defining commitment of the Communication discipline: to study human symbolic action in the various contexts of its performance (Cronkhite, 1986). We signal here our root assumption that qualitative research in communication involves *the performances and practices of human communication*. By *performances*, we mean expressive communication whose immediacy and skill transcend the status of "messages" as transparent vehicles of information (Bauman, 1986). Performances are local and unique interaction events. Their execution is collaborative and their significance is negotiable. They emerge in a productive tension between participants' expectations for good form and content in particular situations and the unpredictable human powers of creativity and improvisation. *Practices*, however, form the generic, routine, and socially monitored and enforced dimension of communicative acts. They are comparatively abstract and standardized. They form the coherent action that is indexed by the material features of performance, and they are understood by participants as an expression of motive and interest. When performances are ambiguous (e.g., in clichéd action-film dialogue: "Was that a *threat?*"), practices are invoked as a way of sorting things out (e.g., "No. It's a *promise.*"). While individuals author performances, their status as exemplars of practice makes them property of the group. Performances and practices, then, constitute the textures of our everyday life experiences. Through them we enact the meanings of our relationships in various contexts. Virtually any act of communication can be studied as a kind of performance, which can in turn be viewed as a skillful variation on a practice. Taken together, these elements make the social construction of meaning virtually indistinguishable from "communication."

In this chapter, we provide a brief review of the intellectual foundations of this assumption. Although it may not be immediately apparent to a novice, research methods form the practical technologies of larger systems of belief about the nature of reality (*ontology*) and about how that reality may be known (*epistemology*). Although these beliefs are often only implicit in specific projects, they form an important code by which communication researchers assert their work—and recognize the work of others—as the product of a particular tradition. This recognition generates a cascade of expectations about the form and content of that research. When these expectations are satisfied (or transformed), research is judged to be legitimate and authoritative. It becomes the credible engine of disciplinary evolution. Researchers who ignore the history and philosophy of science use methods at their peril. They usually experience frustration and produce confused, unsatisfactory results.

To avoid those outcomes, we proceed by contrasting three paradigms that have shaped the development of qualitative research. We also distinguish between some key terms that are used to characterize qualitative research. After that, we review the history of qualitative research within Communication, and assess its impact in several subfields. We conclude this chapter by outlining the remainder of the volume.

Postivism, Post-Positivism, and Interpretivism: A Brief History and Survey of Qualitative Communication Research

In 1975, communication historian and theorist James Carey outlined a vision for qualitative research influenced by the tradition of American cultural studies:

> To seize upon the interpretations people place on existence and to systematize them so they are more readily available to us. This is a process of making large claims from small matters: studying particular rituals, poems, plays, conversations, songs, dances, theories, and myths and gingerly reaching out to the full relations within a culture or a total way of life. (p. 190)

At the time of its publication, Carey's vision opposed a long history in which communication research (particularly the social-scientific variety) was dominated by *positivist* assumptions. These assumptions have been alternately demonized, caricatured, and debated in a variety of forums by speakers using distinct yet related labels (e.g., *objectivist, empiricist,* and *rationalist*). At the center of this commotion lie the following interrelated claims (Anderson, 1987, 1996a; Lincoln & Guba, 1985):

- Reality is singular, a priori, and objective (i.e., independent of the knower).
- True knowledge arises from observation of empirical phenomena that form the tangible, material traces of essential reality.
- The concepts and methods of natural science are—with some necessary modification—a legitimate model for the conduct of social science.
- Essential reality constrains the range of possible knowledge claims. Those claims should aspire to exacting correspondence with reality.
- In observation, the complexity of phenomena should be reduced to clarify their underlying structures and isolate the existence of (and relationships between) specific elements.
- The logic of measurement and quantification (e.g., in the use of statistics) is best for formalizing empirical observations (e.g., as amount, frequency, or rate).
- Researchers should search for, and explain, mechanisms of cause and effect.
- Human behavior is determined by such mechanisms. Researchers should facilitate the prediction and control of that behavior.
- Researchers should aggregate subjects (e.g., as population samples) based on their possession of a specified trait, attribute, or performance.
- Theory is best developed deductively and incrementally. Researchers should proceed by systematically proposing and testing explanations based on existing, verified knowledge. Hypotheses inviting confidence are to be added to theory.

In the field of Communication, as in most social sciences, the historical impact of positivism has been manifested in a variety of institutional practices. Principally, these have included a search for external and psychological causes for communication "behavior," a focus on predicting and controlling that behavior, and the use of objective, quantitative methods in artificial settings (e.g., experiments and surveys). There are numerous examples that could be cited here; research on media "effects" has been especially prominent and resilient. Although positivism is powerful—Anderson (1996) estimates that it is reflected in over one-half of all published communication research—its hegemony has never been total or simple. Communication researchers affiliated with positivism have never been completely unified about the appropriate goals and strategies of research. Further, as a relatively young and interdisciplinary field, Communication has tended toward pluralism and diversity (although this tendency has not been evenly distributed across subfields; Bochner & Eisenberg, 1985; Pearce, 1985; Peters, 1986).

Finally, communication researchers responded in various ways to the critiques of positivism mounted in the postwar era that emerged from innovations in the natural and social sciences. These critiques challenged a number of positivism's core premises and practices, including the conflation of the discovery of phenomena with the verification of explanations; the premise of "facts" generated independently from theory, values, or terminology; artificial constraints imposed on the goals and purposes of research; and ethical dilemmas arising from a commitment to detachment in the face of human evil and suffering. As a result, many communication researchers affiliated with a *post-positivist* paradigm based on the following premises (Guba & Lincoln, 1994; Miller, 2002, pp. 32-45):

- The physical and social worlds are composed of complex phenomena that exist independently of individual perception (a "realist" ontology). Human beliefs about these phenomena, however, are inevitably multiple, partial, approximate, and imperfect.
- Humans interact in patterned ways. Those patterns "reify" beliefs about phenomena, and infuse them with consequence.
- Knowledge is best created by a search for causal explanations for observed patterns of phenomena. Causes are assumed to be multiple, interactive, and evolving.
- While absolute truth and value-free inquiry are unattainable, the reduction of bias in research (e.g., through peer review) is both attainable and desirable.
- Discovery and verification are equally valued as logics of research.
- The "emic" intentionality and experience of social actors should be preserved in explanations.
- Research conducted in natural settings is useful for documenting contextual influences on social action.
- Both quantitative and qualitative methods are legitimate resources for conducting research.
- The use of multiple methods enhances explanations of complex phenomena (e.g., by "triangulating"—comparing and contrasting—their outcomes).
- Qualitative methods are valued for their contribution to highly structured (and potentially quantitative) analysis. The use of statistics by qualitative researchers, however, is more likely to be basic and descriptive (e.g., frequency counts) than complex and inferential (e.g., regression analysis).

Again, while examples abound, one that is notable includes a research program organized by Brenda Dervin and her associates (Dervin & Clark, 1999) devoted to "sense-making methodology." Researchers in this program utilize both qualitative and quantitative methods to study fundamental practices of expression and interpretation in diverse contexts, such as public communication campaigns, health communication, and religious communication.

A few words are in order about this disciplinary sea change. First, we should emphasize that it is not total or universal. Some elements of classical positivism—such as a belief in value-free inquiry—persist in a qualified, modified form. And although certain practices of objectivist research—especially the uses of variable-analytic designs and probability statistics—have been challenged (Bochner, 1985; Craig, 1989), they are not defunct. Funding institutions, for example, continue to prefer positivist and post-positivist research formats, thereby sustaining the authority and legitimacy of those formats. In this sense, the potent residues of positivism circulate with the emergent phenomena of interpretive and critical inquiry. This condition is messy, but it is rarely boring, and it forces us to be reflective and explicit about our intellectual commitments.

Second, professional and geopolitical contexts mediate the local occurrences of post-positivism. There may be no bigger tent in the academic world than the field of Communication, which serves as a master-professional identity for multiple, component subfields and interdisciplinary affiliations. And although it is an international field, as one travels between institutions within a single country (where some departments are dominated by humanistic traditions, and others by social-scientific traditions), or between countries, there is both variation and similarity in what counts as "communication studies." Canadian scholars, for example, are primarily oriented toward media studies, and are rarely accountable to U.S. speech-communication traditions. In Australia, Communication has only recently been formalized as a field, and its curriculum draws uniquely on American traditions and British cultural studies to serve both critical/theoretical and professional/applied interests in a postcolonial cultural context (Putnis, 1993). These examples indicate that it is best to consider occurrences of post-positivism in Communication as diverse, local events shaped as much by intellectual history and institutional politics as by a consistent disciplinary identity. If post-positivism is like a language, it has many dialects. The wise traveler develops a sharp ear.

Finally, we note an aftermath of specialization and fragmentation. Specifically, there is a growing sense that discipline-wide agreement about the goals and epistemology of a communication science may not be achievable. Communication research, whose topical ambition (all symbolic performances, anywhere, anytime) is nothing short of astounding, now accommodates many different theoretical traditions and styles of inquiry. These traditions cohabit in various states of tension and harmony. Some accept this situation reluctantly, others welcome it, but all communication researchers struggle to maintain a comprehensive understanding of, and adequate *lingua franca* for, the discipline. Gone forever, it seems, are the days when communication "generalist" was a viable career path, and one could proclaim "the state of the field" without risking the appearance of being narrowly read or self-serving. In reviewing recently published qualitative research for this volume, we have been struck by the increasing centrifugal force of these influences. Perhaps the best that researchers can do under these conditions is to keep up with developments in their major areas of interest, while monitoring the seismic tremors in outlying areas as opportunities for innovation and collaboration (Van Maanen, 1995a).

In regard to qualitative methods, this change occurred largely through the persuasiveness of argument. That is, the pluralism we now see came about by a process of passionate debate among communication scholars. The success of qualitative researchers in this process hinged on two elements. The first was their advocacy of the *interpretive paradigm*, a strategic punctuation of metatheory that overlaps with related accounts such as the *naturalistic paradigm* (Anderson, 1987; Denzin & Lincoln, 2000; Guba & Lincoln, 1994) and *hermeneutic empiricism* (Anderson, 1996a, 1996b). As an ontological and epistemological foundation for qualitative methods, the interpretive paradigm developed from the convergence of several 19th- and 20th-century intellectual traditions, including German idealist philosophy, phenomenology, hermeneutic philosophy, and American pragmatism (C. Taylor, 1977). We will explore these traditions further in Chapter 2, but for now we can identify the following commitments of interpretive (see Cheney, 2000):

- The "human sciences" concerned with experience and social action are inherently different from the natural sciences.
- Realities are plural, simultaneous, and local phenomena.
- Realities are socially constructed by and between human beings in their expressive and interpretive practices. Meaningful realities are emergent, collaborative, and symbolic in nature.
- Research should privilege deep understanding of human actions, motives, and feelings. It should illuminate how cultural symbol systems are used to attribute meaning to existence and activity.
- Knowledge of social realities emerges from the interdependence of researcher and researched. The researcher does not use methodological instruments. The researcher *is* the instrument.
- Knowledge claims are inevitably positioned and partial. As a result, researchers should reflect on and account for the contingencies of their claims.
- True knowledge is gained through prolonged immersion and extensive dialogue practiced in actual social settings. Intimate familiarity with the performance and significance of social practices (e.g., involving membership) is a requirement for adequate explanation.
- Evidence for claims about social action should be recorded and expressed using verbal and narrative means.
- Knowledge claims should preserve the subjective experience and motivations of social actors in their meaningful performances.
- Theory should be developed inductively through the iterative testing of tentative explanations against the experience of ongoing interaction with group members.

Theory should create increasingly "expansionistic" understandings of phenomena within and across the sites of their performance.
- Researchers should continuously reflect on the ethical and political dimensions of their research activities.

During the 1980s, one forum for advocacy involved the publication of several compelling "experiments" in the use of qualitative methods. These articles, special journal issues, and edited volumes helped to shape new possibilities for communication research (e.g., Benson, 1985; Dervin, Grossberg, O'Keefe, & Wartella, 1989; Gerbner, 1983). They continued to emerge during the 1990s, penetrating the remaining bastions of quantitative research (Tracy & Gallois, 1997). At their best, these exemplars demonstrated not that objectivist science and quantitative methods were *faulty* modes of inquiry but that—because they did not value the study of situated and reflexive social action—they were *insufficient* for those purposes (Deetz & Putnam, 2000; Schwandt, 1989). As they unfolded, these developments were not unique to Communication. In fact, they mirrored (or, more often, followed) similar changes in other fields. Scholars looked outside the behaviorist tradition of American communication science for fresh inspiration: to sociology for its symbolic interactionist and phenomenological traditions; to literary theory for new ideas about the relationship of readers and texts; to feminist and political theory for alternative explanations of power, agency, and social structure; to cultural studies for ways to integrate theory and method in the study of cultural communication.

There were also obstacles on the path. Until recently in the history of Communication, empirical qualitative studies were consigned to the margins of research activity and graduate training (Delia, 1987, pp. 69-73). Qualitative research was viewed by many as *soft science*, characterized by imprecise instruments, biased observations, and selective reporting of data. In addition, it appeared to practice insufficient controls against random effects (and other threats to internal validity), representative sampling, generalizability, and the falsification of hypotheses.

This is not to say that no qualitative studies were done before the late 1970s, or that a qualitative emphasis was not evident in some types of inquiry. Indeed, Wartella (1987) traces some important, although neglected, field studies of children and media (mostly comic books, radio, and movies) from the first half of this century. Nearly all of those studies, however, were conducted by sociologists and social psychologists, rather than by self-identified communication scholars. In 1984, Anderson's survey (cited in Anderson, 1987) of published ethnographies in communication journals yielded only 16 examples over the prior five years. Even if we add to this count work that appears in books and in the journals of other social scientific disciplines, and under descriptors other than ethnography, it is still true that until recently most qualitative communication research was done by a persistent few. Further, because qualitative inquiry did not immediately produce unambiguous benefits, its legitimacy was questioned.

This questioning was often directed to topics of qualitative inquiry associated with organizations, subcultures, families, groups, and individuals. These topics can be selected as much for their relevance for the researcher's inner world as for sanctioned communication theory. Some topics, such as professional-academic gender inequity, are chosen because they represent problems in the politics of communication. These topics often arouse (sometimes thinly disguised) resistance among the members of groups whose privilege is threatened by such studies (Blair, Brown, & Baxter, 1994). Other topics attract attention because of their striking—and controversial— cultural character. The topic of fan subcultures whose members use media texts to create oppositional narratives (Jenkins, 1988), for example, seems trivial to some because it concerns an esoteric practice by a small number of seemingly eccentric people. Such research might be judged irrelevant to the development of universal propositions about media effects. As an argument for textual indeterminacy and audience agency, it may also be judged political heresy in the wake of cultural tragedies, such as the 1999 Columbine High School massacre, and other spectacles, such as the appearance of a uniform-clad *Star Trek* fan in the jury pool for an Arkansas trial involving the president of the United States (Jenkins, 1996, 1999). In these moments, researchers have to swim upstream against the visceral emotion, the search for scapegoats, and the anti-fan bigotry that animate public discourse about media effects. Questions about the potential fitness of topics, then, can add to the notoriety of doing qualitative research.

Within Communication, however, this skepticism has lost much of its edge and energy since the time of Carey's essay, and sentiment appears to have swung in the other direction. In their recent survey of communication graduate programs, for example, Frey, Anderson, and Friedman (1998) found that—although its rate of offerings lagged behind those for quantitative methods and rhetorical criticism—almost half of the responding departments offered some form of instruction in qualitative methods. They judged this to be a positive indicator for such a recent arrival. Although the definitive study of growth remains to be done, our own experience—and the talk among our colleagues—is that cultural and interpretive research are claiming an increasing share of disciplinary resources. One significant indicator of this trend is journal space allocation: Pardun's (1999) analysis of a prominent media studies journal between 1978 and 1998 found a publication incidence of

26% for qualitative research articles (although her broadly inclusive criteria may have inflated this figure). Our recent search of one Internet database (ComAbstracts) of articles published in communication journals returned 50 entries for abstracts containing the keyword "ethnography." It also returned over 200 entries for "qualitative" (although its coverage of journals is only partial, and these figures lump "pure" studies with those using mixed methods and with methodological or theoretical commentaries). Outside of academe, growing interest among corporations and other institutions in the value of qualitative research for product design, program evaluation, and marketing purposes is also fueling its growth (Arnould & Wallendorf, 1994; Baba, 1998). Clearly, the times are (still) changing.

Looking back on the rise of the interpretive paradigm in Communication, at least two key impacts can be identified. First, members of the discipline have gained increased understanding of the purposes and methods of interpretive, cultural, and critical approaches. Most communication scholars now acknowledge that studies of contingent meaning can produce useful insights about the human condition. They also acknowledge that qualitative methods are more suitable than quantitative methods for addressing certain (but not all) questions about culture, interpretation, and power. For these purposes, the flexible and accommodating aspects of qualitative inquiry—its relational style of fieldwork, its inductive mode of analysis, and its resistance to closure—are strong attributes indeed.

Second, qualitative scholars can now publicize their work in an affirmative (as opposed to defensive) tone—even if they do so in many different voices. Although some reactionary sentiment persists (as discussed in Chapter 9), qualitative scholars will not find much sympathy for claims of categorical discrimination. As always, one needs to have access to the resources of communication to be able to say anything, much less be heard. But the boat of qualitative research has been lifted with Communication's rising tide as a discipline. Although conditions are far from ideal, few would argue that the discipline's visibility and sophistication have *declined* in recent years. The institutionalization of qualitative interests appears in various ways. One significant development involves the recent creation of an Ethnography division within the National Communication Association, ensuring conference panel slots for, and specialized discussion of, presentations of qualitative work. An increasing number of journals (some communication-based, some interdisciplinary) either accommodate or prefer qualitative, naturalistic, and cultural studies (see Chapter 3 for a detailed list). Although the receptiveness of a particular journal can vary with the appointment of a specific editor (and is always dependent on the quality of the work submitted), and some journals are traditionally more open than others, most have continued to display broad perspectives in their editorial policies and review boards. Further, several university and academic-oriented presses have actively sought and published volumes of cultural and critical communication studies. Increasing numbers of bibliographies, reviews, anthologies, and methodological texts also have contributed to this critical mass.

Coming to Terms

Having won the battle for legitimacy, then, qualitative research in Communication has now entered a period in which it can enjoy the associated fruits. In this process, however, it also assumes the responsibility of maintaining its legitimacy by producing perceived benefits. Shortly, we will explore various trajectories of research that have emerged in key disciplinary subfields. First, however, we conclude this section by drawing distinctions between three terms that are commonly used to describe methodologies that derive from the interpretive paradigm: *naturalistic inquiry*, *ethnography*, and *qualitative research*. These terms are often used interchangeably, producing confusion among both advocates and critics (Potter, 1996). While we cannot resolve confusion in the literature, our distinctions signal how these terms will be used in this volume.

Naturalistic Inquiry

The term *naturalistic inquiry* is often used interchangeably with *naturalism*, which takes cultural description as its primary objective. Naturalism proposes that the indigenous behaviors and meanings of a people can be understood only through a close analysis of "natural" settings (Hammersley & Atkinson, 1983, pp. 6-9). Natural settings are the customary arenas of activity for those being studied (e.g., shopping malls for teens engaged in "hanging out"). According to Denzin (1977), "Naturalism implies a profound respect for the character of the empirical world. It demands that the investigator take his [or her] theories and methods to that world" (p. 31).

The naturalist's injunction that social actions be studied in their own contexts does not mean that all contrived situations, such as interviews, are to be avoided. On the contrary, many data-gathering techniques are used in naturalistic study, including informant interviews, maps of settings, and artifact analysis. The naturalistic researcher combines different techniques to compensate for the limitations of each individual technique.

However, in their quest for "ecological validity," naturalists sometimes ignore the effects of research itself on outcomes (Hammersley & Atkinson, 1983, pp. 10-14). They try to document what is going on "out there," but the "there-ness" inevitably includes their own research presence. Even in naturalistic inquiry, the researcher cannot claim a privileged position separate from the phenomena being studied. It is to the credit of interpretive forms of inquiry that this reflexivity is accepted explicitly. The practice of *reflexive* analysis—accounting for the researcher's own role in social action—sensitizes the researcher to the different orders of reality in a scene (Myerhoff & Ruby, 1982). As we will discuss in Chapter 5, this mode of qualitative research is becoming increasingly popular. Naturalism's success, then, may be measured in its assimilation as an implicit premise in qualitative research. Its importance is increasingly historical and—for researchers reluctant to leave the laboratory but curious about alternatives—conceptual.

Ethnography

The term *ethnography* does not imply any single method or type of data analysis, although participant observation is a strategy that nearly all ethnographers employ. Nor do ethnographers (particularly the post-positivist variety) disavow the use of quantification. On the contrary, they often use surveys and statistical procedures to analyze patterns, determine who or what to sample, and triangulate findings (e.g., Silverman, 1985). Ethnographers also sometimes employ diagnostic tests, personality inventories, and other measurement tools (Pelto & Pelto, 1978). Basically, ethnographers will turn to any method that will help them to achieve success.

Typically, that success involves describing and interpreting observed relationships between social practices and the systems of meaning in a particular cultural milieu. This commitment is encoded in the term's roots, *ethno-* (people) and *-graphy* (describing). Ethnography usually involves a holistic description of cultural membership. As such, it differs from *ethnology*, which involves the more abstract comparison and classification of cultures (Spradley & McCurdy, 1972). Traditionally, ethnography is also holistic in that it tries to describe all (or at least most) relevant aspects of a culture's material existence and meaning systems. "Thick" description—specifically, of the contextual significance of actions for their performers—is a key attribute of ethnography (Geertz, 1973). The more detail that goes into the description, the richer our understanding, and the more value the account holds for the reader.

Although ethnography descends from centuries of imperial exploration and colonization of "primitive" life-worlds (a tainted heritage whose consequences we explore in Chapter 2), its academic institutionalization dates to the 1920s, when anthropologist Bronislaw Malinowski conducted a number of studies of the Trobriand islanders. As a result of Malinowski's pioneering studies, ethnography became identified with "living intimately and for a prolonged period of time within a single native community whose language [the researcher] had mastered" (Wax, 1972, p. 7). Prolonged engagement of the researcher with a culture, culminating in the production of a lengthy written account addressing the theoretical significance of observations, became not only the norm but the *sine qua non* of ethnographic fieldwork. Subsequent generations of anthropologists dutifully traveled to far-off locales to undergo the same disciplinary baptism through fieldwork. In sociology, however, ethnographic practice is more commonly described as "participant observation," which similarly connotes intensive, long-term immersion in a social scene. Sociologists have been less concerned with exotic sites of global diversity, however, and more focused on domestic folk, urban, and deviant subcultures, as well as social movements. Typically, sociologists focus on the consequences for these life-worlds created by the social, political, and economic changes associated with modernism and post-modernism (e.g., immigration, urbanization, the rise of the mass media, and consumerism). Also, sociology and anthropology have traditionally been concerned with matters of social structure and function. Although these traditions have been disrupted by the paradigm shifts described earlier in this chapter, they nonetheless form a legacy that distinguishes, in comparison, Communication's use of ethnography to *directly* focus on symbolic practices (see Hammersley & Atkinson, 1983; Sanday, 1983; Vidich & Lyman, 2000).

Like Malinowski before them, ethnographers live intimately inside the life space of the cultural members. Within that space, they must decide on the appropriate mix of perspectives through which cultural phenomena are studied. However, these decisions must be made *with* (not for) cultural members, because it is they who admit the ethnographer into their midst and risk the consequences of scrutiny. Ultimately, the documentation of social life can be realized only through negotiation with the people being studied.

Finally, in ethnography, process and product are joined closely. Ethnography is textual in the dual sense that (a) writing is a key activity in all phases of field research, and (b) writing "fixes" cultural analysis within the dialectic of field relations worked out between researcher and cultural members. What is left in and what is left out, whose point of view is represented, and how the scenes of social life are depicted become very important matters for assessing the "poetics and politics" of the ethnographic text (Clifford & Marcus, 1986). These issues are central to our discussion of writing and reading qualitative research in Chapter 9.

Qualitative Research

Fundamentally, qualitative researchers seek to preserve and analyze the situated form, content, and experience of social action, rather than subject it to mathematical or other formal transformations. Actual talk, gesture, and so on are the raw materials of analysis. This distinctiveness is often muddied, however, by a tendency for scholars to define qualitative research by what it is not (i.e., quantitative and statistical; Anderson & Meyer, 1988, p. 247) and as an "umbrella term covering an array of interpretive techniques which seek to describe, decode, translate and otherwise come to terms with the meaning, not the frequency, of certain more or less naturally occurring phenomena in the social world" (Van Maanen, 1983, p. 9). The term "qualitative research" vexes those with a low tolerance for ambiguity (Potter, 1996) because it crosscuts disciplines, it contains ambiguous phenomena that bridge theory and method, it has no particular defining method, and its meanings have changed dramatically over three centuries of practice and debate (Denzin & Lincoln, 2000). Because referential precision is not one of this term's virtues, we focus pragmatically on how this term is used, and by whom.

Central here are the nonnecessary relationships between qualitative research, naturalistic inquiry, and interpretivist epistemology. That is, qualitative methods are often—but not always—employed in the service of interpretive and naturalistic premises. Observation of interaction, for example, may be conducted for the purpose of validating a deductively derived coding scheme. The link between epistemology and methods is also conditioned by the history of a particular discipline. As described above, ethnographers practicing in anthropology and sociology have traditionally affiliated with positivist and post-positivist projects (Potter, 1996, p. 34). Unlike naturalistic inquiry, qualitative research is not always carried out in the habitat of cultural members. For instance, many qualitative studies eschew participant observation and are based solely on interview data (Kleinman, Stenross, & McMahon, 1994). Unlike ethnography, qualitative research does not always immerse the researcher in the scene for a prolonged period, adopt a holistic view of social practices, or broadly consider their cultural and historical contexts (Press, 1989). In fact, studies using qualitative methods often focus only on a partial set of relationships in a scene. Whether this is specificity or reductionism becomes a matter of debate.

Despite these differences, qualitative research has a great deal in common with both interpretivism and naturalistic inquiry. Most communication scholars, for example, consider *qualitative research* to be the broadest and most inclusive term for these phenomena (Frey et al., 1998), and so it is the default term that we use throughout this volume. Two perspectives help to clarify this resonance. The first, offered by Lofland (1971), defines qualitative inquiry in terms of the kinds of questions it asks:

> What kinds of things are going on here? What are the forms of this phenomenon? What variations do we find in this phenomenon? That is, qualitative analysis is addressed to the task of delineating forms, kinds and types of social phenomena; of documenting in loving detail the things that exist. (p. 13)

This definition emphasizes empirical and descriptive elements of qualitative inquiry that are consistent with—but not exclusive to—interpretivism. Denzin and Lincoln (2000), however, emphasize the distinctiveness of craft employed in qualitative research. They liken qualitative researchers to *bricoleurs*—workers who assemble useful and valuable forms from available, fragmentary resources to meet situational needs. This process—as those of quilt makers and jazz musicians—is as much creative, intuitive, and improvisational as it is systematic. Qualitative researchers, they argue, commonly use the aesthetic forms of *montage* (in which images of social life are juxtaposed to create a larger narrative) and *pentimento* (in which obscured elements of social life are restored for consideration). Again, these practices may be employed in natural settings to serve the goals and premises of interpretivism—but not necessarily.

These characteristics—a logic of discovery and attention to the diverse forms and details of social life—are shared by nearly all qualitative approaches that are interested in human understanding. These approaches converge on issues of how humans articulate and interpret their social and personal interests. For the purposes of this book, then, qualitative research is understood to be an approach that subsumes most of what goes by the names of interpretive, ethnographic, and naturalistic inquiry.

Looking Closer: The Conduct of Qualitative Research in Communication

As discussed earlier in this chapter, Communication is a complex field whose diversity encourages multiple and competing claims about its identity. Much of the day-to-day work in the discipline is organized around subfields. That is, although scholars may identify with the discipline as a whole, that identification is more abstract (and potentially weaker) than the bonds developed between colleagues who share a particular research topic or a methodological or theoretical approach. Discussion of these contexts is useful for several reasons: Senior communication scholars typically socialize junior scholars to develop primary affiliations; scholars evaluate each other's work as contributing to particular subfield agendas; and epistemological shifts ultimately get played out within subfields as matters of local relevance. Further, this last process is not uniform. Different subfields have different histories and cultures that mediate the outcomes. To illustrate this, we provide a brief survey of qualitative research conducted in nine subfields, with a list of associated exemplars. The first six subfields are identified by the context of communication studied (interpersonal communication, language and social interaction, group communication, organizational communication, intercultural communication, and media and cultural studies) and the last three subfields are identified by topic and genre (performance studies, applied communication, and health communication). Our discussion focuses on the themes and issues that characterize the impact of qualitative research in each subfield. The exemplars listed illustrate, but do not exhaust, the scope and depth of qualitative research conducted in each category. In reading, we encourage you to note the opportunities and challenges that characterize not only your own subfield(s) but also those of your colleagues. This broader understanding can form the spark of innovation and collaboration.

Interpersonal Communication

As a traditional bastion of quantitative and positivist and post-positivist research, this subfield has been relatively slow and cautious in accommodating interpretive epistemology (Leeds-Hurwitz, 1992). Groundbreaking qualitative studies have treated personal relationships (e.g., family and friendship) and episodes of interaction (e.g., conflict) as situated accomplishments of speech and nonverbal (Ray, 1987) communication (e.g., Jorgenson, 1989; Rawlins, 1983, 1989). In their premises and practices, most of these studies reflect the influence of social-constructionism, "conventional" explanation, and "grounded theory." Personal identities and social realities are viewed as constructions of language use, culture is treated as a central context of interaction, and explanations are developed through the inductive analysis of data generated in intimate observation (Poole & McPhee, 1994). Interest often centers on the ways in which people describe their relational bonds, and the dilemmas (e.g., dialectics created by incompatible goals) they encounter in maintaining and transforming them. Somewhat more elaborately, the contributors to a recent edited volume (Carter & Presnell, 1994) bring idealist, hermeneutic, phenomenological, and critical perspectives to traditional topics of research, such as understanding, competence, listening, and self-disclosure. The contributors to another volume (Morrill & Snow, 2003) argue that mainstream research on personal relationships has been too narrow in selecting types of relationships (e.g., emotionally invested, highly interdependent, enduring, and "private"), in sampling populations, and in using methods. They advocate a form of "relational ethnography" that focuses on cultural contexts, registers variation in interdependency, and expands the range of relational types and sites studied. Exemplars include Arnold (1995), Bochner and Ellis (1992), Bruess and Pearson (1997), Sabourin and Stamp (1995), and Stamp (1999).

Language and Social Interaction

This term describes a "diverse, squabbling family" (Tracy, 2001) of communication researchers influenced by the traditions of psychology, sociology, linguistics, and anthropology. They share a general commitment to interpretive social science, but they differ strongly over procedures for gathering and analyzing data and for reporting findings. At least four groups are represented:

- *Conversation analysts* focused on conversational structure as the display of strategies by which speakers coordinate and interpret utterances
- *Discourse analysts* concerned with analyzing oral, written, and visual texts produced in a variety of contexts
- *Ethnographers of communication* focused on cultural codes and rituals (e.g., for places, times, and styles of appropriate speech) that organize characteristic, routine communication between the members of "speech communities" (e.g., Carbaugh, 1988a; Philipsen, 1975; Sigman, 1986)
- *Microethnographers* practicing fine-grained analysis of both verbal and nonverbal practices to create holistic portraits of embodied, situated interaction

Generally, language and social interaction (LSI) researchers are committed to precise and detailed study of everyday talk occurring in natural contexts, recording and documenting that talk (e.g., through transcription), and using excerpts as evidence for knowledge claims. Although hybrid forms of research are not unknown among this group (e.g., Jarmon, 1996; Tracy & Tracy, 1998), LSI researchers typically diverge from ethnographers in favoring a more detached researcher role, limiting evidence for claims of contextual influence to explicit features of recorded interaction, and "glossing" the biographical complexity of actors to foreground the material features of interaction as exemplars of social practice. Exemplars include Beach (1996), Buttny (1997), Fitch (1994a), Hopper (1992), and LeBaron and Streeck (1997).

Group Communication

Frey (1994c) has argued that interpretivism may help to revive a somewhat stagnant field of research that has traditionally used quantitative methods to study zero-history groups of college students in one-time, laboratory events involving the solution of artificial tasks assigned by researchers. Alternatively, qualitative methods can be used to expand the range of groups studied (e.g., bona fide groups characterized by extensive history, shifting boundaries, and interdependencies with other groups; Putnam & Stohl, 1990), the types of communication studied (e.g., the construction of group identity), and the types of evidence used to support claims (e.g., exemplars derived from fieldnotes and long-term observation). In addition, Dollar and Merrigan (2001) argue that qualitative studies can validate and extend existing group communication theory (e.g., by clarifying its boundary conditions), generate new theory (e.g., concerning the dialectic between individual and collective interests experienced by group members), redress traditional neglect of topics (e.g., meaning construction), and problematize conventional wisdom (e.g., surrounding the necessity of shared goals for group status). In addition to these benefits, however, Frey (1994a) notes that qualitative research also creates dilemmas involving negotiation with group members of agreements concerning access, inclusion, confidentiality, and mutually beneficial transactions. Exemplars include C. Braithwaite (1997), Conquergood (1994), Croft (1999), Della-Piana and Anderson (1995), and Lesch (1994).

Organizational Communication

Researchers in this subfield turned to interpretive models and philosophies in the early 1980s, partly out of frustration with the barrenness of rationalist and functionalist explanations (Putnam & Pacanowsky, 1983). They learned from their colleagues in management (as well as from popular authors and their own experiences as paid consultants) that organizations can be likened to cultures: they ritually initiate members and sometimes expel them; they create and share evocative stories designed to inspire and terrify members; they carefully manage the flowering of difference and opposition in subcultures; and they relate to external entities through both mundane commerce and imaginative superstition. Researchers' initial studies focused on topics such as the scripted and performative dimensions of organizational roles, the metaphors used by organizations to represent their identity and cultivate productivity and commitment, and the messy, nonrational practices underlying the gleaming face of the corporate machine (e.g., Goodall, 1991; Kelly, 1985; Pacanowsky & O'Donnell-Trujillo, 1982; Smircich & Calas, 1987).

Generally, qualitative methods were valued as a means for creating fine-grained and preservationistic accounts of organizational symbol use (Schwartzman, 1993). These findings contributed to theoretical knowledge about a variety of topics, including employee socialization, commitment and identification, leadership, ethics, implementation of new technologies, diversity, and organizational innovation. Potentially, this knowledge helps organizational members to identify and resolve pressing problems, reflect on the premises that guide their sensemaking, and develop cultures that successfully balance the tension between individual and organizational goals (Kreps & Herndon, 2001). In addition to embracing interpretivism, organizational communication has recently adopted a variety of "critical" and "postmodern" theories concerned with politicizing organizational power and control, and with transforming conventional understandings of "organization" and how it should be studied (Taylor & Trujillo, 2001). Exemplars include Bantz (2001), Eisenberg, Murphy, and Andrews (1998), Ruud (2000), Taylor (1999), and Wendt (1995).

Intercultural Communication

Under this umbrella term, researchers are variously concerned with interaction among and between the members of different cultural groups (Martin & Nakayama, 1999). Traditionally "functionalist" research in this subfield has been affiliated with the practical interests of foreign relations and international business. Related research has conceptualized national culture as relatively coherent and stable, and sought evidence of its causal influence on communication (e.g., as reflecting "individualist" and "collectivist" traits). Since the late 1980s, intercultural communication has been a fertile ground for interpretive research grounded in the traditions of anthropology and sociolinguistics; significant overlap exists between members of this subfield and ethnographers of communication. Interpretive research here focuses on reciprocal and emergent relationships between communication and culture. It emphasizes the social construction of cultural knowledge and identities (e.g., membership is a performance not a trait), and the importance of researcher accountability for how claims are constructed in overlapping academic, historical, and socioeconomic contexts. An exemplary research program involves the use of focus group interviews by Mary Jane Collier (1998) and her associates to develop "cultural identity theory." Related studies examine

the relationship between respondents' self-identified affiliation with national, racial, and ethnic groups, and the extent to which respondents share such identity patterns as in-group norms, experiences with out-group discrimination and prejudice, and constitutive ideas and strategies for managing conflict. (Collier, 1998, p. 139)

This subfield has recently been influenced by postmodern and critical perspectives (most notably feminism and postcolonialism), in which scholars reflect Western culture's often imperial gaze back on itself and subvert its conventional wisdom regarding homogeneity, assimilation, rationality, and consensus. Whether focused "at home" or "abroad," this research emphasizes unequal power relationships; diversity; the simultaneity and partiality of ethnic, class, and gender identities; and the dissolution of clear geopolitical boundaries (e.g., within and between nations) in the context of globalization (Collier, 2000). Recent exemplars include Bailey (2000), Bradford, Meyers, and Kane (1999), Gareis (1995), Lindsley (1999), and Starosta and Hannon (1997).

Media and Cultural Studies

In this subfield (formerly known as "mass communication"), audience ethnography attained prominence mainly as a result of two different events: the recognition by critical theorists of the limits of purely textual and political-economic analysis and the dissatisfaction of many American communication scholars with the limits of empiricist models of audience research. Both communities found their own paths to the discovery of qualitative inquiry: critical theorists through what is called cultural studies (heavily influenced by semiotic and poststructuralist theories), and American mass communication researchers through social phenomenology and other interpretive social science approaches (this is a simplistic account, because both communities borrowed from each other's ideas). The rapid development of audience ethnography has produced insights into the social uses and rules of media and the interpretation of meanings in mainstream media texts (Anderson & Meyer, 1988; Corner, 1999, pp. 80-92; Geraghty, 1998; Lindlof, 1991; Morley, 1992). Murphy (1999b) notes, however, that the postmodernist turn has produced excessive critique of ethnographic textuality by scholars who do not themselves practice fieldwork. Less charitably, Bird (1992) describes this scholarship as "narcissism." Central here, in any event, has been the naturalistic move to study actual reception practices (e.g., television viewing) in the context of audience members' daily activities (e.g., the domestic routines of home-based women). Some researchers have conducted "resistance studies" of specialized subcultures (e.g., fans) whose members appropriate media texts to serve local needs and motives (Fiske, 1991a;

Jenkins, 1992). Others have focused on "interpretive communities" in which media-use is a ritual performance through which users maintain their status and membership (e.g., in performing interpretations of content that conform to communal mythology). The rise of resistance studies and textualist critique has in turn produced a backlash that rejects populist celebration of audience opposition as—at best—premature, and calls for more grounded study of audiences as the material objects of institutional knowledge and power (Morley, 1997).

The rise of media audience studies has also affected an ancient and venerable subfield in Communication—rhetorical studies. As the fields of rhetorical criticism and cultural studies increasingly overlap (Rosteck, 1999), the former now struggles to revise its tradition of *speculating* about textual influence on audiences. That is, cultural studies challenge rhetorical criticism to *document* that influence by participating in and observing its actuality (Blair & Michel, 1999; Stromer-Galley & Schiappa, 1998).

Finally, two other areas of research may be mentioned here. The first is development communication, in which ethnography is seen as an approach that can study local realities and needs without imposing the value assumptions of traditional media effects research (Bourgault, 1992). The second is the production of content in media organizations. Here, participant observation work has examined the social construction of news in the routines of journalists and newsrooms (Lester, 1980; Rodriguez, 1996; Tuchman, 1991) and in the processes of producing entertainment programs (Gitlin, 1983; Levine, 2001; Saferstein, 1991). Other exemplars of qualitative research in this subfield include Beck (1995), Geiser-Getz (1998), Huesca (1995), Ling, Nilsen, and Granhaug (1999), and Rockler (1999).

Performance Studies

Conquergood (1991) argues that

> performance-centered research takes as both its subject matter and method the experiencing body situated in time, place, and history. The performance paradigm insists on face-to-face encounters instead of abstractions and reductions. It situates ethnographers within the delicately negotiated and fragile "face-work" that is part of the intricate and nuanced dramaturgy of everyday life. (p. 187)

This definition signals the exquisitely reflexive use of the performance paradigm by scholars in this subfield. It designates sites and modes of expressive practice that form the object of study: dance, play, sport, food, ritual, ceremony, music, theater, and so on. The focus here is on how performers interpret culturally authored scripts and on how they artfully collaborate with audiences in the construction of cultural identities. The unique move that follows is to appropriate performance as an epistemological allegory in which corresponding elements of the research process are reconfigured as performer, audience, script, and theater. In this view, performance is not merely the *object* of research, it is also the *mode* of research, in which the presentation of self (e.g., by the researcher to the group) is central, inter- action is semi-scripted but also improvised, and knowledge emerges from the contingencies of situated, collaborative interaction. This allegory cul- minates in the conversion of qualitative research findings into aesthetic formats of public, oral, and written performance: poems, short stories, per- sonal narratives, and even staged productions (Welker & Goodall, 1997). These performances vividly clarify for audiences that social meanings are inherently precarious (e.g., immigrant folkways threatened by assimilation) and are preserved through embodied acts of will and skill (Denzin, 1997, pp. 90-125). Perhaps more than any other subfield described here, perfor- mance studies has been influenced by feminist and postmodern theories emphasizing the contingency of cultural identity, the persistence of both subtle and brute forms of oppression, and the role of performance in creat- ing spaces and moments in which authentic experience can be creatively asserted against dominant ideologies (e.g., through irony, parody, carnival, etc.). These perspectives break from traditional dramaturgy in emphasizing paradox, conflict, ambiguity, and instability over coherence, structure, and consensus. Exemplars include Bell and Forbes (1994), S. H. Jones (1999), Shue and Beck (2001), and Valentine and Matsumoto (2001).

Applied Communication

This subfield includes highly motivated and focused research projects, which are undertaken for at least two purposes. The first purpose is to assist real-world individuals and groups in the diagnosis and solution of practical problems hindering their ability to achieve communication goals. The second purpose is to use these opportunities to build and test communi- cation theory. These studies potentially combine quantitative (e.g., surveys and experiments), qualitative (e.g., interviewing), and textual-critical meth- ods to meet situational needs. They are uniquely characterized by collabo- ration between researchers and clients intended to define problems, set goals, identify contributing factors, formulate methodological strategies, and implement solutions. One example of such research is the growing employment of qualitative researchers by marketers and product design- ers to intimately observe consumers in the "fields" of their homes and workplaces (Osborne, 2002)—an alternate career path that is proving increasingly attractive to academics addicted to the ethnographic life (Thornton, 1999).

Qualitative methods are especially helpful in managing the naturalistic elements of these projects (Frey, O'Hair, & Kreps, 1990; Seibold, 1995). Denzin and Lincoln (2000) note that applied qualitative research

> is the critical site where theory, method, praxis, action, and policy all come together. Qualitative researchers can isolate target populations, show the immediate effects of certain programs on such groups, and isolate the constraints that operate against policy changes in such settings. Action-oriented and clinically-oriented qualitative researchers can also create spaces for those who are studied (the other) to speak. (p. 23)

Exemplars may be found in volumes of the eponymous *Journal of Applied Communication Research*.

Health Communication

This subfield provides a distinctive exemplar of applied qualitative research. It has traditionally been dominated by a functionalist focus on assisting health care professionals to identify and overcome perceived communication problems. These problems are variously interpersonal (e.g., the presentation of diagnoses to patients), organizational (e.g., inadequate training of staff), and media related (e.g., the assimilation of telemedicine systems) and affect the delivery and quality of services. Health communication researchers have used both quantitative and qualitative methods to help professionals predict and control patient attitudes and behaviors (e.g., their conformity to treatment regimens) and to achieve preferred outcomes (e.g., reduction in rates of illness). Arguably, however, this focus has reproduced the hierarchical authority of medical professionals over patients and obscured patients' experiences. Qualitative methods have recently been used to restore the integrity of patient experience and action in medical encounters (e.g., by redefining "effective outcomes" in patient-centered terms such as quality of life, respect, and advocacy). This research emphasizes the situated performances that form the referent of variables such as "self-efficacy." It also focuses on the importance of gender, class, and racial identities in the co-construction of often-competing meanings for pain, discomfort, health and illness, the body, mind and spirit, and mortality. Researchers have used methods of interviewing, observation, and textual analysis to foreground the voices of patients (e.g., personal narratives of illness) and professionals engaged in the profoundly challenging and rewarding encounters that constitute the social life of medicine. These methods are particularly useful in capturing "the ground truth" behind controversial, large-scale change in health care institutions, such as that currently surrounding "managed care" (Gillespie, 2001; Sharf & Street, 1997; Vanderford, Jenks, & Sharf, 1997). Exemplars include Ellingson and Buzzanell (1999), Geist and Gates (1996), Hirschmann (1999), Orbe and King (2000), and Whitten, Sypher, and Patterson (2000).

Conclusion

In this chapter, we have reviewed some key commitments of interpretivism that underlie much of what we recognize as qualitative research in Communication and compared them with those of positivism and post-positivism. We've had our first look at some specific procedures that logically derive from interpretivism and noted the fact that these methods may also be made to serve positivist and post-positivist purposes. It should by now be crystal-clear that what distinguishes qualitative research is not so much the particular methods employed as the epistemological purposes to which they are put. These relationships between method and epistemology are not easy to articulate (at least not at first), but novices become experts when they work at increasing their precision and fluency in these accounts. Qualitative researchers at any career stage who ignore this responsibility risk the loss of credibility. Finally, we've taken a quick spin around the large city known as "qualitative research in Communication." We've looked in on some different neighborhoods (we hope yours included) and seen some important differences in how qualitative research is used to serve local interests. Along with those differences, though, we also saw central arteries that cut across and connect these neighborhoods: rich, detailed descriptions of human experience, dialogic encounters between the self and other, and the inductive development of theory from intimate knowledge of situated practice. In the next chapter, we continue the orientation begun here by exploring the theoretical traditions that energize qualitative communication research (particularly critical theories that we have so far only mentioned in passing). As we will see, these theories form "scientific" and "professional" narratives adopted by the members of disciplinary subfields to legitimate their qualitative research.

2

Theoretical Traditions and Qualitative Communication Research

Communication as a Human Science

A study belongs to the human [sciences] only if its object becomes accessible to us through the attitude which is founded on the relation between life, expression, and understanding.

— Dilthey (1944/1974, pp. 16-17)

This chapter considers qualitative communication research as a project of the human sciences, as broadly conceived by the 19th-century German philosopher Wilhelm Dilthey. For Dilthey, the human sciences included historical studies, social and psychological sciences, moral theory, legal and political studies, and literary criticism. All of these fields share a concern with problems of choice, value, and understanding, and their influence on the activities of expression and interpretation. In this way, Dilthey's decision to group the social and psychological sciences with literary criticism rather than the "hard" sciences of physics and chemistry was revealing. As Ricoeur (1977) has noted, one way to unpack the significance of social action is to assume that it embodies intention just like a *written* text (even if it turns out to be stubborn and devious). Like a literary text, social action "constitutes a delineated pattern which has to be interpreted according to its inner connections" (p. 322). Just as we understand a particular text by tracing the allusions it makes to *other* texts, qualitative researchers understand communication through its indication of motives, thoughts, and feelings that connect actors to each other.

We open this broad intellectual umbrella here to shelter a wide-ranging discussion of the theoretical traditions that shape qualitative communication research. At the outset, we concede some healthy concerns. One such concern is that the scope and complexity of theory in the discipline has grown so considerably in recent years that our discussion can only sketch the key commitments that distinguish particular traditions. Even this goal is complicated by several factors. One complicating factor is that theories can be highly contested narratives. Craig (1999) notes that, partly because of their multidisciplinary provenance, the discipline's subfields differ sharply as to which communication theories they include and how they include them. Additionally, there is often as much disagreement within particular theoretical traditions (e.g., about founders' contributions) as there is between them. Because sketches cannot preserve this complexity, we recommend that readers consult primary sources as needed to learn more. Further, in practice scholars can be vague and implicit when discussing how theory informs a particular study—especially when they are addressing like-minded colleagues. Sometimes, the choice of a particular publication venue—with its inevitable editorial biases—can influence which theories are used and how they are used. In both these cases, theory is a matter of both intellectual logic and practical rhetoric. These factors complicate attempts to trace the "natural" evolution of traditions. Finally, Communication's entrepreneurial heritage and the porous boundaries between disciplines mean that many recent studies display a bricolage—or creative combination—of theoretical narratives. This means that a survey like this artificially distinguishes narratives that are often blended in practice. Clair (1998), for example, combines the resources of feminism, modernist critical theory, and poststructuralism to examine the interrelated dialectics of speech and silence and oppression and resistance. And in her study of Sea World, Davis (1997) blends political-economic and cultural studies perspectives to analyze the connections between corporate hegemony and environmental degradation displayed in its commodification of nature. Significantly, *there is often no prior consensus* about the acceptability of such blends (Alvesson & Deetz, 1996)—only the researcher's responsibility to demonstrate their appropriateness for specific sites and purposes.

Despite these obstacles, this is still a valuable survey to undertake. Learning to use a methodology without being grounded in its intellectual traditions is like learning a musical instrument (say, blues guitar) without knowing the artists (like Robert Johnson) who have shaped its use, or the performance styles (like Delta blues) that make a particular artist (like Susan Tedeschi) both traditional *and* innovative. You may be able to pick up some mechanics, but fundamental things will be missing. Further, learning these intellectual traditions helps new qualitative researchers to make better choices. Because the formal use of theory is typically deferred in qualitative research (a condition discussed further in Chapter 7), inexperienced researchers may not consider its relevance until after they have made important and constraining choices. Even though theory is carefully invoked in data analysis and presentation, we believe that it should also inform all phases of qualitative research as a resource for rationalizing decisions. Finally, as mentioned above, researchers increasingly combine theoretical traditions—with varying degrees of coherence and success. Some combinations are more logical, harmonious, and successful than others, and learning these traditions can help researchers to understand why.

Our discussion, then, will focus on how six key traditions—ethnomethodology, symbolic interactionism, ethnography of communication, modern and postmodern critical theory, feminism, and cultural studies—have each been adapted to qualitative communication research. Our goal is to be, if not comprehensive, at least useful. Like you, probably, we are fans of "musical" research. We begin by building a bridge between the discussion of interpretive epistemology in Chapter 1 and the more specific traditions treated here. The foundations of this bridge include a concept (*verstehen*, meaning "understanding") around which several interpretive philosophers have historically converged and the ideas of a social theorist (Alfred Schutz), who advanced a conceptual basis (social phenomenology) for interpretive science.

Verstehen

For interpretivists, it is axiomatic that we need to see social action from the actors' point of view to understand what is happening. In this way, interpretivism takes understanding as its principal topic and methodological wellspring. It was Dilthey who called this way of gaining an empathic insight into others' attitudes *verstehen*. But the origins of *verstehen* reach back to the 18th century, a time when the influence of Cartesian rationalism was rippling through intellectual discourse. During this period, philosopher Giambattista Vico's "New Science" proposed that a proper understanding of human nature and artifacts requires inductive, historical study of cultural forms. Vico was one of the first to see a basic disjuncture between the aims of the natural and human sciences. In 1781, in *The Critique of Pure Reason*, Immanuel Kant (1929) extended Vico's argument by maintaining that our perception of the world, although active, is nonetheless mediated by conceptual categories. These categories provide the "presuppositional" framework by which knowledge and questions about empirical reality develop.

As a concept, *verstehen* developed mostly as a reaction to philosophical and scientific arguments (e.g., by John Stuart Mill and Auguste Comte) favoring the application of positivism to the study of human behavior. During the 19th century, confidence rose that universal laws of behavior could be derived through the study of how human beings respond to their environments. These principles would specify the psychobiological elements and mechanisms that determine the complex particulars of human life. The rapid movement during the late 19th century of positivist science into areas that had traditionally been the preserve of the humanities caused significant alarm in the academy. It bred a phase of competition among explanations of social behavior (Martindale, 1968, pp. 310-311).

By the early 20th century, the concept of *verstehen* and debates about its use in science formed the basis for a science of social phenomenology (as discussed further, below) and other ways of doing interpretive research. In the field of *hermeneutics*, which originally concerned itself with interpreting ancient scripture, the work of Wilhelm Dilthey, F. D. E. Schleiermacher, and, much later, Hans Gadamer, formalized the techniques and broadened the scope of textual study (Palmer, 1969). The hermeneutical method involves interpreting the meaning of a text by empathically imagining the experience of its author and by engaging in a circular movement that alternates between textual features and context to generate holistic knowledge (Ricoeur, 1977; Schwandt, 2000). Although this practice can be used in any situation where one wishes to recover historical meaning, hermeneutics is far more than a method. As a philosophy, it emphasizes understanding as a central element of the human condition. It also advocates an ethic of dialogue in which the experience of otherness (i.e., of meaningful engagement with the unfamiliar) can clarify, and perhaps transform, the biases that influence the production of knowledge.

At both levels, hermeneutics has strongly shaped qualitative scholarship. One example is its influence on the paradigm of social constructionism, which holds that "human beings do not find or discover knowledge so much as we construct or make it . . . against a backdrop of shared understandings, practices, [and] languages" (Schwandt, 2000, p. 197). Another example is the "interpretive turn" promoted by the cultural anthropologist Clifford Geertz (1973). Geertz argued that cultural meanings were encoded in public, symbolic forms (e.g., rituals, artifacts, and calendars) that were best understood through acts of "reading." Interpreting these "webs of meaning" requires researchers to produce "thick descriptions" of performances and their local significance (or, in Geertz's terms, rendering "the said" from "the saying"). Geertz argued that sufficiently artful and compelling interpretations could relativize cultural understandings and facilitate "mutual intelligibility" between the members of different cultures.

Another figure significant to the development of *verstehen* was Max Weber. Weber was responsible for grounding sociological theory in the study of meaningful social action and specifying the methodological uses of *verstehen* (Morris, 1977; Winch, 1958). By arguing that subjective motives direct human conduct, Weber (1968) tried to rid *verstehen* of its mystical quality and put it on a scientific footing. In his view, institutions, authority, and policy all arise from the expression by actors of their motives in interaction. Potentially, a sustained study of motivated conduct could lead to the discovery of *ideal types* (i.e., of identities) that orient the subjectivity of actors in a given situation. Contrary to many interpretivist thinkers, however, Weber continued to believe that science should seek value-free, causal explanations of conduct. Weber's ideas provided Schutz with a foundation for his concepts of motive, coordinated social action, and "the natural attitude."

A final figure to discuss here is Edmund Husserl, who had perhaps the greatest impact on the development of a science of interpretation. Although Husserl is not directly associated with the concept of *verstehen*, his belief that *intentionality* and *consciousness* should be central concerns of any scientific investigation connected him to other figures with a similar interest in subjective experience. Husserl's philosophy of *phenomenology* sought to define the "essence" of the objects of our perceptions (see Husserl, 1931; Kockelmans, 1967). He argued that human consciousness orders the ways that we understand the physical nature of the world. Human consciousness is a fundamentally intentional activity, in the sense that intentions are always directed toward objects. For Husserl, consciousness is always consciousness *of something*. Objects are defined in terms of our practical intentions when we encounter them.

Husserl argued further that each of us lives in a world of objects, people, actions, and institutions that is constituted in a characteristically taken-for-granted fashion. This *lebenswelt*, or "life-world," is the unique world of being for all humans. Though it appears arbitrary and transient when analyzed, the life-world is typically experienced as timeless and natural. Husserl called this sense of objectivity and inevitability the *natural attitude*. This term describes how social actors create meaningful order by standardizing, and abstracting from, the unique specifics of recurring situations. When shared by participants, this orientation reduces the complexity and increases the predictability of interaction.

One *practical* problem with the natural attitude is that its routines often become taken for granted, creating inflexible communication patterns. The primary *scientific* problem is how things get to be that way: *how* the life-world acquires the quality of naturalness. The method Husserl developed to address this problem is called the *epoche* (or "transcendental reduction"). Phenomenologists using this method "bracket" the structures and appearances of the life-world. They seek to make strange what otherwise seems normal and to characterize the essence of a phenomenon that endures once its specifics are discarded. Through a series of bracketing exercises, phenomenologists can understand how common objects of perception are meaningfully constituted. As Anderson (1987) has written, Husserl's epoche "is a purified form of scientific induction" (p. 239). In effect, it permits a systematic study of how intentional activity creates meaning.

Schutz and Social Phenomenology

In many ways, Alfred Schutz synthesized Weber's and Husserl's efforts to explain the subjective basis of social action. But in Schutz's work we also find much more than that. In his writings on intersubjectivity, Schutz established nothing less than a conceptual basis for the interpretive study of communication.

In his analysis of the life-world, Husserl encountered a problem that he never solved: How do humans *learn* to construct a life-world that can be shared? How do they create continuity in their actions? What Husserl was puzzling over was the problem of *intersubjectivity*.

In *The Phenomenology of the Social World*, Schutz (1967) approached this problem by claiming that individuals unquestioningly accept that a mundane world exists and that others share their understandings of its essential features. Schutz argued further that individuals orient to objects and actions by assuming that others can and will reciprocate their perspective. That is, in communicating with others, we take a leap of faith: "If you were to trade places with me, you would see situations in the same way I do, and vice versa." This "presupposition" supports a natural attitude toward the social world.

In every interaction, individuals are phenomenologically located—they actively take up positions in space (e.g., in a "long-distance" relationship) and time (e.g., in "working for the weekend") that make events meaningful. Schutz was interested in how we develop, manage, and apply *stocks of knowledge* in this process. These stocks include all the facts, beliefs, desires, prejudices, and rules we have learned from personal experience, as well as the ready-made knowledge available to us in the culture into which we are born. The former kind of knowledge is unique to each of us and is locally developed in face-to-face interaction. The latter knowledge comes in preformed *typifications* of experience that are widely available to cultural members. Typified knowledge consists of myths, frames, scripts, and common sense. Changes in our biographical situations and stocks of knowledge change the aspects of experience that we consider relevant.

A dramatic example of this process involves the interpretation by (mostly young) women of traumatic—and initially ambiguous—sexual encounters as "date rape." Aside from showing how typifications of events can trigger associated typifications of identity (e.g., "victim"), this example suggests that phenomenology is relevant for the analysis of urgent communication problems. Health communication professionals, for example, encourage potentially vulnerable women to assimilate this typification (and thus change their natural attitude toward sexual encounters) *prior* to putting themselves at risk. Phenomenology also clarifies the gender politics of legal definition. Defense attorneys in some trials have characterized the time period in which this interpretation emerges, and its status as retrospective sensemaking collaboratively developed by victims and their counselors, as evidence that "date rape" is a fabricated, and therefore an invalid, typification. Finally, this example indicates that typification can be a multilayered, contested— and highly consequential—social practice. Whether the plaintiff and the accused in a date rape trial can agree about the event in question may ultimately be less important than the consensus achieved by jury members.

Whatever its outcomes, intersubjectivity is always produced in the relationships that we develop with others. In this primary "we-relation," persons mutually occupy a time and place. Their actions are geared with respect to a common system of relevance. In Schutz's phrase, social actors "grow old together," with each actor defining self and other through a negotiated relationship. Poignantly, Schutz noted that we imaginatively construct these relations not only with our contemporaries (whether known or unknown) but also with our predecessors (our cherished and feared dead) and successors (e.g., in the "Seven Generations" taken into account by some Native American tribes in their decision-making processes). Although these last two modes may not involve face-to-face communication, they all influence our evolving self-understanding.

Schutz embraced Weber's concept of action as meaningful behavior, but went on to clarify *how* it becomes meaningful. Schutz (1967) defined meaning as "a certain way of directing one's gaze at an item of one's own experience . . . Meaning indicates, therefore, a peculiar attitude on the part of the Ego toward the flow of its own duration" (p. 42). In other words, *only when attention is reflected toward the self does experience become meaningful.*

Schutz also distinguished "action" from "act." An action, he argued, is a project that is in process. An action becomes an act when individuals direct their gaze on the action and thus make it meaningful. To put it another way: "Action is subject-bound, it builds up in temporal development, and its full significance is always on the far side of the actor's intention. The act is a unitary phenomenon which is object-oriented and whose meaning is graspable" (Natanson, 1968, p. 222). The meaning of any action can be grasped only in its actual or projected completion (i.e., when we imagine the fulfillment of a desire).

We gain insight into people's motives for action by engaging them through their acts—primarily, acts of speaking. Schutz argued that these motives are of two types: *in-order-to motives* (e.g., "I joined the Army to get a good job") and *because motives* (e.g., "I joined the Army because I was hanging around with the wrong people"). These two types of motives can be differentiated in terms of their temporal nature (Bernstein, 1978, p. 155). In-order-to motives concern projected acts; because motives account for past experiences.

Schutz's overall analysis of action, act, and motive is historically significant because it clarified previously vague notions of interpretive research. In *The Phenomenology of the Social World* and his other works—most notably the essay "On Multiple Realities" (Schutz, 1962)—he shows how individuals actively construct numerous, overlapping life-worlds. Schutz provides a sophisticated analysis of how we gain access to each other's subjectivity, an issue with real significance for methodology.

In summarizing this section, we can say that the work of Weber, Husserl, and Schutz converged around the problems of understanding lived experience and social action, and created the foundation for many concepts that would later become central to interpretivism. These include the *social construction of reality* (e.g., Berger & Luckmann, 1967; Garfinkel, 1967), the *rules of language use* (e.g., Cicourel, 1974), and the *self in social life* (e.g., Goffman, 1959). The work of these figures continues to influence nearly all of the human sciences, and we turn now to some particular descendants.

Ethnomethodology

In developing phenomenology, Husserl considered its implications for the disciplines of psychology and sociology. Specifically, he believed that empirical science should be *eidetic*, or concerned with essential objects and relationships. Instead of assuming consensual meanings for constructs like "family" and "organization," an eidetic sociology would go "to the things themselves" and try to account for their existence as entities in human discourse. In Husserl's view, without a fundamental understanding of how social life comes to have significance, empirical work would be fruitless.

Husserl's philosophy, however, did not provide the resources needed to actually study the social realities that people share. Schutz theorized how intersubjectivity *should* operate, but he went no further in probing its actual occurrences. In this way, both writers arguably adopted an objectivist stance toward the life-world as "out there," a product of the natural attitude (Kinchloe & McLaren, 2000).

The empirical program that has come closest to a true eidetic science is *ethnomethodology* (EM). In fact, of the many varieties of phenomenologically based sociology that have appeared, only EM has hewed closely to the original purpose of bracketing mundane social practices (Heap & Roth, 1973). As a term and a research program, EM is the invention of Harold Garfinkel, whose seminal work is *Studies in Ethnomethodology* (1967). In simple terms, EM seeks to understand how the taken-for-granted character of everyday life is actually accomplished. The *methodology* in the term refers not to the scientific variety but to the methods and procedures people use to construct sensible and orderly ways of doing things. Going to work, grocery shopping, viewing television—these are all usually experienced as coherent events because we perform our parts skillfully and because we expect (without really having to think about it) that others will do the same. The question that inspires most EM research is, How do they do it? Significantly, the "it" in this case is not the *activity* as such but the *participants' emergent sense of its objectivity, factuality, and orderliness* (Maynard & Klayman, 1991; O'Keefe, 1980). EM scholars are fascinated with how "appearances" in interaction are sufficient to sustain participants' belief in the reality of the interaction. For Garfinkel, there is nothing behind the appearance: The practice of creating a consistent, convincing appearance *is* social reality.

As a sociological approach, EM is peculiar. It forsakes the usual path of developing theories of human behavior. Conventional social science starts with topics (such as "family") that are shot through with other common-sense meanings (such as kinship, obligation, and trust). These tacit associations are normally not problematized in most sociological studies (Atkinson, 1988), nor is it clear how participants use constructs and their tacit meanings to coordinate their behavior.

EM enters this gap by focusing on the local construction of meaning through social—particularly conversational—practices (Sacks, 1963). The *content* of these practices is of little, if any, consequence. What *are* consequential are the situational resources and the sequence of activities used to construct the coherence of a given practice. A classic example from research by Garfinkel and his associates on scientists illustrates this difference between "topics" and "resources" of interaction (see Garfinkel, Lynch, & Livingston, 1981; Lynch, Livingston, & Garfinkel, 1983). Rather than examining the epistemology or outcomes of scientific research, these researchers focused on scientists "doing science" (e.g., in actual laboratory work). They found that scientists' technical and occupational languages contained important, "self-explicating" understandings that guided this activity. That is, the nature of their work was found not in their results or their expressed ideologies but in their observable practices (like using instruments). Specifically, the EM researchers noted that the scientists' espoused value of rationality was often belied by their use of unofficial working practices (e.g., "rules of thumb") for interpreting and reporting ambiguous data. Topics such as "validity" among scientists were in fact complex resources for improvisational performances whose correspondence to official dogma was at best approximate. EM principles have been similarly employed in studying settings such as classrooms (e.g., Mehan, 1979), computer centers (e.g., Johnson & Kaplan, 1980), and newsrooms (e.g., Tuchman, 1991). The common theme in these studies is that social actors uniquely organize the resources and activities of particular settings. The focus is on how people engage in an activity in ways that implicitly define it for them *as* that activity. This perspective can be disconcerting (particularly for participants) because it violates the conventional belief that persons, objects, and events possess an a priori function or status.

We will take a closer look at two key concepts to complete this summary of EM. The first concept emerges from the fact that social life is enacted in contexts. The practical reasoning in which people engage depends upon their use of the resources available in specific situations. Expressions that draw upon particular aspects of a local context to establish orderliness and factuality are *indexical*. These expressions help us to organize the information available in settings as a resource for interpreting their emergent interaction. For example, a risqué joke told among coworkers around the grill at a company cookout engages situational resources: the participants' spacing, orientation, posture, vocal capabilities, and so on. From the EM stance, what makes this event "joke telling" is not a summary of the joke but its characteristic activities: the teller's bidding for the group's attention, pausing to emphasize significant content, gesturing to illustrate verbal symbolism, integrating narration with food preparation and service, and soliciting affirmation from sympathetic audience members. In telling the same joke to a religious leader while leaving a worship service, one would have to negotiate a very different set of contextual resources (e.g., the reduced availability of the audience). Indexicality, then, involves the artful and reflexive organization of behavior to create a meaningful act. By invoking context, indexical expressions ensure the production of subsequent indexical expressions. They sustain context as a guide for evolving interaction.

The second EM concept emerges from the need of social actors to make their practical reasoning somehow "visible" to each other. In some cases, this may mean keeping the reality of the situation clear to everyone. In other cases, the situation might require keeping some participants in the dark. According to Garfinkel (1967), "The activities whereby members produce and manage settings of organized everyday affairs are identical with members' procedures for making those settings 'accountable' . . . [that is,] observable-and-reportable . . . available to members as situated practices of looking-and-telling" (p. 1). In this way, EM scholars find evidence for social order in people's (usually verbal) *accounts* of their activities. Much EM research consists of close analysis of "talk-as-accounts." EM scholars view talk as a central means by which actors construct their shifting, yet objective, realities (Heritage, 1984). Accounts are a form of practical action. As such, they frequently economize on (or "gloss") what they purport to explain or coordinate. In fact, an enormous amount of what we say is vague or incomplete. We rely on others to do a great deal of work to figure out what we mean—or might mean.

When they elicit accounts, EM researchers may follow up with questions designed to get more detail or justification (which of course results in more accounts). This quest to define the actor's *background expectancies* (another term for the natural attitude) by generating and interpreting accounts has been criticized as solipsistic—that is, explaining only a solitary, experiencing self (Mayrl, 1973). But this criticism is misguided: EM has in fact shunned subjectivity as a concept that is not useful for its purposes. Instead, it seeks to describe the concrete methods people use to create and sustain an *intersubjective* reality. Recently, EM researchers have expanded their description of the sequences of coordinated activity (the how) to focus on the links between rules, ideology, and social structure (the what) (Atkinson, 1988; Gubrium & Holstein, 2000).

EM has affected Communication's research agenda in at least three ways. First, and perhaps most directly, it has shaped the development of *conversation analysis* (CA). This focus, which was briefly introduced in Chapter 1, derives its methodological and conceptual impetus from the work of Harvey Sacks and his associates (e.g., Sacks, Schegloff, & Jefferson, 1974; Schegloff, 1968), who were fascinated with microscopic features of ordinary talk: how conversations open, the order in which speaking turns occur, and, in general, how it displays skillful collaboration (Gubrium & Holstein, 2000). While CA's overriding interest in the structure of talk leaves little room for consideration of its relational, affective, or cultural aspects, it rigorously clarifies speakers' local organization of coherence (Hopper, Koch, & Mandelbaum, 1986). CA scholars typically rely on transcripts of discourse recorded in naturalistic settings and diverge from ethnographers in preferring the analysis of talk features to detailed descriptions of its context (Nelson, 1994; Spencer, 1994).

Second, some strands of EM, particularly those influenced by the work of Aaron Cicourel (1974, 1980), have emphasized the significance of *rules* in communication. Following Schutz's ideas rather more closely than Garfinkel's (O'Keefe, 1980), Cicourel viewed order in everyday interaction as emanating from sets of cognitive rules he called "interpretive procedures." He argued that rules embody an ongoing schema of social structure and provide actors with guidelines concerning appropriate and effective action in situations. Traditionally, rules concepts in Communication hold that the regularity of action in situations results from the social-cognitive rules learned by actors. Rules explanations have proven durable partly because they offer ways to explain both creativity and conformity in interaction. They also fit very well with the idea that communication relies on intersubjective codes of meaning. Historically, the most prominent of these explanations in the interpersonal area have been the consensual rules perspective of Cushman and his associates (see, for example, Cushman, 1977; Cushman & Whiting, 1972) and the Coordinated Management of Meaning perspective of Pearce and his associates (e.g., Pearce & Cronen, 1980; Pearce & Pearce, 2000). A third tradition, deriving from the ethnography of communication, investigates the rule-like character of language performance (e.g., Philipsen, 1975; Sigman, 1980). Although a full discussion of communication rules cannot be pursued here, it should be noted that the area continues to struggle over a number of issues, including how intentional and conscious social actors are when they carry out rule-governed behavior, whether or not people can verbalize the rules they "follow," what degree of creativity is involved in rule use, how specific a rule statement should be, and how universally applicable rules are (see Morris & Hopper, 1987; Shimanoff, 1980).

Finally, one growing area of study influenced by EM involves "talk at work" (Drew & Heritage, 1992). This body of research assumes that talk is the principal means through which actors conduct goal-oriented activities in professions and organizations. It examines the connections between talk in institutional settings (e.g., job interviews, courtrooms, academic colloquia, emergency call centers) and their larger structures and ideologies.

Frequently, it depicts speaker identities as collaborative works in progress and the negotiation of inevitable tensions between individual agency and organizational constraint (Banks, 1994; Mellinger, 1994; G. Miller, 1997; Tracy & Baratz, 1993). In Communication, this project attracts researchers in the subfields of language and social interaction and organizational communication.

Symbolic Interactionism

In a phrase, *symbolic interactionism* (SI) is the study of how the self and the social environment shape each other through communication. Several SI concepts originated in the philosophy of pragmatism. Despite a good deal of diversity among its founders (William James, John Dewey, George Herbert Mead, and Charles Sanders Peirce, who coined the term), pragmatism can be summarized in a few propositions. In pragmatism, meaning is invoked in practical consequences. For example, the difference in meaning between two terms (e.g., *Spanish* and *Hispanic*) arises out of the ways that they are used in concrete situations (e.g., in choosing from identity options available on census forms). In this way, different meanings grow out of different procedures for anticipating and orienting to the social world. The semiotics developed by Peirce laid the groundwork for the study of signification (meaning-making) as a social process (Jensen, 1991). Also, pragmatism rejected the rationalist belief in an objective reality and behaviorist methods. Rather, it claimed that reality is *indeterminate*. In other words, the world that we perceive and act in consists of multiple, emergent realities that are always in the process of changing. These realities are formed in negotiations conducted between the self and various people, objects, and events. By *negotiation*, we mean that it is only through engaging their environment that individuals define the limits of their knowledge—especially of the self (Dewey, 1929/1958; Mead, 1934). Finally, in disavowing scientific knowledge as an end in itself, pragmatism embraced the analysis of concrete social problems. Pragmatists' belief in the mutual constitution of self and society led them to advocate progressive reforms in labor and education to mediate the destructive effects of industrial capitalism. Pragmatists such as Dewey (1927/1954) were particularly sensitive to the moral imperative of open discourse for fostering democracy. Many SI founders, especially the Chicago School of sociology, took up this legacy to study the ecology of urban communities, ethnic assimilation, and disenfranchised groups (Rock, 1979; Shalin, 1986).

SI is often associated with George Herbert Mead, whose model of the self strongly influenced its development. According to Mead, communication is fundamental to the development of the self. He viewed society as realms of group life premised on cooperative interaction. In these interactions, participants ascertain each other's intentions through the use of *significant symbols*. These are gestures (verbal or nonverbal) that "implicitly arouse in an individual making them the response which they explicitly arouse, or are supposed to arouse, in the individuals to whom they are addressed" (Mead, 1934, p. 47). Using significant symbols involves more than signaling our internal state to others; it also evokes in us the anticipated response of the other. In this experience (also known as "taking the role of the other"), we momentarily imagine how we are seen. We encounter our selves, then, only through the eyes of others. In order to perform this *role taking*, an individual must understand all the roles making up the life of a particular group. Mead's famous example involves the ability of baseball players to execute their own positions because they understand the roles (and thus anticipate the actions) of their teammates. Hickey, Thompson, and Foster (1988) arrive at the same conclusion from the opposite route: They depict the anxiety of a young man who, after being hired to play the Easter Bunny at a shopping mall, discovers that both the script for this role and the feedback from his audience are ambiguous at best. Both examples demonstrate that we learn who we are, and what parts to play, by perceiving others' attitudes toward us (Goffman, 1959, 1967).

In Mead's theory, the self embodies an expressive component (the "I") and an evaluative component (the "me"). The "I" directs our creative expression, whereas the "me" imagines the attitudes of others (either general or specific) in ways that adjust the "I." This ongoing interplay between action and reflection enables us to engage in a controlled exchange of significant symbols. By taking the role of primary other (such as a parent) and generalized other (such as an educational institution), one learns to act flexibly in different social situations. The self is inevitably shaped by this saturation of expectations, but so too is society. The complexity of socialization creates selves that are capable of both conformity and innovation.

Herbert Blumer (1969) played a significant role in developing the implications of Mead's social psychology. Blumer argued that meaning arises directly from social interaction. In fact, meanings are the *only* basis people have for acting toward things or other people. People align their actions based on shared meanings for symbols, and also on perceived differences. Successful alignment is generally known as *joint action* (Denzin, 1969, 1977). The types and range of acceptable joint action are influenced by relational rules of conduct and by civil-legal codes (e.g., for ownership of property). Although these constraints have real force for group members, they can also be changed through joint action. In terms of methodology, Blumer encouraged researchers to directly immerse themselves in settings via participant observation. He believed this was the only way for researchers to understand the meanings of joint action. The "documentary" investigations of urban life directed by Robert Park, Ernest Burgess, and others from the sociology department of the University of Chicago in the 1920s and 1930s (Delia, 1987; Kurtz, 1984) characterized this style of inquiry. Those studies combined survey, census, document analysis, and observational techniques to document changes in the human ecology of Chicago neighborhoods and ethnic groups, and in the working lives of marginalized people.

Like ethnomethodology, SI strongly resonates with Communication's defining commitments. It emphasizes the role of symbolic expression in both affiliation and conflict. It explains relationships among actors' understandings, motives, and message design practices. Most important, it opens up for scrutiny the *meanings* inherent in social phenomena, lest they be otherwise objectified as structures and functions (Duncan, 1962; Faules & Alexander, 1978). Historically, SI has influenced the development of the *constructivist* approach to interpersonal communication (e.g., Delia, 1977; Delia & O'Keefe, 1979). Constructivism seeks to explain how persons adjust and adapt their communicative strategies by means of such cognitive assessments as perspective taking. This approach is particularly interested in how cognitive complexity affects responses to different communicative situations. Constructivism has borrowed widely from various theories; from SI it draws on concepts such as role taking, the definition of the situation, and the emergence of meaning in interaction. Qualitative studies, however, have played a small role in constructivism. Traditionally, the approach relies on structured coding systems applied to simulated social situations.

Elsewhere, SI has influenced—often implicitly—the study of topics such as socialization, social cognition, role and identity management, and relational negotiation. Chatham-Carpenter and De Francisco (1997), for example, show how SI bridges the contexts of interpersonal and intrapersonal communication in their study of women's integration of self-talk and relational experiences to produce healthy self-esteem. Scheibel's (1992) study of identity negotiations between underage female bar patrons and male gatekeepers is a classic study in the "dramaturgical" tradition. SI concepts have also influenced studies of group and organizational communication as cultural phenomena (Bantz, 1993; Frey, 1994b). The interpretive debts of these studies are quite eclectic, but their emphasis on the performance of myth, ritual, and everyday interaction, as well as their focus on conflict, belies the influence of SI (e.g., Pacanowsky & O'Donnell-Trujillo, 1982,

1983). Bastien and Hostager (1992), for example, directly applied SI concepts in their study of cooperation between jazz performers, and Scheibel (1994) studied the graffiti of film school students as a text of their artistic and professional identity construction. In the field of media studies, SI researchers have historically studied the impact and interpretation of motion pictures (see Wartella, 1987), and Blumer (1969) wrote a fine essay on the misguided nature of media effects research. Some theoretical work has argued that media formats (comprising elements of symbolization, story, and technology) provide important material for audience members' constructions of reality (Altheide & Snow, 1988; Anderson & Meyer, 1988; Chesebro & Bertselsen, 1996). However, current audience studies only occasionally claim an interactionist perspective (e.g., Frazer & Reid, 1979; Lindlof, 1987). The rich possibilities of SI for studying communication sites and events have clearly not been exhausted.

Ethnography of Communication

Our third tradition draws from a rich heritage of anthropology, sociolinguistics, folklore studies, and (arguably) semiotics. Ethnography of communication (EOC) conceptualizes communication as a continuous flow of information, rather than as a segmented exchange of messages. It views social actors as simultaneously using multiple channels (e.g., verbal and nonverbal) and codes to create meaningful interaction (Sigman, 1987). By "codes," we mean rules that inform cultural members how to use and interpret particular categories of signs (such as fashion and food). Although many of its studies focus on linguistic practices, EOC research has encompassed a broad range of communication media, genres, and contexts, including spitting (Knuf, 1992), griping (Katriel, 1990), television talk shows (Carbaugh, 1993), family photographs (Musello, 1980), personal scrapbooks (Katriel & Farrell, 1991), museum exhibits (Katriel, 1993), subcultures of orality and writing (Baxter, 1993), membership rituals (Braithwaite, 1997), terms of personal address (Fitch, 1991), and organizational symbolism (Carbaugh, 1988a).

What unites this diversity is a concern with the relationship between symbolic practices and social structure. As a theoretical matter, this concern is played out when researchers preserve evidence of cultural "particularity" in communication (e.g., in statements of the specific requirements for locally competent performance). This allows researchers to inductively develop "acontextual" formats for comparing data and discovering patterns in cultural communication (e.g., in the use of silence; Braithwaite, 1990)

(Philipsen, 1989). In this process, EOC researchers are guided by recurring questions: How do communication practices reflect local preferences for its form and content? How do those preferences operate systemically to organize particular identities and relationships among participants? How do these practices work to constitute general forms of social reality (Carbaugh, 1995)? In response, EOC studies produce highly detailed analyses of communication codes (e.g., for acceptable expression) and their moment-to-moment functions in various contexts. In these analyses, speech communities are constituted in local and continuous performances of cultural and moral matters.

This broad focus may be traced to the work of scholars such as Ray Birdwhistell (1970), who developed the study of kinesics (human movement) in social context, and Edward T. Hall (1959), who pioneered the cross-cultural study of communication codes such as proxemics. The influence of sociolinguistics and anthropology is evident in EOC's concern with the relationship between linguistic forms (e.g., vocabularies and grammars) and their social uses (particularly as requirements for cultural membership). The influence of folklore studies is evident in EOC's collection of examples of artful, situated performance to develop an understanding of its origins and functions. Schely-Newman (1995), for example, showed how storytelling helped Israeli women of North African heritage to negotiate the domestic politics of gender and intergenerational relationships.

The largest influence on EOC, however, is that of Dell Hymes (1962), who initially named the field the "ethnography of speaking" and defined its agenda: the field study of language pragmatics in social contexts. Hymes pioneered a radical empirical focus on "speaking as an activity in its own right" (1962, p. 16). Stewart and Philipsen (1984) have summarized three implications of Hymes's work: (1) that community speech can be studied as if it is a system of rule-guided practices; (2) that investigators should examine significant cross-cultural differences in the forms and functions of speech; and (3) that emic (or communal) meaning structures should constrain researcher claims. Collectively, these assumptions shift research focus from speech as an abstract code to speech as a situated and practical *event* whose understanding requires ethnographic investigation. Hymes later revised his model of the speech event as a framework of elements encapsulated in the acronym SPEAKING: "*S*etting, or *S*cene; *P*articipants, or *P*ersonnel; *E*nds (both the goals or purposes and the outcomes); *A*ct Characteristics (both the form and the content of what is said); *K*ey (the tone, manner, or spirit in which an act is done); *I*nstrumentalities (the channel and code); *N*orms of Interaction and of Interpretation; *G*enres (the categories or types of speech act and speech event)"(Bauman & Sherzer, 1975, p. 100). This framework was then used by researchers to engage topics such as speaker competence and cultural attitudes toward speaking itself.

Three sets of distinctions should be noted at this point. First, although *ethnography of speaking* was the original designation for this tradition, many of its researchers have since adopted the term *communication* in describing their focus. This term is more expansive and connotes the study of mediated and nonverbal discourses in addition to speech. At the same time, most EOC researchers consider "speaking" to be a prominent—even primordial—means of communication and thus invoke this designation when speech is the principal phenomena of study (D. Carbaugh, personal communication with Bryan Taylor, September 27, 2001). Second, while EOC shares some aims and methods with conversation and discourse analysis, it also possesses two distinctive characteristics: its ethnographic heritage and its interest in analyzing speech performances to reveal role structure and enactment. Finally, as an interdisciplinary enterprise, EOC diverges from the primarily sociological traditions of ethnomethodology and symbolic interactionism.

As a research community, EOC emerged in the 1960s and 1970s marked by several field studies, programmatic statements, and anthologies (see Bauman & Sherzer, 1975; Leeds-Hurwitz, 1984; Philipsen & Carbaugh, 1986). During this period, journals such as *Language in Society* were established for the express purpose of studying speech in social life, and several other journals (such as *Language, Research of Language and Social Interaction,* and *Text and Performance Quarterly*) have since emerged that regularly publish EOC studies. Within Communication, EOC is commonly associated with the figure of Gerry Philipsen, who, in a long and distinguished career at the University of Washington, has trained many of its leading practitioners (e.g., Donal Carbaugh and Tamar Katriel). Philipsen's 1975 study, "Speaking Like a Man in Teamsterville" is a landmark study that examined the codes (e.g., when, how, and to whom to speak) underlying male role enactment in a working-class urban neighborhood. As part of a Chicago trilogy, this study was later followed by analyses of locations for gendered speech (Philipsen, 1976) and of the codes of dignity and honor used by politicians to construct and defend local interests against interlopers (Philipsen, 1986).

Cumulatively, EOC researchers have provided Communication with a clear and influential model for qualitative research. The perspective is particularly systematic in its linkage of data analysis and theory building, and it demonstrates how good research can grow out of practical necessity. (Philipsen's Teamsterville studies, for example, were one response to the challenges he faced as a social worker trying to perform effectively in an alien culture.) The EOC tradition is also valued because it provided an alternative to the psychologism and positivism that dominated Communication during the late 1960s and 1970s. Recently, however, postmodern and cultural studies scholars have criticized the implicit modernism in EOC's theories and methods (Fiske, 1991b; Neumann, 1994). They argue that its rational emphasis on order, stability, and consensus emphasizes abstract forms over complex processes, disguises the researcher's active role in constructing the appearance of cultural coherence, and suppresses the realities of fragmentation, ambiguity, and paradox created by ongoing struggle among social groups. In their defense, EOC researchers argue that claims concerning power and conflict should not be imported a priori, should be limited to explicit evidence of their relevance for speakers, and should not preclude the depiction of how order is achieved despite contingencies (Carbaugh, 1991; Fitch, 1994b). Huspek and Kendall's (1991) study of the political vocabularies of loggers, for example, shows how an EOC focus can produce counterintuitive findings (e.g., regarding speakers' rationales for their expression) otherwise missed by simplistic theories of domination. This controversy concerning the nature of cultural communication and how it should be studied will, along with the continuing need for direct studies of interaction (Carbaugh, 1995), shape the future of EOC.

Critical Theory

The term *critical theory* invokes a rich, lively, and often vexing body of work. Centrally, this work involves an ethically heightened and politically reflective study of the relationships between power, knowledge, and discourse that are produced in contexts of historical and cultural struggle. Of all the theoretical traditions discussed in this chapter, this one is the most densely packed. For heuristic purposes, we punctuate its multiple strands using the categories "modern" and "postmodern." These two categories signal important differences in the topics that critical theories address, the premises they invoke, and their implications for qualitative methodology. As an orientation, here is one summary of critical theory premises:

> That all thought is fundamentally mediated by power relations that are social and historically constituted; that facts can never be isolated from the domain of values or removed from some form of ideological inscription; that the relationship between concept and object and between signifier and signified is never stable or fixed and is often mediated by the social relations of capitalist production and consumption; that language is central to the formation of

subjectivity . . . that certain groups in any society are privileged over others, and, although the reasons for this privileging may vary widely, the oppression that characterizes contemporary societies is most forcefully reproduced when subordinates accept their social status as natural, necessary or inevitable; that oppression has many faces and that focusing only on one at the expense of others often elides the interconnections among them; and finally, that mainstream research practices are generally, although most often unwittingly, implicated in the reproduction of systems of class, race, and gender oppression. (Kinchloe & McLaren, 2000, p. 291)

We can begin to unpack the implications of this quote by distinguishing between a general definition of critical theory and a more specific one. The former involves a broad "orientation towards investigating exploitation, repression, unfairness, asymmetrical power relations . . . distorted communication and false consciousness" (Alvesson & Deetz, 1996, p. 192). When qualitative researchers operate from this general definition, they reflect on the political influences that shape their agendas (e.g., managerial sponsorship of organizational consulting) and commit to the production of knowledge that provides disadvantaged groups with new resources for thinking and acting (a process also known as *emancipation*). Here, researchers presume that their chosen sites are shot through with tensions produced by conflicts between the members of resident groups (e.g., over access to the means of self-expression). These tensions, which evolve out of incompatible group interests, may produce overt conflict and coercion. More typically, however, they are managed in subtle and normalized practices of domination that diffuse the possibility of organized resistance (e.g., in denying the members of minority groups access to education that would promote their economic advancement). This approach is inherently concerned with communication as a medium through which social actors produce and deliberate knowledge claims, and realize their potential for self-understanding and determination. Qualitative researchers working in this vein are witnesses to, and potentially change agents in, the pivotal moments where dominant and subordinate groups influence each other by expressing their interests (Thomas, 1993).

Modernist Critical Theory

The preceding "general" definition of critical theory is distinguished by its permissive scope. A more restrictive definition, however, involves a "modernist" tradition that derives from work conducted in the early and mid-20th century by members of the so-called Frankfurt School (e.g., Max

Horkheimer, Theodore Adorno, and Herbert Marcuse) and by their successor, Jürgen Habermas, the famous theorist of rationality and public deliberation. As neo-Marxists, these scholars were specifically concerned with forms of authority and injustice that accompanied the evolution of *industrial and corporate capitalism* as a political-economic system. In this process they wrestled with the failure of traditional Marxism to anticipate the success of capitalism—aided by positivist social science and commercialized mass media—in socializing cultural members to passively accept oppressive conditions (e.g., militarism) as if they were objective and inevitable "facts." Specifically, they identified sites where the Enlightenment value of rationality (i.e., systematic means-ends reasoning) and the potential benefits of technology had been manipulated to create systems of domination and alienation. Within these systems, powerful groups enforced "technical rationalities" that displaced traditional forms of community life (e.g., those valuing empathy, intuition, spirituality, and authenticity). These rationalities suppressed the collaborative deliberation of goals and compelled conformity to routines. Generally, these rationalities promoted a narrow range of "instrumental" values, such as efficiency, productivity, profit, and control. The tendency of these rationalities to reduce human beings to human doings was memorably satirized in the 1936 silent film, *Modern Times*, in which Charlie Chaplin's impish character struggles with a relentless factory assembly line, endures management harangues delivered via closed-circuit television, is force-fed by a malfunctioning machine, attempts to escape *into* the machinery, and is ultimately consigned to a mental institution.

Although the Frankfurt School critics indicted capitalism as a condition of social ills, they did not assume that it directly or solely determined human existence. Instead, they opened up to scrutiny the role of cultural institutions (such as media, science, and industry) in producing ideological discourse. This discourse, they argued, subverted the ability of cultural members to fully understand or transform their "imaginary" (ideologically shaped) relationships to the "real"(e.g., political-economic) conditions of their existence. Historically, this move to conceptualize ideology as a circulating narrative has been central to cultural and critical studies (Hall, 1982; Jameson, 1977). It has enabled scholars to identify the specific communicative practices (e.g., reification) by which elite groups normalize arbitrary arrangements and generally distort the processes of public debate (Shapiro, 1988; Sholle, 1988). In this process, critical understanding of ideology has shifted. Rather than being viewed as a distorted mode of "false consciousness" (which presumes an objective reality behind the veil), ideology is now viewed as a *productive* force of "reason" and "common sense" that *constitutes* knowledge. It does so by selectively depicting what is "natural," "possible," "good," and "inevitable" (as well as their opposites) in social life. In this view, there is no "outside" to ideology—only a pervasive field of contesting narratives. French theorist Louis Althusser contributed to this view by connecting emergent Freudian theories of identity formation to Marxist theories of political-economic influence on cultural life. Althusser argued that the discourses of "institutional state apparatuses" (e.g., the church, family, workplace, and school) "hail" cultural members to assume various "subject positions" (e.g., to view themselves as "consumers") whose practical reproduction is essential for the maintenance of dominant institutions (a process also known as *interpellation*). So positioned, cultural members become conscious of themselves, each other, and their world through a complex—and often contradictory—field of forces, including obligation, permission, and constraint. The actions of cultural members, and their consequences, are generated within this field of forces (Strinati, 1995).

The Italian philosopher Antonio Gramsci made yet another significant contribution to this project in developing the concept of *hegemony* (Mumby, 1998). Gramsci argued that cultural members are neither dupes nor victims of dominant ideologies. Instead, he viewed them as objects of intensive ideological operations seeking to create their active consent (e.g., through fear-mongering, inducements, etc.) to the conditions of domination. In negotiating their relationship with dominant images and voices in their culture, "the governed" become complicit in reproducing structures that are not in their interests *and* are not of their making. This deeply ironic process occurs, Gramsci theorized, as cultural members make choices in the context of a life-world whose options for meaning have always already been shaped by ideology. They experience themselves as exercising agency in making choices and sometimes even as resisting cultural authority. They are not aware, however, of the options that have been rendered literally unthinkable by dominant ideologies—moved beyond the rim of the conceivable or legitimate. As a result, there is little guarantee that their actions will be truly authentic or radical, or that the logic controlling their understanding of their choices will be transformed. This is especially true in light of the remarkable abilities of dominant groups to identify and appropriate subversive movements for their own purposes (e.g., when radical politics are sanitized and recycled in advertisements as an aesthetic of "individual" and seemingly defiant consumer choice). In Gramsci's phrase, a complex "war of position" ensues in which the members of subordinate groups use tactics (e.g., labor strikes and sabotage) to expand their "margin of maneuver" in oppressive systems, while dominant groups exploit their control of resources (e.g., plant lockouts, pressure brought to bear as advertisers on commercial media outlets) to contain social meanings and practices (e.g., those generated in news coverage).

Significantly, for qualitative researchers, this process is inherently communicative: Its shifting terrain involves animated dialogue between the proponents of multiple narratives of social reality. These narratives materialize and circulate through mundane cultural practices of expression and interpretation. Embodied as texts, they alternately promote and challenge the legitimacy of particular ideologies. Qualitative researchers influenced by critical theory bear witness to this struggle, seeking to clarify—and perhaps transform—encoded linkages between representation, power, and the formation of identity (Strine, 1991). Struggles of meaning around cultural terms (such as "terrorist"), then, involve far more than mere "semantics." They represent ideological attempts to interrupt and refashion the "signifying chains" of conventional associations that underwrite institutional authority (Hall, 1985). Because of the textual density of this conflict, even small performances (e.g., the preservation by a married woman of her maiden name) can produce rippling, unpredictable consequences.

Postmodernist Critical Theory

The object of celebration and scorn among intellectuals, *postmodernism* is both a powerful theoretical resource and a cultural cliché. Its ambiguity stems from the enormous work that it is called upon to perform by various audiences: adequately conceptualizing and engaging the complex phenomena of *postmodernity*. This latter term is used to punctuate a number of dramatic, interrelated developments in 20th-century global politics, economics, and social life (Alvesson & Deetz, 1996; Foster, 1983; Mumby, 1997):

- The disintegration of colonial systems ruled by imperial nation-states, and the subsequent dispersal of people, information, and products at accelerated rates across geopolitical boundaries
- The decline of industrial capitalism, and the rise of an information-age economy premised on the ruthless consolidation of corporate control and the commodification of symbols and knowledge
- The rise of global mass media systems whose relentless, commercialized operations collapse traditional boundaries of space and time, and whose programming erodes conceptual distinctions between "high art" and "popular culture," "citizen" and "consumer," "reality" and "simulation," and "authenticity" and "irony"
- A continuous dismantling and reassembling of artistic genres and media to produce creatively combined bricolage and recycled -but- familiar pastiche
- A general loss of faith in "foundational" meta-narratives of institutional authority (e.g., of religion, politics, and science) and an ambivalent embrace of marginalized cultural voices that challenge traditional values (e.g., of rationality)
- The erosion of traditional identities premised on stability and essence (e.g., "individual") in favor of those premised on ambiguity, fragmentation, and simultaneity

(e.g., "cyborg") so that identity is not the *referent* of communication but, rather, the *effect* of discourses that construct and enforce preferred narratives for understanding the self and other (including the discourses of "theory") (Lannamann, 1991)

Although this list is not exhaustive, it begins to establish some implications of postmodernist critical theory for qualitative research. Generally, postmodernism requires researchers to politicize social problems by situating them in historical and cultural contexts, to implicate themselves in the process of collecting and analyzing data, and to relativize their findings (Charmaz, 1995). A related development is that the contemporary juggernaut of globalization has destabilized ethnographic traditions of conceptualizing and engaging research sites. In this era of "flow" (in which, for example, international combatants watch the same real-time broadcasts of military operations on cable news networks), the cultural distinctiveness of even geographically isolated sites is no longer guaranteed. As a result, qualitative researchers are revising their fields as "multi-sited" (Marcus, 1995). In these studies, researchers depict large-scale social forces by comparing and contrasting their local manifestations in particular, interrelated scenes.

Throughout this process, qualitative researchers confront the challenge of engaging a cultural zeitgeist of crisis, schizophrenia, and nostalgia. These jagged forms of feeling emerge from the rapid transformation of social structures that make meaning itself a precarious accomplishment. Postmodern researchers can vacillate between ecstasy and despair in a world saturated with swirling signs: the rate and intensity of social action increase, and communication itself moves front and center as a social problem. At the same time, disorientation and emptiness haunt the research process: more (signs) is not necessarily better, or even enough. Rapid mutation (e.g., in continuous organizational change) can be either liberating or terrifying, depending on who is controlling the process and how it is being controlled. Diverse voices gathered by researchers may indeed relativize authority and emancipate the oppressed; they are just as likely, however, to raise vexing problems of "undecidability" around compelling yet incompatible narratives (e.g., those associated with alien abduction and "recovered memories" of sexual abuse). In this stormy epistemological climate, field-based research engaging the actual use and abuse of texts *in context* becomes *more*—not less—important (Charmaz, 1995; Trujillo, 1993).

Another consequence of postmodernist critique for qualitative research involves a general *crisis of representation* in the human sciences (Marcus & Fischer, 1986). This crisis stems from theoretical innovations that emphasize the centrality of discourse in shaping human understanding. A major influence here is that of poststructuralism, which rejects traditional claims that individuals "author" discourse as expressions of their unique essence and that the material elements of spoken and written language (signifiers) have stable referents in objective reality (signifieds; Chang, 1996; Hawes, 1998). Poststructuralism focuses on the way in which signs depend for their meaning on arbitrary, unstable (and often suppressed) relationships *with other signs* (e.g., racial identities such as "white" that invoke other racial identities as a basis for contrast). In this view, culture is a giant "rhizomatic" (rootlike) field of interrelated sign systems; the meaning of any particular sign is stabilized only through rhetorical processes that constrain its "polysemic" potential for competing or subversive meanings. One implication of this argument for qualitative researchers (explored in Chapter 9) is that their work products (e.g., fieldnotes, monographs) may no longer be considered objective depictions of a stable other. Instead, these texts may be subjected to critical scrutiny concerning their ideological productivity (Clifford & Marcus, 1986; Manning, 1995; West, 1993). Consequently, many qualitative researchers have chosen to abandon traditional forms of narration (e.g., "realism") to explore alternatives that encourage reflection about the "politics and poetics" of their work. In these accounts, the embodied, collaborative, dialogic, and improvisational aspects of qualitative research are clarified (Conquergood, 1991; Presnell, 1994)

Having covered some traditions of critical theory, we conclude this section by noting a historical conflict between critical theorists and qualitative researchers. The accusations in this conflict have been two-way. For their part, critical theorists claim that ethnographers (as the principal offenders) display naïveté in their "integrationist" depictions of cultural order, mistake cultural members' *consent* to dominant arrangements for their *endorsement*, and ignore the political complicity of a "neutral" research stance (e.g., one that depicts the cultural exotic as an aesthetic spectacle for pleasurable consumption). In this way, critical theorists fear that qualitative researchers may perpetuate oppression for no other reason than that they fail to conceptualize and oppose it. Alternatively, by presuming that social life is saturated with irony, paradox, absurdity, and cruelty, critical theorists seek to "expose" and "awaken" rather than merely "describe" (Hawes, 1983; Ortner, 1997; Putnam, Bantz, Deetz, Mumby, & Van Maanen, 1993).

Not surprisingly, these claims have generated strong reactions among interpretivists, who argue that a critical-theoretical agenda is both flawed and inappropriate for the conduct of qualitative research. Hammersley (1992), for example, has indicted critical theorists for failing to prove that emancipation is itself an undistorted or falsifiable ideal and for oversimplifying the operations of power in actual cultural practice. Even critical theory's sympathizers have noted how some of its key elements discourage qualitative researchers from taking up its banner: *intellectualism* (favoring abstract concepts), *reductionism* (e.g., "reading off" people's identities from their class positions), *elitism* (presuming that people's sensemaking is inherently flawed), and *negativism* (identifying problems without providing viable solutions) (Alvesson & Wilmott, 1992).

This conflict is not intractable, however. Qualitative researchers studying organizational communication, for example, are increasingly using sophisticated critical theories of identity and power to frame their studies of the evolving systems of workplace control (Barker & Cheney, 1994; Deetz, 1998; Holmer-Nadesan, 1996). Some critical theorists (Forester, 1992), in turn, are sympathetic to using ethnographic methods to produce careful and empathic descriptions of everyday life. In addition, both groups have been affected by the fallout from postmodern theories of discourse: ethnographers cannot accuse critics of "only" working with "texts" when their own work products (e.g., fieldnotes and monographs) are no longer presumed to be objective accounts of social action. These trends indicate that although the tensions between critical theory and qualitative research are not easily resolved, debating them can generate innovative research.

Feminism

Although feminism is clearly a strand of critical theory, its controversial status and rich contributions to qualitative research warrant a separate (even if brief) discussion. Like critical theory, feminism is not a single theory or method but a highly charged field of competing narratives about the nature and consequences of gender identities (Eichler, 1997). These narratives include *liberal feminism*, which is primarily concerned with the inclusion of women in the rights and benefits traditionally afforded to men; *ideological* or *Marxist feminism*, which links female oppression to the system of social organization under capitalism; *radical feminism*, which celebrates women as fundamentally different from and better than their male oppressors and emphasizes sexual separatism; *standpoint feminism*, which argues that women's marginalized position as other provides a resource of difference useful in critiquing and transforming oppressive institutions; and *poststructuralist* or *postmodern feminism*, which analyzes discourse to understand how gender identities are constructed and deployed as a political process. This last perspective diverges from other feminisms in not presuming, a priori, inherent differences between the sexes (M. G. Fine, 1993; Hallstein, 1999; Ollenburger & Moore, 1992; Tong, 1989).

Although they share some core values (e.g., the emancipation of women from patriarchal structures), these feminisms bring different resources and priorities to qualitative research. Any single study may blend these elements in different ways. Also, although qualitative methods are uniquely suited to feminist research goals, the criteria for producing "truly" feminist research are highly contested. This means that feminist researchers establish their legitimacy through a variety of formal procedures and rhetorical strategies: constructing research questions (i.e., that directly address gender concerns), sampling subjects (i.e., so as to include women), choosing and employing methods (e.g., anticipating the influence of participants' gender identities on interviews), interpreting data (e.g., preserving the nonlinear and affective dimensions of personal narratives), presenting findings (e.g., incorporating subjects' voices into research narratives), and putting research to practical use (e.g., as a resource for deliberations on issues affecting women's lives). Although feminist research goals may be realized in the use of either quantitative or qualitative methods (or in their combination), there are particular sites of affinity between feminist theory and qualitative research. Let's review six of these.

First, feminists hold that since the production of knowledge is an act of power, qualitative researchers and subjects should be equal partners (Gergen, 1988). Ideally, the research process should evolve as cooperative and nonhierarchical. The traditional authority of researchers to define problems, determine methods of inquiry, and interpret findings is interrupted in order to pursue alternatives: the collaborative development of goals and procedures that directly meet the needs of women and that value women as authorities on their own experience.

Second, feminist qualitative researchers are decidedly *not* objective (Mies, 1981). Although this stance is a general article of faith in interpretivism (see Chapter 1), it is inflected here by a critique of the historical relationships between patriarchy and science and of the suppression of women's voices that is rationalized under the guise of neutrality and detachment (e.g., in deriving benchmarks for the attributes of general populations from studies of male subjects only). This stance has produced at least three specific consequences. One consequence is that feminist qualitative researchers are committed to reflecting about their investment in their work (e.g., as a function of their class positions, sexual orientations, and personal histories). In her call for greater introspection among media audience researchers, for example, Lotz (2000) urges a clarification of their contingent identities: "Did we ever belong to a different class? Have old friends who are positioned differently than we are? Have access to a specific regional mind frame? Have we belonged to organizations ... that present us access? Are our families' subjectivities different from our own?" (p. 460). In addition to this reflexivity, feminists also consider the ethics of their qualitative research and its consequences for those they study. Potentially, this commitment leads to a dilemma involving incompatible goals: the question is how feminist researchers can simultaneously affiliate with their women subjects, protect these women's intimate "secrets," and publicize relevant findings (Marshall, 1993; Stacey, 1988). This dilemma clarifies that, while women are uniquely positioned to inform qualitative researchers about their negotiation of patriarchy, they also face unique risks of exposure and punishment in this process. Finally, rejecting objectivity has led feminist researchers to develop alternate narratives of validity that support their claims "without falling back into positivist standards that measure acceptability of knowledge in terms of some ideal, unchanging body of knowledge" (Olesen, 2000, p. 236).

Third, qualitative research assists feminists in grappling with the politics of diversity. Feminist researchers frequently cite the importance of achieving adequate understanding of the relationships *between* the elements of class, race, nationality, and so on, and gender (Oleson, 2000; Ollenburger & Moore, 1992). Because qualitative methods are oriented toward holistic understanding of social action, such methods are one resource for studying the *simultaneity* of sexism, racism, and class discrimination in the globally dispersed yet interrelated contexts of postcolonialism, capitalism, and patriarchy. In particular, contemporary feminist researchers are sensitized to the urgency of de-centering knowledge that privileges the experience of white, middle-class, Western, heterosexual women. One partial solution is to increase qualitative study of the "nontraditional" settings, experiences, and activities of lesbian, working-class, nonwhite, and so-called Third World women (Ashcraft, 2000).

Fourth, feminist qualitative researchers are profoundly sensitive to the ways that *all* forms of research are affected by sexism, racism, and class discrimination that inhibit the achievement of feminist ideals. Qualitative researchers, potentially, face challenges such as the following: academic rituals (such as "the literature review") that constrain the questions that researchers may ask within an established universe of patriarchal discourse; institutional preferences for funding studies of "traditional" topics using quantitative methods; and academic policies for retention and promotion that encourage reproduction of the status quo (e.g., high numbers of rapidly produced, "well-placed" journal articles) and discourage women from performing time-intensive field-based research (e.g., in addition to their traditional responsibilities for childbearing and child-rearing) (Moore, 1991; Podsakoff & Dalton, 1987).

Fifth, feminists hold that since qualitative data are produced in the context of a relationship (i.e., as a mutual process of sensemaking between researchers and subjects), they should be recorded and interpreted accordingly. Kaufmann (1992), for example, argues that *qualitative interviews are not simply a means to produce data* (e.g., a transcript that displays theoretical concepts and formal features of social action). Instead, *they are in and of themselves data—* that is, they are collaborative performances of an evolving, politically inflected relationship between the participants. For this reason, the complexity of interviews should be preserved in their interpretation, not stripped for the purpose of aggregation with other abstract indices.

Finally, feminist commitments dramatically influence the form of qualitative research narratives. As will be discussed in Chapter 9, these narratives are often explicitly autobiographical. They vividly and sensitively use lyricism, affect, nonlinearity, and the juxtaposition of different textual fragments to subvert the positivist premises of detachment, monologic authority, and non-contingent Truth. Ronai's (1992) account of her fieldwork as a topless dancer, for example, is a searing depiction of how researchers and performers in the sex industry negotiate the relationship between their "real" and stage *personae*. Richardson (1992) renders data from her interviews with unmarried mothers as a long poem. These examples demonstrate the politics of style in feminist qualitative research—the ways in which narrative innovations can expose and disrupt patriarchal institutions. This form of qualitative research also serves as a medium for feminist researchers to work through the ambiguity, trauma, and contradiction associated with their autobiographical experience (Martin, 1989; Weil, 1989).

In summary, feminist theory and methods influence qualitative communication research in at least four ways. First, they reinforce the interpretivist commitment to collaborative and inductive research that preserves situated accounts of human experience. Second, they direct that commitment to serving the real needs of women. Sexual harassment in organizational settings, for example, has recently received intensive and sophisticated analysis by communication researchers (Clair, 1998; Townsley & Geist, 2000). In addition, Ashcraft and Pacanowsky (1996) have explored the potential for "cattiness" by the members of female groups that actively reproduces the conditions of gender oppression. Mobilized for these purposes, qualitative research can identify the sources of oppressive communication, clarify its complex dynamics, and increase participants' options for change. Third, feminist theory and methods expose taken-for-granted research practices so that gender differences may be considered at every opportunity. Finally, the feminist emphasis on the relationship between representation and lived experience has encouraged qualitative researchers to experiment with the form and content of their research narratives. In so doing, it has fueled the critical interrogation of academic knowledge as a rhetorical discourse.

Cultural Studies

Cultural studies (CS) is an international and interdisciplinary field that is often at the center of controversy (Slack & Semati, 1997). This tendency stems from a commitment by CS scholars to realize the implications of critical theory for working in academic and cultural (i.e., arts and broadcasting) institutions. This commitment produces a heightened tendency to reflect on and critique the conventional management of cultural matters. This opposition to the status quo has generated significant backlash from traditionalists, and CS has become a lightning rod for popular debate about the contemporary status of critical intellectuals.

CS has generated a rigorously eclectic body of theory (Barker, 2000; Tudor, 1999). This theory draws from and transforms many of the critical traditions discussed earlier in this chapter, particularly neo-Marxist, feminist, psychoanalytic, and poststructuralist theories of hegemony and identity formation. CS theory has evolved to engage *the totality* of structures and practices that constitute living and feeling in a modern (or postmodern) world (Nelson, Treichler, & Grossberg, 1992). Particular manifestations of this totality (such as Internet-based systems for exchanging music files) are opportunities for understanding the interaction between two opposing social forces: those of political-economic determination (e.g., when artists and recording companies seek to preserve music copyright) and those arising from individual or group desire for self-determination (e.g., when computer users circumvent copyright to increase their options for consumption). CS researchers freely combine textual-critical and qualitative methods to study this process (Frow & Morris, 2000).

For many CS researchers, culture is the site of profound struggle between the members of dominant and marginalized groups. This struggle evolves through the circulation of textual forms within communities (such as San Francisco "punks"; Lull, 1987) whose members share particular class, gender, and racial affiliations. In this view, cultures (and subcultures) are also "economies" in which texts form the medium for evolving relationships among producers, performers, and consumers (or audiences). In invoking the term *cultural economy*, CS scholars blend the traditional meanings of *text* and *commodity*. They explore the relationships between an object's *official* value in a financial or cultural economy (e.g., its price, or prescribed function) and its *unofficial* potential for generating meanings and pleasures within local systems of value and belief. Conquergood's (1994) study of a Chicago youth gang, for example, depicts its members' appropriation of a popular beer logo as a sign of their gang identity. Outsiders are often unable to detect the semiotic hijackings that underlie these surface appearances, and that is exactly the point. In general, the potential for textual meaning is shaped by a number of factors. These include the imperatives of the dominant political economy (e.g., the creation of profit in capitalism), the existing desires of cultural members (which are always already conditioned by textual circulation), and the condition of *intertextuality*. This term describes how cultural forms become meaningful based on their reference to prior and external texts (e.g., in their practices of quotation, allusion, and parody; Bennett & Woollacott, 1987; Johnson, 1986-1987).

In studying cultural activity, CS scholars emphasize a number of historical influences, including revolutionary advances in technology; the industrialization of mass production; the rise of consumerism; dramatic urban and suburban growth; the development of mass media and now of *new* media systems; the growth of powerful, bureaucratic nation-states; the rise and decline of Western colonialism; and the drastic fluctuation in the international commodity markets (Berman, 1982). CS scholars are interested in how these historical developments—and their aftermaths—are registered in cultural symbol systems (such as architecture) and how they influence the reproduction of identities, relationships, and communities. As a result, CS shows how power and knowledge are discursively produced in the crucible of centripetal (i.e., traditional and unifying) and centrifugal (fragmenting and subversive) conditions.

CS was loosely formalized in postwar Britain as an anti-elitist, radically contextual, and multimethodological project concerned with emancipating the working class. CS scholars sought to legitimate working class cultural practices (i.e., in opposing the tyranny of "high culture") and to mobilize their authenticity as a resource for social revolution. Over time, CS scholars expanded this focus to incorporate questions about race and ethnicity and about gender and sexuality. Their scope of inquiry expanded to include the sites of globalization, postcolonialism, pedagogy, youth subcultures, aesthetics, history, and many others. Within Communication, CS was initially framed as a critique of the discipline's traditions of empirical and quantitative study of media institutions and effects. But CS also offered humanistic resources for analyzing media texts as cultural artifacts (Kellner, 1993).

In this view, texts are complex (and contested) artifacts of ideologies that work to determine their symbolic form and content. In this tradition, textual meaning (i.e., that encoded in television programs during their production) is "overdetermined." This condition occurs, for example, when program producers who wish to appeal to the widest possible audience incorporate the elements of multiple ideologies. Because these ideologies inevitably conflict, however, they create ambiguity, contradictions, and omissions in texts. These conditions in turn create the possibility for multiple interpretations by audience members (i.e., polysemy). Audiences actively engage (or decode) these features in local contexts and in routines of media use that are shaped by specific purposes (e.g., domestic viewing of evening newscasts by married couples). During this process, they bring the skill and knowledge that are generated by their social positioning (i.e., their "cultural capital") to bear on texts. These "readings" may confirm, adapt, or reject the dominant ideological influences encoded in texts. Such outcomes, of course, hold significant consequences for cultural hegemony (Hall, 1981).

While the British tradition of CS emphasized class struggle, an American branch developed somewhat differently. This American CS was grounded in a pragmatic, liberal-pluralist tradition. It opposed the dominant positivism of media effects research and de-emphasized class to focus more broadly on the social practices by which diverse groups (i.e., in the context of an immigrant nation) achieved relative stability and consensus (Carey, 1989). The populist impulse in this tradition has been further developed by CS researchers such as John Fiske (1991a), Janice Radway (1984), and Lawrence Grossberg (1997). Their work foregrounds the everyday practices of ordinary cultural members, and it rejects simplistic theories of direct media effects and political-economic determination. In this view, cultural practices have at least some political effectiveness and some autonomy from economic determination. Currently, CS scholars are struggling to accommodate the increasing interrogation of so-called First World cultures and research by postcolonial voices uniquely concerned with the dialectic of globalization (i.e., cultural imperialism) and localization, diaspora, hybrid identity, and the nature of human rights (Hegde, 1998; Kraidy, 1999; Saenz, 1997; Shome, 1996).

Initially, the radical implications of CS suggested a bifurcation of academic fields (CS and Communication) and research topics (culture, media, and communication). As principles for organizing qualitative research, however, these distinctions appear increasingly false and unnecessary. Amid sharp debate, they are gradually being supplanted by a tolerance for holistic and multiperspectival research that illuminates the relationships *between* political economy, textual polysemy, and audience reception (Kellner, 1993). Thus, although the influence of CS on qualitative communication research is increasingly broad (e.g., in studies of racial identity; Nakayama & Krizek, 1995; Warren, 2001), it continues to be central in shaping the subfield of reception and audience studies. One practical implication of polysemy and the encoding/decoding tradition has been to shift researchers away from positivist methods that presume audience passivity and strong media effects toward qualitative methods capable of depicting (or at least speculating about) audience production of meaning (Anderson & Meyer, 1988; Jensen, 1991; Lindlof, 1988; Morley, 1992). In these qualitative studies, the basic protocol has been for researchers to question people who have seen or read a media text about their thoughts, perceptions, inferences, and feelings. Patterns of interpretation revealed in their answers are then compared to certain features of the text and context. The demonstration of diverse readings is just one analytic step. Researchers may also conceptualize the logic by which readers embrace, negotiate, or resist textual influences. In her study of female viewers of the television program *Beverly Hills, 90210*, for example, Rockler (1999) focused on their use of "realism" as a criterion for evaluating its relevance to their experience. This lay theory constrained them, however, from more deeply engaging the program's ideological dimensions. Finally, researchers may explore how particular reception practices are linked to the social positions of audience members (e.g., as lesbian and feminist viewers of heterosexist science fiction; Jenkins, 1988).

Currently, the use of qualitative methods in audience studies appears to be entering an awkward adolescence. Following a spate of enthusiastic adoption, researchers are turning to a sober evaluation of the results. Among the loudest opponents are political-economic scholars who vehemently oppose populist qualitative research on the grounds that it fails to adequately address the structural determination of cultural practices (e.g., Ferguson & Golding, 1997). Their strongest judgment is reserved for critics who *infer* the *actuality* of audience opposition to hegemony from their discovery of its *potential* in textual polysemy. They also caution that a materialist ethnography of contextual constraints should not be neglected in favor of idealistic ethnography that mistakes localized idiosyncrasy (e.g., in the practices of fan subcultures) for widespread emancipation.

In addition, several commentators have noted a gap between the traditional ideal of ethnography (i.e., as practiced in cultural anthropology) and the watered-down version more typically practiced in audience studies (Tudor, 1999, pp. 167-178; Murphy, 1999b). This gap results from misapplication of the term *ethnography* to describe a culturally informed criticism of textual materials (i.e., published ethnographies) and from failure to perform participant observation in studying audiences (i.e., in favor of interviewing). Even when it is performed, these critics note, observation is often limited only to scenes of actual media use, thus missing the broader integration by audiences of media use into their whole way of life. In her study of the reception of proto-feminist soap operas among Egyptian village women, Abu-Lughod (1997) attempts to reverse this trend by situating it in a series of overlapping contexts. These include the tensions between cosmopolitan media producers and "peasant" audiences, husbands and wives in Islamic marriages, and nationalist and transnationalist ideologies and their local appropriations. These critiques indicate that the status of qualitative methods in CS is far from resolved.

Conclusion

This chapter has reviewed six theoretical traditions that inform qualitative communication research: ethnomethodology, symbolic interactionism, ethnography of communication, modernist and postmodernist critical theory, feminism, and cultural studies. We have traced the development of these traditions from the historical influences of Kant, Dilthey, Marx, Weber, Husserl, Schutz, and others. Inevitably, this discussion is partial and reflects strategic choices in the selection of figures, traditions, and exemplars. Nonetheless, we hope that it has heightened your appreciation for the gravity of tradition in qualitative communication research. If nothing else, it should indicate that these traditions are constantly interacting with and transforming each other. Symbolic interactionists, for example, have recently explored areas of mutual interest with other traditions such as cultural studies and postmodernism (Becker & McCall, 1990). The fruits of this integration include Neumann's (1993) study of the organization of identity and community in alternative tourism. In the subfield of organizational communication, qualitative researchers increasingly blend interpretive and critical traditions to explore the impact of hyper-capitalism on various spheres of contemporary work life (Cheney, 1999; Wendt, 2001). To borrow a popular saying, these works reflect a productive tension between a theoretical commitment to "think globally" (i.e., to conceptually expand claims beyond their immediate applications) and the qualitative commitment to "act locally" (i.e., in depicting situated practices). Rabinow and Sullivan (1987) state the matter more eloquently when they note a growing interdisciplinary awareness that "all human inquiry is necessarily engaged in understanding the human world from within a specific situation. This situation is always and at once historical, moral, and political. It provides not just the starting point of inquiry but the point and purpose for the task of understanding itself" (p. 20). Our next four chapters explore what this statement implies for the actual practice of qualitative inquiry.

3

Design I

Beginnings: Searching for a Research Idea

Alyssa Eckman was searching for an idea for her dissertation. She soon found it within one of the major problems engaging the contemporary media: the encroachment of commercialism upon the sanctified ground of news. Facing no shortage of examples of this problem, she chose "advertorials" as her topic (Eckman, 2001). Advertorials are "products that look like news and read like news but are . . . often bought and controlled by advertisers" (p. 10). These advertiser-driven stories are written in the guise of editorial content in order to seem credible and objective. Alyssa was less interested in the stories than in the people who produce them. She wanted to understand how they produce this content, what values and standards guide their work, and what role dilemmas they encounter within the newspaper company.

Why did Alyssa focus on "advertorialists"? Her decision was based in part on reading the research literature. She found a few studies of advertorial content and reader perceptions, but none on the context of production. Thus, her review suggested an area where she could make a contribution. But this does not explain the full story of how Alyssa came to her topic. There is another side, which is best told in her words:

> My first job in journalism after my college-level training was at a small-town newspaper. One of my first assignments was to write an advertorial-type piece

about a local veterinarian. The only problem was that I didn't know what an advertorial was, or that such things even existed in the newspaper world. And the publisher didn't refer to it as an advertorial, or content separate from the rest of the newspaper. My publisher simply told me: "We need a feature story written each week about each business that is listed around the outside of this ad on the back cover of the front section."

I approached the assignment like a journalistic feature story. I interviewed the veterinarian, I sat in on surgery as he repaired a cow's hernia, I took photos, and I went back and wrote what I thought was a solid feature story. The publisher then passed the story to the veterinarian, who proceeded to edit and rewrite the piece. I was astonished and a bit angry, because I didn't grasp the concept of the advertorial. The veterinarian had paid for the story and had every right to perform surgery on it. To me it was a news story; to the veterinarian and the publisher it was an advertisement.

This happened more than 15 years ago, and it remains a memorable event in my professional development. I silently swore to myself that I would never let someone other than an editor review a news story before it was published. I believed the publisher's actions—driven by the power of advertising dollars— had somehow compromised the integrity of the newspaper's total content. . . .

Now, many years later, I found myself entrenched in the world of advertorials. I was promoted and found myself serving as the editor of several advertorial publications. . . . I took pride in the positive relations I worked to establish with my target markets. As part of my job duties, I served on boards and committees of the local trade associations that represent realtors and builders . . . Each time I was named to a new board or committee, I would report it to my supervisor, who would react with praise and record my accomplishment in my personnel file. Establishing such relationships as serving on the boards or committees within my coverage area would be considered "conflicts of interest" for journalists. But I was no longer a journalist. I had become an advertorialist.

The story Alyssa tells is a familiar one of lost innocence. But on another level, the story brims with irony. Alyssa was now doing the very thing that she once despised (although she did not despise herself as a result). Her journey from journalist to advertorialist gave her a deep understanding of who advertorialists are and what happens when someone steps into the role and begins to perform it. Though proud of her success as an advertorialist, the veterinarian story was still etched in her memory, and she knew that the code of the journalist was widely perceived as purer, more respectable. With the concepts and methods learned in her doctoral studies, she looked forward to locating her own transformation in a larger narrative of the media industries.

Stories of how scholars find their research ideas can become the stuff of oral legend. But they are seldom told publicly. According to the conventional view, a study begins in "a clean, well-lighted place" (to quote the title of a Hemingway short story). This place is the world of theory and all of the empirical works relevant to a project. It is the author's responsibility to argue persuasively about how the study adds to the body of knowledge. Research questions or hypotheses are the final moves in this opening argument.

No one would dispute that these elements should be prominent in the conduct of research. However, researchers' choices also derive from their experiences, desires, interests, and opportunities. The story of who we are includes the story of what we study. This chapter describes how most qualitative projects actually begin. Our intent is not to displace or devalue the role of theory. Rather, we want to acknowledge the diverse sources from which ideas spring and indicate how the process of forming ideas can be done more consciously and productively.

Qualitative research design can be divided into two broad phases: *planning*, which is the process of research problem development, and *getting started*, which is the implementation of the researcher presence—negotiating access, gaining entry to a setting, becoming known to the participants, and applying a sampling strategy. In this chapter and the next, we portray research design as a stage of pre-fieldwork decisions that are finished by the time the researcher begins to collect data. This portrayal is realistic up to a point. Most design decisions are in fact made well in advance of going into the field. However, qualitative research is an evolving framework of questions and tools. Plans sometimes change, and adjustments in methods and problem focus may continue right up to the time that one leaves the field. Through the course of this book, we will reveal more of the twisting, turning character of actual qualitative design.

This chapter takes us through the components of the planning phase: (1) the sources of research ideas; (2) questioning our selves; (3) questioning the scene; (4) the research proposal; and (5) human subject protections. First, we examine the process of qualitative inquiry as a whole.

The Qualitative Research Process: An Overview

The idea of research design has different meanings for those who do qualitative research and for those who do quantitative research in the hypothetico-deductive tradition. The latter tend to follow a linear order of activity, in which what precedes all else is the choice of a theoretical perspective from which testable propositions can be deduced. From the writing of hypotheses to the operationalizing of variables, from the selection of a sample to the conduct of an experiment, the project's linkages are clear every step of the way. Researchers do not return to an earlier step unless the move is already built into the design. And the steps to follow seldom deviate from the original plan. Importantly, most quantitative projects depend on a high degree of control by the researcher. For the quantitative researcher, testing propositions about behavior, cognitions, or attitudes would be futile without the ability to control some factors while allowing others to vary. Ensuring the integrity of the research instruments (validity and reliability) is also critical to this control. So is the profound separation of the researcher from the human subjects.

Qualitative research, on the other hand, is known for being primarily inductive, emergent, and—well, somewhat unruly. Very little is linear about it. Very little of it can be controlled in the strict sense. As Lincoln and Guba (1985) advise, "Design in the naturalistic sense . . . means planning for certain broad contingencies without, however, indicating exactly what will be done in relation to each" (p. 226). In other words, we plan on making decisions about issues we haven't yet discovered. We usually begin with a sense of purpose and some broad questions. We may also have read the research literature, made some personal contacts, and found a way to enter a social world. Otherwise, we cannot predict—in fact, we usually refrain from even trying to predict—how the study will turn out.

Bogdan and Biklen (1982) provide a more defined view of a typical qualitative study:

> The start of the study is at the wide end: the researchers scout for possible places and people that might be the subject or the source of data, find the location they think they want to study, and then cast a net widely trying to judge the feasibility of the site or data sources for their purposes. . . . They begin to collect data, reviewing and exploring it, and making decisions about where to go with the study. They decide how to distribute their time, who to interview and what to explore in depth. They may throw aside old ideas and plans and develop new ones. . . . Their work develops a focus. The data collection and research activities narrow to sites, subjects, materials, topics, and themes. From broad exploratory beginnings they move to more directed data collection and analysis. (p. 59)

This process is *cyclical* in its basic movement; that is, most qualitative studies cycle many times through the same steps (e.g., with researchers doing scouting, data collection, data review and/or analysis, and interpretation, then doing them all over again). The process goes on until the researcher "gets it right"—until an insightful interpretation has been achieved.

A similar approach to design has been proposed by Agar (1982), who sees ethnography as a problem of resolving interpretive difficulties. To understand another culture, the researcher pursues a series of tasks aimed at clarifying meaning. The series begins with an early schematic understanding by the researcher of a performance or practice—a proto-schema of its forms, contexts, and meanings. Failure to make sense of an observed event causes a "breakdown" in the researcher's sensemaking; that is, the researcher's schema (or explanatory model) has proven in this instance to be inadequate. Some of these breakdowns happen serendipitously in the field and are what Agar called "occasioned" breakdowns. Others are "mandated" because the researcher intends to test how well she or he has reconstructed the cultural knowledge of the group. Different methods, sources, and sites can be used in different ways to mandate a breakdown. In the normal course of fieldwork, schemas will break down many times, and new schemas will be built from new data, until a ritual or some other act becomes understood.

Now, let's look at the process through the viewpoint of the one who performs it. Among the metaphors for the qualitative researcher are that the researcher is an intelligent "homing device" (Lincoln & Guba, 1985), a cultural "detective" (Goodall, 2000), and a "professional stranger" (Agar, 1996). If we move past the nuances of each characterization, what remains are researchers who are resourceful and inventive. Every scene is unique and dynamic, and calls for flexible strategies. Any technique is allowed that may help the researcher gain a purchase on the social realities of communication.

Qualitative researchers are also disciplined. They must learn when to watch, when to listen, when to go with the action, when to reflect, when to intervene tactically (and tactfully). Their awareness of their own and others' actions and motives is an act of inner control fully the equal of the external control of the hypothetico-deductive researcher.

They are also inquisitive. Question crafting lies at the core of conducting qualitative research. Early on, they ask questions about the research literature, the world around them, and their own selves. At this point, they use questions to get a footing in a new, exciting area. Once they are in the field, qualitative researchers use questions as navigational devices to find their way around the social terrain of the scene. Researchers ask questions out loud, to one person at a time or an entire group. This question-answer process begins to produce a structure for their knowledge. Many other questions are silent and fugitive, jotted into fieldnotes or a journal. The questions that grip researchers in the middle passage of the project may scarcely resemble the ones that motivated them in the beginning. By the end of the project, they are curious about how to put it all together. They ask, What is the best way to tell the stories in this study as well as the story of this study?

As in any overview, much has been left out of this presentation. Chapter 4 will fill in many of the operational details regarding the design and deployment of the research plan. The next section focuses on how to develop ideas for research, an essential step for all that follows.

Sources of Research Ideas

Qualitative communication researchers can usually be found at work or play in the fields of signification. What leads them there in the first place is a sense of curiosity about how people use and interpret signs to create the meaningful worlds in which they live. Of course, we are all curious about the sensemaking that swirls around us. How people relate to their pet cats, for example, may be a subject of passing interest to a household guest. But how people relate to their pets—conceived as a general problem deserving the close study of specific performances—could hold special fascination for an analyst of relational communication.

This section tours the wellsprings of most research ideas: theory and research literature, public problems, personal experiences and opportunities, and funding priorities. Initially the idea may be brief, half-formed, a sprawl of notes meaningful only to the author. Too much editing can defeat its growth at this stage. What is important is that a path of inquiry has been foreshadowed.

Theory and Research Literature

Most studies that use qualitative methods intend to contribute to a theoretical understanding of communication. Whereas hypothesis-testing research derives its focus from a theory, or a competition between theories, qualitative research can be more flexible in its use of theory. We will describe briefly several sources of this flexibility.

As discussed in Chapter 2, the cultural hermeneutics paradigm posits an indefinite range of collective social realities. We may be more sensitive to the form and content of these realities if we realize that "preordained theoretical perspectives or propositions may bias and limit the findings [of case study research]" (Eisenhardt, 1989, p. 536). At the same time, our preexisting perspectives lose the power to enhance our sensitivity if we fail to acknowledge them. In other words, by thinking in advance about potentially relevant concepts, we can use them as "sensitizing" probes of the scene (Glaser & Strauss, 1967) and do not have to commit to them until later, if at all. In like manner, we can delay the use of a "name-brand version" of theory (Anderson, 1996a, p. 27)—standpoint epistemology? social action theory? phenomenology?—until we know more about what aspects of the cultural scene become important.

A second source of flexibility in qualitative research theorizing is in our ability to construct theory around local communicative practices. These "activity theories" can account for the practices documented in the field and also orient us to future observations (Carbaugh & Hastings, 1992).

Finally, qualitative research is an arena in which "poaching" is common. In poaching, an analyst "[uses] diverse, even contradictory, theories in order to advance an argument" (Anderson, 1996a, p. 7). The use of any concept or theory to explain field data—alone or in combination—is one more example of the flexibility found in qualitative research.

What role, then, does theory customarily play in helping researchers to come up with fruitful research ideas? A good place to start looking for the answer to this question is Lincoln and Guba's (1985) distinction between types of studies in which the investigator "knows what he or she doesn't know," and therefore can project means of finding out, and situations in which the investigator "does not know what he or she doesn't know," in which case a much more open-ended approach is required" (p. 209). The first type refers to situations in which the investigator is well aware of what needs to be done to extend a body of theoretical or disciplinary knowledge. This is the type of study in which theory and the research literature play a large role in creating the idea. (The second type is more likely when one starts a study out of personal interest or opportunity.)

The more familiar one is with a research literature, the more readily one can identify the inconsistencies, contradictions, or gaps in current theory. Recall that Alyssa Eckman found a yawning gap in the literature of media organizations concerning the production of hybrid content forms. The presence of a gap does not in itself tell the researcher what idea to create. At most, it reveals that some part of a theory or knowledge domain is underdeveloped. One would be well-advised to think carefully about why no one has yet done work in this area. Perhaps the field has simply not caught up with increasing, real-world convergence (and mutual transformation) of media systems and content genres; perhaps the area is fraught with methodological challenges. In any case, if researchers are intrigued by an unmet theoretical need, they must respond to this opportunity with an idea that is compelling on its own.

Occasionally, an area seems to suffer from a lack of new thinking or exciting empirical work. This can open the way for a new approach. For example, Janice Radway (1984) was one of the first scholars to introduce the "interpretive community" concept to media audience theory and research. The notion of the interpretive community had been circulating among literary theorists for years, but it was new to communication studies. Her study of women's romance reading practices, published as *Reading the Romance*, was hailed as a fresh way to think about the interpretation of popular text. It was also one of the first major studies to take seriously the female audience for "low brow" content. As such, she was able to comment simultaneously on the popular taste hierarchy and on cultural patriarchy.

The research literature does not speak with one voice. It is simply too diverse to set out a unified agenda of problems. Given the time lag to publication, it may also be a dubious source of the most urgent problems to study. Journals sometimes publish theoretical critiques that can be extremely useful as a guide to the controversies in an area. A good critical article can set disciplinary brushfires that take years to quench or die down. Valuable cues to research needs can be read in state-of-the-art review essays such as those published in *Communication Yearbook* or similar volumes. Edited books bring together diverse views and approaches in ways that most journals cannot offer. Though the chapters can be uneven in quality, at least one provocative idea can usually be found.

At scholarly conventions, the best and the brightest convene to exchange views on cutting edge issues. Such sessions frequently deliver the goods. The opinions of influential scholars tend to attract more attention than those of scholars who are new to the field. However, newcomers are often the ones who "break out" an exciting new concept or methodological practice. Scholars should read journals in communication and allied disciplines to keep up with the latest developments in their interest area. Table 3.1 lists some key journals that publish qualitative articles. The articles can be appreciated as exemplars of field strategy, data analysis, and authorial style, as well as for their content and substantive ideas. As a research idea develops, a search of research literatures and databases should be done to help frame questions, find background material on the topic, and understand the use of research tools and techniques (Helmericks, Nelsen, & Unnithan, 1991; Rubin, Rubin, & Piele, 1999).

At the end of the day, deciding what needs to be done next is always a subjective assessment. A new research idea should build in some way on what is already known, but knowledge is ever-evolving, not static. This organic view of theory, as an ongoing conversation, makes it easier to think of how any one of us can contribute. The ideas we derive from theory can

Table 3.1   Scholarly Journals That Regularly Feature Qualitative Studies

Communication
Communication Theory
Critical Studies in Media Communication
European Journal of Communication
Howard Journal of Communication
Journal of Communication Inquiry
Media, Culture & Society
New Media and Society
Research on Language and Social Interaction
Studies in Visual Communication
Text and Performance Quarterly
Written Communication

Anthropology
American Anthropologist
American Ethnologist
Anthropological Quarterly
Cultural Anthropology
Current Anthropology
Ethnology

Cultural Studies
Cultural Studies
European Journal of Cultural Studies
International Journal of Cultural Studies

Education
Anthropology and Education Quarterly
International Journal of Qualitative Studies in Education

Language Analysis
Discourse Processes
International Journal of the Sociology of Language
Language in Society

Qualitative Research (Multidisciplinary)
Ethnography
Journal of Contemporary Ethnography
Qualitative Inquiry
Qualitative Research
Studies in Qualitative Methodology

Organizational Analysis
Academy of Management Journal
Journal of Management Studies
Organization Studies

(continued)

Table 3.1 (Continued)

Sociology
    Qualitative Sociology
    Sociological Quarterly
    Symbolic Interaction

Other
    Family Process
    Human Studies
    Journal of Consumer Culture
    Public Culture
    Qualitative Health Research
    Semiotica
    Signs
    Theory and Society
    Women's Studies International Forum

---

be just the sort of leverage we need to start a project and to continue to find meaning in it as we move into the field.

Public Problems

Public problems in society can also be rich sources of research ideas. The pathbreaking studies of the Chicago School of qualitative sociology, early in the 20th century, focused on a variety of urban problems. Later classic studies, such as Erving Goffman's *Asylums* (1961), Elliott Liebow's *Tally's Corner* (1967), and Paul Willis's *Learning to Labour* (1977), depicted the lives of people struggling for dignity and self-determination—mental institution inmates, the black underclass, and working-class boys, respectively. Ethnography, generally, is well-suited for digging deep into the lived experiences of the poor, disenfranchised, and outcast. Such studies enable socially invisible or silenced groups to be seen and heard. They may also comment indirectly on the failures of public policy or society's institutions. A communication study in this tradition is Mara Adelman and Lawrence Frey's *The Fragile Community* (1996), an ethnography of people living with AIDS and supporting each other as they come to terms with their mortality.

Other studies focus a high-beam light on subjects already well-known in the public sphere. Their goal is to uncover sides of the subject other than those familiar to the public, and perhaps point to "problems" where none were thought to exist. For example, *Life on the Screen* (1995)—Sherry Turkle's best-selling study of how young people use the Internet to explore issues of identity—was released just as popular fascination with the Internet was in full lift-off.

Public problems also exist in policy debates, legal controversies, human rights issues, social movements, politics, organizational crises, and so forth. At the core of these problems is a conflict between two or more parties. The nature of the conflict usually hinges on differences regarding goals, status, rights, and resources. For example, the problem of abortion involves contention between pro-life and pro-choice advocates in such areas as the rights of women, the rights of the fetus, state and federal legislation, and the availability of medical and other resources. Faye Ginsburg's celebrated work, *Contested Lives* (1989), used ethnographic fieldwork and women's life histories to examine abortion conflict at the grassroots level in Fargo, North Dakota. Of particular interest to communication researchers is the role of discourse and other symbolic forms in the way in which conflictive issues are understood by participants and audiences.

Of course, the mass media offer a nonstop supply of problems, most of which are packaged as conflicts. However, the attention a problem receives in the media can be two-edged. On the one hand, media attention does assure one of the problem's importance and can enable the researcher to learn quite a lot about it prior to fieldwork. On the other hand, all of the media play could be misleading in some nonobvious ways. The researcher might become blinded to aspects of a situation that are truly problematic. When using public problems as the basis for a study, it is important to think first about why they are problems at all—apart from the publicity or news coverage surrounding them.

Personal Experiences and Opportunities

Alyssa Eckman's story illustrates how research ideas can originate in one's identity or life experiences. However, it is not simply the fact that we experience something that matters. What matters is how we think and feel about the experience. In other words, *we problematize our experience*. A disturbance in the smooth running order of our own or others' sensibilities is sometimes all that is needed to jump-start an idea. Like so much else in qualitative research, this involves asking questions. Why did things "have to happen" the way they did? Why were my assumptions proven wrong in this instance? What aspects of the event did I not see or hear? How and why did others perceive the event differently? Why is one person's performance seen as a "success" and another's performance seen as a "failure"? What is considered a valued interpretation among these people?

As these questions suggest, we problematize experience by noticing gaps and dislocations in our own explanations. We might sense an *incongruity*, an *irony*, a *contradiction*, an *ambiguity*, or a *mystery* in a situation. Or we find ourselves in a new situation, one that defies our ability to explain it. Or we imaginatively put ourselves in the place of others who are confused or mystified. Or we experience moments that prick at our moral conscience. We might notice that when a teacher leads her class in a discussion of race relations, she turns first to students of color to ask their opinions. The students' embarrassment becomes our own. This situation, too, may stimulate a research idea.

Perhaps the best practice for developing this orientation, if it is not already strongly present, is to seek a variety of experience in one's life. Many ethnographers thrive on new and unexpected experiences (Goodall, 2000). Encounters with different cultures or lifestyles, or new ways of doing things, can confront us with our own stereotyped thinking and give us insights into others' lives. This is an important lesson for academicians. For all of its intellectual freedoms, the university campus can still be sheltered from much of the strife, pain, and rough justice of the world. Of course, few of us would want it any other way. The larger point is this: The more exclusive our experience, the less acute our ability to sense new ideas in the world.

The identity and role conflicts one experiences can also be a source of research ideas. These quandaries are most salient for people whose identities— for example, ethnic, age, gender, political, religious, or sexual—have been challenged in local, societal, or global contexts (Conquergood, 1991). One of our graduate students, for example, decided to study the media "policy" and rhetoric of his own church. He became interested in this topic because, in his role as a pastor, he felt uncomfortable telling new members about this aspect of church doctrine. He also wondered about the ambivalence he felt when he rented videos.

These motives are not always documented in journal articles. Perhaps they might be perceived by readers as a threat to the "impartiality" of the work. Traditionally, the discourses traversing the researcher's identity and the field find expression in such formats as the essay (e.g., Lindlof & Grubb-Swetnam, 1996; Taylor, 1997). Even so, authors are increasingly devoting space in research reports to their personal investments (as discussed further in Chapter 9). One example comes from Yount (1991), who studied how women coal miners manage sexual harassment on the job:

> My interest in conducting this study was generated by my commitment to feminism, the pressing need to facilitate the entry of blue-collar women into higher-paying jobs numerically dominated by men, and the relative paucity of

data in the literature on these women. I was drawn to coal mining in particular because I was born in a small coal mining town where a number of my male relatives worked in the mines. (p. 398)

Probably few of us resolve an identity issue by studying it. But researchers often use the project to unite their personal concerns more closely with their professional lives. It is important to know that feeling passionate about our research is not just "okay" but the best way to live the scholar's life.

Researchers' lived experience can also be a source of *opportunity*—a "found" topic. There are abundant examples of researchers happening upon a time, place, and people that set the stage for a study. In most cases, the door of opportunity swings in both directions: The researcher and the researched both get something of value from the project. Of his entry to W. L. Gore & Associates, Michael Pacanowsky (1988a) writes:

I got in because my brother was a trusted associate of seven years' tenure. . . . I also got in because W. L. Gore & Associates had in the previous three years tripled in growth. . . . It was easy for them to see that they had, if not outright problems, at least opportunities for improving their communication practices. (p. 358)

Gerry Philipsen (1975) was a social worker in "Teamsterville," on the south side of Chicago, when he began to consider the male performances of speaking in that area. Similarly, Eleanor Novek (1995) lived in the urban neighborhood that became the scene of her ethnography; a succession of teaching jobs led her more deeply into questions about the chances for success of the community's young people. However, remember that settings don't come equipped with research questions. The researcher who makes opportunistic use of a scene must still devise an idea with some theoretical import.

Funding Priorities

Research requires material and human resources, and not many colleges and universities can afford to absorb all of these costs. More importantly, academic institutions, particularly those designated as research universities, play a critical role in the knowledge needs of federal and state governments, corporations, and nonprofit organizations. Enormous sums of grant money are dispensed every year to academicians who are willing to respond to the priorities of these entities. These funds do not hinder intellectual freedom in any direct sense, but they do have the effect of encouraging activity in some research areas more than in others. This primary effect in turn creates ripple effects in the academy. For example, the late 1990s' surge in funding for health communication arguably contributed to the growth of faculty positions and graduate programs in that area at many universities.

Most funding priorities call for quantitative projects, and qualitative investigators in all of the social sciences are often believed to suffer a disadvantage in getting grants. This situation is especially true of funding sources that are oriented to short-range problem solving. Qualitative researchers cannot always produce conclusive answers to focused questions, or even guarantee that the questions they set out to study will be the ones they report on at the end of the fieldwork.

Yet many qualitative researchers manage to get their studies funded by learning as much as possible about the grant application process, by "networking" with funding agency officers and successful grant-getters, and by being willing to adapt their interests to the types of projects that agencies and foundations want to fund. (See Agar, 1996, for a thorough discussion of these points). There are in fact many enticing topics to be found in *requests for proposals* (RFPs). For example, an RFP from the Society for Information Management describes an interest in projects that "[uncover] effective . . . practices and behaviors relevant to the management and use of information technology to achieve business objectives" (Advanced Practices Council, 2001). Further reading into the Web site announcing this program reveals this "success hint": "[Successful research teams] use qualitative research methods (i.e., interviews, case studies, focus groups) as the foremost elements of research designs." An organizational communication scholar with a qualitative-methods skill set and an enterprising impulse might see an opportunity here.

Becoming adept at writing proposals and winning grants brings many benefits to the researcher. Fieldwork is labor-intensive and a grant often allows an investigator to buy out time from teaching. A grant can pay for travel to research sites and for hiring graduate assistants to help out in the field or do tasks like transcribing and coding. Grants are prestigious in themselves. They burnish the reputations of both the investigator and the university. Administrators like the "indirect costs" that come back to their units and will often reward the grant-getter for these windfalls. Finally, researchers who seek funding often find themselves engaging real-world issues. They may even see their research result in changes in social practice or policy. This can be a source of satisfaction for those who want to make a difference in areas outside the academy.

Questioning Ourselves

As practicing ethnographers, we ourselves have entertained many ideas for research that have yet to go beyond written or mental notes. At some time in the future, these ideas might be set into motion. But in all honesty, most of them never will be. Often the reasons why we do not act upon an idea have little to do with its conceptual merits. Maybe we don't feel ready to commit to a grueling schedule of interviews or fieldwork; maybe other projects command our attention; maybe we simply cannot muster enthusiasm for the idea. Of course, some ideas do meet our criteria of the moment and go on to become successful projects.

Researchers should confront several key questions early in the design process. Is this idea congruent with my personal and researcher identities? Can I sustain my interest in this project over the long haul? Is this an idea that will yield the type and quantity of research products that will advance my professional goals? Thinking in these ways about an idea may help the researcher learn the answer to the big question: Is *this* the right project *now*, for *me*?

The first of these questions—Is the idea congruent with my personal and researcher identities?—may have already been answered by the time the idea has been articulated. As we have already discussed, research ideas frequently arise from quests for self-understanding. Indeed, the interpretive approach appeals to many who want to study their own social worlds. For example, non-Euro-American graduate students ("foreign students") in anthropology often return home to do research to achieve deeper understandings of their nation's identity or sociopolitical issues, among other reasons (Bakalaki, 1997). Communication researchers also find it natural to engage topics close to their interests. In their study of music bootlegging, Mark Neumann and Timothy Simpson (1997) explain basic techniques of bootlegging by referring to their own experiences in making concert tapes. It seems reasonable to think that the authors' professional identities (as cultural studies scholars) and personal pursuits (as enthusiasts of concert taping) dovetailed at some point to create a research idea.

But what about research ideas with which we do not identify or sympathize? Going outside the safe harbor of friends, family, and associates always poses some risk. An extreme case is Blee's (1998) study of women in American racist and anti-Semitic groups. Not only did she not share their racist beliefs or condone their activities, she had to develop ways of negotiating with informants "in which fear became a visible component in the research relationship" (p. 390). Identity congruence, or its absence, becomes a highly salient issue because qualitative researchers must devote energy and artful care to their self-presentations. And because changes in the self produce much of the interpretive insight during fieldwork, researchers need to assess their ability to register subtle changes in their knowledge, emotions, and competencies.

Among the questions one can ask are these: Can I manage an effective dialectic between what I personally feel as events happen around me and how I present my researcher face to others? Can I recognize and set aside any biases I have of the subject? Can I create a constructive interpersonal dynamic out of the apparent "differences" between me and the other? We may not be able to answer these questions with certainty early in the idea-shaping process, but they are worth considering with whatever information we can marshal.

The second question—Can I sustain my interest in this project over the long haul?—is related to the first, because a subject with which one feels compatible seems likely to sustain interest. But this is not always the case. It can be hard to feel the thrill of discovery when studying a mundane scene. Conversely, encounters with the unfamiliar can be adventurous, even "white knuckle" experiences. Reflecting on her interviews with female racists, Blee noted the frightening situations that occurred and the death threats she received as she penetrated the subculture. Of course, most research situations are not that intense. On the whole, fieldwork is not that different from any other kind of work. One will face stretches of time in the field that will be boring, confusing, disagreeable, or even pointless. Some student projects we have supervised foundered because the students somehow lost interest in what they set out to study. Some could not get past the seeming banality of what they were observing day in, day out. For most researchers, however, the prospect of practicing their craft on an interesting problem is enough to carry them through even the most arduous project.

Finally, one should ask, is this an idea that will yield the type and quantity of research products that will advance my professional goals? Since not many of us do qualitative research solely as a leisure pursuit, it makes sense to ask whether the end result will be worth all of the time and effort. Refereed journal articles are considered by many to be the "gold standard" of scholarly production. Untenured faculty members, in particular, are encouraged to make their mark in journal publishing. Because qualitative research can take a long time to finish, there may be an incentive to optimize the articles that come out of a project. These may include one or more data-based articles comprised of different slices of the collected material, a methodological article, a piece with a theory orientation, and articles that explore policy, practice, and pedagogy. Those in tenured positions may feel better able to engage in longer projects, even ones that are open-ended.

At this stage of these scholars' careers, writing books becomes a viable option. More will be said about these products in the final chapter. For now, though, it is enough to say that any good research idea should promise payoffs in the "currency" required by the field and by the institution in which one labors.

Questioning the Scene

As a general principle, any communicative action can be studied. We should be able to operate as a "human research instrument" anywhere and insinuate our way into anyone's space. We should be able to join any group and become anyone's newest, most trusted friend or researcher. We should be able to learn any local idiom, follow any tribal rule. There is no reason not to be optimistic about any of these matters. However, what is possible in principle may not always be achievable in practice. Keeping this caution firmly in mind, one should ask questions about the scene of study. Given the resources I have, is this scene researchable? Can I start the project with confidence in its ultimate value?

First, we need to draw some important distinctions between three related terms: *field, site,* and *scene.* The term *field* refers to the general intersections of the topic and territory in which research takes place. It is the broad scope of theoretically relevant events in which researchers operate as working professionals. Tom's field, for example, has included any home where family members are using media, and Bryan's field any organization whose members are talking about nuclear weapons. Researchers usually work more than one field over the course of their careers. The concept of *field* differs from that of *site* (or *setting*). This second term refers to a specific, local, physical place in which the researcher and the social actor coexist. Bryan, for example, has studied controversy surrounding exhibits located in the Bradbury Science Museum at the Los Alamos (New Mexico) National Laboratory. Tom is currently studying the controversy surrounding the 1988 film *The Last Temptation of Christ* at the sites of Universal Pictures, movie theaters, and many other venues. The aforementioned two terms can in turn be distinguished from a third, that of the *scene.* This final term refers to actors' self-defined scope of social action. Scene is a construct fashioned by participants as a frame for coordinating their immediate accomplishments. It is meaningful as a context in which a particular, recurring episode of social action takes place. At this level, Tom has studied the scene in which family television viewing is enacted, and Bryan has studied the struggle between "orthodox" and "progressive" groups over the form and content of nuclear-historical narratives.

In playing out these distinctions, we see that a field can consist of many sites but that not all sites are equally valuable for studying the scenes that structure the social reality of a particular group. Researchers, then, must assess whether they have selected sites containing scenes that yield data responsive to the research questions associated with their fields.

As a first step in this process, the researcher performs a reconnaissance of the scene to be studied that is known as "casing the scene." The researcher does this by going to one or more sites of the potential study and looking, listening, touching, and smelling. The researcher can get a sense of how his or her research presence could fit in, and also glean information about its material dimensions, the people who inhabit the site or sites, and the forms of activity that seem to prevail there.

Scene casing, like any fieldwork procedure, calls for the researcher to assume a role that is acceptable to the cultural members. If it is a public setting, the researcher can hang out simply as someone who has a right to be there. Of course, it is often not as simple as that. Many public places, such as a neighborhood bar, have their unspoken rules of behavior, which one would be wise to recognize and adapt to from the start. More restricted settings—factories and homes are examples—usually do not allow strangers inside to wander about at will. In these situations, researchers will have to accept the role of guest. They might avail themselves of a generic tour designed for outsiders. Better yet, they may be able to take a behind-the-scenes tour guided by a native member. These special tours often allow for closer inspections of the scene and the chance to have questions answered with more candor. Another option would be to "shadow" one or more people in their daily rounds. Shadowing permits even more of an insider view because one is walking literally at the elbow of people who are participating in the action.

If one is already a native member, the home scene does not need to be cased in the conventional way. Instead, one should deconstruct (or "bracket") existing ideological or emotional commitments and evaluate whether the demands of the member role also allow a researcher role to be performed.

In casing a scene, the researcher should look through both *emic* and *etic* lenses. When we take the *emic* view, we see the scene through the meanings that the members attribute to their own communicative actions. Pelto and Pelto (1978) characterize emic analysis by the injunction that "the native's categorization of behavior is the only correct one" (p. 56). "Correct," as used here, means correct in the cultural sense; that is, what is moral or true for the culture member is the correct categorization of morality and truth in this instance. We not only take a walk in the natives' shoes but also understand what shoes mean to them. For example, what is the activity called "teaching"? The nonteacher's notion may be the classical one of leading students in learning activities in a classroom. Teaching, for the one who teaches, could involve meanings that overflow into diverse situations. Talking with students over coffee at the student center, reading a journal article, setting up a Web page—all of these may be part of the construction of teaching. They can be discerned, emically, as "teaching" only by aligning one's understanding closely with that of the teachers themselves.

So, how does one identify a scene—the scene as the member defines it—before actually starting to study it? This is indeed a problem for qualitative researchers as they stand at the opening edge of a project. Tours or shadowing can give the researcher access to meaningful action, but the researcher should hedge these observations with the reminder, repeated like a mantra, that the guest role does not permit much more than a guess at the full range of actions that are most meaningful to the members.

Scene casing also involves an *etic* perspective. When we take the etic view, we see the scene through categories derived from disciplinary knowledge and theory, or in terms of settings, behaviors, and other objective characteristics that are important to our purposes as a researcher. The researcher thus examines a social world as a purposeful observer, not as a participant. Etic analysis is useful at this early stage in order to relate the idea to theoretical interests. Applying the etic view to teaching, we might go into a school looking for "knowledge transfer," "discovery," or other constructs. We also think etically when we categorize objects or properties of the research site. We might look, for example, for evidence of the prominence that a school gives to scholastic versus athletic achievement—trophies, ceremonies, press releases, and so on.

Schatzman and Strauss (1973) articulated several goals of the researcher's scene casing that are etic in their basic orientation:

> (1) to determine as precisely as possible whether this site does, in fact, meet his [or her] substantive requirements—a question of *suitability*; (2) to "measure" some of its presenting properties (size, population, complexity, spatial scatter, etc.) against his [or her] own resources of time, mobility, skills, and whatever else it takes to do the job—a question of *feasibility*; and (3) to gather information about the place and people there in preparation for negotiating entry—a question of *suitable tactics*. (p. 19)

The latter goal, tactics, will be taken up in Chapter 4. However, the first two of these goals—suitability and feasibility—are helpful for interrogating potential scenes and thus will be discussed here. A *suitable site* should encompass most, if not all, of the criteria in the emerging research problem.

For example, Lindlof (1987) set out to study prison inmates' uses of media. The kernel of his idea was that in long-term confinement persons relate to media content and technology in distinctive ways. He thus knew that jails and detention centers would not qualify as sites for his study. He also knew he wanted a site that had a fairly liberal media policy for inmates—whatever *that* meant. It was actually an abstract notion until he began to look at possible sites.

Scene casing will often modify a priori notions of what is suitable. For example, Lindlof took a walking tour with the deputy superintendent of the prison, interviewed him, and examined prison documents. He found, among other things, that the prison had a multiethnic inmate population of whites, blacks, and Hispanics. He also learned that prison officials had developed methods for trying to avert situations of racial conflict. Some of these methods involved the use of media. The ethnic and racial aspects of prison life then became part of the research idea. The point of this example is that scene casing can act as a tool for reframing the research problem.

Feasibility is the decision space where two broad concerns meet. The first of these is what Schatzman and Strauss (1973) call "presenting properties"—observable characteristics of a scene that affect the researcher's ability to establish a presence and operate effectively. Presenting properties include the size of a site, its population and structural complexity, and the intimacy and spatial scatter of interactions. The second concern is the researcher's own resources of time, cultural capital, and personnel. Here are some questions concerning feasibility that have been faced, and resolved, by qualitative researchers:

- Can we understand rules of stranger interaction in scenes like television viewing in public places? (Krotz & Eastman, 1999)
- Can we track the action and social actors in an organization housed in three buildings at two sites that are five city blocks apart? (Carbaugh, 1998a)
- Can we understand the interpersonal communication of people involved in stressful work, like 911 emergency call centers? (Tracy & Tracy, 1998)
- Can we analyze a tightly coordinated team of people who work in conditions of physical danger and low tolerance for error, such as an aircraft carrier flight crew? (Weick & Roberts, 1993)

Time is always a critical resource. A shortage of time can prevent one from achieving full insider knowledge of a role, practice, or performance. A demanding scene can also steal time from writing fieldnotes, studying the notes, and other obligations of a project in progress. If external factors—such as the length of a semester or a conference paper deadline—limit the time we can allot for fieldwork, the study may have to be scaled down in scope. For example, an interest in studying impression management strategies in several retail settings may be far too ambitious for the 10-week window allowed for a project. A customer service department of one store may have to suffice instead.

The ways in which the rhythms and cycles of a scene mesh with the researcher's resources of time can also tell us how feasible the research idea is. Most of the routines in a scene are predictable—so predictable that it is a simple matter to gauge whether and when one can observe the phenomenon of interest. For example, one of our graduate students, Bruce Berger (1998), wanted to study the world of "simulcast racing and betting, who [the gamblers] are and why they are here, and what is the meaning of here in the context of everywhere else in their lives" (p. 2). Fortunately, simulcast racing was going on near him at the Red Mile track, so Berger was able to go to the track for 20 evenings of on-site observing and interviewing. He could even count on regular interaction with 13 "frequent" gamblers.

In some settings, events may happen so rarely or unpredictably that it is well-nigh impossible to set a schedule. Another of our graduate students wanted to study how Hispanic women communicate their health problems to English-speaking health care providers at a local clinic. It turned out that these women visit the clinic much less often than others. Due to this timing difficulty, the student had to shift the research problem to the providers' perceptions of Hispanic women's communication, relying on an interview approach with the providers.

Another presenting property of the scene concerns the cultural codes that one must understand. Culture codes are the sets of knowledge that people use to perform their roles in a scene. Codes constitute and regulate different orders of conduct, such as occupational (e.g., technical codes), public interpersonal (e.g., politeness codes), private interpersonal (e.g., relational codes), and media-related conduct (e.g., interpretive codes), among others. Every scene is made up of coded knowledge. Some codes are tacit and known widely—what anyone should know almost intuitively—while many fewer people may know and practice other codes. To use a simple example, "everyone" knows how to purchase a ticket for a baseball game, but not everyone knows the best ways to bargain with a ticket scalper.

Hierarchies of codes usually exist in organizations that respect or enforce hierarchies of rank. However, normal markers of status do not always coincide with cultural capital. Most people of the baby boomer generation are oblivious to, and quite inept at interpreting, the popular culture references of teenagers. Scarce cultural capital is one reason why a cross-generational study can be challenging.

One purpose of scene casing, then, is to estimate how long it might take to learn the many layers of code knowledge. Ethnographers often pride themselves on their quick uptake of cultural procedure, but there are certain codes that are hard for anyone to crack in a brief period of time. The actors may even try to keep communicative codes from being learned. Bruce Berger, for example, found lying to be rampant at the Red Mile simulcast-racing scene. But trying to decode the ways and reasons gamblers lie was a delicate matter, because lies are part of a gambling strategy that bettors do not always wish to disclose. The researcher must also try to evaluate how the effort involved in learning codes will influence relations with the social actors. Some scenes forgive a novice's efforts more readily than others.

Personnel considerations also arise when the nature of the membership seems to call for a particular set of skills, status, or experience. As we will discuss in Chapter 5, studying people who share some of our own characteristics (e.g., women studying women on women's issues) has real advantages. However, ethnographers are often able to interact with people unlike themselves, as in cases of adults studying the cultural world of children (Fine & Sandstrom, 1988) and white academics studying urban black people (Liebow, 1967; Rose, 1987). Approaching people with genuine respect can overcome most socially marked differences. If handled correctly, studying these differences can actually lead to strong insights. The use of a research team—in which member roles vary by age, gender, ethnicity, or other characteristics—is another solution to the issue of researcher-scene difference.

Finally, scene casing does not need to be a lone pursuit. It can be useful to exchange views of embryonic ideas with colleagues and experts. These people can be consulted when little published information exists on a topic or when researchers feel that a live conversation will answer their needs better than other means will. Scholarly conventions, for example, are events in which we meet our colleagues face-to-face to talk about projects—ours, theirs, or the ones on which we might collaborate. Thanks to the Internet, the colleagues we don't know can be approached at almost any time or place—by e-mail, in Usenet news groups, through inquiries posted to the National Communication Association's CRTNET.

At the local level, one can usually locate individuals with vital expertise or experience in the scene. For his prison media study, Tom consulted with two faculty members at Penn State University. One regularly donated his time and services to the prison and was able to sketch a verbal picture of inmate life. The other was an expert in criminal justice and suggested ways of scripting the approach to the prison officials. The advice given generously by these two individuals shortened Tom's learning curve in that study.

Colleagues and peers can also act as sounding boards or support groups (Ely, Anzul, Friedman, Garner, & Steinmetz, 1991). They can respond to our ideas, give us encouragement, and stimulate new thinking. We might seek feedback from different persons or groups. One colleague may be a source for methodological insight, while another helps with the conceptual side of things. Such "debriefings" can also be built into the project as part of the analysis protocol (Lincoln & Guba, 1985). In the best spirit of these consultations, a peer's advice should be freely given, and freely taken or not taken.

The Research Proposal

In the normal course of research development, a formal proposal is written and presented to one or more audiences: a thesis or dissertation committee; a grant review panel; an institutional review board; gatekeepers at the research site. Aspects of the basic "script" can be highlighted, expanded, or downplayed in order to meet the interests of each group.

Regardless of the audience, the basic goals of research proposals are the same. First, a proposal aims to *inform* others about the study's purpose, rationale, procedures, and intended outcomes. The author is more likely to be successful if the proposal is written clearly and coherently and the study is portrayed as justified and procedurally sound. A research proposal also aims to *persuade*. The audiences who read a proposal will usually take some form of action on it. For example, a dissertation committee decides whether to approve it (often with amendments); a funder decides whether to support it with a grant; a gatekeeper decides whether to allow the researcher into the site. Authors can increase the chances of a positive reception if they can convey the study's benefits and their own ability to carry out the research plan.

Finally, the proposal serves a purpose for the proposer. A proposal "nails down" elements that up to that point had been only discussed or speculated about. It is a moment of truth when the study is finally articulated. The research proposal, then, is one way that most of us commit to doing a project.

Title

A good title should concisely reflect the topic and its context. Some titles include a nod to the methodological, theoretical, or philosophical approach of the study. For example, the title of Alyssa Eckman's dissertation, *Negotiating the Gray Lines: An Ethnographic Study of the Occupational Roles and Practices of Advertorial Producers at a Medium Market American Newspaper*, tells readers about the topic, context, and method.

She also employed a trope in the main title to put across her viewpoint rather colorfully (at least in a monochromatic sense).

Abstract or Summary

Next, the author presents a capsule description of the project: What will be studied, how the investigation will be conducted, and what outcomes are expected. This statement, typically several sentences in length, comes at the beginning of the proposal and cues the reader to the key points that follow in the main text. The nature of the intended audience will usually dictate the desired format for this statement (e.g, abstract, executive summary, or introductory summary paragraph). Often, this statement is written after the rest of the proposal has been completed.

Rationale

A section devoted to the study's rationale should answer a question present in many readers' minds: Why does this need to be studied now? The author should present the research problem clearly and gather the strongest possible arguments for doing this research. It is particularly important that the arguments relate to, or build upon, each other. This section loses its power to persuade if the reasons for the study seem scattershot, overblown, or naïve. Here are some types of rationale that are often used in qualitative research proposals:

1. Trends in society, or in societal sectors (e.g., the media, education, labor, religion), indicate changes that are not understood very well.

2. A communication phenomenon has yet to be described.

3. The cultural variations in a well-known communication phenomenon have not been well documented or explained thus far.

4. The meanings that circulate among specific cultural members have not been studied extensively, or with a particular focus.

5. Ambiguities, weaknesses, or potentials in a theory or construct need to be examined.

6. A theory or construct has not yet been validated.

This list does not exhaust all of the rationales that may be used. Although the key arguments usually arise in some way from the original idea one had, the literature review will often add new reasons or reshape the previous ones. If the audience does not share the author's deep knowledge of the topic, special attention may have to be devoted to explaining or defending its relevance. If the audience is known to be skeptical or uninformed about qualitative inquiry, this may be the section in which to argue for its suitability.

Conceptual Areas of Inquiry

Readers look forward to learning about the conceptual logic for a study. A thesis committee or grant review panel in particular will want to see how the study fits into the existing work in an area—especially those issues known to be important and unanswered. Readers want to know whether there is a road that the proposer intends to travel—a road that has at least a few recognizable landmarks. Here is part of the conceptual discussion in the proposal for Alyssa Eckman's (2001) dissertation study:

> In *Ideology and Modern Culture*, Thompson (1990) characterizes media messages as symbolic goods, going beyond the surface meanings and impacts of particular messages. . . . These symbolic goods are commodities produced by media organizations according to conventional rules, such as successful situation comedy formats or news story formats. Following these formats ensures that mass audiences will continue to be receptive to the goods produced by media organizations and to attach value and expectations to those goods. This production of symbolic goods (content), according to McQuail (1994) is most often approached by examining the producing organization's role in society and its reflection on the culture it operates within. Researchers have also addressed the "media organizational routines and procedures for selecting and processing content" (McQuail, 1994, p. 186) and the influences those processes have on the symbolic goods that are ultimately produced and disseminated to an audience. This second emphasis—on examining the organizational processes that create media content—is the focus of this study of advertorialists.

Alyssa not only leads us through the thinking underlying her choice of the topic, she also points us in the direction of the study itself. Some familiar terms are mentioned: *rules, routines, formats, audiences*. The term *symbolic goods* seems especially important because it combines the notions of *symbol* and *commodity*—a key move in how she defines the advertorial product. She also tells the reader of her interest in the production process of media organizations—a key move in how she plans to study advertorials. She goes on to expand these ideas in the proposal, but here we can see a basic thrust of her overall conceptualization.

We can also see who she cites. The literature one cites reveals the perspective that one values most out of all of the available scholarship. Sometimes the author tells us what sets of literature are less useful for the research and the justification for excluding them. This strategy can be an effective way of persuading readers of the study's conceptual soundness. If only a few works are cited, the informed reader may wonder why other works, particularly competing ones, were not considered. In the worst case, the author is unaware of key works in the area of the proposed study—a weakness that could have unfavorable consequences for the proposal.

Hypotheses or Research Questions

Formal hypotheses are rare in qualitative research. Because qualitative inquiry usually sets out to interpret the qualities of social phenomena, there is little reason to predict the relationships between variables. This is not to say that the researcher cannot sort good interpretations of data from ones that aren't so good. Rather, these judgments can only be made once the researcher has been in the field long enough to generate substantial and credible data.

Far more common in qualitative research are research questions. Research questions articulate the researcher's *expectations*. Research questions are open-ended probes that, with the benefit of theoretical reasoning and some scene casing, orient the investigator's interests to the scene. Just as there are many ways to cross a river but only one can be chosen, there are many ways to enter a cultural scene but only a few (at most) can be chosen. Thus the need for research questions to guide one's entry. Here are two of Alyssa Eckman's research questions, out of the total of five written for her proposal:

> Q1: What occupational tenets or value systems guide the work of advertorialists, how do they develop, and how do they relate to occupational practice?

> Q3: How do advertorialists "fit" within a media organization? How do they negotiate the gray areas between advertising and news?

The questions she crafted are good ones not only because they grow out of her literature review but also because they don't confine her much at all. For example, she does not yet know how the "negotiation" of gray areas actually gets done, or even what this "gray area" might be. But for the purposes of starting out, the intent of the latter question is clear enough. Later, if a research question turns out to be less relevant than it was before, it can be either dropped or rephrased to better approximate social reality.

Methodology, Protocol, and Logistics

From the conceptualization and research questions, researchers should be able to anticipate what they need to learn and how to go about learning it. This section should go into some detail about how the selected methods and the data they produce will address the research questions. Because qualitative studies are usually multimethod designs, the proposer should explain how each method will operate relative to the others. For example, if participant observation, interviewing, and document analysis are all used, they ought to be described in terms of their interrelated purposes. Sampling (or case-selection) strategy is also a component of the methodology and should be included in this section of the proposal. In all, methodology is best explained in the proposal as *strategies* linking research goals to the type and sequence of methods to be used.

Protocol refers to the way in which methods will be implemented: How entry to the field sites will be accomplished; how informants will be approached; how visits to the scene will be scheduled; the social contexts of observing or interviewing. Much of what is considered research protocol is a matter of how one plans to perform the field role (see Chapters 4, 5, and 6). Protocols may change as researchers become involved in the scene, but by describing the protocol in advance, researchers can think about solutions to potential problems.

Logistics concerns the acquisition and management of resources, such as computers, tape recorders, tapes, disks, photocopying, transcriber costs, field-worker wages (or graduate student stipends), payment for human subjects, travel, and so forth. If the research is not complicated, the costs can be absorbed by the academic institution or the researcher. However, if one is applying for a grant or fellowship, it may be necessary to itemize most or all of the resources in a formal budget, including the value of the investigator's time.

Analysis

In the overview of qualitative inquiry presented earlier in this chapter, we saw how the design of a project anticipates the analysis and interpretation of field materials. However, most readers of research proposals will want to know about coding systems and analytic procedures. They may also want to know whether data analysis software will play a role and how reliability and validity will be assessed. Detailed guidelines to analyzing data are presented in Chapter 7. Chapter 9, which concerns qualitative texts and writing, considers analysis from the view of the final integration of data, arguments, and claims.

Schedule

The final element of most proposals is the schedule for completing the project. Again, the nature of the audience determines which components should be projected. For example, the timetable for dissertation proposals often includes these events: the dissertation proposal defense; Institutional Review Board (IRB) approval; the period for data collection; a period for data coding and analysis; due dates for completed chapters; a period for revisions; the final draft to the committee chair; and the dissertation defense. The time element in qualitative research tends to be more elastic than it is in quantitative projects. This is not as much an issue for dissertation committees as it might be for funding agencies and gatekeepers. Overestimating the amount of time needed to finish each stage of a project is a way, but by no means a foolproof one, to spare oneself the anxiety of missed deadlines.

Human Subject Protections in Qualitative Research

The writing of a research proposal is also an occasion for thinking about the ethics of the project. The ethical decisions of greatest importance concern the people who participate as human subjects. Concern about their welfare does not begin and end with the proposal, but this is the stage when procedures for engaging with people in the field must be made explicit.

The use of formal ethical guidelines for the conduct of scientific research is a relatively late development. Revelations of atrocities committed against prisoners of war by Nazi physicians in World War II led to the adoption of the Nuremberg Code by the original member nations of the United Nations. The Nuremberg Code set forth two key conditions for justifying research that continue to this day: The need for voluntary informed consent of subjects and a scientifically valid research design that could produce fruitful results for the good of society (Guidelines for the Conduct of Research, 1995). In later years, the growth of federal funding for social and medical research, and the occurrence of several well-publicized cases of clinical research abuse, prompted federal agencies to refine the protocols for protecting human subjects. Colleges and universities adopted the federal model in most respects, even for unsponsored research. Today, it is widely accepted that society has a stake in the ethical conduct of science.

Nearly all academic institutions require students, faculty, and staff scientists to submit their research plans to an IRB for review and approval. The human subjects office at one's institution usually offers group workshops and individual consultations on the IRB review process, and the National

Institutes of Health (NIH) now requires all researchers conducting human subjects research involving NIH funds to complete a Web-based training program (see http://ohsr.od.nih.gov/). The major purposes of the IRB review are to ensure that the rights of human subjects are properly respected and that subjects will not be placed in undue physical, psychological, social, or economic risk by a study's procedures or outcomes. The IRB board members, who are drawn from the ranks of the faculty, try to assess the ways in which a study might compromise a participant's status or rights. The investigators themselves may not recognize all of the risks. And, of course, lay people don't often think of themselves as "subjects" who need protection. Even if they did, they would probably not be able to tell whether a study follows sound practices. Thus, the IRB review acts as a third-party guarantor of a study's responsibility to those who participate.

Every academic researcher who embarks on a qualitative study should apply for and receive IRB approval. In our view, this is a "given." It is true that some people do decide to go forward with their studies without submitting their proposals for review. Their reasons are varied. They may think that there isn't enough time before their fieldwork must start, that the IRB's judgments are habitually capricious, that the IRB doesn't understand qualitative research, or that "there's nothing harmful about my study." Perceptions of the IRB process as an exercise in bureaucratic hoop-jumping are not uncommon, either, even among those who comply with it. However, these "reasons" evade the key questions that an IRB review poses: Is there anything about the treatment of human subjects that could be improved? Is there anything about the way that data and reports are handled that could be improved? An IRB review functions as a critical reading of a study's ethical orientation. It also helps to sensitize researchers to aspects of their studies that could be perceived differently by those who participate.

It is also important to know that the IRB review exists to protect the researcher. In the event of legal actions brought by individuals who claim damages from their participation, a university will usually come to the aid of faculty or students who follow an approved protocol. The investigator who elects to conduct research without IRB approval, for whatever reason, may not have access to the services of the university's legal counsel if a problem arises.

The ethical obligations of qualitative researchers are no different in most respects from those of other social-scientific approaches. However, by virtue of the contexts in which qualitative studies typically take place, as well as the interactive relations enjoining investigators and participants, qualitative inquiry does present special challenges. The following sections examine the major areas addressed in IRB reviews of qualitative research.

Informed Consent

The influential Belmont Report's principle of Respect for Persons affirms "the dignity and autonomy of individuals," and "requires that subjects give informed consent to participation in research" (Guidelines for the Conduct of Research, 1995). Anyone who participates in a study should do so on a voluntary basis; be able to understand what the study will demand of him or her; be able to understand the potential risks and benefits of participation; and have the legal capacity to give consent. These tenets should guide the construction of any informed consent text. Figure 3.1 presents an example of an informed consent form, the one used by Alyssa Eckman in her dissertation study of advertorial producers.

The protocol for interacting with potential subjects is at least as important as the content of the informed consent. Only those persons who give their consent verbally *and* in writing should be allowed to participate. The researcher should eschew technical terminology in favor of language that the lay person can understand easily. Potential subjects should be able to ask questions about the project and their participation, and have them answered satisfactorily. Subjects should know that they can leave the study at any time without negative consequences. Coercion or pressure tactics of any kind are totally inimical to the concept of human beings as autonomous agents.

As a matter of principle, the time to obtain the informed consent is before the subject contributes usable data to a project. Recording conversation or behavior before consent is given violates the spirit and policy of consent. There are also good practical reasons for having an early consent briefing. Because qualitative projects can be lengthy, emergent affairs, researchers may not be able to forecast the nature of all of the information that will be needed. It is far better for people to decide not to cooperate at the start, due to their hesitancy at the commitment that is expected of them, than to drop out midway through the study. In our experience, once we discuss the rationale and basic operation of qualitative inquiry, people usually understand why we cannot predict exactly how the project will unfold. They may even appreciate the "benefits" of participating. Of course, they may still choose not to consent.

Some qualitative researchers believe that the informed consent procedure can damage rapport with the potential subjects. Like a prenuptial agreement, goes this line of thought, the informed consent might remind them of what could go wrong and therefore spoil the "romance" the researcher is trying to create. However, one can cultivate good relations in an initial meeting and then sit down with the person for an informed consent briefing. The spirit of good faith that informed consent promotes may even help the process of building rapport.

Consent for research study: *Negotiating the Gray Lines Between Advertising and News: An Ethnographic Study of The Occupational Roles and Practices of Advertorial Producers at a Medium Market American Newspaper*

I, _____, agree to participate in the research being conducted by Alyssa Eckman, under the direction of Dr. Thomas Lindlof, University of Kentucky, College of Communications and Information Studies.

The purpose of this research is to examine the occupational roles and practices of newspaper advertorialists and how they relate to the mass media products that they produce.

Participation in this study is completely voluntary. It is not part of your job and will have no effect on your job or any employment evaluations.

Subject's work practices will be observed by the researcher during the research project to analyze the roles and practices of those who produce advertorials. Subject may agree to participate in a one-hour interview, which will be tape recorded and transcribed by the researcher.

Throughout the project, subject's real name will not be revealed and confidentiality of subject's responses and actions will be maintained by the researcher. You should know, however, that there are some circumstances where the researcher may have to show information gathered from you in this project to other people. Someone from the University of Kentucky may look at or copy records that identify you.

There are no foreseeable risks to the subject stemming from this research. Subjects will receive no monetary compensation for their participation.

_____   _____
              subject   date

For questions about this study, contact the principal investigator, Alyssa Eckman [phone number], or her advisor, Dr. Thomas Lindlof [phone number]. For questions about your rights as a research subject, call the Office of Research Integrity at the University of Kentucky [phone number].

I have explained and defined in detail the research procedure in which the subject has consented to participate.

_____   _____
        principal investigator   date

Figure 3.1   An Informed Consent Form

Some skeptics claim that the permeable boundaries of social scenes undermine the orderly pursuit of informed consent (Fleuhr-Lobban, 1994). For example, in Tom's studies of media and family life, friends and relatives of those he was studying would show up unexpectedly. Even if he had had informed consent forms with him at the time, it would have been awkward to administer the procedure then. It is usually not a problem to seek consent if newcomers become key social actors in the scene, or if new methods are adopted for new research questions. In this regard, Fleuhr-Lobban (1994) notes that "consideration of informed consent can be built into the regular progress and monitoring of social research at various logical steps along the way to the conclusion of research and its aftermath" (p. 7).

Exemptions from informed consent are usually granted for studies of public behavior. Because social actors in settings like shopping malls and street corners are anonymous to the researcher, there is little risk to them from the research activity. However, this does not mean that as researchers we can always reserve the right to decide when and where a public situation exists. Are meetings of Alcoholics Anonymous, a gay student group, and the city council all equally "public" events? Which group, if any, might be harmed if we reported its discourse without permission? The social value of the research and the researcher's power to record others' behavior should be weighed carefully against the members' own sensitivity to what they want to disclose about themselves.

Many of the uses afforded by communication technologies also function as public spaces (see Chapter 8 for a discussion of Internet research). Researchers who merely observe scenes of Internet communications such as Web sites and Internet chat rooms often choose not to notify site managers or users that a study of their discourse is in progress. These researchers treat Internet discourse as they would stranger interactions at a shopping mall. Decisions of whether to seek consent become less clear-cut when the researcher begins to take part in the virtual action. One-to-one communications like e-mail disclose both user identity and private information to the researcher, and thus require informed consent. Other types of virtual communication, such as restricted-access news groups and MUDs (Multi-User Dungeons, text-based virtual environments in which users manipulate commands to create and perform unique characters), offer the opportunity to discern patterns of self-reference that may emerge over time. Some researchers find ways to inform users without disrupting the social life of the site, as in Elizabeth Reid's (1996) study of MUD environments:

> My solution was a virtual approximation of a tape recorder: My MUD characters' personal descriptions included mention of a tape recorder, notebook, or

other device suitable to the particular milieu of the MUD. Moreover, since the ability to log sessions was an integral feature of the client software commonly used to connect to MUD systems, I felt that I was not behaving unethically in logging sessions. . . . I felt that this pragmatic, perhaps even utilitarian, approach satisfied my obligations to the individuals who made up each MUD userbase. (p. 170)

A serious difficulty of seeking informed consent in cyberspace is that the potential subjects may present themselves in a variety of guises (Jones, 1994; Lindlof & Shatzer, 1998; Marx, 1999). Moreover, virtual actors tend to underestimate the potential consequences of agreeing to participate in research (Reid, 1996). Definitions of "public" and "private" remain fluid on the Internet, and with privacy and commercial intrusion still hot political issues, it will probably take some time for consensus to develop around rules of informed consent for virtual communities.

Instruments

Researchers are usually required to submit the instruments they use—questionnaires, measures, tests, stimulus materials, and so on—to the IRB for review. In the case of participant observation, the researcher *is* the instrument. Subjects may need to adjust to the presence of a researcher in their space, but for the most part participant observation does not place major demands on the members of a culture because they are only doing "what comes naturally." Covert observing in nonpublic situations—for example, a researcher who is in a familiar relationship with the subjects records their behavior or discourse without their knowledge—requires special justification because the subjects usually cannot be debriefed when the study is over. At a minimum, the IRB will want to know why a covert approach is necessary and whether anyone will be negatively impacted by the situation.

Interview studies are often exempted from review because they are seen as low-risk methods. However, the IRB will examine a list of interview questions that delves into highly personal areas, illegal activity, or the lives of people who belong to a vulnerable population (see the next section). Even if interview questions are not problematic for the IRB, care must still be taken with how the interview is conducted. It is not uncommon for respondents to reveal emotionally charged information whose disclosure was not foreseen at the start of the interview (LaRossa, Bennett, & Gelles, 1981). Certainly it is unethical to use tactics that are meant to cause distress. In any event, researchers need to be careful not to enter into any form of exploitative relationship with subjects in order to obtain information.

Vulnerable Populations

Certain categories of people are considered to be vulnerable and thus qualify for special protections: children, the homeless, medical patients, prison inmates, and persons with physical or mental disabilities. Because individuals in these populations may not understand the concept of voluntary participation, or may live in institutions where "voluntary" connotes a different meaning, it is critical for the researcher to find the most effective way to communicate the core ideas of informed consent. Under no circumstances should the researcher act coercively to gain access to a vulnerable group or allow institutional agents to coerce on his or her behalf. In the case of minor children, parental assent to their children's participation must be obtained. In general, the IRB wants to know why a vulnerable population is needed for the project.

Additionally, IRB definitions of vulnerable populations may reflect assumptions that strike researchers as odd or biased. Many institutions, for example, require interviewers of gays and lesbians to provide information about resources where interviewees can obtain counseling in the event that discussing their sexuality proves traumatic. Such regulations send mixed signals that reflect mixed motives—IRB's are genuinely concerned about protecting human subjects and also about protecting their institutions from potential lawsuits. Anticipating rare and extreme outcomes can lead IRB's to advocate measures that seem, at best, awkward. In this case, the rules potentially sustain a homophobic stigma that the mental health of "out" homosexuals is precarious.

Data Access

Participants in research projects sometimes notice that a lot of data about them are accumulating in fieldnotes, tapes, and transcripts. They may become apprehensive at what they imagine to be a bulging FBI file. Potential subjects should be reassured that everything recorded or collected in the project will be confidential. This can be explained to them in a general way: "No one but me (or my research assistant) will have access to the interviews and fieldnotes." The IRB will want to know the specifics: Where the data will be kept (e.g., stored in a secure location, such as a university office), who will have access to the data, in what media they will be stored, and how long they will be kept.

Textual Representation of Subjects

The publication of any qualitative study carries the potential to reveal group or individual secrets, affect reputations, or expose "uncomfortable realities" that may upset the subjects when they see them in print. One may wonder why people would be surprised at reading what they chose to say or do in the presence of a researcher. The fact of the matter is that a great deal of our conduct seems innocent enough until it is reported in an interpretative context far away from our control. Not to put too fine a point on it, but researchers and subjects almost never reach a lasting consensus about the nature of the research project, because they each hold to rather different sets of values and are answerable to different constituencies (Becker, 1964). Unless informed consent (or another agreement) screens out the use of certain materials, the researcher has a great deal of latitude concerning the use of data. Some researchers give participants an advance look at a piece of the analysis, or even the entire report—perhaps as part of a member-check procedure (see Chapter 7)—but it is seldom a good idea to allow them an editorial role concerning how their words or actions are interpreted.

How then should the researcher handle the representation of human subjects for publication? In most cases, the subjects' actual identities—their names and other identifying information—should be withheld and some other means used to refer to their actions or expressions in the text. Pseudonyms, chosen by either the researcher or the subject, are a popular option. The researcher should never be careless about protecting participants' identities.

Research participants sometimes want their names to appear in the report. The researcher can agree to accommodate these wishes, but only after the subjects have been fully informed about the detailed nature of qualitative narratives. Certainly the subjects and the researcher can decide to amend any earlier agreement about how they are represented. In historical case studies, specific persons, institutions, or events must be identified if their significance is to be fully realized. For example, Tom's study of the controversy surrounding the film *The Last Temptation of Christ* entailed interviews with motion picture industry artists and executives, many of whom are public figures. These individuals were informed that they might be quoted "on the record," unless they wanted certain information to be "not for attribution" (quoted, but not by name).

Conclusion

The pre-fieldwork activities described in this chapter allow us to locate and shape a research idea. We also begin to understand how the subject of the idea can be engaged in the cultural scene. In the planning phase, this design process culminates in a written research proposal. Only when an idea has been characterized in some form—usually, but not always, written form—do sources and materials related to the idea begin to pull together in suggestive relationships. In this way, the researcher becomes sensitized to the idea. Theoretical sensitivity involves "having insight, the ability to give meaning to data, the capacity of understanding, and capability to separate the pertinent from that which isn't" (Strauss & Corbin, 1990, p. 42). The possibilities of the idea expand further as the researcher begins to implement the project in the field. We will continue discussing this next phase of research design in Chapter 4.

Exercises

1. A prominent source of research ideas is our own personal experiences. Researchers often begin a project—or even an entire research program spanning many years—from their explorations of a personal memory, issue, dilemma, or current involvement. Think of at least one experience you have had that might form the basis of a qualitative communication research study.

- What significance does it hold for you? Why did you think of it as a potential research topic?
- Who else (types of people) may have had a similar experience? What characteristics do these people have in common?
- What kinds of "research questions" might develop out of this idea? Is there a research literature—or are there other sources (including novels, biographies, poems, films, etc.)—that would help you understand this experience further?

2. In this chapter, we discussed the distinctions between field, site, and scene. These are "concepts," to be sure, but they are also important in a practical sense at the start of a project. As you begin to gather information, see if you can define your study concretely in terms of scene, field, and site or sites. Do you think a member of this scene would agree with your descriptions?

3. Write a reconnaissance survey of the scene you want to study.

- What are the characteristics of the research settings?
- What are your initial impressions of the settings, people, and research points of interest?
- What are your impressions of field entry and personal involvement issues?

4

Design II

Today, we can no longer be sure that any field site can contain the action we want to study, or that the "field" is even a valid construction (see Gupta & Ferguson, 1997; Marcus, 1995; Markowitz, 2001). Transnational ethnic migrations, global flows of image and capital, and the explosive growth of media technologies have combined to create worlds of competing discourses and multiple, unstable identities. The researcher's identity is also arguably more fluid and negotiable—with cyberspace ethnography as a prominent example, as we will discuss in Chapter 8. Yet most qualitative studies are still built upon the trust engendered in relations with others, whether in face-to-face or virtual modes. Questions about access, self-presentation, and strategy continue to be key issues for qualitative research.

Picking up where we left off in Chapter 3, this chapter explores the considerations of contacting the scene of study and using exploratory methods to probe aspects of the scene. This process moves us into a new arena of questions: Where is the site? Whom do I contact for access? How should I present myself and my purposes? How do I negotiate with the participants? What tools should I use in understanding the scope, coherence, and qualities of the scene? What aspects of the scene do I sample, and with what kind of strategy do I sample them?

Contacting the Scene

The first days or weeks, in some researchers' view, are the "most uncomfortable stage of field work" (Wax, 1971, p. 15). We suspect that this discomfort is due in large measure to the vulnerability felt by both parties to the project. Researchers feel vulnerable to the possibility of being rejected by the group they want to study. Key members may opt not to cooperate, and those who do so may be less forthcoming than ideally desired. Researchers must also adjust to a new style of living. They may have to visit field sites miles away, and their usual routines must now compete with blocks of time turned over to writing fieldnotes or transcribing tapes. Just beneath the researcher's calm exterior may lie insistent questions about where all of this will lead.

A different vulnerability is felt by the participants, who are now objects of scrutiny by someone they do not know well. Unless they have offered to host the project, or have happily embraced the wish of their trusted leader to cooperate, many of them may regard the researcher's arrival with unease, if not suspicion. On the surface, they are polite to the newcomer and smile pleasantly. But questions about what the researcher wants to know, and why she or he wants to know it, will run through their thoughts and coffee breaks.

This preamble is not the only story that can be told about the first days or weeks. It is an archetypal story, however, and one that resonates with many of our own forays (with some license taken in telling the participants' side). In one study, for example, Bryan recalls fumbling to respond to suspicions among employees at a nuclear weapons laboratory that he was a spy for a rival design facility. We bring up this "story" only in the spirit of full disclosure, not to demoralize readers who are starting on the path of inquiry. In truth, moderate levels of vulnerability are actually useful. The mild anxiety felt by the researcher and noticed in others can be a telling sign of the insider-outsider distinctions that normally operate in the scene or at its boundaries with other scenes. In Bryan's case, what he first thought to be a ludicrous accusation was a revealing statement about the historical rivalry among proud communities surrounding weapons production facilities. In large doses, however, anxiety can have a crippling effect. Researchers already have a demanding ontological position to cope with: They have made it their professional business to enter another social world in order to study and explain the discourses, actions, motives, or understandings of the people who live there. Constant worry about the big picture—for example, whether the project is worthwhile—or about the smallest details, especially without just cause, can only deflect attention from the truly important activities of research.

In this section, we discuss key issues of field entry. Every scene has its own mix of challenges, so broad generalizations can take us only so far. Therefore, we will consider some of the situations that call for improvising a response. We hope that the ideas we propose, when applied in the field, will help reduce researchers' tremors of vulnerability to the scale of "speed bumps."

Negotiating Access

Early in the research process, one must negotiate access to the sites of study. Often these negotiations happen as the research idea is being developed. Indeed, many research proposals will not be considered seriously until the researcher has obtained at least tentative permission from the group or organization being studied. Sometimes, access can be worked out concurrently with entering the field. Regardless of exactly when permission is sought, the terms of access that are usually up for discussion include how long the project will take, what kind of role the researcher can or should assume, the areas available for study and those that are off-limits, when the researcher can enter and exit the scene (or how many interviews can be done), and the kinds of resources the researcher may need. In some ways, these points are related to human subjects protection issues—and in actual practice, the two areas are often discussed together—but negotiations for access focus more on the pragmatic needs of the project and the extent to which the host culture is able to satisfy them. The types of people with whom researchers first negotiate access are called gatekeepers and sponsors.

Gatekeepers. Negotiations usually start with a *gatekeeper*, who controls access to the desired research sites. "Gatekeeper" is not an official title in any organization of which we are aware. Rather, the term describes the person or group who has the authority to negotiate and approve research access in a group or an organization. The researcher's first step in securing a research site must be to find out who the gatekeeper is. Some organizations—such as public school systems—take requests from academic researchers on a regular basis; they have developed policies that define the kinds of research that are normally permitted, and they depend on a standing committee to review these requests. Although committees may act as the arbiters of access, it is not unusual for final approval to come down from the highest levels of an organization. In organizations where research requests are less common, one person may be pressed into service as the gatekeeper, who will probably consult with others who may potentially be affected by, or interested in, the proposed study. In any case, written proposals, perhaps accompanied with the investigator's curriculum vitae and other supporting documents, are normally expected.

Many other scenes are much less formal in their handling of research queries. In research on families, for example, one or both parents are normally approached first. The researcher comes to their home, she or he explains the research, and the discussion flows easily. Children can be influential voices, but they hardly ever act as true gatekeepers. Deliberations in small groups can be just as delicate as in a formal organization, but decisions can also happen surprisingly fast. One of Tom's doctoral students, for example, was seeking a public site of interaction for members of the vinyl record collector community. He found a store that stocked a major vinyl record inventory and approached "Pops," the owner, about observing the patrons. A couple of minutes into the student's spiel, Pops interrupted and said yes to the request. Gatekeepers who are accountable to no one but themselves may be more prone to rapid decision making, and their personal affinity for the topic—and/or the researcher—can be a decisive factor.

An important aspect of relations with gatekeepers that the researcher should bear in mind is that the researcher needs the approval of the gatekeeper far more than the gatekeeper needs the research. Gatekeepers can blithely ignore or turn down such requests, because the group or organization often stands to gain little from the project and potentially has much to lose. Commercial businesses, in particular, often act cautiously. They keep their guard up, perceiving little practical benefit for them if they grant access, or even fearing that it may intrude on the proprietary nature of their products or services. Therefore, the researcher almost always bargains from a weaker position. The investigator is forced to argue persuasively for the family members, peer group, club, or company to create a space for research activities that may be somewhat alien to their social routines. If the site is unique, the need to present the study effectively only increases. The steps described next may increase the researcher's chances of gaining access to a scene, and, in the best case of all, on the terms the researcher seeks.

Study the group or organization and tailor the proposal to fit its interests as closely as possible. By becoming familiar with the history, mission, and needs of the group or organization, the researcher can begin to understand the perspective of the gatekeeper (usually a *management* perspective), speak more credibly about the practical value of the project, and lay the groundwork for good relationships over the course of the project. It is probably not wise for the researcher to suggest that the project will directly diagnose or ameliorate the problems of the group or organization. (That is more properly the role of a consultant, and the consultant and independent researcher roles don't mix very well.)

Devote care to the ways in which one's self and the proposal are presented. Ultimately, the success of most negotiations depends on whether the gatekeeper feels good about placing trust in the person asking for access. Researchers should give the gatekeeper every reason to think that they are competent, organized, true-to-their-word individuals who will respect the culture of the group or organization. Researchers should make it clear that they will conduct research in a fair, thorough manner. If the research requires access to many different processes, levels, or sectors of the group or organization, a strong rationale for this range of investigation should be given. (Many organizations are loath to permit researchers free rein to roam through and inspect all of their operations.) The researcher should be prepared to tack to the group's internal timetables; likewise, good gatekeepers will ask about any deadlines that the researcher must meet and try to accommodate to them. Candor and goodwill on both sides can go far toward avoiding future misunderstandings about what is needed to complete the study.

It may come as no surprise that gatekeepers are often unenthusiastic about hosting a project that could reveal the group's problems to a public audience. Researchers who intend their projects to critique the goals, ideologies, or practices of the group or organization (as many communication researchers' projects do) should consider alternative ways of presenting this purpose (e.g., making it a secondary element of the request for entry). Here, "alternative" does not mean "deceptive." If judgment is the agenda, hiding the knife doesn't make the eventual cut any kinder. Most "critical" research goals are not synonymous with "adversarial" goals; they may often be restated as "seeking the full range of opinions" or "exploring alternate solutions."

Be willing to consult with or ask permission of others in the group or organization. In some scenes, more than one gatekeeper will be involved in the negotiation. Even when one person exercises the authority to grant access, others may be brought in on the process in some fashion. Also, access decisions made by group authorities typically devolve to the responsibility of specific handlers and contacts occupying lower levels and local sites where the research actually takes place. Researchers should remember that achieving formal sponsorship does not relieve them of responsibility for building trust with these immediate contacts.

Kahn and Mann (1969), for example, developed a procedure they call "contingent acceptance decisions," in which the permission line moves downward through a hierarchy until all agree to participate. They note that "it is implicit in this method that a higher level within the authority structure will not veto the study if the researcher can gain the acceptance of those at successively lower levels" (pp. 48-49). Methods like this can have the dual political benefits of broadening the field of stakeholders and ensuring that the researcher does not align too closely with a power nexus. Seeking wide support for a project is almost always a desirable strategy.

Make only those promises that can be kept. Researchers should resist the urge to promise too much in order to win approval from gatekeepers. The people who grant access often monitor the project's progress closely, particularly if it is consuming resources from the group or organization. Naturally, they will be concerned if the original promises miss their mark widely. Asking the gatekeeper to accept an open-ended commitment is one way to avert this situation. Overestimating the time required for completion of the project is another way; if the gatekeeper balks at the estimates given, one can then downsize it to a more realistic level.

To close this discussion on a note of reassurance: *Refusals are seldom final in the game of access requests.* As long as researchers show a sincere willingness to respond to sticking points, most gatekeepers will cooperate in the search for a solution.

So far, our discussion has centered on those gatekeepers who, primarily on their own authority, enable the researcher to enter a scene. But there are other situations in which the researcher must go to the members and appeal to them directly for cooperation. Referring to ethnographic studies of television usage in families, Lull (1985) observes that "contact through some agency of importance to the family is usually necessary to gain access . . . [including] religious and educational institutions, places of work, community service groups, and clubs" (p. 81). Following approval by a committee or executive board of the agency, the researcher then tries to reach the membership through such means as telephone calls or a brief pitch at a membership meeting. These direct appeals are more common in groups or organizations in which democratic self-governance by members is the norm.

Sponsors. Most gatekeepers do not invest much of their own or their organizations' capital, reputational or material, in the projects they approve. They probably view research access as something of a public service gesture—with the possibility of useful information coming back to the organization. In contrast, a *sponsor* is someone who takes a very active interest. In addition to granting access, a sponsor usually goes around to others and personally introduces the researcher, vouches for the project, and helps the researcher find informants or resources. Sponsors may even act themselves as key informants about the local customs, speech norms, history, power structure, and so on. Sponsors and researchers mutually invest in the project, and their bond may become a close, productive relationship.

Sponsors are key figures in many studies. Their timely appearance often enables the researcher to become an ally and valued member of the scene. Patrick Murphy (1999b), for example, tells of finding a sponsor in the person of Eladio, leader of a conchero dance group in the San Francisquito barrio of the city of Queretaro, Mexico. By Murphy's own admission, his ethnography of Mexican families' interpretations and uses of television had not been going well. His efforts at publicizing his study locally had yielded few volunteers willing to let him into their homes. However, a chance meeting with Eladio during the dance troupe's bus trip to a religious festival—and Eladio's surprising response to the researcher's "contribution" to the cost of the trip—cemented their friendship. In Murphy's words,

> [Eladio] decided to support my research with all the seriousness and respect that he wanted his dancing to receive. Moreover, as I increased the amount of time that I spent with Eladio and his family, I was increasingly associated by many Queretanos with *el barrio* of San Francisquito. (p. 487)

As this story illustrates, the intervention of a sponsor can greatly aid the progress of a study, but the researcher also becomes identified with the sponsor's constituency—a result that may or may not pose a risk to the study.

Negotiating Research Relationships

Obtaining permission from a gatekeeper or sponsor does not guarantee a successful entry to the scene. A good start also depends on finding out *who is willing to cooperate*. The parties involved—the researcher and the persons who live in this scene—have their own individual and communal interests to look after; ipso facto, the researcher should be ready to engage them in dialogue about how and why their interests will be served by participating in the project.

One argument that researchers frequently use concerns the "social good" of research. By this, we mean that researchers try to show participants why it is important to study the nature and processes of communication. The social-good explanation is likely to be more persuasive if the researcher can clarify the connections between research and teaching or between theory and praxis. The researcher can explain that the knowledge that comes from this project may help ordinary people become more skilled communicators or may equip all of us with tools and insights for understanding interpersonal and mediated communication in social life. Given its intellectual tenor, this line of argument by itself may not gain much compliance. Conceivably it carries more cachet with audiences who already appreciate the role of social science. Still, if it is delivered with conviction, the social-good pitch needn't be elitist in nature.

One variation on the social-good theme is to claim that the study will focus on a practice or issue of critical importance to the group itself. If the study is funded by a federal agency or foundation, the researcher can tell participants that the final report might contribute to policies or techniques that will improve the well-being of their families or communities. This moves the study's rationale closer to the participants' own interests. Of course, this claim can't be mere "window dressing"; the study must actually prove its relevance to a practice or issue that the group or organization considers important. Describing the genesis of his study of a longshoremen's union, David Wellman (1994) wrote that he was motivated by theoretical questions about postwar, postindustrial changes in working-class consciousness. As he discussed his study with colleagues and others who interacted with labor unions, Wellman began to realize the value of grounding his inquiry in the grievance process—thus situating the study at a locus of struggle between capital interests and organized labor, and also creating a "research story" that would make more sense to the longshoremen than "the larger meaning of working-class consciousness" would (p. 571). Wellman described how this reasoning was received:

> The stated reason for studying the union resonated with longshoremen. Many of them were angry about the grievance system; they were critical of it. Thus, my presence was interpreted as giving legitimacy to, if not endorsing, their point of view, and I was actually welcomed aboard.

> "I'm very glad you're doing this," said a dock steward after learning of my reasons for being at a union meeting. "The goddamn grievance machinery sure as hell needs looking into. I would do it myself, if I had the time and know-how."

> One of my first discoveries, then, was that many longshoremen wanted me to be there. I was expecting resistance and reluctance, and was therefore prepared to plead and justify. Instead, I found openness and encouragement. (pp. 571-572)

Participants may also be impressed with the researcher's desire to understand their expertise, their thoughts and emotions, or the interesting qualities of their world. The research project, then, can be framed as a chance for people to display, or talk about, their skills or forms of understanding to a sympathetic outsider—someone who wants to be taught important truths and who will not judge them. Many people welcome the opportunity to spend time with someone who shows genuine interest in them. Sometimes they are flattered at being selected. Bryan's status with the nuclear laboratory employees rose dramatically when he announced midway through his study that he had received some federal funding. As frequent competitors for research funding themselves, they knew that only studies of legitimate topics qualified for such funding. In these positive reactions, some members might even disclose to a researcher aspects of their lives that aren't shared with their spouse, other close relatives, or friends. On the other hand, some individuals take this opportunity to exaggerate their role or to advance a personal or professional agenda. The researcher should be careful not to encourage self-serving motives that could negatively affect the quality of an interview narrative or the researcher's relationship with a group or community.

Investigators can also argue that research is simply part of their job, and in order to do this job well, they need willing participants. This line of argument does resonate with many people. After all, we all have jobs to do. And this job—the research—has to be done *here*, *now*, and with *these people*, if it is to achieve its aims. This appeal may be more well-received when it comes from students, who are literally required to do a project as a course (or degree) requirement, and with many fewer resources than their professors.

Finally, some form of reciprocal agreement between researcher and participant may form the basis for cooperation. It is natural for any interpersonal relationship to involve exchanges of time, effort, and services. Relationships that develop in qualitative research are not much different in this regard, because personal interests are expressed, affections are felt, and trust is shared. Getting along with an informant, or becoming an accepted member of a scene, may depend on knowing what—and when—to give and take. Researchers have been known to give car rides to participants, buy them meals or drinks, or help out with household chores. Most of these circumstances involve acts of courtesy; others are more obviously performed in exchange for access or data.

Cash payments are a special case of rewarded cooperation. Cash has the advantage of being fungible; that is, money establishes a scale of value for all forms of research participation. Cash payments can be effective when people have little intrinsic interest in the topic of the study, when they have a real need for money, or when the researcher wants a high rate of cooperation. The size of the payment often depends on how hard it is to recruit from a certain population (e.g., those in high-status occupations). Probably the type of qualitative inquiry in which monetary rewards play the largest role is focus group interviewing. For the most part, though, payment-for-participation is not nearly as common in qualitative research as it is in quantitative research. The primary reason why qualitative researchers shun cash payments is that it is not regarded as a preferred way to start a personal relationship with someone. With money as the basis for the time people spend together, relationships get off on a peculiar footing, to say the least. A secondary reason is that qualitative researchers often are not externally funded, or if they are, the funding is not at a high level.

More common is the exchange of small favors and tokens of gratitude. Usually, as in the examples cited above, these are not significant enough to make anyone feel awkward, and they may in fact build a sense of fellowship between researchers and those they study. However, like cash, some favors do have the potential to affect the relationships with participants or the judgment of the researcher. For example, a student in one of Tom's graduate seminars decided to study the scene of new car sales—in particular, the situated practices by which salesmen categorize customers and engage them on the car lot. The student selected as his field site a dealership where he had recently purchased a car. His stint of participant observation went well. During the last week of the semester, Tom was watching television at home when a commercial for this dealership appeared. There, featured in the 30-second spot, was the student giving a hearty endorsement for the dealership. The student later explained that it only seemed natural in his field role to go along with management's request for him to play the part of a satisfied customer in the commercial. After all, he did enjoy his car-buying experience! The student performed his part in the TV ad with admirable brio, yet in doing so, he risked being co-opted by the people he was studying.

Clarifying the Commitment

Among the most practical interests of potential subjects, and rightfully so, is the extent of their involvement in the project. Most would like to know how long their participation will last, how many field visits or interviews they should expect, and how much time all of this will take. Many of them—being busy people when they are not being human subjects—would like to minimize the time they devote to the project. The researcher, on the other hand, would like their commitment to be open-ended and for them to be maybe not "on call" but at least available for "call backs." Somewhere between these two sets of interests lie the grounds for negotiation.

If the researcher has portrayed the project in the most compelling *and* realistic light (no small task), the participant should be ready to sign on. The first meeting or two, then, should focus on how the subject's involvement will unfold. Usually, the opening phase of the research will be defined in more detail than the middle and end phases. The researcher can say, "I'd like for us to talk about Topic A at our first interview. At the second and third interviews, we will get to Topics B, C, and D. If we don't finish everything by the third meeting, we can talk about having a fourth interview." The researcher should not be cavalier about trying to accurately estimate this time frame. If interviewees find themselves still discussing Topic A at the third interview, they might get frustrated and bail out of the project.

Long-term cooperation seems to be enhanced when participants view the study as relevant to their interests, and when their relationship with the researcher becomes more personalized and equal in perceived status as time goes on (Thornton, Freedman, & Camburn, 1982). If the experience goes well for both parties, it is usually not hard to extend the involvement beyond what was envisioned initially.

Another issue to clarify concerns when and where research data are collected. In qualitative studies, *anything* can become data. The unwary person can be forgiven for thinking that "research" only happens at certain well-marked times, and at other times, the incidental topics they discuss won't be recorded or used for publication. Qualitative folklore, for example, holds that researchers should be especially attentive to comments made by interviewees after they believe an interview is concluded, because they may still be simmering, impulsive, and lulled into greater disclosure.

Probably the most responsible approach is simply to agree upon when the research activity is "on" in their common life-worlds. In one version of this understanding, any and all of the participant's contacts with the researcher may produce usable data. That is, "research" interests and "personal" interests merge in any situation of co-presence. In another version, data may be recorded only when the researchers and participants see each other at designated field sites. For example, if they pass each other while jogging and stop to talk, the research project is *not* "on" at that moment. In still another version, data will be created only when the tape recorder is rolling; nonrecorded comments can be used only if the subject gives explicit permission. Whatever version the researcher and participants jointly adopt should be used for *all* participants (although in some cases, special rules devised for individuals or subgroups may be warranted).

Generally, the simpler the ground rules defining the act of research, the better. Complicated rules can potentially lead to mistakes in their use and erosions of trust. If the researcher and participants are comfortable with how they treat each other, particularly if the researcher exhibits discretion in the scene, the participants will probably trust the researcher to "do the right thing." Of course, the informed consent—especially, the subject's right to know about the study's instruments, protocols, and access to data—should answer most questions about how information is gathered and used.

Constructing a Perspective

As negotiations with gatekeepers, sponsors, and participants bring the researcher to the brink of entry, the researcher begins to enact a view of the action. "Adopting a perspective," writes Anderson (1987), "means that the analyst references his or her behavior within [the] group. Choices in dress, ways of speaking, and the like are directed by that group's alternatives" (p. 307). Whether a study centers on one family, a dozen respondents, or a whole community, the researcher always creates a perspective. A highly practical interpretive device, a perspective defines what will be seen and heard, noticed, and reported. It is used as a sensemaking device for experiencing action in the field and is similar to, but not the same as, the participants' own perspective. However, perspectives are not neutral, morality-free vantage points. Researchers must often contend with factions and rivalries within a group in deciding how to develop their way of looking, listening, and participating.

Participants will search for clues to this perspective, because it is a matter of interest to them—very keen interest—to know where the researcher stands with respect to their issues and identity claims. They expectantly await the researcher's answer to the unspoken question, "Whose side are you on?" One researcher we know answers this question with, "The side of Truth and Beauty, of course!" Her strength of conviction typically squelches further interrogation, although not everyone is advised to employ a retort. An alternative is to treat the question as an opportunity for further learning about members' experiences: How many sides are there? Who's on them? Nancy T. Ammerman (1982), who began a participant observation study of a Fundamentalist Christian congregation, phrased the dilemma this way: "How different can I be and still maintain access [to] and communication with the group?" (p. 23). The nature of the group's belief system raised the stakes for this question:

> For Fundamentalists, there are only two kinds of people: the saved and the damned. Until people are saved they can neither be part of the church nor even understand the "things of God." . . . In my case, the problem was not whether or not I was "saved," but whether or not I also accepted the Fundamentalist version of the One Truth. My solution to that dilemma was to emphasize my identity as a saved person and keep as silent as possible about my differences. (p. 25)

Ammerman's circumspection was not severely tested, in part because she was willing to sing when they sang, pray when they prayed, and dress as the women dressed, "but most of all" because she "used their language" (p. 25).

The participants will sometimes try to impose their own idea of the researcher's perspective. In many cases, these attributed identities can be redefined during the course of a study, as Ruth Horowitz (1986) relates in her study of Chicano gang members:

> The first dimension of my identity that I discovered they were constructing was as "a lady" which placed me in a respected but somewhat distant position from them. A "lady" implied that a woman was unobtainable sexually. . . . However, "ladies" do not sit in the park and are not interested in gang members' lives. Social workers might be "ladies" who asked questions, but there were no outsider-social workers in the community, and the Lions discarded that category for me because I was at the park on evenings and weekends and did not try to make them do anything that would threaten their way of life. Finally, about four weeks after I arrived, one of the gang members declared that I was like Lois Lane, the reporter (Superman's girlfriend). It was an identity that transcended gender. . . . This provided them with the necessary identity with which I could ask about their activities and they could readily respond. Often they would seek me out to relay new stories of gang activities and, later on in research, when someone wanted a story retold, to say, "Ask Ruth, she's been writing it all down." (pp. 414-416)

As these excerpts show, a research perspective develops and flourishes as the researcher works into a role (e.g., scribe) that both makes sense to the participants and satisfies the intent of the project. The role that they arrange will open up a particular view of the scene, but this perspective also constrains the researcher from sensing, or making full use of, alternate realities. Alert, reflective researchers will feel and observe the tension between the perspective they have chosen, or been permitted to utilize, and the views that are closed off to them. We will say more about observer roles in Chapter 5 and about interview rapport in Chapter 6.

Exploratory Methods

The self-questioning and scene-questioning activities discussed in Chapter 3 enable researchers to decide whether they should embark upon a project. Once a commitment is made, more systematic means of sizing up social scenes can be used by researchers to inform research design, especially with regard to sampling. These exploratory methods are useful when little is known about a scene in advance or when the social action is too elusive to document directly; some of these methods—such as the use of visual media and documents—may play a central role in the investigation.

Maps

In any project, researchers swiftly learn that their field sites are "human gathering places" in the fullest sense. Any spaces in which social actors live or work are turned into *places* that uniquely express their preferences. Arrangements of walls, windows, doors, hallways, and rooms large and small—accented with lighting, floor coverings, window treatments, and so forth—not only channel flows of activity, they also create a distinctive social ambience. Think, for example, of the vast, fluorescent territory of a Wal-Mart superstore and the narrow aisles and charming clutter of a neighborhood grocery, and how these differences influence the tone of the shopping that occurs in each place. Objects and artifacts also help construct a sense of place by revealing the history, values, and aesthetic sensibility of its occupants.

Making maps is a way for researchers to explore the spatial dimensions of a site. Denzin (1978) notes that maps

> give the researcher a working picture of the temporal, ritual, and routine features of the persons or social organizations under study. Representational maps are also graphic. They pictorially display the recurrent and stable features of the social worlds under examination. Typically these graphic maps will describe the ecological and physical layout of concrete social settings. (pp. 95-96)

Early in a project, maps help the investigator understand how social actors gather, move, and orient to each other in relation to space and objects. Maps are useful in team projects for facilitating discussion among team members about their ongoing work in different settings. Later, maps can help track the growth or decline of social action or changes in the spatial configuration of field sites (e.g., changes in furniture or remodeled office spaces). Data can also be fed into the production of new versions of maps in order to represent key incidents or types of social activity. As an example, Figures 4.1, 4.2, and 4.3 depict three maps from research conducted by Joel Kailing when he was a doctoral student at the University of Kentucky. As we discussed in Chapter 1, the Burgin post office was the site for his research of small town communication rituals. The first map renders the physical layout of the Burgin post office. The other two maps show the participants (icons standing for specific people) and their positions in the post office for the key incidents labeled, respectively, "*Black Beauty*" and "Boys' Club." Maps such as these can help readers visualize the orientations of the people described in the report.

For researcher-designed maps, drafting skills are not required. These maps usually do not have to be drawn to scale, and rough sketches done

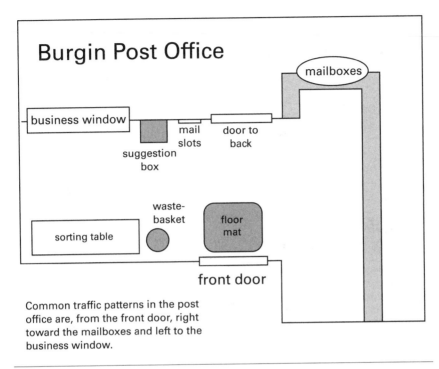

Figure 4.1   Burgin Post Office

on-site will work well for many situations. However, some researchers, like Joel, take their sketches back to the office and make cleaner versions using software tools. Hypertextual modes of representation also allow computer-generated (or scanned-in) maps to be integrated into analyses of data.

Finally, maps are to be valued not only because of their representational value but also because their very construction may become part of the research relationship. Bryan's nuclear-laboratory study mentioned above, for example, took place in the facility's museum. Although his study had been sponsored by the museum's professional staff, he had no legitimate role to play with the older, patriotic (and initially suspicious) docents who worked on the museum floor. In order to break the ice, he began his fieldwork by constructing a detailed map and narrative account of the museum's many exhibits. Bryan's viewing, drawing, and writing activities entailed asking the docents about the function and history of the exhibits and the accuracy of the map. This interaction proved invaluable to establishing a working relationship with this group.

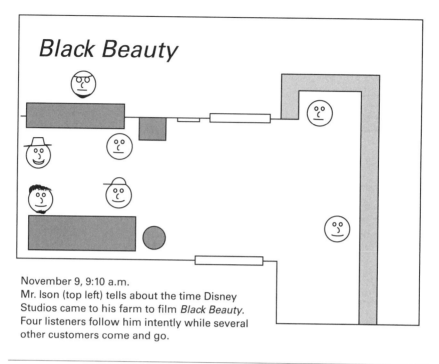

Black Beauty

November 9, 9:10 a.m.
Mr. Ison (top left) tells about the time Disney
Studios came to his farm to film *Black Beauty*.
Four listeners follow him intently while several
other customers come and go.

Figure 4.2   Black Beauty

Visual Media

Motion pictures, video, and still photography have been common data collection tools in anthropology for more than 70 years. These media have in fact been used to produce entire ethnographies of cultural life or specific rituals (Harper, 2000). Researchers in sociology sometimes use video cameras to observe public behavior openly (or covertly in some cases) or to record spoken narratives (Barnes, Taylor-Brown, & Wiener, 1997), and focus group interviews are often videotaped from behind one-way mirrors to capture interviewees' gestures and facial expressions. Film and video are also well-suited to micro-ethnographic studies that examine the orderliness of routine interaction in fine-grained detail (e.g., Ruhleder & Jordan, 1997) and replay increments of behavior in motion that would escape the real-time notice of the most acute observers. However, visual media have rarely been used in qualitative communication research. Ethnographers in this discipline seldom resort to the use of images as primary data (but see the discussion in Chapter 9 of documentaries

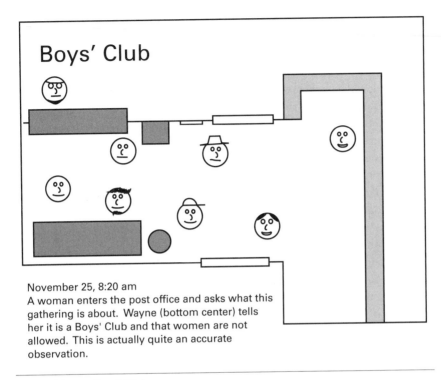

Boys' Club

November 25, 8:20 am
A woman enters the post office and asks what this gathering is about. Wayne (bottom center) tells her it is a Boys' Club and that women are not allowed. This is actually quite an accurate observation.

Figure 4.3   Boys' Club

produced by Communication ethnographers), and the use of photographs has mainly been confined to an illustrational role in published Communication work.

Despite this history, there are many features of visual media that commend their use. Human beings are constrained in observational ability by their limited visual memory and their self-consciousness in social situations. Cameras easily overcome the first limitation by making a permanent, high-fidelity record of an event. In the case of video, events can be played over and over at various speeds, or frame by frame. Cameras are also implacable observers. They do not respond differently to social and nonsocial situations, as humans do. Cameras can take in the whole action of a scene or isolate and follow specific parts of a scene. Digital still and video cameras have even greater advantages over cameras that run emulsion film stock. Digital cameras are now extremely compact and lightweight. They run quietly, shoot in very low-light situations, and do not require expensive processing. More importantly for data analysis and authoring applications, digital images are easily downloaded into computer files, where they can be edited, manipulated in endless ways, combined with other media for placement on Web sites, and shared electronically with distant users.

Although the imagery is static, still photography is not inferior to moving-image media for all purposes. With photography, we can carefully compose images of objects in which we have a special interest, or we can set a high shutter speed to stop a "moment" in a stream of action. Researchers who combine visualization skills with social sensitivity may be those most likely to produce useful pictures in the field (Ball, 1998). As widely used, low-tech devices, still cameras can be part of a researcher's presence from the first days in the field (Prosser & Schwartz, 1998). Pictures can help "map" the research sites early in a project, and important artifacts can be photographed in their natural contexts. Still cameras also probably cause less self-consciousness and anxiety in the scene's participants than video cameras do. Some participants enjoy having their pictures taken as they carry out their activities, and it can be valuable for participants' understanding of their lives for them to photograph the settings, artifacts, and people that they consider most meaningful (Ginsburg, 1995). All of this suggests that images can enter directly into the researcher's interpretational process. As Becker (1986) notes, "photographer[s] will be alert for visual embodiments of [their] ideas, for images that contain and communicate the understanding [they are] developing. . . . [Their] theories will inform [their] vision and influence what [they] find interesting and worth making pictures of" (p. 249).

It is also important to consider the risks that can accompany the use of visual media in fieldwork situations. Like anyone else, research participants may experience a heightened sense of being watched when cameras are present and may even feel that their personal space has been invaded. If the researcher first establishes a good-faith presence, and only then asks for permission to photograph or videotape the participants, the camera may be much less socially problematic. Of course, some people will object to having their pictures taken under any condition. Their wishes should be respected above any other consideration. Another issue is whether visual records are more "objective" or precise than data obtained by other means. Think of the camera as an extension of the human who operates it: The camera is aimed in the direction, and with a lens setting, that the researcher prefers; the picture frames the person or object that the researcher is interested in. Why would we think of the image as any less tainted by the researcher's personal and conceptual interests than are other data? Perhaps the main difference is that, unlike a fieldnote, pictures are nondiscursive and therefore may be more open to diverse (and uninformed) interpretations in the hands of people who do not possess the researcher's own experience.

Documents

Even as we find ourselves more and more ensconced in a world of electronic messages, paper documents (or in current parlance, "hard copies") remain critical to the functioning of organizations, groups, and individuals. To the qualitative analyst, documents are very important because they are the "paper trail" left in the wake of historical events and processes. Among other functions, documents in an organization indicate what the organization produces; how it certifies actions (e.g., a license or deed); how it categorizes events or people (e.g., membership lists); how it codifies procedures or policies (e.g., manuals); and in what ways it informs or instructs the membership (e.g., newsletters and shareholder reports), explains past or future actions (e.g., memoranda), memorializes its own history or achievements (e.g., yearbooks), and tracks its own activities (e.g., minutes of meetings). The personal documents of individuals—for example, letters, diaries, journals, notes, scrapbooks—can provide insights into the construction of personal beliefs, identities, relationships, and communicative styles (e.g., Banks, Louie, & Einerson, 2000; Katriel & Farrell, 1991; Otnes, Kim, & Kim, 1994).

By themselves, documents are usually of limited significance. But when they are related to other evidence, they have much to offer the qualitative analyst. First, documents can be linked to the talk and social action contexts that the researcher is studying (Miller, 1997). For example, an ethnography focusing on the "careers" of documents within the International Monetary Fund (Harper, 1998) shows how intraorganizational communities form in part through their semiotic engagement with documents.

Second, documents can help researchers reconstruct past events or ongoing processes that are not available for direct observation. Although documents are often relatively accurate (because groups and individuals depend on them for functioning effectively), it is still vital to evaluate their reliability and accuracy, especially if one is interested in them for their historical value.

Third, documents reflect certain kinds of organizational rationality at work. They often embody social rules—but not necessarily the reasoning behind the rules—that govern how members of a social collective should behave. For example, the memoranda written by chief executive officers can be read for signs of hegemony, and the responses written by low- and middle-level managers can be read for signs of compliance or resistance.

When working with documents, researchers should try to gain access to the originals, but photocopies will suffice for most purposes. Clearly, researchers do not want to be barred from using a document at all, so requests must be crafted carefully. The format and content of a document should be characterized by the same devotion to detail that the researcher gives fieldnotes. The researcher should try to describe the document's origins and history, who issued it, when and how it was circulated (or read), and how it was used in communicative action. Separate files and indexes of document exhibits should be set up for analytic purposes.

Research Diaries

Some activities happen so spontaneously or rarely that attempts to observe them would be inefficient. The activities of interest may also be secretive or solitary. A field probe used for documenting activities like these is the diary method—or "diary-interview" (Zimmerman & Wieder, 1977). Diaries are often thought of as blank-paged books in which people confide their innermost thoughts. However, in most studies, participants are given instructions regarding the kinds of experiences to be recorded in the research diary, and of course, they are aware that these descriptions will be read by an outside party.

The diary is normally kept by the participant for a standard period of time, such as a week, then collected by the researcher. The participant may be instructed to simply note the occurrence of events of a certain type (including details about when, where, who, and how). This approach to diary keeping allows the researcher to analyze patterns of events for a sample of people, such as a family or peer group members, and subsequently schedule sessions of participant observation when the event seems to occur with greatest regularity. Interviewers can use diary data to inquire about how and why the recorded incidents happened.

Participants may also be asked to describe their own attitudes or impressions in the diary, usually in a free narrative. In this sense, diarists act as "informants" on their own personal lives. For example, McKinney and McKinney (1999) placed diaries with 77 people ranging in age from 18 to 23, for a one-week period, in order to understand the role of prayer in their everyday lives. The directions on the inside cover of the diary instructed the subjects to

> keep a record of all of their thoughts and activities related to prayer, as well as of their feelings before, during, and after praying. They were given additional suggestions as to what might be included such as the time of day, the place,

whether they were alone or with others, the length of time spent praying, to whom they prayed, the reasons for praying, etc. (p. 283)

The diary is capable of yielding a wealth of information about people's daily lives. It is also one of the few methods in which the participants are relatively free to determine the nature of the data. But with these strengths come risks. Because it can be easy for people to forget about their diary-keeping duty, the researcher should prompt them to record in the diary regularly and make complete, truthful entries. Researchers should also be prepared to follow the diary period rather quickly with interviews so that participants can recall the contexts, motives, and consequences of the incidents they recorded.

Quantitative Resources

As we discussed in Chapter 1, quantitative methods and data need not be antithetical to the conduct of qualitative studies. Indeed, they can add precision to design efforts at the front end of a project. Surveys in particular can be a valuable exploratory method. Due to their ability to capture demographic, behavioral, and attitudinal attributes, surveys can offer a comprehensive look at an entire social unit. A survey—even one administered quickly by e-mail, for example—may return enough responses for a baseline evaluation of key population variables. Variable analysis in this sense is a means, not an end, for conducting a qualitative inquiry. Surveys and depth interviews can also be used in a two-stage design in which the survey provides public normative opinions about a topic while the qualitative study yields data about actual practices and processes (Mason, 1994).

Surveys can also track opinion, technology use, or a host of other social indicators over time. Investigators may find it useful to compare trend data with "on the ground" changes noted from the qualitative component. Because panel studies are often expensive to conduct, an alternative to such studies might be for researchers to avail themselves of existing sources of data, such as census data, public polls, privately commissioned polls, or institutional records.

Finally, researchers may find surveys useful for reaching specific persons for intensive study; that is, the investigator, in addition to analyzing a sample statistically, may want to examine the questionnaires individually in order to select those who fit the criteria for a qualitative study. This can be a good way to identify "social outliers." As we will see in the next section, qualitative analysts are often interested in studying extreme cases (or typical cases, for that matter) in a social universe. Those who use survey data would do well to remember that quantitative data are only as good as the validity and reliability of the measures used to collect the data.

Briefing Interviews

Conducting interviews with key informants is another way for researchers to explore the scene prior to field entry. These interviews can be considered *briefings* in the sense that they educate (brief) the researcher on such matters as a group or organization's current goals, mission, personnel, recent history, and prospective agenda. Thus, what one gets from a briefing is a detailed overview of the group or organization. Briefings also afford the researcher an opportunity to raise any remaining issues about the study's method. Because the person who gives the briefing is typically not a methodologist, the researcher is mainly interested in knowing from this informant how practical it would be to engage in certain field tactics. The informant's intimate knowledge of the scene usually puts that person in a good position to say whether a tactic would work well or poorly.

Informants are chosen on the basis of their deep knowledge of the scene. They should be willing to give articulate, detailed responses and even foresee what the researcher should know or ask when the researcher hasn't thought of it. Ideally, briefings should go beyond the "official line," and offer glimpses of the many unofficial realities that await the researcher. Chapter 6 will look more closely at who informants are and how to conduct effective interviews with them.

Sampling

No qualitative project can capture every event as it unfolds. Even if this Godlike feat were possible, the amount of information produced would be so vast that it would take a cadre of analysts years to code and interpret it. This brief fantasy of "total field coverage" underscores a key issue facing qualitative researchers as they begin a project: how to use their time and resources. Many qualitative researchers use a *sampling strategy* that guides their choices of what to observe or whom to interview. An intelligent sampling strategy enables researchers to make systematic contact with communicative phenomena with a minimum of wasted effort.

Researchers who do immersive, participatory ethnography often enter the field with few preconceived ideas of how they will spend their time. The roles they create (see the discussion in Chapter 5) will open up opportunities for experiencing social life that are more natural than the formalized, even forced, nature of a sampling strategy. These "opportunistic" decisions may seem more intuitive than mindful, but they are still sampling decisions. The need to make choices in the field is inescapable, and the logics of sampling we discuss here are in fact used by nearly all qualitative inquirers, albeit not always consciously.

Sampling Units

First, we review the sampling units that are most common in qualitative inquiry—sites, settings, people, activities, events, and times. These units represent distinctive frameworks for sampling communicative performances. Although we discuss them individually here, in most research designs some combination of these units will be used to devise a sampling strategy.

Sites and *settings* are geographic (or simulated) places that have social and cultural meanings for people. A field site—for example, a theme park—is composed of many settings (e.g., rope lines, plazas, walkways, rides, concessions). Sites and settings are most important as sampling units when one wants to study how people interact with natural or built environments (the social ecology of communication) or how acts of communication exhibit regularity or variation in terms of where they occur. Multisite case studies bring the comparative sampling of action and discourse directly into the heart of project design.

The value of *persons* as a sampling unit is most obvious in interview-based studies. The researcher recruits persons for qualitative interviews because they have had experiences, or possess knowledge and/or expertise, that are important to the research questions. Focus group interviews, for example, often bring together individuals who share in an activity (e.g., newspaper reading) or in a status or an attribute (e.g., children in blended families). The positions that persons occupy in an organization, a group, or society at large can be the basis for interview selection; in most such cases, these persons are actually a surrogate for discourses gathered from different locations of a social structure.

Activities and *events* can be treated together because they are closely related sampling units. Activities are the doings of individuals or groups—extended social performances, often ritualistic, enacted in specific settings and time periods. For example, "batting practice" is a type of rehearsal activity of baseball players that takes place on a baseball field before a game begins. Events are episodes of behavior that, together, constitute an activity. We see an event as a discrete part of an activity when one or more of the participants recognizes it as such or when we analytically detach an episode from the stream of activity. Schatzman and Strauss (1973) identify three types of events: routine events, special events, and untoward (or emergency) events. In the case of batting practice, the pitcher throwing a pitch to a batter would, in most instances, constitute a routine event. But a non-team member—for example, a celebrity—taking swings at batting practice would be considered a special event, and the celebrity getting beaned by a pitch would clearly qualify as an untoward event. Often one samples activities with the ultimate goal of gaining access to a certain type of event—the most logical way to proceed because events are embedded in a stream of activity.

By itself, *time* is not a very meaningful dimension. However, when it intersects with settings, persons, activities, or events, time can become a highly salient unit to sample. Productive participant observation often depends on knowing the rise and fall of activity cycles and the time frames in which key events are likely to occur. The researcher may also need to know the personal schedules of culture members in order to track their activities and use of settings. As we have already mentioned, exploratory methods such as diaries can be used to chart the temporal contours of a scene and thus lay the groundwork for a sampling strategy in which time plays a central role. In interview studies, time enters into decisions about the best order in which to interview respondents. In the interview itself, time can be sampled by asking the interviewee to recall critical events from her or his past.

Sampling Strategies

Most sampling decisions in qualitative inquiry are not based on procedures of random probability, in which every element of a population has an equal and independent chance of being selected. Therefore, the results from qualitative studies cannot legitimately be extrapolated to the population from which they were drawn. This is not normally considered to be a problem in interpretive social science for two reasons: (1) Qualitative studies do not produce data that can be subjected to statistical procedures that allow generalization to a population; and (2) qualitative studies focus on the social practices and meanings of people in a specific historical or cultural context. The second reason is possibly the more compelling one. Because social phenomena are studied for their unique qualities, the question of whether they are normally distributed in a population is not an issue.

Most qualitative studies are guided by *purposeful sampling*. The rationale for this nonprobability approach has been described by Schwandt (1997) as follows: "Sites or cases are chosen because there may be good reason to believe that 'what goes on there' is critical to understanding some process or concept, or to testing or elaborating some established theory" (p. 128). Thus field research is carried out according to criteria of selection that flow logically from the objectives of the project. Each strategy presented in this section is designed to address a different research need—although the outcome of using one sampling strategy can often resemble the outcome of using another, and occasionally more than one strategy is applied in a study.

Maximum variation sampling. A common strategy in qualitative research, maximum variation sampling taps into a wide range of qualities, attributes, situations, or incidents within the boundaries of the research problem. As the name of this strategy suggests, the researcher seeks to study the variation in a communication phenomenon.

In maximum variation sampling, the researcher simply seeks to find exemplars of a wide range of characteristics. The purpose of finding and studying these exemplars is to build a conceptual understanding of the phenomenon. It is not as important if the number of exemplars does not match their actual distribution in the population. In fact, we may have little evidence at all of how prevalent they are, especially if the behavior or discursive formation being studied is elusive or ambiguous in some way. Maximum variation sampling is most useful at addressing these kinds of questions: What different forms does this phenomenon take? Do communicative performances vary in terms of settings or time periods? What themes emerge when different participants discuss this text, genre, relationship, issue, or dilemma?

In her study of female readers of self-help literature, for example, Debra Grodin (1991) knew that the typical profile of this audience was middle-class women with at least some college education. However, because she wanted to learn about a range of circumstances and experiences of self-help reading, Grodin sought to diversify her sample. The 11 women who were interviewed (for at least five hours each) reveal the outcome of her efforts:

> Participants who were interviewed ranged from 22 to 55 years of age. Ten respondents were white; one was black. . . . Their occupations ranged from secretary to university administrator, from community organizer to computer systems analyst. Four of the women (all in their 20s or early 30s) had never married. Of this group, one was living with her male partner, and another was a lesbian. Three of the women were currently married, one was widowed, and the rest had been divorced and were now single. (p. 408)

With these 11 respondents, Grodin was able to relate the practice of reading to differences in age, race, occupation, marital status, and sexual orientation. She "maximized variation," although of course her small sample could not hope to match the demographic richness of all self-help readers. In any qualitative project, claims can be warranted only within the scope of the researcher's engagement with the scene.

More complex versions of this approach have been developed in other fields, notably in applied anthropology. Arcury and Quandt (1999) designed a "site-based" method for arriving at "a representative or stratified sample for qualitative research in large community-based studies" (p. 129). Their five-step procedure begins with specifying desired sample characteristics and generating a list of sites (churches, social clubs, clinics, community centers, etc.) "selected to maximize coverage in terms of characteristics important to the study" (p. 129). The next steps involve estimating the clientele at each site and contacting the respective gatekeepers who will help in the recruitment of site members. Sample building then develops in a dynamic fashion through the use of spreadsheets that display the changing patterns of subjects in the key "cells" of interest (see also Trost, 1986). Another approach (Carlson, Wang, Siegal, Falck, & Guo, 1994) combines targeted sampling (triangulating drug use data from informant interviews and other indicators), snowball sampling, and proportional sampling quotas to get access to community-wide networks of injection drug and cocaine users. Arguably, these approaches come closer to achieving a representative sample, although they are still purposeful (nonprobability) samples.

Snowball sampling. Used exclusively in interview studies, snowball sampling "yields a study sample through referrals made among people who share or know of others who possess some characteristics that are of research interest" (Biernacki & Waldorf, 1981, p. 141). Several situations commend the use of this method. Snowball sampling may be the only way to reach an elusive population (e.g., illegal drug users) or to engage people about a sensitive subject. It is also a method well-suited to studying social networks, subcultures, or dispersed groups of people who share certain practices or attributes.

The sample is started when the researcher locates someone who is willing to serve the dual role of interviewee and guide to potential new interviewees. This person recruits (or refers the researcher to) people from the community or his or her circle of acquaintances who fit the criteria for the study sample. Some of the interviewees in this second group may then be asked by the researcher to provide referrals to others who will make up a third group of interviewees. These chains of referral create an expanding pool of respondents—a "snowball" growing larger over time. Figure 4.4 charts two waves in the growth of interview subjects in Tom's study of the 1988 film *The Last Temptation of Christ*. Actually, his total sample contains several snowballs, each reflecting different networks of people. The snowball shown in the figure started with a public relations consultant who was willing to put Tom in touch with former Universal executives and others. This sample had the effect of opening up a new area of the study (the studio's response to the crisis).

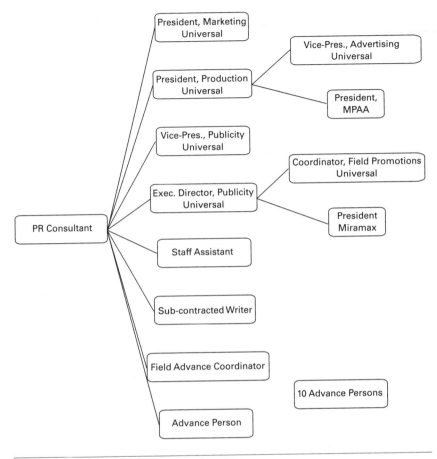

Figure 4.4   Snowball Sample

Contrary to popular belief, snowball samples do not always roll easily toward a satisfactory result. Locating members in a population of low social visibility, and training them as "research assistants" in the recruitment of other respondents, can be time-consuming and uncertain work. It is not uncommon for the snowball to hit a dead end ("freeze") or to "melt" prematurely. Researchers also need to monitor the sampling process in a disciplined manner. The speed with which some snowballs grow can create backlogs of untranscribed tapes or problems with the quality of the interviews (Biernacki & Waldorf, 1981).

The snowball method can be managed carefully in ways that increase a sample's diversity. For example, in her study of Filipino Americans' constructions of racialized sexuality, Yen Le Espiritu (2001) started by interviewing

Filipinas whom she knew and then asked these women to refer her to others they trusted in the San Diego Filipino community. She used this method to go beyond a narrow spectrum of social characteristics— "To capture the diversity within the Filipino American community, I sought and selected respondents of different backgrounds and with diverse viewpoints" (pp. 417-418). Her eventual sample of nearly a hundred Filipinos was evenly divided between first-generation immigrants and those who had been born or raised in the United States; their socioeconomic backgrounds ranged from "poor working-class immigrants who barely eked out a living [to] educated professionals who thrived in middle- and upper-class suburban neighbor-hoods" (p. 418). As this example shows, the use of multiple snowballs can result in a sample as variegated as one designed by the maximum-variation method.

Theoretical construct sampling. If a research project is driven by a theoretical interest, then persons, activities, events, or settings can be selected according to the criteria of key constructs. In other words, theoretical construct sampling builds a sample on the basis of the study's theoretical interests. Of course, the methods we have already examined also set forth criteria to guide selection. Grodin screened out people who didn't read self-help books of a particular kind; Espiritu only wanted to talk with Filipino Americans.

What is different about this sampling strategy is that it originates in the researcher's own theorizing. Before going into the field, the researcher forecasts what sort of communication phenomena will achieve the goal of a theory-informed sample. Cultural diversity among respondents, for example, may not be important unless "diversity" itself is central to the construct.

William Rawlins's (1983) study of "close friendships" is a good example of theoretical construct sampling. He argued that friendship functions as a dialectical tension between openness and discretion, and that friends man-age this bond through strategies of discourse. Interviewees were selected in part on the basis of this conceptualization of friendship:

1. Subjects could not be known personally by the investigator.

2. Subjects had to regard each other as "close friends." Siblings, spouses, coworkers, lovers, and engaged individuals were screened out.

3. Subjects had to have been close friends for at least two years.

4. Subjects had to engage in voluntary interaction outside of settings where they were required to be together, such as work or school. This requirement reflected theoretical conceptions of the voluntary character of friendship.

5. Subjects had to be 20 to 29 years of age.

6. Subjects had to appear interested and involved in close friendships.

7. Subjects had to be articulate enough to function well in in-depth interviews.

It is plain to see that these criteria satisfy the theoretical requirements of the study as well as some practical research considerations.

Theoretical construct sampling can also operate in more scene-sensitive ways. In Goldsmith and Fitch's (1997) study of contexts in which advice is given and requested, the participant observation component entailed that six members of a research team keep fieldnotes on instances of advice-giving that arose naturally in their daily lives. The sampling unit was thus the event of someone giving advice. The authors decided to "[rely] on participant observers' . . . understandings of what would and would not be instances of 'advice' rather than providing an a priori definition of this concept" (p. 473). In this way, team members were used both as data collectors and as participants in the articulation of what advice means in everyday life. The authors relaxed their a priori hold on the construct to allow concepts of advice to emerge from the scenes of performance.

Typical or extreme instance sampling. Often researchers study only certain ranges of the available persons, settings, activities, events, or time. The instances selected may be *typical* or *extreme* in some sense.

Typical-instance sampling seeks out the normative or the "expected" in an area of social life. This strategy makes the claim, which may be explicit or implicit, that the selected instances represent a type of behavior that normally occurs in a scene. For example, Lemish (1982) studied the social rules of television viewing in public places. She chose locations—bars, student lounges, retail settings, and so on—according to a plan that maximized variation of settings, program content, and viewership. But she selected times to observe

> according to the level of expected activity. For example, bars were studied in the evenings with special care to be present when sporting events were televised; students' lounges were studied during soap opera time; dining areas during lunch time; shopping areas during the weekends, etc. (p. 760)

In other words, the times to observe were chosen on the basis of when people usually view television. Lemish provided no evidence in support of the idea that these were in fact the "expected activity" at these settings, but most readers have enough experience with public TV viewing to be able to accept or reject her claim. It is vital to recognize that the goal of typical-instance sampling is "*not* to make generalized statements about the experiences of all participants. The sample is illustrative, not definitive" (Patton, 1990, p. 173; emphasis added).

Qualitative communication researchers also study the rare, the dangerous, the excessive, the extraordinary, and/or the controversial. In other words, one seeks instances that fall outside the ambit of the normative. These instances often represent a "critical test" of an idea or explanation. In some studies, the communication skills under study may be highly expert, elaborated, or quintessential versions of the skills that all of us perform (see Eisenberg, 1990; Weick & Roberts, 1993). (It may be the case that in the communication literature, we have far fewer studies of "best practices" than we do of dysfunctional or oppressive ones.) The atypical instance is often chosen because it is an extreme form—or even pathology—of everyday social conduct. Ironically, the study of atypical instances tells us quite a lot about the norms that usually hold "reality" steady in society, organizations, groups, or the popular imagination. Studies of fringe groups sometimes reveal how closely they resemble "normality" or how such groups have influenced our world (e.g., McGirr, 2001). Of course, unusual phenomena can be exotic subjects and attract our research interest on that basis.

As an example of this sampling strategy, Kerry Ferris (2001) studied the encounters that fans have with celebrities. Rather than try to represent the full range of these encounters, the author chose to focus on "active fans" whose devotion extends deeply into their lifestyles, social relationships, and consumption practices: "The fans who participated in this project were exceptional in many ways; they were conspicuous members of the television audience. Their activities, however exceptional, are versions of more common pursuits and as such are instructive in understanding fan-celebrity relations at many levels" (p. 29). Ferris assured readers that "by standard sociological measures of social anchorage, none of the respondents had the profile of a social isolate" (p. 29), but on the question of whether this "fact" made the sample more or less atypical of active fans, the author is silent.

Sample Size

We conclude with a question often raised by students but seldom answered—and sometimes even avoided: How big should the sample be? In quantitative studies, sample size is critically important to making decisions about statistical tests as well as calculating statistical power. But sample size is the terra incognita of qualitative sampling strategy. No tests or coefficients exist to tell the researcher when the sample is big enough. Sample sizes of N=1 are not unknown—for example, Oscar Lewis's 1961 study of one Mexican family in the 499-page *The Children of Sanchez*. And some qualitative studies have gathered data from hundreds of persons. Neither extreme is inherently better or worse than the other.

In qualitative research, sample size is usually considered to be a factor that can't be decided until much later in the course of a study. We sample persons, settings, activities, and so on until a critical threshold of interpretive competence has been reached—when, for example, we cease to be surprised by what we observe or we notice that our concepts and propositions are not disconfirmed as we continue to add new data. (These issues of deciding when to leave the field will be taken up in Chapter 7.) These may not be satisfying answers if we face a practical necessity for projecting sample size. Funding agencies or dissertation committees, for example, may want to know when closure will be brought to the study.

In the absence of formal rules, rules of thumb tend to guide practice. Projects that focus on a bounded system, such as a fan club or a hospice, can simply deal with the whole group rather than draw a sample. Projects that extend deeply into cultural history, or whose research interests range across a complex social entity, generally require a larger number of data sources. Projects that seek to describe a diverse population tend to collect larger samples. Projects that study hard-to-find participants are more justified in having smaller samples. Although there is no rule for a "correct" sample size, the researcher can develop an estimate by considering the scope of the project, the complexity of the research problem, the accessibility of potential participants, and the time and resources that are available for working in the field.

Conclusion

Qualitative design is guided by acts of questioning and dialogue. In the communication discipline, these questions are distinguished by their interest in how signs, symbols, and discourse are used for social and cultural purposes. Chapter 4 sketched some of the ways in which we prepare. We negotiate with gatekeepers or sponsors; we establish constructive, ethical relationships with subjects; we may use exploratory probes; and we conceive a strategy for sampling. These pre-fieldwork strategies move us into the field, ready to perform a role among a group of social actors. We are poised for a path of discovery. The next two chapters introduce the methods—participant observation; interviewing—that engage us with communicative performances and practices.

Exercises

1. When negotiating with gatekeepers—or with people you wish to interview or observe—it is often helpful to write a "script" about your study that contains talking points for interacting with these individuals. This is an exercise in putting the reasons for cooperation into a concise form that not only reads well but also "speaks well." Write one or two paragraphs that distill the essence of what you are studying and how the individual (the gatekeeper or potential participant) can help. This script should be audience centered and written in conversational style.

- Try it out with someone else and get feedback about how natural and persuasive it sounds.
- Think about how someone you would like to approach for the study might respond. What questions is the person likely to ask? What if she or he begins to show some hesitation? How might you respond?

2. This is an exercise—with three options—in the visualization of settings. The setting you choose should be a public place where people congregate but are not necessarily in familiar relationships. Examples are retail settings (e.g., shopping mall, movie theater); nonretail settings (e.g., airport terminal, church); and outdoor spaces (e.g., plaza, soccer field).

Option 1: Write a description of this setting *without visiting it first*. Focus on creating a visual representation—through words only—of the people, objects, decor, spatial dimensions, and so on. You can also include other sensory information, but exclude conversational stimulus.

Option 2: Visit the setting for a limited amount of time, then leave and create a map. As with Option 1, focus on creating a visual representation—albeit in graphical terms only.

Option 3: Visit the setting with a still or video camera. Spend a limited amount of time in the setting while capturing what you consider to be important visual elements. No arrangement of individual photos or editing of the video should be done. (Of course, this option is only for those settings that will tolerate the presence of a photographer or videographer.)

Regardless of the option you chose, ask yourself these questions after completing the visualization task:

- How did your perspective—physical and social—affect what you chose to visualize? How would you describe your perspective?
- What parts of the setting did you describe most densely, or attend to most closely— and why? What parts did you choose to ignore, or pay less attention to—and why?
- Were there aspects of the setting (including the participants) that you felt were inaccessible or somehow closed off to your efforts to visualize?
- Can you tell a story of the social action in this setting by referring to your visualization?

5

Observing, Learning, and Reporting

A Field of Adventure

The cultural pattern of the approached group is to the stranger not a shelter but a field of adventure.

— Schutz (1944, p. 506)

Since we can only enter into another person's world through communication, we depend upon ethnographic dialogue to create a world of shared intersubjectivity and to reach an understanding of the differences between two worlds.

— Tedlock (1991, p. 70)

In the first passage above, Alfred Schutz is writing about the situation of immigrants entering a new culture. As a German who had recently relocated to New York City, Schutz was deeply aware of the challenges facing "strangers." Immigrants, for example, needed to quickly learn alien ways of thinking and acting. Ideally, this hardship was partly offset by the benefit of gaining new resources. The unique qualities of cultural scenes, Schutz knew, could produce memorable "adventures" for those motivated to enter them. In the second passage, anthropologist Barbara Tedlock reminds us that strangers learn by *communicating*—by asking questions, expressing understandings, forming relationships, and so on. In this way, qualitative researchers—who are professional strangers—are saturated by symbolic interaction. These phenomena form the *object* of study, the *means of studying* that object, and the *means of expressing* hard-won knowledge to others. In this process, researchers must do more than simply acquire the linguistic rules of their new culture—they must also learn new forms of feeling. As Schutz puts it elsewhere in his article, "In order to command a language freely as a scheme of expression, one must have written love letters in it; one has to know how to pray and curse in it and how to say things with every shade appropriate to the addressee and to the situation" (p. 505). Behind every new language, then, are social usages that can be learned only *in vivo*—in the living of them.

Together, these quotes establish the scope of this chapter, which covers three principal methods of fieldwork: observation, participation, and field-note writing. Here, we build on knowledge developed in Chapters 3 and 4 about the selection of research sites, the negotiation of access, the protection of human subjects, the formulation of research questions, and the sampling of opportunities for observation. In turn, this chapter focuses on the concepts and skills that help qualitative researchers to develop, maintain, and—when necessary—change their roles throughout the course of a study. Leaning how to use these tools can help researchers to achieve inclusion, credibility, and rapport at their chosen sites. As we will discuss, however, this process is not easy: Fieldwork requires researchers to deliberately abandon their certainty and expertise. It obligates them to adopt a stance of curiosity and openness to the unexpected that may leave them feeling frustrated, humbled, and vulnerable. Additionally, fieldwork requires patient attention to the routine features of social action. This can occasionally be boring and exhausting. We present these caveats *not* to dissuade you from undertaking qualitative research but to reassure you that such reactions are normal, unavoidable, and temporary. They are also necessary: As the saying goes, the only way out is through.

Our approach here is best captured by Weick's (1985) notion of a "soft technology of systematic observation" (p. 568). *Soft technology* refers to the total sensory and conceptual equipment used by a human investigator. By "soft," Weick means that observing is carried out through loosely structured, adaptable rules. In this process, observers compare and contrast the unique features of a particular person, object, or event with other related phenomena. They begin by noting the apparent identity of an object—such as an organization member's job title and duties. This framing permits observers to notice how an object functions in "the first instance" of its natural contexts— such as a person's style of talking to superiors, peers, and subordinates.

By "systematic observation," Weick means "sustained, explicit, methodical observing and paraphrasing of social situations in relation to their naturally occurring contexts" (p. 569). Let's unpack this definition one term at a time. In essence, it means that observers do the following:

- They engage the phenomenon for a prolonged period of time (*sustained*).
- They account for how the observing is done (*explicit*).
- They observe in an alert, proactive manner that also allows them to improvise (*methodical*).
- They focus their attention in ways that combine their professional training with personal instinct (*observing*).
- They selectively focus on complex phenomena and summarize their observations (*paraphrasing*).
- They ground their observations in the relationships between places, actors, and activities (*social situations*).
- They try to distinguish the immediate and specific features of social action from their abstract and remote influences (*in relation to their naturally occurring contexts*).

Weick's definition helps us to understand what is required for "mindful" observation. This activity differs from the more casual, sporadic, and "mindless" looking that we often perform (e.g., in commuting to and from work). Additionally, this "way of seeing" (Wolcott, 1999) differs from deductive schemes that rely on predetermined rules for sampling, categorizing, and coding the features of events (see McCall, 1984). Here, the interpretive premise is that the observer's own emotional, cognitive, and cultural frameworks are *open* to change during the course of the study. In this way, the success of observing depends on what the observer *learns* through participation and the uses to which that knowledge is put.

Traditionally, *participant observation* is the term used to describe the professional craft of experiencing and recording events in social settings (Gans, 1999). Although the term is sometimes used as a synonym for the total gestalt of qualitative research, it more accurately refers to specific methodological practices: being in the presence of others on an ongoing basis and having some status for them as someone who is part of their lives. These components may or may not be joined in a particular project with other methods, such as interviewing and document analysis. Liberman (1999) explains the process this way:

The craft [of fieldwork] consists . . . of *hermeneutic practices* that permit the researcher to understand the indigenous world close to the way that it appears to the people themselves . . . to ascertain the interpretive schema that informants employ in knowing their world, to be able to communicate with them in ways they find immediately recognizable, to discern in detail the way one's subjects fit meanings together, and to appreciate the horizon of meaning they bring to bear on what they are still in the process of understanding. (p. 53)

By getting involved in the life of a scene, then, researchers seek to perform their roles in ways that make sense to its social actors. They notice what is going on and try to join in as responsible and contributing members. In this process, researchers draw on their experiences to imagine what the actors' motives might be for performing these actions. What researchers end up with are descriptions of these interactions. These descriptions include how the participants account for each other's presence (e.g., as legitimate or illegitimate) and evaluate each other's performances (e.g., as competent or incompetent).

A major part of participant observation is talk. This form of talk is distinguished from interviewing by the fact that it is embedded in the accomplishment of episodes other than interviews (these two methods can certainly overlap, however; informal interviews are often conducted during events in which participants experience "slack" or "down" time). Our focus here, then, is on ways that researchers can interact with others effectively and appropriately.

Effective Participant Observation

The validity of participant observation derives from researchers' *having been there*. Observing and participating usually work in concert, even if not always seamlessly. As a result, researchers' competence develops along two parallel paths: (1) They become increasingly skilled at performing in ways that are honored by group members, and (2) they create increasingly sharp, detailed, and theoretically relevant descriptions. This growth curve is not automatic, and the occasional false start, misfire, and reversal are often disguised in research reports (and outright failure usually sinks without a trace). However, there are certain attributes and skills that increase the chances of success in fieldwork.

Tolerance for Marginality

Participant observers occupy uniquely liminal positions, in which they are situated—both literally and existentially—*between* various social groups, psychological states, research goals, and so on. This experience is usually filled with contradictions, and working through them often shapes the agenda for a particular study (Eastland, 1993). Fieldworkers often take up position on the margins of a social setting, where they can have good vantage and some—but not overwhelming—involvement. In these cases, where they periodically arrive for brief sessions of fieldwork and then leave for home, class, or work, researchers usually operate as minor players in the scene. Sometimes, however, they adopt a more central role (e.g., in assuming formal leadership), although this inevitably affects the unfolding of events in ways that must be carefully documented. Even when researchers are prominent, the duration of their stay may be only temporary. Further, as researchers move between center and periphery, the nature of their commitment to a group's goals may change accordingly. It's harder, for example, to express reservations about a group's ideology when you're in its spotlight. Adams (1999) provides a rich example of the dilemmas associated with fieldwork positions in reflecting on her ethnography of Uzbekistani folk culture. In that study, she found herself occupying a "mascot" role in which, with mixed feelings, she traded control over her research agenda for the information and access provided by her official "hosts." These valuables, however, came at significant cost. Her hosts used her status as a female American academic fluent in Uzbek—and frequently made her "perform" in front of audiences—to promote their own standing and agendas.

Researchers feel another sense of marginality internally. Specifically, their personal identities may undergo profound slippage and refashioning over the course of a project. This occurs as researchers accept—and are transformed by—the obligations of group membership. This may happen when researchers try to honor a professional commitment to fairness while group members insist on total commitment to their ideology (e.g., Robbins, Anthony, & Curtis, 1973). It can also happen when researchers perceive that they have more in common with a group than they first thought. As we will discuss below, the degree to which these become problems depends on the type of role adopted by the researcher. In almost every qualitative project, researchers try to negotiate between one world that is considered "home" and another (i.e., "the field") that is adopted and temporary. Although the boundaries drawn between these sites are often arbitrary and unstable (Taylor, 1997), it is the field that usually draws more selfishly and directly on researchers' psychic reserves. As a place where they regularly confront professional challenges, the field tends to prey on researchers' thoughts even when they are physically "away" from it. An ability to tolerate marginal status, and treat it as an opportunity for learning how groups manage their membership, thus seems essential for effectiveness in the field.

Requisite Variety

Imported from cybernetics, the concept of *requisite variety* holds that biological and social systems should possess elements that are *at least* as diverse as the elements in their environments. According to Weick (1985):

> The specific link between requisite variety and observing occurs through a twist on epistemology. Rather than assume that seeing is believing, we assume that believing is seeing. This inversion suggests that beliefs are the medium through which the world is examined. Therefore we want to know the size, connectedness, and external orientation of an observer's belief system. An observer who knows many theories, metaphors, images, and beliefs and who has had varied experiences has more elements than an individual who has less content. (p. 581)

The final sentence here is key: It implies that researchers must be sufficiently complex in their resources and abilities to successfully engage the complexity of their chosen field. We hinted at this in Chapter 3, in discussing the personal origins of research ideas. Suppose, for example, that a researcher wants to study how the leaders of a particular religion create "advisories" specifying "appropriate" media content for members. The leaders and members probably embody a variety of beliefs and experiences that are activated in this process. However, if researchers identify only—or even strongly—with just one group's perspective, they will miss the full range and nuance of these beliefs.

Researchers who possess different beliefs and broad knowledge, then, will pick up more from complex environments (and there are few simple ones) than those with lower levels of knowledge and simpler belief systems. Further, as Weick (1985) suggests, the more *competing* beliefs a person is able to entertain, the more open that person will be to the mystery of real social action. "Requisite variety" is another way to express what some call "tolerance for ambiguity." Or, as the saying goes, genius is the ability to hold two (or more) contradictory ideas at the same time.

Embodiment

A visual bias pervades both the practice of fieldwork and methodological writings about it. The very terms we use—such as *observation* and *watching* (Schatzman & Strauss, 1973)—imply that what is done in the field primarily involves looking, gazing, glancing, and fixating. It has even been said that participant observers should try to mimic the behavior of a camera, as though the goal was to emulate visual technologies. Recently, this discourse has been critiqued for its connection to the gendered fantasy of a disembodied, omniscient—and inherently voyeuristic—masculine subject (feminist philosopher Donna Haraway, 1991, calls this "the God trick"). In addition, the Western cultural practice of visually objectifying others (for example, as "exotic") has contributed to a repugnant history of colonial oppression (Rusted, 1995).

Although these are serious indictments, the primary *methodological* problem of visualism is that it represses a whole range of other sensory modes that can be useful for fieldwork. What is significant here is that researchers are *bodies in fields* (Conquergood, 1991). Their sensual, visceral, and emotional experiences are only arbitrarily detached from the allegedly more valuable contents of rational cognition. Although this does not mean that every stomach gurgle is significant, it does mean that researchers are themselves the products of cultural institutions that have historically worked to discipline the experience of embodiment (e.g., so that impulses are "appropriately" and "productively" expressed). These "hygienic" forces, which encourage us to ignore or moralize a variety of "dirty," "noisy," and "smelly" phenomena, are dubious regimes. They are composed of codes that often embody racism, sexism, and class biases. Researchers are thus encouraged to monitor how these biases operate in their perception and interpretation of events. Noted sociologist Patricia Adler, for example, requires her fieldwork students to complete a series of writing assignments in which they systematically manipulate the relationship between sensory modes. In a "sight without sound" exercise, they record all the features and potential inferences yielded by a scene they can see but not hear. A "sound without sight" exercise reverses these conditions. The learning experience can be quite powerful, and it speaks volumes about implicit discrimination against the knowledge claims generated by differently abled researchers (one is hard-pressed to find studies conducted by hearing-impaired or visually impaired fieldworkers).

In this way, significant differences in the experience of embodiment may be *exactly* what researchers need to appreciate about a scene. For example, Barbara Myerhoff (1978) was so moved by the frailty of the older adults she was studying at a Venice Beach community center that she conducted a personal experiment to achieve greater empathy. She donned thick glasses to distort her vision, earplugs to impair her hearing, weights to bend her posture, and bulky orthopedic shoes to slow her gait. As a result, her writings were informed by a vivid and ethical awareness of how frailty affected interaction with older adults. In a very different example, James Gibson (1994, pp. 170-192) provides a vivid account of how being trained in combat pistol shooting—a highly rigorous process that involves remaking the body as an efficient killing machine—transforms Americans into ideal (but paranoid) warriors in post-Vietnam War culture.

The visual bias thus tends to convince us that the act of gazing embodies the organizing principle by which the environment is set up. If we are not careful, we may mistakenly believe that it is our habits of seeing that determine how events are meaningful for their participants. Two practical implications follow. The obvious one is that, as Stoller (1989) points out, we should open up our sensing to include the tastes, smells, tempers, touches, colors, light, shapes, and textures of the cultures we study. Effective observers should become connoisseurs of the particular sensory combinations that are valued by group members (e.g., the youthful participants in all-night "raves"). The second implication is that fieldworkers' bodies are important research instruments and should—as much as possible—be treated well (e.g., through adequate rest and a healthy diet) so that their sensitivity is not compromised.

Spontaneous Decision Making

Fieldworkers should develop a talent not only for noticing things but also for noticing them *as evidence* (e.g., as an example of a particular pattern). Deciding that something is evidence involves a complex, rapid—and often instinctive—process. Those instincts are shaped by continuous reflection, however, and the goal of this process is to organize the emerging evidence toward the best possible explanation—even if it ends up weakening researchers' initial assumptions. The first line of analysis occurs as observers experience and sift events in real time. One challenge of observing is that the relevant and irrelevant events are all equally ephemeral; distinguishing between them can only occur as they are disappearing. Researchers never get a chance to notice any particular event again. To be effective, observers must be able to decide what is and what is not important according to criteria that are themselves only gradually being understood. Although this sounds paradoxical, we will look more closely at how this works later in this chapter.

Being an Ethical Person

Like medical professionals, fieldworkers should at least aspire to "do no harm." But this is easier than it sounds. Fieldwork typically involves ongoing struggles between researchers and participants over whose interests will take precedence at a particular moment. This process is not necessarily primary, continuous, or destructive. Conflict can also be subtle, occasional, and even highly productive for the relationships involved. But whatever form it takes, ethics are the norms and values employed by participants to resolve these struggles. Moments of potential conflict can be extraordinarily revealing: One piece of ethnographic folklore involves a fieldworker whose covert study of a malevolent occult group was exposed. Hauled before the group's leader, the fieldworker braced for an angry denunciation (and worse). He was surprised instead to find amused tolerance and an offer of even greater inclusion: "What a perfectly *evil* thing to do!" Whether the story is true may be less important than the lesson it offers.

In this process, fieldworkers must acknowledge that they have been socialized to accept a number of "lies" (or myths) about their professional ethics (Fine, 1993). These myths depict researchers practicing universal informed consent, consistent empathy, honest disclosure, accurate reporting, and unobtrusive observation. Behind these myths, however, are the harsh realities of improvised consent, mutual dislike, strategic deception, creative reconstruction, and intentional shaping of events. Shulman (1994), for example, recounts a number of strategies gained from his study of private detectives that can assist fieldworkers in verifying "dirty" (i.e., dubious) data provided by deceptive informants (including going through their trash). The danger, then, lies not in aspiring to ethical ideals: it is in assuming that their attainment is easy or predetermined.

To help fieldworkers anticipate ethical challenges, Punch (1986) has listed a number of temptations they typically face. These include (1) inappropriately claiming to have witnessed a scene; (2) depicting either observation of or participation in an event, when the opposite was the case; (3) claiming direct knowledge of events learned through indirect means; (4) depicting contrived events as spontaneous; and (5) misrepresenting strategy as authenticity. To these, Shulman (1994) adds ethically "gray" practices such as

> using purposely ambiguous entrée letters, glancing at or acquiring documents lying on desks that subjects would not have wanted seen or sometimes covertly acquiring them from other subjects, overhearing privileged conversations during observations because researcher status was not announced, and pretexting informants "about what others said." (p. 249)

Punch (1986) acknowledges that, as a matter of self-protection, all fieldworkers will inevitably practice *some* deception (although the types and amounts are unique). What may be more important, he concludes, is for fieldworkers to continuously reflect on their motivations for doing so and to carefully monitor the consequences. When it seems likely that a course of action will injure participants or spoil the field for future researchers, fieldworkers should *always* take the higher road. In this enterprise, we serve at the pleasure of a group's membership, and our ends do not justify our means (Angrosino & Mays de Peréz, 2000). When we fail, the consequences for our personal careers, our employing departments and institutions, our profession's reputation, and our participants' trust can be both deep and lasting (Allen, 1997).

Generally, fieldworkers can avoid (or at least minimize) a number of these dilemmas simply by acting in an open, warm, and unpretentious manner. Being an ethical person also means giving people the benefit of the doubt, getting along by going along, and not being overly contentious (Fine, 1993). These are all time-honored strategies for engendering goodwill, and they may in turn lead to researchers being included more in member activities and embedded in relationships characterized (mostly) by honesty. As Guba puts it, "Good guys [sic] get better data" (quoted in Weick, 1985, p. 585).

Difference Matters

Increasingly, the impact of researchers' cultural identities (note the plural) on fieldwork has become a topic of inquiry (see Burgess, 1984, pp. 88-92; De Andrade, 2000; Warren, 1988). Here, *identities* refer to the partial, multiple, and simultaneous conditions that distinguish fieldworkers as types of human actors and knowers. These conditions include race and ethnicity, gender, class, age, sexual orientation, and so on. Much of this inquiry has been spurred by contemporary social theories that view identity not as a stable "individual" essence but as a process and product of interaction. In this view, identity is symbolically constructed as participants draw on available evidence to make attributions about themselves and each other. Whether or not they are explicitly exchanged through talk, these attributions help participants to resolve the ambiguity of particular situations and to stabilize their relationships. It is useful, then, to view fieldwork as a process in which researchers and participants put the various components of their identities into play as tokens of status and bids for attention and inclusion. In this process, the meanings of these components are up for grabs; interactions will variously serve to affirm and subvert preferred identities. This process, further, is not a level playing field. It is shot through with power relations (e.g., racism and sexism) in which groups have historically defined and performed their identities to secure their social, political, and economic advantage. A central contribution here has been made by feminist standpoint theories that emphasize how "knowledge is socially located and arises in social positions that are structured by power" (Hallstein, 1999, p. 35). Although standpoint theories are particularly useful for examining the complex positioning of female researchers, they implicate *all* researchers in the need to account for how their knowledge claims are shaped by historical and cultural conditions (e.g., masculine privilege). In this process, the fantasy of a unitary, "individual" subject is discarded in order to foreground the affiliations that tug at researchers. In its place arises an image of partial, contingent, and conflicted—but no less useful—knowledge.

These conditions create a number of implications for fieldwork. The primary implication is that researchers should assess the ambiguous gifts of their physical characteristics (e.g., skin color, hair style), social attributes (e.g., education levels), and "cultural capital" (i.e., insider knowledge of group meanings and practices). As these elements uniquely manifest themselves in fieldworkers, they establish axes of difference and similarity with corresponding configurations in. the group members being studied. Fieldworkers and participants subsequently read each other as texts. As these texts interact and transform each other, they create challenges and opportunities. The fact that one is a certain age, gender, or ethnicity, for example, frequently determines the possibility of even *entering* a scene. Although power is not a simple phenomenon, it is undeniably true that whiteness, wealth, and masculinity have historically operated to protect elite social groups from research scrutiny—particularly when conducted by members of other groups (Hertz & Imber, 1995). And sadly, elites have no monopoly on exclusivity or bigotry.

Potentially then, a researcher's identities create the basis for affiliating with others who share those attributes. This potential often encourages researchers to consider studying groups and topics that are familiar: women should study women's issues, African American researchers should study scenes populated by African Americans, and so on. Such pairings can smooth entry, promote empathy, and enhance the quality of data. Researchers usually benefit from having advance, detailed knowledge about at least some elements of the scene.

But affiliation is no guarantee of success. Here, we should remember that there is often as much diversity *within* as *between* groups. Although some identity components are more salient for membership than others (and codes can vary in the granularity of their distinctions), the similarity between group members on any one component frequently leads to consideration of how that component is configured with others. In her study of older, working class Chicanas, for example, Facio (1993) matched her informants on ethnicity and gender, but their class and age differences created a number of dilemmas affecting her access and inclusion. Even after they have been accepted as a group member, then, fieldworkers should anticipate how they will respond to the following questions, when (not if) they are posed (usually implicitly) by others: "*What kind of member* are you?" and "Are you *my kind* of member?" Researchers should treat these moments as opportunities to map the internal complexity that is often glossed by the rhetoric of group identity.

In addition, what may seem at first glance to be a special endowment of a class of people may instead be a set of styles, codes, social skills, and understandings that others *could* learn if they had the opportunity. It is an ethnographic truism, for example, that outsiders are able to achieve unique (and perhaps superior) understanding of a culture's taken-for-granted elements. As we have noted, *some* form of difference between fieldworkers is inevitable, and there are many different ways to be an outsider. A fascination with borders and conflicting loyalties (e.g., among cultural members who leave their home, later to return as researchers) is often the motivation for a study.

One would be badly mistaken then to think that identity issues are any less charged in fieldwork settings than they are elsewhere. The truth is just the opposite. However, we have no simple or blanket prescriptions. Researchers must case themselves just as they case the scenes of a potential study. They should carefully consider the possible consequences of their culturally ascribed identities for the ethics and politics of conducting research.

Adapting Roles

Researchers often enter the field seeking to become the proverbial fly on the wall: seeing and hearing without being seen or heard. They attempt to "blend in" by practicing civil inattention in public places or by being deliberately passive in the midst of a provocative, busy scene. But even a fly on a wall has a role, and so does the novice who—inevitably—bumps into someone or otherwise gets noticed while trying to blend in.

By this, we mean that every role has a *generic* character: a range of actions, obligations, and rights that go with being in a certain relation to others in a social system. A role also has a *situated* character involving adjustments of the self to specific people in specific situations. Participant observers often start by taking on a role already available in the setting or by modifying one for their own purposes (Olesen & Whittaker, 1967). Sometimes a new role can be created solely for them to inhabit, with the assent and help of the scene's actors. In either case, though, role adapting should not be construed as operating under false pretenses. Rather, it is *through the role*—living it and working through its particular problems—that certain kinds of observing become possible. Two broad ways of considering research roles are presented in this section: roles based on degree of participation and roles based on social function.

Roles Based on Degree of Participation

Conceptions of fieldwork roles often come to us as typologies. The best known of these are based on the degree to which the researcher participates in the scene. For example, Schwartz and Schwartz (1955) distinguish between the "passive" participant observer, who tries to operate as anonymously and unobtrusively as a scene permits, and the "active" participant observer, who tries to mix with participants as much as possible. These two types involve different assumptions about the researcher's presence. Passive observers believe that high levels of participation provoke "unnatural reactions" and are thus to be avoided or minimized. Active observers accept that some reactivity is inevitable and that passivity is as artificial and generative a performance style as any other. They believe that by decreasing the status and activity differences between themselves and participants, they can gain a better understanding of the scene. A more refined—and classic—typology has been developed by Gold (1958), who proposes four "master roles": *complete participant, participant-as-observer, observer-as-participant, and complete observer.*

Complete Participant. For complete participants, pretense and, arguably, deception create the dominant motif: Participants are fully functioning members of the scene, but they are not known by others to be acting as researchers. They are known only through a role that has no revealed purpose other than the one that is immediately understood in the scene itself. One example of how this is performed and justified involves a classic study by Thomas W. Benson (1981), who—at the invitation of a former student—decided to join a film crew for a few days to shoot some political commercials. When he arrived in "Sunbelt City," the principal scene of his research narrative, Benson began meeting the people with whom he would be working. Soon enough, he was asked to explain himself:

> The drink ordered, Clark turns to me with a smile. "And who are you in real life?" This is exactly the right question, and defines the situation. But I am not prepared for this directness, and the anonymity that Gary [Benson's friend] offered me so vaguely seems out of place, not really an option, since Gary is not here, and my host has asked a friendly and direct question. The situation settles my doubts about how to represent myself. "I'm a professor of Speech Communication at Penn State University." (p. 358)

In some cases, revealing one's research identity does not seem like a good option, for reasons such as impracticality or group expectations of privacy. In Benson's case, complete participant status was more ambivalent. He joined the film crew to get close to the action of an unfolding campaign. His research interest was only hinted at to the crew, and the initial anonymity he worked out in advance with his sponsor, Gary, was fleeting and inconclusive. Benson found that he needed to improvise his identity at the site. But as this excerpt indicates, revealing who he was "in real life" did not elicit much more than further small talk. Soon after, he allowed the press of events to shunt the issue aside.

A complete participant role allows researchers to use the self to understand behavior in a natural setting. In that sense, it holds real promise for getting inside the subjectivity required for meaningful communicative action. Certainly there is no better path to knowing the feelings, predicaments, and contradictions of others than to be with them in an authentic relationship. And for scenes characterized by guarded access, or by belief systems that do not easily admit critical elements, acting in the complete participation mode may be the only viable way to get in.

Once inside, the researcher will often become involved in situations not usually available to outsiders. Private information is revealed because only a private relationship is assumed. It is important to note, however, that the complete participant's presence *does* influence what goes on in the scene. The other social actors respond to the researcher as a fellow actor rather than as someone with a research agenda.

For several reasons, qualitative researchers do not embrace the role of complete participant as often as its benefits might suggest. First, in this role researchers' freedom of movement and their ability to tailor specific relations with other members are severely curtailed. The scope of their own movements is limited to what they can experience in the member role, which necessarily spans only a part of the total activity of the group. Further, a covert role does not permit the use of strategic and directive techniques such as interviewing or the solicitation of "member checks" to test working hypotheses.

Second, compartmentalizing the researcher identity is a difficult and precarious achievement. Worries about having one's cover blown often attend this mode of fieldwork. To cope with frustration and distraction, complete participants frequently need to retreat and regroup (and here, we are reminded of espionage lore about the double agent who needed to rise at 5:00 every morning for the two hours of meditation required to keep his increasingly elaborate lies straight). Even with such attentiveness, it may not be possible for researchers to maintain psychological control of their situation. This, then, is another reason that complete participation does not yield perfect, total, or nonreactive observation.

Third, researchers deprived of the opportunity for extensive and collaborative reflection may lose their analytic detachment. This phenomenon, known as "going native," covers several trajectories in which researchers over-identify with a group's ideology, participate unreflectively in its rituals, advocate its interests uncritically, and fail to document what is happening to them. In some cases, researchers fail to complete their study or even return from the field. But few go this far. In concluding his study of political advertising, for example, Benson (1981) expressed the more common experience of returning home to realize that he had been partly transformed, that he had acquired new eyes to see with.

Finally, the complete participant's pretense raises urgent questions about the ethics of role concealment. Although there is ongoing debate in the human sciences about the potential appropriateness of deceptive and covert research (Punch, 1986), it is typically seen as a violation of the faith that people place in each other's motives in everyday situations. It may signal a breakdown of the code of human subject protections that was described in Chapter 4. Benson, for example, did admit who he was, but in terms of occupation only; he did not mention the research thrust of his participation. One could rationalize, after reading his entire account, that his deception was justified because the political campaign scene is one in which candor is neither expected nor especially valorized. In this regard, Douglas (1976) argues that successful inquiry may call for covert tactics—for example, when group members regularly practice evasion, "fronting," and outright lying. Sometimes these rationalizations are conducted post hoc: Pierce (1995) felt less guilty about conducting covert observation in her role as a paralegal after being sexually harassed by the male lawyers employed at her firm. In Benson's case, it is not easy to see what he gained by hiding his research goals, except that he avoided raising alarms about his trustworthiness in the competitive context of a political race—a fear that was only anticipated, not tested. In this way, some researchers—whether through laziness or timidity—justify their covertness on the possibility that members *might* reject them. In this vein, it's worth considering that the veil of pseudonyms Benson employed for the people and places of Sunbelt City would probably yield rather easily to motivated inquiry.

If one believes that ethics should be situational, then one may view some performances of complete participation as more justified than others. However, many practitioners believe that *all* covert study is exploitative, and thus that it is never justifiable (Anderson, 1987; Dingwall, 1980). Suffice it to say that all researchers considering the role of complete participant need to thoroughly think through their motives and the potential consequences. We also recommend consulting trusted colleagues for a second opinion.

Participant-as-Observer. In the role of participant-as-observer, researchers enter a field setting with an openly acknowledged investigative purpose. As a result, they are able to study a scene from the vantage point of one or more positions within its membership. As the name of this role implies, observing flows from the perspective of participating. Here, researchers complete the pre-fieldwork activities outlined in Chapter 4 and check out the available positions to determine which ones provide the best view of the culture. Whereas complete participant is less a role than a full immersion, participant-as-observer is a role that is, in a very real sense, rewarded with involvement. Everyone who interacts with this type of researcher knows in some way that the transaction of interests underlies participation. The relationship with group members that makes this possible can be an enduring one, lasting for weeks or months.

Unlike the complete participant, the participant-as-observer does not operate as a member who is fully integrated into the routines and subjective realities of the group. Participation is part of a "deal" negotiated with gatekeepers (or sponsors) and usually involves a special status—usually a part-time, temporary, voluntary, and/or "play" role. As a result, the responsibilities that go with *real* participation in the group are not complete, constant, or binding on the participant-as-observer. As Gold (1958) puts it, "The role carries with it numerous opportunities for compartmentalizing mistakes and dilemmas which typically bedevil the complete participant" (p. 221).

For researchers adopting this role, participating in a scene proceeds on the basis of being lightly supervised—or even protected to some degree—by other responsive and accountable participants. Under normal conditions, these participants might not suffer fools gladly. But for the participant-as-observer, normal rules do not apply. In this situation, researchers are free to act like naïve visitors or inexperienced "boob[s]" (Weick, 1985, p. 585). Such an appearance (which may not have to be faked) can be useful when the researcher wants to be taught things by members, especially at the start of a study. However, as Weick points out, this persona has a brief window of legitimacy: too much naïveté displayed for too long may convince members not to trust researchers with important information or tasks. Researchers should instead seek to gradually become useful (in some way) as time goes on, so as to be included in increasingly complex or interesting areas of social life. During this process, researchers can enjoy cooling-out periods when they need to, taking time to write fieldnotes or attend to their real-life responsibilities.

As an example of this type of role performance, Trujillo and Dionisopoulos (1987) wanted to examine the drama of routine police work. They worked from the premise that popular notions of "police work" obscure the communication actually performed in the daily grind of "life on the street." By participating in "ride-alongs" during work shifts, they were able to witness and describe how police officers used language during key events—"cruising the streets, responding to dispatched calls, joking at the station house, and drinking at 7-11. Informal interviews were conducted with the officers, but we mostly watched, listened, and made written notes of their activity" (p. 200). Their interpretations included the cops' use of labeling ("scrotes," "dirtbags," and so on) to distance themselves from perceived negative elements of the public and their ritual of "talking tough" to verify that all officers were sufficiently skilled and resolved to protect their colleagues from danger. Trujillo and Dionisopoulos's protocol involved adopting vantage points (the front seats of patrol cars) and attitudes (receptivity) that enabled them to hear the stories of the cop world. In their report, they do not offer many details about the status of their participation, or the times of day they rode along, or how their involvement was greeted and interpreted by the officers. Yet one senses that they must have made innumerable decisions about such matters: with whom and when they should ride along, what to do in case of emergencies, and so on.

For this role, then, achieving an insider's insight may require more complicated procedures than is needed in the role of complete participant. The researcher's involvement in the scene demands ongoing adjustments in terms of participation. Group members, for example, must be brought up to date and reassured about any changes in the participant-as-observer's evolving role. Researchers' contacts with their informants enable them to gain the trust of key sectors of a group and to sample among its various subcultures. None of this may be very trying for the typical group member, but for researchers it makes building and maintaining trust a key issue over the entire course of a project.

To summarize, a greater degree of informed reciprocity distinguishes the participant-as-observer role from the role of complete participant. In this process, researchers and group members negotiate a space to cohabit and a relational ethic. In disciplines practicing qualitative research, this role has gained increased legitimacy during the past three decades (Angrosino & Mays de Peréz, 2000; Tedlock, 1991). This shift, which is part of the general decline of traditional myths about objectivity, has involved a pragmatic acceptance of the benefits generated by researchers' immersion and inclusion in the scenes they study. Here, participation is viewed as facilitating—not subverting—valid data.

Observer-as-Participant. In the observer-as-participant role, participation derives from a central position of observation. In other words, the agenda of observation is primary, but this does not rule out the possibility that researchers will casually and nondirectively interact with participants. Although this role is traditionally favored as an acceptable compromise between the competing goals of detachment and familiarity (Angrosino & Mays de Peréz, 2000), Gold's (1958) lack of enthusiasm is evident: "Because the observer-as-participant's contact with an informant is so brief, and perhaps superficial, he [or she] is more likely than the other two to misunderstand the informant, and to be misunderstood by him [or her]" (p. 221). Undoubtedly this is true, but only up to a point. The observer-as-participant may value *verstehen,* but mainly as a way to enter the scene, to foster goodwill for the duration of a study, or to validate propositions at the very end. Researchers adopting this role negotiate with gatekeepers in a manner different from that used by participant-as-observers. They can often describe in advance what kind of information is needed and the amount of time and other resources needed to obtain it. Gatekeepers can grant access to these researchers with confidence that group life will not be overly disrupted and that the study will not stray into unforeseen areas. For the observer-as-participant there is much less uncertainty about what counts as data than there is for researchers adopting other roles.

Interviewing is a common method for doing an observer-as-participant study. Researchers can administer a schedule of questions with clear goals fairly easily, and participants can usually resolve superficial misunderstandings—about the intent of a particular question, for example—on the spot. Researchers in this role, then, can efficiently sample a relatively large number of incidents, time periods, persons, or groups.

Because this role involves fleeting contact with real participants, it is tempting to say that the observer-as-participant role falls short of the criteria for interpretive social science. Clearly it does not engage the researcher in an intimate, prolonged study of a culture. However, the role does allow conclusions about communication to emerge over time. And the analysis that results from its use does integrate regularities of behavior or discourse with theoretical problems concerning the attribution of meaning. Nevertheless, researchers who observe with minimal participation run the constant risk of reading too much of their own conceptions into what they see. Such ethnocentrism, or blindness to the perspective of the other, is the opposite of good qualitative work—or to good scientific work of any kind, for that matter.

Complete Observer. "You can observe a lot just by watching," Yogi Berra is supposed to have said. This kernel of wisdom from the former baseball great is highly relevant for the last role of this typology, the complete observer.

Complete observers take the role of observer-as-participant to what might be its logical conclusion: they observe without being "present" to the participants. Not only do participants not recognize complete observers as researchers, they do not recognize them as part of the scene *at all*. This is the least palatable style for many qualitative researchers, because the absence of an analyst's "presence" runs counter to the value of "accountable human as research instrument." It is also the rarest role in the literature, for logistical as well as ontological reasons.

The complete observer role can be usefully compared with its opposite, the complete participant role. Both are hidden roles; no one in the scene reacts to a research project. However, there are striking differences in the experience of performing the complete observer and the complete participant roles. The complete participant enacts a research agenda through a self that is naïvely accepted by others in social relationships. The complete observer, in contrast, is in a nearly a solipsistic role, because the researcher's absence of meaningful contact with human participants denies the participants the opportunity to influence the researcher's interpretations. So, whereas the danger of "going native" supposedly lurks within the complete participant's project, the threat of "going ethnocentric" relentlessly stalks the complete observer.

Naturally, complete observers operate best in free-access settings. Crowd scenes offer excellent opportunities for them to operate without the risks of revealing or having to account for their purposes (e.g., Lang & Lang, 1953). Generally, the more remote from the action one can get, the more complete an observer one can be. The technologies of video, photography, audio, and computers, among others, enable remote sensing and recording to be done with a low probability of detection. Knuf (1989-1990), for example, used a camcorder to tape the ritual boundary maintenance activities performed by participants in a sorority rush; operating covertly from across the street, he had no face-to-face contact with the group members.

The ethical situation of the complete observer differs somewhat from that of the complete participant. The complete participant acts in ways that seem sensible and correct within the expectations of the group being studied. This closeness usually brings the investigator to an understanding of, and respect for, the rationality of the members' moral order. In learning what they value, the complete participant can potentially avoid doing things that might harm members' interests. Complete observers, however, have no identity that is explicitly recognized by the social actors under study. As a result, they may have little reason to reflect on how they come to interpret the actions they observe or on the potential consequences of circulating those interpretations. The potential problems are obvious.

Roles Based on Social Function

Gold's durable typology has influenced the thinking of many qualitative researchers, mostly because of its simplicity. However, the adequacy of this typology—and others similar to it—has been called into question. Typically, these critiques seek to more finely distinguish the types and degrees of participation. Adler and Adler (1987), for example, believe that the covert/overt distinction is not useful as it is drawn. It splits the researcher into a participant role that interacts with members and an observer role that gathers data. Adler and Adler urge us to instead think of researcher involvement in terms of differing degrees of *committed membership*. Essentially, they recast two of Gold's roles—complete participant and participant-as-observer—into three new roles: *complete member*, *active member*, and *peripheral member*. These new roles are distinguished by how important their associated performances are for events. They each entail different obligations, liabilities, and chances for experiencing social life:

> Peripheral-member-researchers participate as insiders in the activities of the group they are studying, but they refrain from engaging in the most central activities. . . . [Active-member-] researchers participate in the core activities in much the same way as members, yet they hold back from committing themselves to the goals and values of members. . . . Complete-member-researchers study their topics from the perspective of full members by either selecting groups to study in which they have prior membership or by converting to membership in these groups. (Adler & Adler, 1987, p. 35)

It is important to note that these role types relate to each other through an overarching concept of member positioning. It is easier to see how one kind of member positioning can evolve into another across the span of a project. In rejecting the duality of participation and observation, Adler and Adler argue that going native is not a serious possibility as long as researchers continue to treat the experience of being with participants as an opportunity for theorizing.

This scheme, then, moves the idea of roles to another plane, that of the *social functions* they perform. Thinking of research roles simply in terms of degree of participation in the abstract does not take us far in applying them to specific situations. Making this criticism more directly, Snow, Benford, and Anderson (1986) explain:

> The utility of these classical typological distinctions is limited . . . because they sketch only the broad contours of one or more ideal-typical roles, thereby leaving each role relatively empty, nondescript, and uncodified. . . . They provide prospective field researchers with little direction on how to proceed once they enter a field setting. (p. 378)

Functional roles are designed to address specific problems. In many ways, it is both more meaningful and more practical to conceive of the researcher's role as a particular form of experiencing the self, the other, and the world. For example, Anderson (1987, pp. 315-317) describes several generic strategies for learning member activities: becoming an apprentice, playing, taking a course, and using past experience or present involvement. The first three of Anderson's strategies involve the researcher in learning situations, with differences in the depth of material to be learned and the formality of the endeavor. The fourth strategy—using past experience or present involvement—requires researchers to take a more analytic perspective on something they have already learned, in order to reflect critically on the structure of that knowledge.

Functional roles can also be defined more concretely to fit a specific field site. Snow and colleagues (1986) identify four roles derived from the social movements and marginal groups they studied over several years. These roles include *controlled skeptic, ardent activist, buddy-researcher*, and *credentialed expert*. Two of these can be briefly discussed here. Acting as if he or she is a convert to a religious group, the *controlled skeptic* solicits members' points of view in a naïve, curious yet skeptical manner. An *ardent activist* role—which entails embracing the means, ends, and ideology of a social movement—can be adopted to experience the full potency of the group's beliefs and to explore the backstage regions in which decisions are made (although the associated risk of going native here is high). By treating research roles as having real functions, then, one can better anticipate the kinds of information that specific sorts of experience produce.

Tactical Observing

By now, you should be well primed to begin observing. Although this can potentially feel like sprinting from a standing start, a more accurate analogy might be that it's like running one leg of a relay race. The groundwork of casing the scene and designing an initial role puts researchers in motion toward social action. In starting to observe, they simply use this momentum to move *into* the scene via the opening afforded by a specific role. A particular role strategy will carry with it an associated mode of observing. This condition will in turn shape the amount and types of opportunities for observation at a particular scene.

As you'll recall from our discussion in Chapter 3, initial observing involves understanding where and when the field is and distinguishing its sites and scenes. Typically, researchers begin with an intuitive preference for a particular site but an underdeveloped sense of which scenes it involves and how the scenes occur. Social actors, on the other hand, have a sure grasp of their own scenes (and their associated performances), but it is the field (i.e., the ways in which their scenes and sites are of theoretical interest) that is usually opaque to them. Over time, researchers and participants help each other to learn about these matters, although the flow is relatively one-way (from the participants to the researchers). As Ceglowski (2000) discovered in her study of a Head Start classroom, despite professional calls for increased collaboration, participants do not necessarily desire or benefit from researchers' continuous discussion of their evolving interpretations.

The process of connecting and distinguishing phenomena can be vexing, but it is central to the process of participant observation. The first task of observing is simply for researchers to notice as many persons, objects, and events in the field as possible within their scope of potential action. Observation should be performed in a nonjudgmental fashion, without trying to force closure or prematurely fit what is observed into a theory of how or why it occurs. At this early stage of the work, the researcher should just live the novice experience:

> Novices in research worry too soon about developing salient categories for final analysis, about developing brilliant concepts, and about establishing "patterns of interaction"; in short, they want quickly to prove to themselves and others that they are social scientists. Not so our model researcher; he [sic] is quite content, for a considerable time, to experience the ambience of the scene. He has great patience, as well as a tolerance for ambiguity and for his own immediate ignorance. Far from acting like a scientist and telling himself he is one, he is genuinely busy being a learner—indeed, a novice—and perhaps a participant. (Schatzman & Strauss, 1973, p. 54)

Although it is good to frequently remind yourself of a project's grander, scientific purpose, the above advice underlines the essential, disciplined character of simply being watchful. When researchers start to assert themes of communicative action after only a session or two of observing, they are usually overreaching.

Observers spend most of those first days or weeks accomplishing two objectives: learning to develop a perspective on the field from their initial position and making careful observations of the full range of behaviors and objects in the field. With respect to the first objective, researchers should take direction from members graciously, learning where it is appropriate to sit, stand, and move, and when and how it is appropriate to talk, listen, and act. This, of course, is consonant with the "ethical person" stance discussed earlier. By accepting help from others to reduce the strangeness of their role, researchers quickly develop a perspective for inspecting social action. True, the perspective is usually one that has been tailored—at least in part—for a person who does not yet know all the ropes. Yet it is still a perspective that expresses members' priorities for inhabiting the scene—and is thus deeply meaningful. Researchers are often rewarded for their initial patience in learning how to faithfully perform a negotiated role with the opportunity to perform more varied, natural, and advanced roles.

Researchers achieve the second objective—making careful observations of the full range of behaviors and objects—by working to adopt member perspectives on what is sensed and how it is sensed. The sampling strategies reviewed in Chapter 4 enable the observer to identify the arenas of action in which important observations can occur. The consistent question for researchers at this stage is, What is going on here? Because the scene is new, and probably puzzling in many ways, this question tends to emerge on its own. For this question to be most useful, however, researchers need to ask it in various ways so as to produce descriptive observations (Spradley, 1980). The corollaries discussed below help to orient that activity in the beginning and middle phases of a study.

Who Are the Actors?

Researchers should begin by learning the nominal status of various actors in the scene (e.g., father, mother, son, or daughter; manager, assistant manager, team leader, or line worker). Certain responsibilities and obligations of a formal, legal, or "natural" kind go with those statuses. For example, one might ask: What are these workers' jobs, and how do these job descriptions structure the way they perform that work? Other questions might include: How do workers display "leadership"? What are the understandings about each other's roles that help family members to relate to each other? These are status positions to which people are recruited, hired, assigned, or born.

Mapping status relationships in this way can significantly unpack the structure of a scene. Such knowledge generates initial answers to our guiding questions: What is this person here to do? How are these people *supposed* to function together in this group or organization? Knowing the relative status of social actors tells a great deal about how they (are supposed to) associate with each other. Even if researchers learn these distinctions from a briefing given by a gatekeeper prior to entry, they should strive to evaluate them independently. Organizational reality, for example, rarely matches the official organization chart (and increasingly fewer organizations use charts anyway). Nominal status, then, predicts neither how a role is actually performed nor how its performers are perceived by other actors. Closer observation will reveal that certain norms, expectations, rules, and taboos come into play in certain situations. Observers should focus on the tension between the statuses that actors hold, and how those actors actually perform.

How Is the Scene Set Up?

The choice and organization of artifacts in a scene signifies what is important to members, as well as the images they intend to project to external groups or persons. Examining decor, furnishings, and objects of play or work is useful for understanding social action. There may be times when certain props are needed for certain acts to occur at all. Researchers may learn that certain objects characterize or divide up territory in meaningful ways. Potentially, researchers can also use unobtrusive measures of "physical traces" of a scene's human activity—the ways that people use objects and interact in their physical environments (Webb et al., 1966).

For example, here is Goodall's (1991) description of the office environment of a computer software company he studied:

> One significant aspect of the B-BCSC culture is nonverbally clear: There is a strong tradition of individualizing one's office area or workspace. So clear is this tradition that certain motifs become apparent. The motifs include some ordinary and expected symbols: symbols of family and families with pets, symbols of academic and professional achievement, symbols of recognition and reward. . . . A second motif concerns symbols that are inner pathways to a mindscape of petty fears, rages, senses of humor, and bellicose warnings that coalesce into a collage of general and specific corporate psyches and that oddly enough correspond to the individual positive symbols of home, and learning, and achievement. For example, "Shit Happens" is an emblem, a sort of badge really, that is laced through the building next to degrees and family snapshots, a common source of strategically ambiguous identification with an anonymous but ever-present enemy. (pp. 91-92)

There is more to Goodall's reading of this scene, including the architecture and landscaping of the site and the cultural implications of the cars and trucks parked in the company lot. Goodall also notes key differences in "persons and things" that occur when the company moves to a new building. Such interpretations develop after repeated periods of observing. At the outset, however, a careful descriptive assessment of the material culture can help the researcher to understand how actors understand their scene and the parts they play in it.

How Do Initial Interactions Occur?

Observing persons interact for the first time can reveal much about how a group socializes its newcomers, polices its boundaries, and generally enforces its preferred styles of communication. In public settings such as bars there are many opportunities to observe these critical moments. Here, analysis can include *elements* such as people, the physical environment, key objects, and temporal dimensions (e.g., the sequencing of disclosures) and *processes* such as greeting, asking, establishing an identity, and judging (Ellis, 1980).

In the first phase of a study, researchers will meet many people for the first time. These mini-dramas form key opportunities to establish the researcher role. If carefully noted, researchers can use these experiences (the sweaty handshake, the cutting remark, and so on) as texts for interpretation. Such situations also represent opportunities to generate background information about participants and for developing additional relationships that may prove valuable. For example, while interviewing Mexican mestizos in their homes, Murphy (1999a) found that resident family members would chime in and argue with the interviewees about their responses. These "interruptions" helped him to understand both his interviewees' responses and the social context of media use in these homes.

How Do Actors Claim Attention?

As Murphy's (1999a) study demonstrated, veteran members of a group are often experts on each other's habits and mannerisms. As such, they normally have little need to explicitly reflect on central elements of their stock of knowledge. Instead, their exchanges are often highly coded and nuanced. They may also be notable because they *appear* so routine.

Veterans also internalize a scheme of how lines of responsibility should operate within the group. This means that information that does not apparently concern the group as a whole might circulate only within certain subgroups (and such practices are the foundation of organizational politics). There may also be tacit rules for when a piece of information carries such significance that it needs to be conveyed to the entire group.

These are only a few of the conditions that invite researchers to penetrate the surface of normality. One of the daunting tasks of entering a scene is understanding when and how its actors claim each other's attention. Why do some items incite talk and action while others do not? What are the routes by which messages typically travel? How are these messages recognized? How do actors know what needs to be the object of joint attention and what does not? How is attention alternately focused and expanded? Once evoked, how are such objects of attention resolved in the making or deferring of decisions?

At first, observers should pay close attention to those things that are somewhat confusing to them but clear to others. These may include terminologies, procedures, or nonverbal behaviors. Researchers should ask members, when appropriate, to brief them on the meaning of an item, knowing that even partial, ambiguous, and idiosyncratic explanations can be expanded over time. Less intrusively, researchers can track the flow of information, along with the routine and unexpected responses it generates.

Where and When Do Actors Interact?

In trying to understand social action, observers should note who associates with whom and under what conditions. The ways in which actors meaningfully and purposefully *congregate*—that is, assemble, conduct their business, and then disperse—should be a recurring theme. Observers should note the temporal and spatial patterns of this type of interaction—the dancelike moves and rhythms by which participants co-orient their expressive bodies (Leeds-Hurwitz, 1989; Meyer, Traudt, & Anderson, 1980).

It may take some time for researchers to generalize about another type of interaction—participants' strategic coordination of joint action for specific purposes (e.g., flirting, job interviews, bail hearings). It is very important to note where and when certain kinds of interactions occur among certain individuals. We can safely assume that most interactions do not happen randomly. The location and timing of episodes provide key evidence for understanding their communicative functions. In addition, the observable aspects of interaction tell us a great deal about the relationships among the participants. Two important concepts for identifying relational behavior in public behavior are "markers" and "tie signs" (Petronio & Bourhis, 1987). These are especially useful when we try to define or describe particular social action in open-access places (e.g., among teenagers hanging out in shopping malls). *Markers* are behaviors that position and orient bodies in ways that signify a particular type of relationship. For example, some of the publicly tolerated markers of a familial relationship include handholding, interlocked arms, waist-holding, hugging, some forms of kissing, and immediate and exclusive orientation. *Tie signs* are symbols or artifacts that indicate a type of relationship. Among the tie signs that usually signify "family" are engagement and wedding rings, children (particularly when they continuously solicit the attention of the adults accompanying them), parental gear (like strollers, diaper bags, or toys), and familial forms of verbal address (such as "Hi, son!"). Of course, these concepts assume that the members of relationships are performing in ways that permit observers to make valid inferences (as opposed to, for example, the deception practiced by coworkers who are attempting to conceal their romance). One needs to understand, then, the potentially subtle ways that members of a group use signs to disclose, conceal, and transform their relational status. Using informants to report on and interpret scenes that we do not directly witness is highly tempting here ("You should have *seen* what she was wearing!"). Nonetheless, we should remember that such reports *always* reflect the partial and biased perspective of our informants.

Which Events Are Significant?

Related to the issue of how to define people's relationships is the issue of how to define the communicative events that characterize a scene. Different scenes can accommodate—often simultaneously—a variety of events (e.g., coffee shops that are used by "regulars" as a place to drink and chat and by traveling sales representatives as an impromptu office). Recognizing significant events involves deciding that they *count as* an example of a higher order concept. Over time, observers will build up a supply of recorded motives, accounts, feelings, and actions that can be used to define these events and their properties. Among these properties are openings and closings for interaction, references to membership, sequences for taking turns, and conversational devices for keeping a topic on track (Speier, 1973). Observation involves noticing the form and content of communication for the purposes of reconstructing them as data.

We learn to recognize events by performing in them, by acting in ways that make sense to other participants. We also learn to recognize how events express the various realities of a scene, such as interpersonal conflicts, political power differences, cultural beliefs, and so on. In reporting and analyzing our observations, we learn to clearly *narrate* processes about which we were previously unaware or inarticulate.

Writing Fieldnotes

Fieldwork produces detailed knowledge about scenes of social life. This knowledge is based on observing social action and reflecting about what it was like to be a participant. These acts create the foundation on which research claims are built. But this creation is not automatic. To achieve the status of evidence, participant observation must first be documented in texts known as *fieldnotes*. We use the term *text* to emphasize how qualitative research is inherently concerned with describing and interpreting the symbolic qualities of social action. We discuss this initial phase of data construction below, noting that the process of formally analyzing qualitative data is treated in Chapter 7.

Scratch Notes and Headnotes

Scratch notes (Sanjek, 1990b, pp. 95-99)—also called observational notes (Anderson, 1987) and condensed accounts (Spradley, 1980)—are written by researchers within the immediate field situation, or soon after leaving it. Often recorded hastily and in improvised privacy (e.g., fieldworkers frequently "need" to visit the bathroom), they involve brief notations about actions, statements, dialogue, objects, or impressions that will be expanded later in fieldnotes. The practices of scratch note taking range widely. Some researchers carry small notepads on which they write in shorthand. The use of acronyms, mnemonic devices, abbreviations, and key words is also common. Local customs permitting, this note taking can be done openly. Some fieldworkers may even be able to use portable recording devices that allow them to quietly narrate their impressions without participants being able to hear (Patton, 1990, pp. 248-249). Still another option is to wait until a stretch of fieldwork is over and write scratch notes at the first available moment (e.g., in parked cars).

When scratch note taking is not possible, headnotes may suffice. *Headnotes* are focused memories of specific events, as well as impressions and evaluations of the unfolding project. They are produced through acts of will. Some researchers have impressive memories and do not need to engage in much scratch note taking—they go straight from headnotes to fieldnotes. Others rely on a combination of headnotes and scratch notes, but even scratch notes do little more than anchor a large mass of material residing in memory. For both forms of notes, it is crucial that researchers retrace experiences as quickly as possible in order to stabilize their features. One should not expect to "download" headnotes all at once. Recording them should begin as soon after a field session as possible, but it may take days for all of the residual headnotes to surface. Some may even return allegorically in dreams. Despite our best efforts, there may be furtive images, impressions of dialogue, and other enduring notions about a project that cannot be salvaged.

Fieldnotes

The importance of fieldnotes for studies using participant observation cannot be overstated. Without them, that work fades from memory and is invalidated as a resource for research claims. What are fieldnotes? They are "gnomic, shorthand reconstructions of events, observations, and conversations that took place in the field" (Van Maanen, 1988, p. 123); "this body of description, acquired and recorded in chronological sequence" (Sanjek, 1990b, p. 99); "the product of observation and participation at the research site and considered reflection in the office. . . . They are written so the analyst can reenter the scene of the action and of the research at a later date" (Anderson, 1987, p. 341). In a revealing study, Jean E. Jackson (1990) interviewed anthropologists about their experiences with fieldnotes. Surprisingly, these researchers showed little consensus—and strong ambivalence—about fieldnote writing.

> Most interviewees include in their definition the notion of a running log written at the end of each day. Some speak of fieldnotes as representing the process of the transformation of observed interaction to written, public communication: "raw" data, ideas that are marinating, and fairly done-to-a-turn diagrams and genealogical charts in appendixes to a thesis or book. Some see their notes as scientific and rigorous because they are a record, one that helps prevent bias and provides data other researchers can use for other ends. Others *contrast* fieldnotes with data, speaking of fieldnotes as a record of one's reactions, a cryptic list of items to concentrate on, a preliminary stab at analysis, and so forth. (pp. 6-7)

Despite this faint agreement that fieldnotes are supposed to describe (and at least initially interpret) the field experience, it is less clear what the contents and functions of these notes should include. The mystique that shrouds fieldwork, the absence of any formal tradition or mechanism for sharing fieldnotes, and the intensely personal feelings that researchers attach to their notes (J. E. Jackson, 1990) all tend to obscure our understanding of this vital activity. Recently, however, some authors have attempted to outline specific procedures for producing and organizing fieldnotes (e.g., Anderson, 1987; Ellen, 1984; Emerson, Fretz, & Shaw, 1995; Sanjek, 1990a; Spradley, 1980). Generally, these authors agree that fieldnotes make up the permanent record signifying—and verifying—that field events did in fact occur in particular ways. They objectify events that were situated, ambiguous, and fleeting. Researchers can write notes at any time and in as many versions as they please, but they cannot rewind actual events and play them again. Inevitably, then, the fieldnote *becomes* the event.

Moreover, raw notes are generally not available to anyone but the researcher because of the privacy promised to participants. As a result, these notes will seldom be critiqued. This privileged status places a burden on the researcher to write fieldnotes with great care.

Several principles inform this craft. As mentioned before, fieldnotes should be written immediately after each fieldwork session. The more time that elapses after observing, the more likely that deteriorating memory will dilute the fidelity and detail of the account. Even scratch notes lose their significance if they are not quickly used (and few experiences are more frustrating than trying to decipher these notes after their shelf life expires). Therefore, researchers should regularly schedule some time immediately after field visits to write their fieldnotes. Although some researchers prefer an interim period for rest and "fermentation," this delay should not be much longer than 24 hours. Researchers should also consider—unless they are engaged in team projects, and perhaps even then—*not* discussing the site visit with anyone until they have written their fieldnotes. This will protect them against compromising unique, hard-won understandings. Regarding length, a standard rule of thumb is 10 double-spaced pages of writing for every hour of participant-observation. Although this may sound like a lot at first, writers who accept the burden of description will quickly leap this psychological hurdle, will write until they feel they are done, and will sometimes even enjoy the process!

Fieldnotes should create a *chronological* record of one's involvement in the scene. Important details about all phases of a project, from the initially awkward negotiations with gatekeepers to teary-eyed farewells, should be recorded (Pacanowsky, 1988a). How participants responded to researchers' arrival on the scene and to their evolving roles are all opportunities for reflection about how groups assimilate a foreign body and tolerate curiosity about their operations. Adhering to a chronology ensures that the record will reflect unfolding changes in the participants' individual and group lives, and the twists and turns of researchers' decision making.

Entering a scene in the first days and weeks, researchers may have already developed a number of conceptual interests. In some cases, this may include inventories of specific behaviors, activities, events, and forms of language use. Nonetheless, researchers should resist the urge to apply these checklists to what they observe. Instead, the first order of business is to inductively develop a working grasp of key elements of the scene: the temporal organization of activities, the location and function of artifacts, the identities of key actors, the significance of their activities, the implicit codes of cultural knowledge, and so on. In this process, the researcher learns how to act as if he or she were a member.

Because it happens only once in the life of a study, it is imperative that this often-overwhelming early experience be recorded in researchers' field-notes. In replicating their initial learning curve, researchers should concretely and completely describe *all* the significant details of the scene. They should continuously ask themselves, What is going on here? This question leads quickly to others: Who are these people? What are their roles and their relationships with each other? What is this activity they are performing? How, when, and where is it performed? What artifacts are usually involved? Who uses these artifacts and how is their use determined? The list of questions that can be asked is endless, but in consistently using such questions to spur fieldnote writing, researchers will quickly determine which of them are relevant for the scene in question.

Extensive (if not exhaustive) description of appearances and activities is called for in fieldnote writing. In the beginning, researchers should not try to write beyond their experience of being a novice, an apprentice, or a tourist in a new terrain. "Why?" interpretations can wait. Instead, writers should use the reliable levers of "Who?" "When?" "Where?" and—especially—"How?" to unpack the scene. Researchers should avoid describing events in clichéd or glossy terms; rather, they should break events down into their relevant components. Initially, nothing is too trivial or too obvious to be noticed and documented. Special attention should be given to the sensuous textures of social action: urgent voices, pungent odors, garish colors, bitter flavors, delicate touches, and so on. Writers should try to depict actors' remarks and conversations as close to verbatim as possible. They should not enclose depicted speech in quotation marks unless they are certain they have faithfully captured its grammatical form. Instead, they should use paraphrase to depict the semantic (what was meant) and pragmatic (how an utterance functioned) elements of dialogue. In characterizing these nuances of appearance and action, fieldnote writers should carefully choose their adjectives and adverbs. In this way, language serves fieldnote writers in the same way that tones serve musical composers and color palettes serve painters. Because it forces them to specify the agents of performed actions, additionally, writers should use the active voice as much as possible. At the same time, writers shouldn't hesitate to experiment with different modes of language that can expand our understanding of the scene. Qualitative researchers are inherently interested in making the familiar strange (and the strange familiar). These goals are advanced by creative and meticulous description.

It may help to think of this kind of writing as an effort to convey to someone who is (also) ignorant of the culture being studied how to understand a situation and decode its surface features. Accordingly, initial fieldnotes should be set down in clear, uncomplicated language. A writer's understanding of the scene's communicative action is developed gradually and patiently, from the details up. This disciplined practice of description—for its own sake, day after day—will enhance researchers' capacities for discriminating observation and faithful recall. Researchers will be rewarded with a dense, fact-filled archive that they can later use to create explanations that are informed by theory.

The writing should also capture researchers' personal reactions to learning how and where to fit in. Although these can be recorded in another medium (such as in journals and diaries, as discussed below), appropriate inclusion of the researcher's voice—especially in the form of insights, conjectures, misunderstandings, or baffled responses—can help to document what it was like to try and understand a particular event at a particular moment. Generally, however, fieldnotes are written from the perspective of one who is socially engaged with *others* (e.g., through material practices that can be documented). In this sense, while we prefer the use of the first person voice in fieldnotes because it is relatively direct and accountable, this does not mean that fieldnotes are only (or even primarily) about the writer's experience. This is as much a matter of focus and emphasis as of perspective.

The excerpt below is a good example of how these issues are worked out in practice. It is taken from a fieldnote written by a member of an ethnographic team studying "America Live" in a northern California city. This large site contained a number of integrated, uniquely themed venues for drinking, eating, and entertainment. The excerpt depicts the winding down of a four-hour, Friday-night fieldwork session conducted in mid-project. This session has taken an emotional toll on the author. Her experiences throughout the site have resembled a Dante-esque tour of descending rings in which entertainers and customers collaborate in the performance of "sex and humiliation."

We decided to go into Gators for a few minutes before calling it a night. It was getting close to 12:30 and we were getting tired! (Aren't you getting tired of reading these fieldnotes?) As we entered, it seemed somehow brighter than when we initially made our way through the bar. It was fairly easy to walk through the crowd and as we approached the dance floor, it was obvious why. The majority of Gator's patrons were on the dance floor! Rona said she'd never seen it so crowded. The crowd was definitely different than that we'd encountered in Li'l Ditty's or JA Flats. Most patrons were young (early 20's to early 30's), the crowd was much more ethnically diverse, and was dominated by male attendance.

The music was quite loud, creating that primal pulse. The room was dark, the faces of the patrons illuminated by ultraviolet, red and blue roving lights.

Several "disco" balls adorned the ceiling, evidence of the club's heritage. The dancing crowd caused the floor of the bar to move slightly with the beat. Several couples danced together, although the "withness" I noticed in the JA Flats dancers was not present. It seemed, for the most part, that the couples were "new" to one another, although many seemed to like each other a great deal.

Many women danced together and men danced (for the most part when not with women) alone. On one elevated area perched a man and two women. The man (young, goatee, brown hair, sleeveless hooded flannel sweatshirt and undershirt) danced with his back to his female companion, leading me to think that they were not together. On another elevated area three women danced, again, with their backs to one another (young, cropped t-shirts and sweaters and jeans, long blond and brown hair, which they twirled and fluffed while they danced). On display, these women also slowly rotated in a circle atop their pedestal. . . . They reminded me of a pie case at a coffee shop.

Not long after our arrival, four video screens were lowered in the bar. A scene from the movie *Tombstone* thundered over the speaker system. I haven't seen the movie, but it was a violent scene in which Kurt Russell was "after" someone. He was knocked to the ground and suffered a bloody lip. The bar crowd cheered. Kurt came after the guy, pointing his gun at him. The excitement in the crowd was palpable. The event came to a crescendo when Kurt shouts "You tell 'em I'm coming and Hell's comin' with me." The crowd erupted into a cheer. Rona says that they play these scenes periodically throughout the evening. Are they all violent? What are they meant to do? (While they provide an obvious break in the action, they didn't seem to move people off of the dance floor and to the bar, at least from my vantage point.) How do they intersect with the music and interaction in the club? I'll have to ask Joe when I interview him. This scene was quickly followed by *Nine-Inch Nails* and *The Offspring* videos.

The dancing during the playing of these videos seems intensified somehow. I also notice that it has spilled onto the space below the dance floor. After the videos the screens are retracted. We watched for a few minutes, and then decided to depart. As we exited, a sea of seekers (of attention, affection, ego-boosting) floated past me. The muscular guy in the black vest, the three young men who looked us up and down, the bald guy in the suit who barely acknowledges an enthusiastic hello from a woman, the woman who said "I feel really good about myself" to which her companion (who has his back to her) replies, "You should" without turning around, and a man and woman locked in a passionate embrace, the Bud trough, now empty.

We emerged from the fog of Gators and breathed deeply. We made our way to the escalator, relieved. However, we descended into an even darker (and somehow more sinister) environment. Broken beer bottles chewed at our feet as we came off the escalator. All of the screens in the sports bar were tuned into the main event: the boxing ring dancing. The ring was packed. Patrons seemed a bit older, again ethnically diverse and dominated by men. Donna's metaphor of deer in the headlights felt appropriate here. We hurried through the area, our senses like exposed nerves. I had the "ethnographer's headache" that Nick talked about. We quickly exited and were drawn out into the fresh air and light rain. I was tired, overwhelmed, and a bit disgusted. I have to admit that I did not experience much of the "pleasure" that AL may have to offer. Is it because I did not go there with the anticipation of connecting with someone or because I didn't revel in the inhibition and debauchery made available to me? I don't know.

There is much to recommend about this excerpt. First, we can note the stamina displayed by the author. At the conclusion of fieldwork (and fieldnote writing) sessions, researchers often become fatigued and are inclined to let up on the work of noticing (and recalling) events. Instead, the author has persisted in recording specific details about participants and their actions ("young, cropped t-shirts and sweaters and jeans, long blond and brown hair, which they twirled and fluffed while they danced") right up to the moment where the research team disperses. These details help us to understand the variety of cultural identities ("the muscular guy in the black vest, the three young men who looked us up and down") and practices ("of attention, affection, ego-boosting") being performed at the scene, and that contribute to its zeitgeist of muted despair and aggression ("broken beer bottles chewed at our feet").

Second, note the clarity, economy, and vividness of the author's style. Writing fieldnotes is an opportunity to develop one's literary powers. Beyond basic attention to grammar and spelling, writers should also experiment with ways of depicting experience that readers will find rich and compelling. Here, even in the absence of lengthy verbal conversations, the author has captured organic textures of light, sound, and movement that characterize the contexts and activities of this scene. She uses analogies ("they reminded me of a pie case at a coffee shop"), imagery ("the fog of Gators"), and metaphors ("deer in the headlights") to stimulate readers' appreciation for the symbolic work being performed by both the participants and researchers who were present.

Finally, note the author's sensitivity to the evolving process of ethnographic understanding. In other words, she is conscious of both what she knows and what she does not (yet) know. While her descriptions are rich, they are also appropriately tentative. They do not exceed the available evidence by making dubious attributions about causes and motives. Instead, the author explicitly asks questions (and rehearses possible answers) about ambiguous events ("Are [these video clips] all violent? What are they meant to do?"). She devises plans to learn more ("I'll have to ask Joe when I interview him"). This type of mental work—which is easily forgotten if not recorded—is invaluable in helping researchers to begin linking data to concepts and theories. In exploring the bar patrons' reaction to the film clip, for example, the author has created data that may eventually be consolidated with other evidence to explore a larger question: How do participants in nonverbal interaction draw on the resources of ambient media texts to structure their activities? (Readers who are curious about how the study turned out are directed to the team's coauthored publication, COMST 298, 1997.)

Over time, as a result of growing familiarity, fewer events take fieldworkers by surprise. Their fieldnotes document recurring patterns of social action, and how participants understand them. Gradually, writers turn their attention to situations that resist explanation and to strategies for resolving (or at least respecting) their mysteries. Fieldnotes become an ongoing conversation between enduring questions and evolving explanations. Managing this conversation becomes the familiar—and often pleasurable—work of fieldnote writing. The level of fine-grained, painstaking detail that went into initial fieldnotes is no longer required. Instead, researchers become more *selective* and *intensive* in their writing. Having relied to this point on "What" and "How" questions, writers can now turn to "Why?" Their fieldnotes begin to explore in greater depth and complexity the potential sources of influence on social action. If researchers move into a different role, or enter a new scene, their note taking and writing may again widen in descriptive scope. But before long, the process repeats itself: patterns of action and themes of significance become familiar to the writer, and the focus of writing adjusts to engage the most interesting topics.

Ultimately, fieldnotes should be carefully organized and protected. It is common for researchers to make multiple hard and electronic copies of their fieldnotes. One motive for this practice involves creating redundancy that ensures against the loss of any single copy. We should note, however, that this also increases the risk that loose copies will find their way into unauthorized hands and compromise valued relationships. Security for all copies should thus be a continuous priority. Copies are typically organized in folders or binders reflecting chronological and thematic schema. Fieldnote sets can quickly grow quite large and unwieldy. As a result, the researcher should create an index for notes that lists them according to date, site, and subject or theme. As a matter of formatting, creating wide left- and right-hand margins on the pages of fieldnotes will allow researchers who so desire to make annotations and coding marks. The next steps in the use of fieldnotes—for coding, analysis, and construction of interpretations—will be discussed in Chapter 7.

Journals and Diaries

Fieldworkers often need companions in the field even when there are no colleagues around in whom to confide. Journals and diaries fill this need. As Sanjek (1990b) states, "Chronologically constructed journals provide a key to the information in fieldnotes and records; diaries record the ethnographer's personal reactions, frustrations, and assessments of life and work in the field" (p. 108). Despite this apparently clear distinction, there is significant diversity within these forms of writing and blurring between them (Janesick, 1999). Keeping a journal can be a highly practical project: it can help to manage a rising tide of data by recording field site visits, names of persons met and persons interviewed, and so on. It can also provide a means of reflecting about procedural problems and their solutions. Potentially, it can be adapted to enhance collaboration: researchers and participants can keep a journal *together*, creating an informal dialogue (and highly revealing member check) concerning researcher practices. Diaries are typically an outlet for turbulent emotions, doubts, private prejudices, and other meditations. Being alone is not the only reason to keep a diary, however. It is also a place to vent feelings about interpersonal relationships in the field, where a tight lid usually has to be kept on impulsive reactions.

In practicing these supplemental forms of writing, fieldworkers can create deeply rewarding sanctuaries for cultivating a unique "voice." Writing potentially becomes less of an alien, obligatory, and mechanical task, and more of an opportunity for the practice of focused, graceful, and compelling expression. In this way, diaries and journals have historically been the hidden subtexts of qualitative research—alternate narratives that were suppressed for the sake of professionalism. Their occasional publication has been a celebrated event—for example, with Bronislaw Malinowski's *A Diary in the Strict Sense of the Term* (1967) and Claude Lévi-Strauss's *Tristes Tropiques* (1955/1974)—in which the fallible, complex person behind the ethnographic mask is revealed. As we will explore in Chapter 9, however, the boundaries between personal "journal," and professional "publication" voices are increasingly becoming less clear and stable.

Conclusion

We have covered a good deal of ground in this chapter and hope it has helped to resolve the ambiguity and anxiety that can potentially surround fieldwork. Participant observation and fieldnote writing are as much art as science, but this does not mean that their performance is arbitrary—far from it. They are disciplined activities that draw on uniquely human capacities for noticing, wondering, and understanding. Performed in a faithful, systematic fashion, they yield data that realize the goal of qualitative research: deeper understanding of the significance of social action for those who perform it. Researchers who accept the obligations of this performance can be reassured that—however chaotic things become in the field—they are upholding their end of the bargain.

The next chapter explores the process of discursively eliciting others' experiences. Interviewing offers qualitative researchers an alternate mode of participation, in which they strategically use talk to encourage people to reveal significant thoughts and feelings. As will be seen, interviews can serve either as a self-sufficient research method or as a complement to participant observation.

Exercises

1. The following are three scenarios (adapted from Braithwaite, Dollar, Fitch, & Geist, 1996; used with permission) depicting fieldworkers confronted with ethical dilemmas. For each, decide if you believe the researchers are acting ethically. If not, what specific norms do they appear to be violating? What are the sources of the problems they face? What, if anything, could be changed to ensure ethical performance of the study?

- Keiko is interested in the social construction of gender identities at cultural rituals. She is particularly interested in the relationships between forms of talk, speaker gender, and ritual context (e.g., holiday festivals, sporting events, and political rallies). She is not recording demographic information about speakers except for their gender, but believes that audio recordings of their naturally occurring talk are crucial to her study. She doesn't want to affect her data by openly taping participants' conversations. She chooses instead to covertly tape these interactions.

- Susan is conducting a study of adolescent girls' sexuality for her dissertation. Part of her data is drawn from participant observation of the girls' domestic, school, and leisure activities. In the process of obtaining informed consent, Susan met with the parents of each girl and explained that she would be protecting their privacy by not revealing any information to the parents about the girls' activities. Over the course of the study, Susan has become fond of Laura, the 14-year-old daughter in a devoutly religious family. Laura has eagerly disclosed her own sexual experiences to Susan, including her covert relationship with the 18-year-old son in a neighboring family. Susan is keenly aware that Laura's parents would object to this relationship and worries that her study is encouraging Laura to sexually experiment.

- Jonas is studying the discursive strategies through which members of marginalized subcultures alternately display and conceal their stigmatized identities. He is drawing a number of examples from interviews he has conducted with African American men he knows who are involved in drug sales. However, because Jonas believes that depicting their involvement contributes to racial prejudice against this group, he has decided to misrepresent the racial identity of these participants in publications as diverse. He rationalizes this decision further by arguing that he is more concerned with the abstract practices of managing identity than specific issues of race, gender, or class.

2. If you are currently engaged in fieldwork (and are not already doing so), keep a journal for a week. This activity can be performed either instead of or in addition to writing fieldnotes. Make at least three entries in this journal. They can be as short or as long as you wish. In making entries, choose from the following list of options:

- Make a list of questions that you would like to have answered before your fieldwork is finished.
- Compose a portrait of a key actor in the scene who is particularly interesting or significant. Focus on the person's appearance, style, and habits.
- Imagine that you are a member of the scene who is observing you conduct your fieldwork. Write a narrative of that person's likely impressions of you.
- Write a letter to someone who is involved in your fieldwork either directly (e.g., a member of the scene) or indirectly (e.g., an advisor). Focus on aspects of your relationship with this person that you would like to maintain and those that you would like to change. (Do *not* send this letter.)
- Imagine that your body can talk about how it is being affected by the emotional experience of performing fieldwork. Focus on different locations and sensations where this experience is being "stored" (excited respiration, muscle cramps, etc.). Try to recall exactly when and where these "symptoms" began during specific fieldwork sessions. What are the events that are generating them? What are the feelings that are involved?

6

Asking, Listening, and Telling

Every object in the world can pass from a closed, silent existence to an oral state, open to appropriation by society, for there is no law, whether natural or not, which forbids talking about things.

— Barthes (1957/1972, p. 109)

In their pursuit of meanings in everyday life, communication researchers encounter speech at every turn. So important is oral discourse to all of the interpretivist traditions that it is hard to imagine any of them existing and prospering without a methodology designed to study speaking subjects. Asking questions and listening to others tell what they know, feel, and believe are the archetypal actions of the interview. Interviewing "quite literally . . . develop[s] a *view* of something between (*inter*) people" (Brenner, 1985, p. 148). At its best, the qualitative interview is an event in which one person (the interviewer) encourages others to freely articulate their interests and experiences. Its ability to travel deeply and broadly into subjective realities has made the interview a preeminent method in communication and the other social sciences. Indeed, some sort of interviewing is employed in nearly all qualitative research. This fact alone underscores the importance of studying its forms, practices, and limitations.

The qualitative interview is a remarkably adaptable method. Interviews can be done in a research lab, during a walk along a beach, at a corner table in a restaurant, or in a teenager's bedroom—anywhere two people can talk in relative privacy. The scope of topics that can be covered is limitless. Interviews may dwell on the most personal matters or revolve around the most public, politically charged issues. Also, interviews vary enormously in their (in)formality. They are usually well-marked social events, but interviews can also occur spontaneously in the course of a field study. They can be conducted briskly in a few minutes or at a leisurely pace for two or more hours. In some long forms of interviews, the discourse may evolve in many sessions across weeks, months, or years.

Interviews are usually, but not always, face-to-face encounters. The Internet and the telephone may serve as media of convenience for the researcher and interviewee who already know each other well. In other cases, communication technologies are a necessary starting point for two people to build their research relationship. Tom once received an e-mail at his office from a long sought-after informant, Dennis Walto, then a relief worker in Africa. Dennis's message began, "Dear Tom—Greetings from deep in the bush where although our diesel is running low, we will run our generator long enough to at least allow me to bang out some initial answers to your queries." In the theater of Tom's imagination, he saw Dennis typing alone in a room—the only light for miles on the Sudanese plain, the muffled roar of the generator in the near distance. Thus began a series of exchanges, which shifted into a different mode when Dennis returned to the United States later that year and visited Lexington to continue the interview. Though their first contact was made possible by the Internet, it was as warm and engaging as any that Tom experienced in two decades of interviewing.

The styles of qualitative interviewing discussed in this chapter have been called "conversation with a purpose" (Bingham & Moore, 1959). Indeed, most qualitative interviews take on the form and feel of talk between friends: loose, interactive, and open-ended. Interviewing, however, is not just conversation. According to Norman Denzin (1978), interview talk

> covers a wide range of topics, which are not selected by one of the talkers—the respondent. It is talk that is organized so as to give one person (the interviewer) greater control over the other (the respondent). It is talk that is (typically) furnished for someone else's benefit. (p. 113)

Yet if the interview's purposes and structure lie largely in the hands of the researcher, interviewees can still exert a good deal of influence. They may decide to be more effusive in their replies to some questions rather than others. They may refuse to answer questions, feign memory lapses, or balk at being drawn into a position implied by a line of questioning. On a more positive note, it is not unusual for ideas and perspectives to be shared mutually during an interview. Collaborative styles of interviewing have developed in which the interests and power of the parties are considered to be of equal value. Interviewer and interviewee invest jointly in the project and "coauthor" its purposes and results (Ellis, Kiesinger, & Tillmann-Healy, 1997; Tripp, 1983).

No matter how egalitarian their premise or process, qualitative interviews are always open to the unexpected and the emergent. How this dynamic process affects the researcher has been described eloquently by Marianne Paget (1983):

> What distinguishes in-depth interviewing is that the answers given continually inform the evolving conversation. Knowledge thus accumulates with many turns at talk. It collects in stories, asides, hesitations, expressions of feeling, and spontaneous associations. . . . The specific person interviewing, the "I" that I am, personally contributes to the creation of the interview's content because I follow my own perplexities as they arise in our discourse. (p. 78)

Stated simply, the researcher defines purposes for these conversations to occur and finds people who can contribute to these purposes. The researcher elicits talk about their experiences and invites ongoing revisions of the ideas and questions guiding the interview. This reflexive method enables us to understand the sensemaking that animates communicative performances.

It is often said that interviews are as much art as science. Much of what we present here is the systematic side of interviewing. But the world that lies beyond this chapter—your interview experiences—will invoke your own artful ways of asking, listening, and telling.

Purposes of the Qualitative Interview

At the most basic level, interview talk has a referential purpose (Briggs, 1986). Thus we expect the people we interview to tell us about events, processes, or objects that exist outside the immediate interview context. But we also know that people are not neutral or mistake-free reporters of their own experience. People forget some features of what they see and hear, ignore other features, and lie about still others. They might enlarge their role in an event, minimize it, or tell about it from the perspectives of others who were there. It is in fact the strikingly distinctive ways that people articulate their experience that makes interviews so fascinating and useful.

Qualitative interviewing is predicated on the idea that interview talk is the rhetoric of socially situated speakers. We interpret the "truth value" of interview speech—that is, its truth for the speaker—within a whole matrix of information about the interview event and the person being interviewed. This premise—that interview talk is the participants' rhetorical construction of their experience—undergirds the purposes of qualitative interviewing explored in this section:

- Understanding the social actor's experience and perspective through stories, accounts, and explanations
- Understanding native conceptualizations of communication
- Eliciting the language forms used by social actors in natural settings
- Gathering information about things or processes that cannot be observed effectively by other means
- Inquiring about occurrences in the past
- Verifying, validating, or commenting on information obtained from other sources
- Testing hypotheses developed in the field
- Achieving efficiency in data collection

Interviews are particularly well suited to *understand the social actor's experience and perspective.* Researchers usually select persons for interviews only if their experience is central to the research problem in some way. They may be recruited for their expertise in a skill or discipline, or because their role in a scene or in critical events created a unique fund of knowledge. Interview subjects who occupy a certain status or social category—for example, the elderly or low-income minority groups—may also be selected because of the life conditions or challenges they are presumed to share. The researcher expects the nature of the actor's experience to result in words that can only be uttered by someone who has "been there" (or "is there").

Experiential knowledge is usually elicited in three forms of discourse: stories, accounts, and explanations. Interviews allow us to hear people's *stories* of their experiences. In contrast to propositional modes of cognition, which favor abstractness and generality, narrative shapes human experience in terms of context, action, and intentionality (Baumeister & Newman, 1994). Qualitative interviews are a storytelling zone par excellence in which people are given complete license to craft their selves in language.

Sometimes people provide *accounts* of their experience, which Scott and Lyman (1968) define as excuses or justifications of social conduct. As an example, Hunt and Manning (1991) interviewed police officers during an 18-month field study about the social contexts in which they would lie. They sought the insiders' perspectives on the morality of this activity, especially the police officers' notions of normal or acceptable lies. Instances of police lying to colleagues and in court were found to serve a variety of ends: saving face, retaliating against disrespectful suspects, compensating for an ineffective justice system, avoiding unnecessary paperwork, and protecting fellow officers. In fact, according to the authors, "learning to lie is a key to [police] membership" (p. 54). Interview studies like this one can uncover confessions of motive that participants might otherwise go to great lengths to keep hidden.

Social actors also produce *explanations* of their behavior. They explain how they apply what they know in certain areas of their lives, how they negotiate certain issues, how they moved from one stage of their lives to another, how they interpret certain texts, and so on. The interviewer's goal is to draw out the individual, interpersonal, or cultural logics that people employ in their communicative performances. For example, Bull's (2001) interviews of Sony Walkman users "demonstrate[d] a complex set of Walkman practices with each user engaging in a multiple set of uses, motivations, and responses" (p. 182). His phenomenological analysis showed how mobile audio listening restructures people's relationship to public time and space.

Another purpose served by interviewing is to *understand native conceptualizations of communication*. Interviews can explore the commonsense conceptualizations, or folk theories, of communication that circulate in society. For example, Sheriff (2000) studied the purposeful silences ("cultural censorship") surrounding the subject of racism in Brazil, and Katriel and Philipsen (1981) used interview texts, among other sources, to deconstruct the meanings of "communication" in American speech.

Interviews also enable researchers to *elicit the language forms used by social actors in natural settings*. Becoming acculturated in any realm of social life involves learning one or more languages and their vocabularies and idioms. These language forms serve social purposes such as marking in-group membership, asserting expertise, and controlling emotional expression. For example, Gordon (1983) collected the hospital slang used by doctors and nurses to characterize patients. They concluded that seemingly dehumanizing terms for patients (e.g., the category "grok," which refers to comatose patients and includes other terms like "pre-stiff," "summer squash," "trainwreck," and "vegetable") were used in situations "where social rapport is important but personalized expression of emotion is not" (p. 183).

Researchers ply the techniques of interviewing to *gather information about things or processes that cannot be observed effectively by other means*. Interviewing, as Kleinman and colleagues (1994) note, is "a good way to learn about physically unbounded social realities . . . [and] identities and meanings that cut across, lie outside, or transcend settings" (p. 43). Well-informed participants (or ex-participants) can describe areas of social life that researchers may not be able to penetrate and study on their own. Interviews in this vein encourage the interviewee to be "the observer's observer" (Zelditch, 1962).

Similarly, researchers use interviews to *inquire about the past*. Critical events that alter the course of a community or a person's life are not always captured in eyewitness reports. And because official histories, if they exist at all, often reflect the interests of power holders, interviews can tap a wider field of voices and memories and thus help to inscribe a more nuanced understanding of past events. Betteridge (1997), for example, relied on interviews and informal conversations to reconstruct the role of the telephone in a small island community off the coast of Ireland.

Interviews are often used to *verify, validate, or comment on information obtained from other sources*. An event we observe can occur so quickly, or so inscrutably, that only a good informant can tell us what "really" happened. Even if we hold an observational text in our hands—for example, the minutes of a meeting—we may need a native member to explain who the actors are or how the actors' relationships influenced what each one said. "Member validations" with key persons are often used near the end of a study to *test hypotheses developed in the field*. The role of these interviews in data interpretation is explained in Chapter 7.

Finally, interviews can *achieve efficiency in data collection*. This is particularly true when an interview study is compared with participant observation. Even a project involving dozens of in-depth interviews will usually consume fewer "contact hours" than a typical field study will. However, this efficiency applies only to time in the field. Interview transcriptions take as much (if not more) time and effort than fieldnotes do. Interviews and fieldnotes can complement each other very usefully, but only rarely can one substitute for the other.

In any given study, interviews may be conducted for more than one of the purposes reviewed in this section. These purposes add up to a compelling set of reasons to become adept in the use of interviews. In the next section, we examine some types of interviewing that are commonly used in communication studies.

Interview Types in Communication

The types of interview we discuss in this section differ from each other along several dimensions: the depth and range of topics to be covered; the kind of discourse that is produced; the comparability of one interview's content to that of others in the same study; the length and number of interview sessions for each participant; the relational quality of the interview encounter. We begin with the type of interview that does not operate as a "stand-alone" genre: the ethnographic interview.

Ethnographic Interviews

The ethnographic interview—also known as the *informal conversational interview* (Patton, 1990, pp. 281-282) or a *situational conversation* (Schatzman & Strauss, 1973, p. 71)—occurs while the investigator is in the field. It is the most informal, spontaneous form of interview. A casual exchange of remarks, or a lull in the action, might suggest that the moment is right for asking a "research" question.

The researcher should be able to identify something of interest in what is said or done by the participants and develop a line of questioning on the spot. In such instances, the researcher awaits (or creates) the right opportunity to ask questions. In his participant observation study of political campaigns, Glaser (1996) found it helpful to offer people rides to campaign events and use the travel time to engage them in talk related to his research. The road trips were in fact quite good for this purpose, because "conversations in the car were often less guarded, and . . . some of the most interesting revelations came out in transit" (p. 535). In Murphy's (1999b) ethnography of Mexican television viewing, mentioned in earlier chapters, he employed "conversational interviews" as a solution to problems with his prearranged interviews:

> [These interviews] emerged out of conversations about local life, cultural practices, or politics. Within these informal conversations, I would find an opportunity to ask more television-specific questions and thus initiate an interview about the place of television in their everyday lives without deviating from the topic at hand. "Hanging out" thus became a big part of daily research efforts. This was a key to making these conversational interviews work and to deliver the kind of interpretive depth and introspection that I was really looking for. (p. 492)

The easy informality of ethnographic interviews belies the skill involved in exploiting the moment. Ethnographers should stay alert to situational cues even as they go into the field with an outline of questions in their heads. The advice given in Chapter 5 about "spontaneous decision making" applies to ethnographic interviews, too.

Informant Interviews

During the course of a study, the researcher may meet people whose knowledge of a cultural scene proves to be valuable for achieving research objectives. These people are called *informants* because they inform the researcher about key features and processes of the scene—what the significant customs and rituals are and how they are done, which people exercise the real power, and so forth. The success of an ethnographic project often hinges on the effective use of informants. Nonethnographic types of qualitative study may be designed wholly or in part around informant interviews.

People who make the best informants often display one or more of the following characteristics:

- They have long experience in the cultural scene, perhaps by having "risen through the ranks," and thus can serve as reliable sources of the local institutional memory.
- They have served the scene in many different roles, or currently have more mobility than others, and thus can speak knowledgeably about people's roles and responsibilities and how the social parts work together.
- They are well respected by their peers, superiors, and/or subordinates, and are plugged into one or more key social networks.
- They are facile speakers of the local language forms and can debrief the researcher on contextualized uses and meanings.

In short, the best informants are savvy social actors. Gatekeepers or sponsors sometimes fill the informant role and act as guides to the world the researcher is about to enter. Some informants rank high in the social order, although such persons may be found to be remarkably ill-informed about what actually happens at the lower and middle levels. In this regard, secretaries and custodial workers can make excellent informants—because the former is privy to the information flows and personal habits of everyone in an organization or office cluster, while the latter may be the only employees who daily go into every room of the building. However, secretaries and custodial workers are supposed to be discreet as a condition of their employment, and informants, by definition, allow their discretion to drop a bit when they speak with researchers.

Occasionally, persons whose status is marginal—that is, those who are socially deviant or discredited or who are independent operators of some kind—may serve as interesting informants precisely because they do not live squarely in the cultural mainstream. They may have trained themselves to notice such things as the political machinations of their fellow actors or the episodes of incompetence, cowardice, avarice, and vanity that most others choose to ignore or "forget." On the other hand, the researcher should be wary of the interpretive coloration that these people may add to their stories. The last thing most qualitative researchers want is to be used as an unwitting mouthpiece by alienated social actors.

The researcher who is likable, trustworthy, and eager to learn will usually find willing informants. For example, while studying the ways in which young people use fake identification to gain access to a night club, Scheibel (1992) "befriended the club's doorm[e]n and was subsequently allowed to stand next to them as they interacted with the customers. Near the end of some evenings, doormen would show me fake Ids they had confiscated from customers earlier in the evening and explain why the Ids were 'bad'"(p. 161). Additional interviews with students, customers, and past employees helped the author understand the contexts, experiences, and consequences of fake ID use. These informants offered various insights and sets of information due to their unique roles in a scene. With respect to informant accuracy, cognitive studies suggest that the best informants generally recall stable, long-term patterns quite well, but that they may also produce "false recalls" of details of particular events (Bernard, Killworth, Kronenfeld, & Sailer, 1984; Freeman, Romney, & Freeman, 1987).

Informant interviews often require an hour or more, and range widely across the experiences and knowledge of the participant. Informants are normally consulted more than one time, and the researcher usually comes with prepared questions. When using several informants, one should organize the questions so that the different discourses can be compared and cross-referenced for the data analysis and write-up.

Respondent Interviews

As its name implies, the purpose of the respondent interview is to elicit open-ended responses. Nearly six decades ago, Paul Lazarsfeld (1944) described the general goals of this interview type: (1) to clarify the meanings of common concepts and opinions; (2) to distinguish the decisive elements of an expressed opinion; (3) to determine what influenced a person to form an opinion or to act in a certain way; (4) to classify complex attitude patterns; and (5) to understand the interpretations that people attribute to their motivations to act. Contemporary qualitative studies that identify their interview subjects as "respondents" adopt at least one of these five objectives.

In contrast to informants, who comment on the world surrounding them, respondents speak only for themselves. Respondents are usually asked to express themselves on an issue or situation, or to explain what they think or how they feel about their social world. The respondent interview is commonly used as a stand-alone procedure rather than combined with other methods in a field study. Participation by each interviewee is limited to one or two interview sessions. Although the questions asked can vary from one person to the next, many respondent-interview studies follow a standard order for all interviewees so that responses can be directly compared across the entire sample. Even if the questions are not standardized, other aspects of the interview protocol may be well-defined and formalized. Biographical contextualization of responses is ordinarily not evoked in the analysis.

Appropriate experience in a scene is usually the key consideration in selecting respondents. Those persons who have been through the critical events, career paths, or social routines and rituals of their institutions and groups are likely to deliver a rich lode of information. However, some communication studies require participants who are not yet fully enculturated in the performances under study. For example, Rawlins and Holl (1987) studied teenagers' conceptions of friendship because adolescence is a time when close relationships are being experienced for the first time. They were specifically interested in the incipience of moral thinking in this domain. Maybe the better all-purpose criterion for selecting respondents is: Whose experience is most appropriate for the research question?

For example, Bruder and Ucok (2000) studied art museum visitors' talk about paintings, focusing on the "communicative character of the viewer's encounter with works of art" (p. 338). Patrons were approached at a public gallery so that they could select the paintings they wanted to view and discuss. The interviews lasted 5 to 30 minutes (the average was approximately 10 minutes) and no background data were solicited (in order to preserve the sense of having a conversation). Except for the basic question "What do you think?" the researcher asked only questions "designed to probe for clarity and greater interpretive depth" (pp. 340-341). The study displays most of the key elements of the respondent interview—brief interview encounters, few and/or uniform questions, interviewee anonymity, and a focus on subjective perceptions.

For Lazarsfeld and others who follow the traditional model, respondent interviews are a lens for viewing the interaction of an individual's internal states (social attitudes and motives) with the outer environment. The interview response is treated as a "report" of that interaction. More recently, however, we see the appearance of a new epistemology of the respondent. Under the influence of critical and cultural theories, respondents are now conceptualized as sites of multiple, changing, and often contradictory cultural discourses. The traditional respondent model may still hold sway in Communication, but the wheel is clearly turning. In the narrative interview, we see more evidence of this move toward open, dialogical interviews.

Narrative Interviews

The idea of a narrative interview type presents something of a "category problem" because other forms of interviewing also yield stories, tales, gossip, anecdotes, and parables. What distinguishes the narrative interview is its twofold nature as an empirical approach and as an ontological paradigm. Narrative interviews capture and explicate the "whole story," unlike other types of interviews, which take stories apart and reassemble the parts for their own analytic purposes. Also, it is not incidental that storytelling itself is the vehicle for generating story data. The performance often holds as much interest as the story content.

Through their enduring patterns of representation (dramatic forms, plots, scenes, character types, etc.), stories enable people to make their experiences intelligible to each other. This is undoubtedly what Bruner (1987) meant when he wrote that "life stories must mesh, so to speak, within a community of life stories; tellers and listeners must share some 'deep structure' about the nature of a 'life,' for if the rules of life-telling are altogether arbitrary, tellers and listeners will surely be alienated by a failure to grasp what the other is saying or what he [or she] thinks the other is hearing"(p. 21). Narrative is absolutely central to art, spirituality, community, and a sense of self, and thus encodes human desire at the deepest levels. Narrative interviews are the earliest known form of in-depth interviewing in the social sciences. From early 20th-century American anthropology came biographical accounts of the lives of Indians, and from Chicago School sociologists of the 1920s came the life history method (Langness & Frank, 1981). As described by Heyl (2001),

> life history interviewing fits comfortably within the ethnographic tradition, since it is usually conducted over time, within relationships characterized by high levels of rapport, and with particular focus on the meanings the interviewees place on their life experiences and circumstances, expressed in their own language. (p. 369)

Life histories traditionally document all of the significant streams of a person's life, acting as a prism for understanding larger cultural or historical frames. Linear narrative forms have recently given ground to life histories that mix genres of oral performance (Chambon, 1995; Heyl, 2001). These studies tend to focus on disjunctures in narrative as a way of studying people's identity work and conflicts in their self-presentations. In Communication, the full-scale life history is rare, but scholars sometimes adopt versions that examine the aspects of a life, or several lives, that have compelling theoretical interest.

Two forms of narrative-interview study have emerged in Communication: the *personal narrative* and the *organizational narrative*. Arising out of oral culture traditions, the *personal narrative* uses not monologue but, rather, conversational interaction as its method for producing interesting stories (Langellier, 1989). The personal narrative "[creates] a dynamic interplay between self and others" (Corey, 1996, p. 57). The stories are often told in relation to cultural discourses of race, class, gender, sexuality, and other politicized identities. Feminist scholarship has had an enormous impact in this regard through its explorations of the gendered nature of everyday speech and its theorizing about the dialogical possibilities of interview style. Recent work in the area of personal narrative in Communication includes the study of stories as strategic resources (Corey, 1996) and the use of systematic introspection for telling self-stories (Ronai, 1995).

Boje (1991) defines the storytelling organization as "a collective storytelling system in which the performance of stories is a key part of members' sense making and a means to allow them to supplement individual memories with institutional memory" (p. 106). Organizational narratives do not differ in many respects from the personal narrative. The key difference is that the stories told by organizational members make up a web of collective reality. Moreover, the organizations themselves are sources of stories that become embedded in, or problematic to, the minds and actions of the membership. Recent organizational narrative studies have focused on stories as the discourse of conflict (Ashcraft & Pacanowsky, 1996), stories as a "centering" device (Boyce, 1995), and stories as the commodified fables of company founders (Boje, 1995).

The method of narrative interviews often depends on a close, long-term relationship with participants. It is not unusual for the researcher to study colleagues, friends, acquaintances, or relatives. If the researcher and participant do not already know each other, the researcher may need to take extra time to achieve a frame of equality for the interview (see the discussion of this in the section on rapport later in the chapter). Narrative interviews are among the least structured of all interview genres. The overriding goal is to find the most comfortable grounds for people to tell their stories. Knowing that unforeseen topics could emerge from the conversational give-and-take, interviewers may be reluctant to rein in the participant or place limits on what can be discussed. Narrative interviewers must be able to let go of any urge to control because their role is to facilitate and encourage.

Focus Group Interviews

In the types examined so far, interviewing is a dyadic interaction. However, there are also situations that call for interviewing several people at once. Among a host of group interview methods (e.g., Delphi groups, brainstorming groups, informal group interviews in the field), the *focus group* is unquestionably the most popular (Frey & Fontana, 1991). Versions of focus group interviewing have been used in academic social science for decades (Lunt & Livingstone, 1996; Morrison, 1998), and marketing firms and political consultants rely on focus groups as a tool for probing people's responses to media messages or their experiences with products, services, and candidates. Focus groups are also used in the early stage of survey design as a way to develop questionnaire items. More importantly for our purposes, the focus group has come into its own as a stand-alone data collection method. Accompanying this new role has been a boomlet of methodological studies on focus group design, operation, and data analysis.

The major reason to interview people in groups is to exploit the "group effect" (Carey, 1994); that is, "the explicit use of the group interaction [produces] data and insights that would be less accessible without the interaction found in a group" (Morgan, 1988, p. 12). In the group context, the members are stimulated by the ideas and experiences expressed by each other. What occurs is a kind of "chaining" or "cascading" effect—talk links to, or tumbles out of, the topics and expressions preceding it.

Focus group researchers usually seek one (or both) of two kinds of group effect. First, some studies aim to produce *complementary interactions*. In this mode, the members broadly agree on an expressed view and add their own observations and subtle shades of interpretation to the view. What is valuable about these focus groups is that they often produce vernacular speech—slang, jokes, anecdotes, songs, acting-out episodes, and so on—that vivify the group norms and sensemaking that occur naturally in the participants' world (Kitzinger, 1994). Sometimes, the tone of these interactions is such that people feel willing to express themselves on sensitive or long-repressed topics.

Alternately, focus group studies can set up the possibility for *argumentative interactions*. The use of certain topics or combinations of group members can result in cleavages of opinion, or clashing worldviews, which enable insights into "how people theorize their own point of view . . . in relation to other perspectives and how they put their own ideas to 'work'"(Kitzinger, 1994, p. 113). In all, the focus group can be a useful "social laboratory" for studying the production of interpretations, perceptions, and personal experiences.

The basic protocol for focus group interviews has by now become well codified. The optimal size for a focus group is from 6 to 12 persons. A group with fewer than 6 persons can lead to a less diverse range (and more rapid exhaustion) of useful comments; working more than 12 participants incurs the risk that not as many topics can be covered and not everyone will be heard. Focus group interviews tend to be 90 minutes in length, with one to two hours as the accepted range for interview length. They typically take place in a conference room or some other "neutral" location, but it is not unknown for focus groups to be held in the residence of the researcher or a group member. Some researchers videotape the proceedings—with the equipment either set up in the interview room or hidden behind a one-way mirror in an adjacent room—in order to capture facial expressions, gestures, and attentional behavior.

In media audience research, samples of textual material (e.g., songs, television programs) are sometimes presented to orient the members to the subject matter and provide a "push-off" to the discussion. Representative studies include Delli Carpini and Williams (1994), who studied the use of media referents in group conversations about environmental pollution, and Press and Cole (1995), who held focus group interviews with pro-life women to discern the ways in which they select and interpret "scientific facts" in the abortion debate. Some inventive focus group designs encourage people to verbalize their views as they work together on a project such as a news story (MacGregor & Morrison, 1995).

The interviewer—or *moderator*—plays a major role in the success of focus group interviews. Moderators try to achieve a fine balance between enfranchising individuals to speak out and promoting "good group feeling." (Some commercial research firms are known to recruit people as moderators whose jobs call for talk-facilitation skills, such as bartenders and teachers.) After introductions around the table, the moderator starts with one or two questions intended to tap into the experience under study. Thereafter, the moderator lightly guides the discussion with a list of questions and follow-up probes.

Morgan (1996) notes that "a key factor that makes groups more or less structured is simply the number of questions [the moderator asks]" (p. 145). More questions in a time frame usually mean more structure in the discussion, although little agreement exists about the number and kind of questions that constitute a more or less structured approach to questioning (Morgan, 1996, p. 145). Recent discourse analysis studies of focus group interaction suggest that the moderator's agenda often wins out over the concerns of the participants in determining the flow of discussion (Agar & MacDonald, 1995; Saferstein, 1995). Moderators would be well-advised to study their own performance from tapes and to correct any discussion-leading habits that tend to inhibit or misdirect group members' talk.

Recent advances in the methodological study of focus groups have been made in the area of standardized versus emergent designs and in the effects of intragroup and intergroup diversity on variation in the topics raised in the groups and the quality of the dicussion (see Morgan, 1996). Understanding these factors can be helpful for planning specific kinds of group interaction.

Interview Practice

Interviewing is a multifaceted practice that calls on varied skills. If interviews are the "digging tool" of social science, the interviewer should ask questions in an effective, nonthreatening way. If interviews are partly conversation, the interviewer should be a skilled conversationalist. If interviews are learning situations, the interviewer should be a willing student. If interviews are cross-cultural encounters, the interviewer should be a sensitive traveler through cultures. If interviews reveal secrets and hidden realities, the interviewer should be a trusted user of information.

The researcher may not always perform each skill brilliantly. As with any skill we try to master, good outcomes are never guaranteed and mistakes will happen. But mistakes are usually forgiven when they happen *despite* one's preparation—not in the absence of it.

As Benney and Hughes (1970) observed in their essay on the sociological interview, "There is an enormous amount of preparatory socialization in the respondent role—in schools and jobs, through the mass media" (p. 193). Most people have been interviewed as students and job applicants, had their opinions tallied in surveys, and watched countless celebrity and newsmaker interviews on television. Not all of this "socialization" is helpful to the interests of qualitative inquiry. Mishler (1986), for example, has argued that surveys tend to encourage their human subjects to be obedient to its task demands and to ignore qualities of the research scene.

Qualitative researchers face the challenge of setting a new tone for interviewing. They seek ways of encouraging a sense of empowerment in the participant. They want to help the participant "enlarge on the definition of the situation as interview by reading the interview also as an interesting and satisfying encounter, as a chance to express his [or her] dislikes, disappointments, and ideas" (Brenner, 1978, p. 130). This goal is more likely to be reached if the interview can be framed as a project in which the researcher and the participant work as partners toward a common goal. Stated another way, interviews should invoke a play frame in which the norms and rules of the world outside are suspended (Bateson, 1972).

Paradoxically, we play most effectively and enjoyably when the "as if" action is taken seriously. When people accept the frame of the qualitative interview, the asymmetrical power roles of the interviewer and interviewee begin to even out (though not neutralize completely), and they find ways to speak with each other more as equals. We turn again to Benney and Hughes (1970):

> By offering a program of discussion, and an assurance that information offered will not be challenged or resisted, self-expression is facilitated to an unusual degree [that is] inherently satisfying. In this sense, then, the interview is an understanding between the two parties that, in return for allowing the interviewer to direct their communication, the informant is assured that he [or she] will not meet with denial, contradiction, competition, or other harassment. As with all contractual relations, the fiction or convention of equality must govern the situation. (pp. 194-195)

This "fiction or convention of equality" is no less serious than any other play frame in which special rules apply. Although the researcher continues to guide the interview agenda—especially through the questions asked—this does not deny the agency of the participants (Kauffman, 1992). The participants can raise issues the interviewer did not think to ask, suggest other ways of navigating a topic, ask to clarify a point, and so on. Often the participants begin to see that they have a stake in the project and kindle an interest in "getting it right"—producing the information, stories, and accounts that will help the researcher to understand their world. In the next pages, we discuss some of the settings and means for achieving this consensual frame. Ultimately, the investigator's bridge to the participants' world is the act of listening with genuine interest to what is being said and how it is said.

Interview Context

When and where to conduct interviews can be consequential issues in a project. *When* interviews should be conducted varies across people and situations. Generally, one should find "protected times" for doing the interview. These are times when outside pressures on the participants are low and they aren't edgy about the next thing on their calendar. The best results are also obtained when participants are relaxed—neither highly energized nor fatigued.

Decisions about *where* interviews should be conducted take similar considerations into account. Thus one usually seeks a space safe from interruptions or the presence of others who might listen in. This does not necessarily mean behind closed doors; certain public settings, like a table at a shopping mall food court, can afford anonymity and enough of a buffer from unwanted interaction for many kinds of interviewing. But most interviews do require a private place in which the needs of comfort and confidentiality can both be met.

Sometimes, researchers ask the participants' advice about where they should meet. Most choose settings that combine convenience (theirs, not the researcher's) and privacy. Often, these will be on their own turf, such as in their homes or offices. These settings have the added benefit of allowing researchers into the participant's habitat, where they can observe artifacts and revealing mannerisms or meet people who are mentioned in the interview stories and accounts. One graduate student we know, for example, interviewed off-duty prison guards at local coffee shops. She quickly noticed that they never sat with their backs to the door and that they remained hypervigilant about potential encounters with ex-inmates or the friends and family members of current inmates. This helped her to better understand the guards' off-duty relationships with inmates.

A third option for the interview setting is a neutral site, such as the aforementioned food court location. The only problems with public sites are that the interview is subject to distractions and the ambient noise can potentially affect the tape recording. Tom remembers conducting an interview during lunch on an open-air patio at the Santa Barbara Biltmore Hotel, while two groups of people laughed and shouted close by, and feeling the high anxiety of going home with a totally useless recording. As the interview went on, Tom nudged the tape recorder closer and closer to his companion until, finally, it was almost in his Cobb salad. Luckily, when the tape was played back later, the interview audio was strong and clear.

Doing telephone interviews can resolve the issue of place altogether. Logistically, telephone interviews are conducted by using a microrecorder with special circuitry into which one plugs the handset cord of the phone. Another, lower tech technique is simply to set an answering machine to record. Most states do not require callers by law to inform the other party that the conversation is being recorded, but of course, it is the only ethical alternative for those involved in academic research. The informed consent procedure should also be discussed on the phone and recorded before the interview proper. (The IRB may want the researcher to obtain written informed consent as well.) It is important to note that in-depth phone interviews are seldom "cold calls." The researcher usually contacts the participant first by letter or e-mail, then follows up with one or more calls in which the researcher and participant discuss the project and negotiate the terms of the interview.

Telephone conferencing has also been used to conduct focus group interviews (White & Thomson, 1995). In this application, "visual cues, which are important in traditional focus groups, are sacrificed for the sake of anonymity [and facilitators] need to be skillful in picking up audio cues and ensuring that all participants have a voice" (p. 261). Interviews conducted in computer environments, a subject that will be taken up in Chapter 9, share many characteristics with phone interviews.

The most frequent criticism of telephone interviews is that they are impersonal and a "poor substitute" for face-to-face meetings. There may be some valid concern about whether people will be candid with a researcher whom they have never met in another context. However, phone interviews can be as intimate and engrossing for the callers, and ultimately as productive, as those conducted in person. (See Bird, 1995, and Sunderland, 1999, for excellent discussions of the value of in-depth telephone interviews.) They often conjure up a kind of "strangers passing in the night" phenomenon; that is, participants disclose private thoughts because they never expect to meet the researcher in person or even hear from the researcher again. The absence of visual cues can also benefit the interview by reducing reactions to the recording equipment or to signs of the researcher's cultural identity and body presentation. Face-to-face interviews may be preferred if all options are equally available, but telephone interviews should not be dismissed out of hand as inferior. For some purposes, the phone interview may do just as well, if not better.

Recording Interviews

Interview discourse must be recorded, of course, and the choices are twofold: note taking or tape recording. The chief virtues of note taking are that it can be done anywhere and does not depend on mechanical devices. Some researchers are capable of recalling conversations in great detail. Author Truman Capote, for example, is reputed to have written up his interviews for *In Cold Blood* almost verbatim from memory. Most of us, however, are not *memoires savants*. We may be able to retrieve the highlights of an interview—maybe even a few exact phrases and snippets of dialogue—but a large amount of the interview is always lost. If the researcher does take notes during an interview, the advice given in Chapter 5 about soon thereafter converting scratch notes into fieldnotes applies in this context as well.

The use of tape recorders has one significant virtue: It enables researchers to capture the interview more or less exactly as it was spoken. We no longer have to worry about remembering a remark or missing it in the first place due to our minds wandering or being distracted momentarily. By transcribing a taped interview, we end up with a text that reproduces the discourse—not only what was said but also how words or phrases were uttered. These interview texts can be imported into data analysis software, and portions of texts can be cut and pasted into research reports. Another important reason to tape-record is that it can free up investigators to participate more fully in the interview.

On the other hand, tape recorders must usually be set in plain view of the participants. Even the smallest microrecorders on the market (e.g., the Olympus Pearlcorder L400, which is not much bigger than the cassette it holds) will be visible. Some interviewees don't seem to care whether or not they are being recorded. With other people, however, it is clear by their glances and what they say that they have carefully noted the fact that they are being tape recorded. The effects of such self-consciousness can be subtle but pervasive. As Whyte (1982) points out, "informants are likely to talk more 'for the record' with the machine than without, even when they have been told that the interviewer is going to write up the interview later"

(p. 118). Thus a certain formality may creep into interviewees' speech. They may "self-censor" their remarks (perhaps without the researcher knowing what has been left out or modified). If they are willing to say something controversial, they may ask the interviewer to turn off the recorder or ask not to be quoted by name. These requests and on-the-spot negotiations interrupt the flow of the talk and can have an impact on the rapport between the interviewer and interviewee, to say nothing of constraining the quality of the interview content.

These potential problems can be alleviated to some degree by a few simple procedures. First, and most importantly, one should take care of the technical aspects—checking that the battery is charged, inserting new tapes, doing a test recording—*before* arriving at the site. Worrying about the equipment inhibits participation in the ongoing interaction, and repairing it in front of respondents can heighten their concerns considerably. (Packing back-up batteries, spare tapes, and even a second recorder are recommended precautions.) Because respondents often take their cue about the importance of the tape recorder from the attitude of the researcher, they are more likely to be reassured if the researcher explains its purpose briefly in a matter-of-fact tone. The researcher should avoid fussing with the recorder during the interview except to change or turn over tapes. Finally, one can offer to send a copy of the transcribed interview to the participant. This offer is a gesture of courtesy, but it also conveys the researcher's good intentions concerning the use of the recording. In some cases, the participants have more to add after reading the transcription.

If only facts, not exact phrasing, are needed from an interviewee, then note taking may win out as the preferred method of recording an interview. Tape recorders can be "deterrents to candor" when highly sensitive topics are explored, such as legally actionable evidence (Weiss, 1994, p. 55). These situations aside, the accuracy and completeness that tape recordings offer make them the medium of first choice.

Rapport

Because the parties usually meet each other as strangers, researchers must do whatever they can to put the participant at ease. Researchers should try to anticipate the images and questions the participant may bring to the meeting: "What does this person want to know about me? What will this 'professor of communication' think of how I talk, of where I live, of how my house looks)? Am I going to be allowed to say what I truly feel and believe? Will I be ripped off by someone whom I will probably never see again? Of what value is this research anyway? Who benefits from it?"

These are all reasonable questions. Perhaps few of them will be verbalized in the presence of the researcher, and some fears or qualms may not be verbalized at all. Nevertheless, researchers should try to put themselves in the role of the participants and prepare to respond to the sorts of issues that concern the participants about the study, the interview, and what kind of professional—and person—the researcher is.

What the interviewer wants to achieve is *rapport* with the interview participants. At one level, rapport means that they may not always agree about the content of the other's viewpoint, but both recognize that the viewpoint is valid and worthy of respect. At another level, rapport means that they agree about matters of communication style such as the turn-taking of the question and answer format, the right to finish a thought without interruption, and the freedom to use any form of expression. This does not mean that they must use the same words to express the same idea. Rather, it means that neither person will be thought worse for *not* using the same words.

Rapport is a quality of a communication event, not of a relationship. As Spradley (1979) notes, "Just as respect can develop between two people who do not particularly like one another, rapport can exist in the absence of fondness and affection" (p. 78). Rapport should also not be confused with "neutrality" on the part of the researcher—even if it were possible to be neutral. Patton (1990) put the distinction this way:

> Rapport is a stance vis-à-vis the person being interviewed. Neutrality is a stance vis-à-vis the content of what that person says. Rapport means that I respect the people being interviewed, so that what they say is important because of who is saying it. . . . Yet, I will not judge them for the content of what they say to me. (p. 317)

Because the researcher has limited time to complete the interview, a high priority is placed on establishing rapport rather quickly. Arguably, this encourages a view of the interview as serving only the researcher's needs (Jorgenson, 1992). Clearly, no one party can "possess" rapport. By its very nature, rapport is a social accomplishment. Still, the researcher is the one who should make the first moves to lay the groundwork for a mutually gratifying conversation.

Rapport begins with the researcher's clarity of purpose. Participants should be given clear, honest reasons for why they have been contacted, what the project goals are, and how the interview will be conducted. Participants can be told that "I want to know how you (or others in your group) think about these topics." The interview will "not be like surveys you might have taken before." Not only are there "no right or wrong responses" to the questions, it is important to hear "your views in your own words."

Participants may be urged by the researcher to "bring up questions or issues that are relevant to the topics, but that maybe I simply didn't know enough to ask." However, the researcher should also let them know that "I have a set of questions that I want to cover in the time we have today."

Because focus group interviews explore many people's perceptions in a defined period of time, they usually follow a protocol for introducing the study and creating the grounds for rapport. Figure 6.1 displays one such "script." Of special interest in this script are the use of humor and the imaginative way in which the moderator explains the concept of opinion equality. It is always important to go around the room for introductions, not only to break the ice but also so that voices can be matched with names for later transcription.

Interviewer self-disclosures are one way to engage the participant's interest and pave the way for a meaningful interview. By saying something about who they are—including, perhaps, their personal reasons for doing the study—researchers concretely signal the equal-footing nature of the interview. This kind of opening gives the participant an idea of how informal the interview will be. Participants may learn enough about the researcher's style and intentions to begin investing some trust in the relationship. If the researcher uses brief personal stories or anecdotes judiciously through the rest of the interview, a sense of reciprocity and goodwill often unfolds.

The researcher might ask for *participant self-disclosures*—for example, asking them to tell about their families, jobs, or other aspects of their lives. One purpose of this tactic is to help participants feel comfortable talking about themselves. Researchers hope that participants will welcome this kind of talk. For the researcher's part, these moments are neither frivolous nor a throw-away tactic: Participants' speech patterns, storytelling performance, and willingness to interact can be noted mentally and used in making adjustments to interview strategy. It may go without saying (but we will say it anyway) that participant disclosures should key in on a positive experience, or at least an innocuous one. Asking about an interviewee's job just after the person has been laid off, for example, is not a good start. Obviously, the goal of building rapport together suffers if negative emotions are brought to the surface.

Demeanor and personal appearance in rapport building also merit some mention. As in the ethnographer's stance discussed in Chapter 5, the interviewer should generally present a positive, nonjudgmental, eager-to-learn face. Interviewers should also be ready to adjust to the tone of the topic and occasion. For example, researchers interviewing men who have undergone prostate cancer surgery should steer a course between bubbly cheerfulness

I. MODERATOR INTRODUCTION

[*Note: A conversational approach sets a tone that relaxes people, making it more comfortable for them to share their intimate thoughts. This part of the script can be easily remembered and delivered naturally by moderators.*]

Hello! My name is _____, and I am working with _____. You were all invited here today because it is important that we hear from young adults like you. However, don't worry that anyone outside of our group will know exactly what you said. No names will be used when your comments are used in our research project. Also, we ask you to respect the privacy of the other group members by not discussing anything that anyone else says. So we all agree that our conversation will be confidential? [*Be sure to make brief eye contact with each person at this point.*]

Let's imagine that you go outside this building and ask someone, "What is the temperature right now at this spot?" There is a right answer that you can check with a thermometer. However, what we are discussing tonight is how you or your friends feel about things, and there could be as many different opinions as there are people in this room. Guess what? Every one of those opinions is right! Remember, we aren't here to convince anyone of something in particular or to change anyone's mind. We are here to discuss things and hear what each and every one of you has to say.

Sometimes, you will find that many people in the room have your opinion, and other times, you will be the only one with that opinion. But it is important for us to learn about all the opinions, because even if you are the only one in this room who holds that opinion, there may be hundreds or thousands of other people in our community who feel just as you do. Most importantly, every opinion counts, so please feel free to share your thoughts.

You will note the carefully hidden tape recorder. [*This is a joke!*] I will be recording our conversation because we want to be able to remember everything you share, and to really listen to you now instead of spending time scribbling notes. The tape recorder does have one problem. It is hard to hear voices when more than one person is speaking. So I'm asking you to please speak one at a time.

(continued)

(*Figure 6.1 Continued*)

If you need to leave the discussion for some reason, please feel free to step outside, but I ask you to hurry back to join us. So, sit back and relax. I know you will find the next 90 minutes very interesting and enjoyable.

II. PARTICIPANT INTRODUCTIONS

First, please turn your name cards so I can see everyone's name. Thanks. I'd like to begin by finding out about your favorite TV show.

[Note: *This is a discussion-training exercise. You call on people by their first name and ask one follow-up question about whatever they say. The follow-up question can be anything that makes it clear you have been listening and that encourages the participant to add something more. That will help get the participants used to your probing for more information. A good approach is to call on people in a seemingly random order, rather than moving around the table, because the randomness better approximates how the focus group discussions happen. Moving around the table sets a different tone and could lead to people patterning their comments after their neighbor who has just spoken.*]

(Courtesy of Suzanne Allard, doctoral candidate at the University of Kentucky)

Figure 6.1   Focus Group Script

and funereal solemnity. One can be far more "bubbly" interviewing young children about cartoons. And whatever people's notions of the academic's dress code may be, interviewers should dress in a way that reflects a sensible reading of the cultural scene. Business attire has its place for some interviews, but so, too, does casual wear.

Finally, it is worth noting that rapport can be more difficult to achieve between dissimilar persons, such as is the case when adults interview children (Weber, Miracle, & Skehan, 1994). The equality frame of interviews is also sometimes disrupted by the interviewees' behavior. For example, when women interview men, especially on topics of gender relations or sexual conduct, some men try to alter the "conversational dance" by asserting their superiority and dominance, denigrating women, asking highly personal questions of the female interviewer, and acts that could be considered sexual harassment (Arendell, 1997; Green, Barbour, Barnard, & Kitzinger, 1993). Such incidents not only threaten rapport, they can also attack the researcher's self-confidence and sense of safety. When they knowingly go into problematic interview situations, researchers should be prepared to use conversational tactics for deflating tensions or terminate interviews if the interviewees become unpleasant or dangerous (see Arendell, 1997; Green et al., 1993).

In any study, researchers must make delicate decisions about how to respond to their subjects. Glaser (1996), for example, tells of being with a White campaign official who told a racist joke. The situation, he wrote, "*required* a response. Silence, interpreted in other situations as approval, was disapproval in this one" (p. 536). Glaser instantly replied, "That's terrible," as if to say that the joke itself was a poor one. His ambiguous response satisfied a moral imperative and avoided a confrontation that might have endangered their rapport. Nonetheless, the author admitted, "It was not the most honest moment in my life" (p. 536). The example reminds us again that rapport can exist even while we disapprove of the other person's ethics, values, or conduct. But achieving it may require us to temper our urge to speak out as we normally would.

Listening

Listening is a crucial—maybe the most crucial—behavior for building rapport after an interview has started. Listening is also a way of eliciting talk. Good listening habits always call forth more and better stories. At its most basic level, listening means "paying attention." Because words can come across as insincere, the act of paying attention can be the purest sign of wanting to hear more. Conversely, looking away from participants is one of the best ways to frustrate them and discourage them from talking.

While paying attention is a form of passive listening, *active listening* is trying to hear the significance of what the interviewee is saying. Figures of speech, emotional nuances, the connections to what was said earlier, the inconsistencies from one remark to the next—these aspects of the conversation and more can be registered through active listening. In active listening, one is actually keeping "a watch on oneself, a self-consciousness" (Cottle, 1973, p. 351). The researcher thinks through the conversation as it unfolds, and silently asks: What am I learning now? What else should I learn? What can I do to help the participants to express themselves? The researcher theorizes about the possible meanings in what the person said or what the person might have meant. These ideas might be urgent enough for the researcher to gently break in with a question. Just the fact that a question is posed *at this point in time* tells the participant that the researcher is listening. These moments often propel the discussion into exciting areas and promote a closer collaboration between the researcher and the participant.

However, one must be careful about when and how to break in with a question. Asking too many questions might suggest that the researcher is not listening closely. And asking questions that were answered earlier in the interview is proof-positive to the participant that the researcher isn't listening at all.

Active listening consists not only of the researcher's questions but is also evident in the head tilts, nods, smiles, looks of concern, and the "Yes," "Uh huh," and "I see" that sustain talk. Rapport always leads to active listening, and active listening promotes rapport. Listening is the vital connective tissue of any interview.

Question Design and Use

Questions are the best-known tools of the interviewer's craft. If the participants have any doubt about the goals of a project when they start, the interview questions will soon cue them to what the researcher is really after. Questions are potent tactics for starting discourse along certain tracks or for switching tracks later. They can be used to open up a shy person or to persuade a talkative respondent to speak more economically. Good questions can even help someone think in new ways about a topic. At their best, interview questions can be essential in producing truly wonderful interviews. At their worst, interview questions can confuse people or disabuse them of any notions they may have had of the importance of the study. The interviewer's questions do not always appear in research publications, but they are objects of concern at nearly every stage of a study. This section considers key aspects of the design and use of interview questions.

Interview Schedules and Interview Guides

Two types of instrument—interview schedules and interview guides—are used by qualitative researchers to prepare for interviews. The *interview schedule* is the more formal of the two. It is used when a project requires uniformity in the wording and sequencing of the questions (Gorden, 1969, p. 264; Patton, 1990, pp. 284-287). The point of the interview schedule is to ensure that all interviewees hear roughly the same questions in the same way—although spontaneous follow-up probes are usually allowed in order to clarify remarks or to ask for elaboration. Interview schedules are best-suited for qualitative studies that call for a more structured approach, such as respondent and focus group studies. Interview schedules are also used to train interviewers who will work in separate locations under minimal supervision. In the view of some researchers, the use of an interview schedule is one way to increase the reliability and credibility of data.

A more informal, flexible approach is offered in the *interview guide*. Interview guides simply consist of groupings of topics and questions that the interviewer can ask in different ways for different participants. There may be a preferred order for asking the questions, but the interview guide does not dictate that order. Nor does the guide dictate how the questions will be asked, because the social dynamics of interviewing change from one participant and context to the next. With an interview guide, the researcher enjoys the freedom to ask optional questions or to go down an unexpected conversational path. Especially when it comes to informants whose experiences and expertise may vary widely, the interviewer can reshuffle topics and questions in order to find the best fit. Interview guides also allow the researcher to adjust to the verbal style of the participant. Questions can be rephrased, broken up into smaller question units, or altered in other ways in order to achieve the goals set out by the researcher.

The difference between the two instruments can be stated this way: "The interview schedule . . . emphasizes the means of obtaining information, [whereas] the interview guide emphasizes the *goals* of the interview in terms of the topics to be explored and the criteria of a relevant and adequate response" (Gorden, 1969, pp. 264-265). In other words, an interview guide allows multiple means to achieve a study's goals, whereas an interview schedule stresses standardization of the method.

In actual practice, interviews often incorporate aspects of both types of instrument. Tom's guide for interviewing members of the "field crisis team," who were recruited from the world of presidential politics to coordinate the openings of the controversial film *The Last Temptation of Christ* (LTC), is shown in Figure 6.2. Not all of the questions were relevant to each respondent, and the questions were sometimes asked in different ways. Yet it resembles an interview schedule in that the questions were usually asked in the order shown.

Nondirective Questions

The last thing that we as researchers want our participants to do is to tell us their experience in terms that they think we want to hear. Thus, general nondirective questions work best at the start of an interview, as well as during many points throughout.

A common nondirective question is the *grand tour question*, which is used to understand how an activity or event usually transpires from start to finish or how a social setting is organized. As the term implies, the interviewer goes

I. Beginnings of Assignment

Please describe your experience in politics and campaign advance work up through summer 1988—and any other experiences relevant to working on the openings of the movie *The Last Temptation of Christ* (LTC).

How did your involvement with LTC begin? What were the specific circumstances?
Did you know anything about LTC beforehand? For example, had you heard of the book?
What were your prior associations with [person #1] and [person #2]?
What do you remember of the orientation in Los Angeles? Please give as much detail as possible.
For example: What did the representatives of Universal Pictures say they wanted the field crisis team to do? What instructions were you given about your role? How were you to handle yourself?
Why would a motion picture company bring political advance people into a project like this?
What professional skills and experiences are most useful in such a situation?
In what ways did your work on LTC differ from other kinds of political advance work?

II. Operational Details

What cities or markets did you work?
Were you matched with these cities or markets for particular reasons that you know of?
Did you do all of them yourself, or did you ever work with a partner?
Describe in kind of a grand tour, from start to finish, how you did a LTC opening.
Did you know what to expect of an opening before you arrived? Was any intelligence done, by you or by [person #1] or [person #2]?
What are your recollections of the security for LTC? Of [security firm name]? Of off-duty cops? Describe the specific security procedures that were used.
Was there anything about the physical aspects of the theaters that was important to your work?
For example: Did you need to find an area for the protesters? Were there shopping mall issues?

What were your involvements with the local news media?

Did you assist the news media in getting good pictures?

Before LTC opened, did you arrange special screenings of the movie (for example, for clergy or religious leaders)? Did you try in any way to generate interest in the movie?

Were there any incidents of disruption, threat, physical injury, or property damage?

How did you communicate with [person #1] or Universal while you were on the road?

Did you have any contact with Universal's field offices?

III. Experiences at the Scene

How would you characterize the people who came out to protest?

What specific details of protester behavior stood out for you?

Did you talk with the protesters? How did you relate to them?

What were your personal reactions to the behavior at the movie openings?

Were there any times at which you were fearful, astonished, amused, enlightened? Were "counter-protesters" at any of the openings?

Did you observe the audiences during showings of LTC?

How would you characterize the theater management and staff—their level of concern, their understanding of the situation, other aspects. Did they understand and/or appreciate your role?

Were you in touch with fellow crisis team members while you were on the road?

If so, did you share experiences?

IV. Closing Questions

What did you think of the movie and the controversy?

Anything else that was notable or interesting to YOU about this experience?

Figure 6.2   LTC Field Crisis Team Interview Guide

---

along on a tour through the word-pictures painted by the participant. Of course, it should be well within the ability of the participant to serve as a tour guide. The participant "educates" the researcher by pointing out the key features—the routines, rituals, procedures, dramatis personae, cycles of group activity, socialization paths, and so forth. The grand tour may also be embellished with telling incidents or brief histories. Indeed, participants may need an entire interview session to finish the tour.

By asking many people the same tour question, researchers may end up hearing basically the same story. But they could also notice differences that are worth following up. These variations on the root tour may reflect differences between generational cohorts, organizational roles, or social standings. The researcher can also ask *mini-tour questions* that go into more depth about parts of the larger activity. Figure 6.3 illustrates the use of a grand tour question—about *The Last Temptation of Christ* field crisis team routine—that then led to a mini-tour question about one of its components. Another view of the activity is provided by the *memorable-tour question*, in which the participant is asked to recount a first experience or a turning-point experience.

If stories are told too quickly or too vaguely, the researcher can try to slow the pace and seek more detail with brief probes like "Tell me how *that* happened" and "And why did you think that?" Sometimes, all it takes is one word like "How?" or "Why?" If the researcher knows about the topic the participants are addressing, some of this information can be used to prompt them to recall more. One can "ask" for details by softly repeating a phrase just spoken by the participant. Repeating a phrase can signal that the interviewer didn't understand completely or would like to hear more. The last question and answer in Figure 6.4 shows this tactic at work. Also, participants usually read the interviewer's facial expressions as they talk, and even a subtle nonverbal sign by the researcher, such as raised eyebrows, can tell them that what they are saying is surprising or not well understood. The key to the use of probes is asking them as unobtrusively as possible.

Grand tours are often temporally grounded, but a more focused way to explore this dimension is the *time-line question* approach (Shields & Dervin, 1993). Here, the participant discusses events on a line moving from some point in the past to a point closer to the present. This kind of questioning is well-suited to studies of the participant's biographical self or the history of a social collective.

Example questions and *experience questions* (Spradley, 1980, p. 80) are also nondirective methods for going deeper into the participant's world. Example questions, of course, ask for an example of, or a case-in-point for, something. In soliciting examples, it is helpful to know whether the example given by the participant is a representative one, the most vivid one, the most influential one, or simply the first one that came to mind. Whereas example questions elicit a case-in-point, experience questions encourage the speaker to go into an incident at greater length and in highly personal, first-person terms.

Excerpt I: Grand Tour and Mini-Tour Questions

Tom Lindlof:	When you would arrive at a city, what are some of the first things you would do?
Respondent:	Well, let's see. Certainly I would meet with the theater owner. In different cases, they were more or less concerned. In some cases, they were very frightened about what was going to happen to the theater and so on. I would meet with the security folks, usually with the local police department, and any other law enforcement. Then I would reach out and sort of be in contact with religious leaders in the city and invite them to come see the movie if they wished. If there was a lot of interest, we might talk at least about setting up a special screening—you know, why don't you come and visit the theater for a showing. I would pretty much basically say, Whether you're thinking it's a good film or a bad film, or positive portrayal or negative portrayal, folks, we'd really like you to see it. Then, no matter what you say, you're saying it based on having seen the movie. And then after people came, if they really wanted to talk to the media—especially on opening night, I'd try to make sure they had ample opportunity to do that. I have to confess I was not hugely aggressive about doing that. Folks back in LA thought that would be a good thing to do, but they never really came out and said, you gotta, you gotta.
TL:	How would you identify these religious leaders when you got into a city?
R:	There's a variety of different ways. You know, a combination of the phone book, people that I might know in the city already. I think I called a university's chaplain, campus folks—usually if you find one religious leader, you can pretty much locate others by networking out. And usually, I'd say 75% of the clergy contacted [came]—and I think I would also invite mayors and city councilmen and people like that as well.

Figure 6.3   LTC Field Crisis Team Interview

Excerpt II: Experience and Compare-Contrast Questions

Tom Lindlof: I kind of wonder whether you, as the field crisis person, were asked hard questions about the movie or about Universal, as the sponsor of this so-called blasphemous movie.

Respondent: Certainly. I mean, not necessarily by the clergy that I was reaching out to, but certainly the protesters themselves were highly emotional, highly confrontational. I was cursed at, questioned vigorously at length—Why are you doing this? Aren't you afraid of going to Hell?

TL: Was it any worse than what you had experienced on the campaign trail?

R: It was more intense. Definitely more intense. There were cases where people were very, very confrontational. Montreal was very peaceful. When I went to Jacksonville, Florida, and Chattanooga, Tennessee, and Atlanta, there I had a real—a highly agitated, very, very aggressive crowd. There was shouting from the crowd, hostile pickets, to put it mildly. We had, in Atlanta, an upscale mall in Buckhead [R speaking softly, almost inaudible], an incident in which a deranged man showed up, handing out neo-Nazi literature. Mall store owners were panic-stricken and called the police, who arrested him.

TL: And he was doing that because the film was there?

R: Yeah. The film was definitely a magnet for all kinds of fringe people. [Named city] was a *very* large protest. The theater was in a mall, but the theater entrance faced out onto the parking lot itself. Very big parking lot out front. And the parking lot was completely filled with protesters every single day. Almost a church revival type of atmosphere. A flatbed truck, full tractor-trailer size, was pulled up to the theater. That was used as a stage. Ministers preaching almost continuously, on and off music. *Lot* of media coverage. Local media coverage, very heavy. You know, *lots* of church groups, other civic organizations, and the Ku Klux Klan.

TL: The Ku Klux Klan?

R: I think their name, their chapter in that area is the [named group], I think. And they were there in full regalia, mostly young guys. A lot of them wearing camouflage, boots, and they have their T-shirts with [name of group] insignia.

Figure 6.4   LTC Field Crisis Team Interview

Tom's first question in Figure 6.4 was intended to ask the respondent for her experience. However, she answered with a few brief examples rather than with the fully fleshed-out experiences that he wanted. The problem here was the interviewer's. He did not communicate what he wanted clearly enough. Questions that ask (usually unintentionally) for yes or no answers do not engage the participant as much as those that presume the respondent had the experience. The question should have been phrased differently: "Tell me about any tough questions you were asked about the movie or about Universal, being the sponsor of this so-called blasphemous movie." Reading transcriptions to see how one asked questions—or didn't ask questions that should have been asked—is always a humbling but instructive exercise.

Social actors' understandings of *motive* are central to many Communication studies. Often, the participant will volunteer ideas about motive in order to justify or excuse the actions of persons mentioned in a story. The question of motive may resolve itself as the interview goes on and the researcher listens to different sides of an issue. However, if it is not brought up, the interviewer may want to probe specifically for the motives of social actors (e.g., by asking "What were you trying to accomplish?" and "Why do you think she said that?"). Motive can be a sensitive subject because it sometimes implies blame or second-guessing, so it should be inquired after with care.

Photo-elicitation interviews (Curry, 1986) employ visual materials, typically photographs, to trigger comments about concrete aspects of a cultural scene. Two lines of questioning seem to be most useful in photo-elicitation work: (1) descriptive questions about what objects (or people) are represented in the picture, what they are called, what the purpose of the activity is, and so on; and (2) questions that use the pictures as a point of departure to ask about the processes, activities, and motives that are not literally represented in the images (Caldarola, 1985). The use of photographs, or other projective devices, can be an effective and enjoyable way of working with participants.

A follow-up question to the grand tour is what Schatzman and Strauss (1973) call *posing the ideal*. Participants are asked to speculate about an ideal state of affairs or goals for their group or organization. Or, the researcher may suggest an ideal—"which pushes an observed process or role to its logical and desired extreme" (p. 81)—and ask participants what they think of it. The tactic can sometimes help participants express deeply held beliefs or ideological leanings. It is a bit more structured than most nondirective questions, but it still gives the participants space to define their own ideas and solutions.

Finally, *native-language questions* (Spradley, 1980, pp. 89-90) encourage social actors to talk about the distinctive language and terms they use in everyday routines. Interviewers generally want to know the meanings of terms, how they were learned, who uses them, and in what contexts they are used. The respondent's reference to "fringe people" in the excerpt in Figure 6.4 was expanded first by discussing the Ku Klux Klan incident and later in the interview with other examples. It can be very illuminating to ask several people how they define the same term; for example: "I've heard the term 'countdown meeting' used by several advance people. Have you heard this term before? What does it mean to you?"

Directive Questions

Nondirective questions are the preferred way to help people talk freely about themselves and their scene. However, there are also reasons to ask questions in a more directive way. *Structural questions* (Spradley, 1980) are used to discover "how informants [organize] their knowledge" (p. 60). For example, by asking the question "How do the managers here deliver 'bad news' to their employees?" the interviewer defines the referent ("bad news") and the relationship (managers delivering it to employees). Presumably this question comes after a series of nondirective questions about the person's role in the organization and what the concept of bad news means. By asking several people the same question, the researcher may be on the way to developing a typology of bad news delivery methods.

A *compare-contrast question* calls on the participant to think of a concept in terms of contrastive (or comparative) experiences or situations. The second question in Figure 6.4 intends to contrast the respondent's work on *The Last Temptation of Christ* movie opening with her experience in advance work in political campaigns. There is a lot left unsaid in the question, but both Tom and the respondent understood from the previous exchange that "hostility" was the referent. What this line of questioning should yield is a finer discrimination of meanings in a person's experience.

Floating an *emergent idea*, and asking participants for their thoughts about the idea, is another technique that builds structure into the question. For example, one could say to a company employee: "I've heard that the top executives here usually begin a 'bad news' talk by saying they have no choice but to do some difficult things in the best interests of the company. Is that the way these talks usually begin? Would you say that's your experience, too?" The interviewee would then voice a viewpoint and cite situations that confirm, refute, or qualify the researcher's emergent idea. Using this approach, much can be learned about what is right or wrong—from the social actor's perspective—with an analytic claim in the making. We emphasize the importance, however, of presenting this claim as tentative, not definitive.

Devil's advocate questions—in which one proposes a view that is unpopular, untrue, or counterintuitive—is another method for prompting participants to respond to an emergent idea. They are particularly useful in eliciting talk about basic assumptions and beliefs. However, there is a tone of confrontation to the devil's advocate question that might produce a defensive or angry reaction. Accordingly, these questions should be used, if they are used at all, only after a good—and spirited—rapport has been established between the researcher and the participant.

Closing Questions

As a rule, *sensitive questions* of a personal or political nature are best left for later in the interview. Not only do researchers want to take some time to develop trust, they may also need to hear the participant speak to several other issues before deciding whether the questions really are justified. This "rule" could be unnecessary if at the beginning of the interview both parties are fully aware of the kinds of subjects that need to be covered. The communicative compatibility between the interviewer and interviewee, such as occurs when women interview women (Finch, 1984), can also lead to intimate discussions sooner than later.

Near the end of the interview, time should be set aside for *loose-ends questions*. These questions usually occur to the researcher during the course of the interview but aren't asked immediately so as not to disrupt the flow of the talk or deviate from the planned order of questions. Loose-ends questions are often prompted by surprising or intriguing remarks, and the researcher may preface such questions by saying "Now, I'd like to ask about something you said earlier" or "I didn't get a chance to ask you this earlier, but I was surprised when you mentioned that. . . ." The researcher should also invite the participant to ask questions or raise issues: "Is there anything we've missed that would be important for me to know?" This is a chance for the interviewee to fill in or clarify, suggest a new area of discussion, or "set the record straight" before the interviewer leaves. If the person is unable to finish then, arrangements can be made to continue in another interview, or by phone or e-mail.

Ideally, these strategies produce a complete and successful interview. Still, however, we note the conventional wisdom among qualitative researchers that the endings of interviews can be surprising and revealing. More than one researcher has discovered that subjects do not necessarily acknowledge the "official" termination of an interview. In a few cases, this is due to researchers' ambiguous closings or to subjects' insensitivity at reading social cues. In most cases, however, this happens because subjects are excited by the interaction and wish to continue. As a result, even when researchers faithfully use loose-ends questions, they should remain attentive to subjects' parting comments and stories, no matter how innocuous or conventional such comments may initially seem. Viewed in retrospect, these contributions may confirm researchers' impressions of how the interview went or reveal something that was transpiring (or still unfolding). In this way, qualitative researchers—along with therapists—apply a famous piece of baseball wisdom to the work of interviewing: "It ain't over 'til it's over."

Transcribing Interviews

Someday, probably soon, voice recognition software will have advanced to the point that computers can be "trained" to recognize and record any number of voices. Until that day of liberation comes, humans must transcribe their interview tapes manually. One way to do this is to simply manipulate a tape recorder. Each brief pass of the tape requires several buttons (play, stop, rewind) to be hit in succession, over and over again—a tedious procedure that tries the patience of anyone who does it for very long.

A far better option is to use transcribing machines that feature foot pedal controls for moving the tape back and forth, thus freeing one's hands to enter text at a keyboard. Machine-aided transcribing significantly reduces the time and frustration of doing this job. Some people can produce a transcript of a 60-minute interview in two to three hours, depending on their skill level and the quality of the recording.

However, even with transcriber machines, the task requires full concentration to do it right. An utterance of moderate length—this sentence, for example—can take two passes to transcribe accurately. Many other utterances are not only longer and more complicated, they are also sometimes unclear. The person might speak too quickly or too softly. The speaker may lean back for a few moments, out of range of the microphone's pick-up. Familiar words might be pronounced quirkily. Two or more speakers might talk at once (which is very common in focus groups), producing several seconds of cacophony. Playing back the problematic section a few times can help to resolve these problems. Some of us have a rule for the number of times we play back a section before we give up on it; for Bryan and Tom, five times is usually the limit. One tactic that works well is to study the semantic and syntactic contexts in which the unintelligible part occurs and try to guess the word or phrase that should fit in that slot. Unfortunately, we sometimes have to let it go untranscribed if its meaning won't come clear.

One decision faced by researchers is whether to transcribe the interviews themselves or hire someone to do it for them. One clear advantage of doing it yourself is that the participants are already known to the researcher, and thus it is easier to recognize their speech patterns, references to people and places, and so forth. Transcribing also allows the researcher to listen to the interview in a more studied way. One can attend more closely to the conversation and pick up certain themes, issues, or contradictions that may not have been noticed in real time. Thus transcribing can serve as a portal to the process of data analysis.

On the other hand, researchers can save much valuable time by outsourcing this work to professional transcribers. (In addition to inquiring about rates, one would be well-advised to inquire about the transcriber's experience and references.) If the sample of interviews is large, there may be no other realistic option but for the researcher to engage a professional's services. Professional transcribers might produce high quality work, but the transcriptions should still be read and corrected by the researcher, especially for names, special terms, and so forth. When researchers have their work professionally transcribed, they are at least partly alienated from the transcription. They encounter it as an unfamiliar product of another's labor, rather than as a familiar record of their own interpretive activities. Our point here is not Marxist but pragmatic: A gain in efficiency is balanced by the loss of intimate understanding that can only be created by hearing—and typing—voices.

While professional transcriber costs can be high, there are strategies for managing this cost against the requirements of the project. For example, a professional might be hired for the tapes that must be transcribed in full; for the others, the researcher may transcribe selected excerpts or write a summary of the topics discussed.

Stylistic matters also call for decisions by the researcher. Notations are sometimes used to indicate aspects of speech behavior. Although the notations used by conversation analysts can be precise and extensive, those used by interpretive scholars tend to be more minimal, as in this set used by Boje (1991, p. 112):

//   Overlapping talk from the first to the last slash.

. . .   A pause of one second or less within an utterance.

(2.0)   A pause of more than one second within an utterance or between turns, the
number indicates the length of the pause.

***   A deletion.

[ ]   An explanatory insertion.

Italics A word or part of a word emphasized by a speaker.

Researchers also decide what level of editing is appropriate. Though some do very little editing, most researchers make some concession to the fact that speech, transcribed literally, is a very messy affair. Editing may mean, for example, taking out a broken start to a sentence, or a stutter in mid-sentence, in order to have a "cleaner" sentence in print. Editing locutions is also common practice. If a person actually says "gonna," for example, we might type it up as "going to," because "gonna" connotes aspects of class and education that might be deemed undesirable. Such minor editing does not usually affect the substance of what was said or cheat speakers of what they meant to say. This level of editing is what DeVault (1990) means when she comments:

> The purpose of editing is to cast talk into a form which is easier to read—and more compelling—than raw interview documents, which are often lengthy, rambling, repetitive, and/or confusing. Another rationale emphasizes the redundancy of talk: the researcher should include only as much detail as needed to illustrate the analytic points to be made. (p. 107)

However, there is another level of editing that does potentially alter participants' meanings. Editing in this sense can involve changes to the represented speech so that it conforms to a standard of grammatical talk. For example, if we polish the patois of American middle-class teenagers—removing the instances of "like" and "you know" and cutting out profanities—are we not also changing meanings of their expressive culture? The kindest interpretation of this sort of editing is that we are trying to make the content of the speech more accessible. Less charitably—and more truthfully—we are performing unlicensed surgery on the participants' culture and identity.

The line between minor editing for the sake of clarity and editing that does some damage to the people involved, and the original social situation, is not always clear. One could argue, for example, that even a broken sentence can reveal something of interest about a person's emotional state at the time. One could also argue for leaving out sentence fragments unless they are integral to understanding the speaker or the dialogue as a whole. Distinctive speech styles are usually vital to the purposes of qualitative studies and ought to be represented accurately. However, it is best to avoid privileging one speech style over another, especially in studies of less powerful minority cultural groups, so as to not perpetuate stereotypes. Consistency in the use of one particular approach to editing should be observed throughout transcription.

Conclusion

Interviewing is a special experience. It is not special because it is rare; interviews, in fact, happen all the time. Interviews are special because participants can be themselves for the benefit of someone whom they barely know. It is an occasion set apart from the webs of status, rank, and obligation that normally enmesh us all. It is a time and place for dialogue to flourish. This dialogue is an achievement of two (or more) people who take their play seriously.

In addition, the practice of interviewing calls for researchers to reflect on their role and identity. The role of the inteviewer may not be as far from that of the participant observer as the separation of chapters in this book might suggest. Through the participant self the interviewer can be in something of an authentic relationship with another person. The interviewer also learns to hear new languages, some of which is the language of the interview situation, and some of which are dialogues drifting in from remembrances of other lived experiences. As an observer, the researcher uses the goals of the "project" to inform her or his decisions about what to ask and how to respond and when to listen; through this observational self the interviewer can be in a theoretic relationship with the spoken discourse.

Exercises

1. Conduct an interview with one of the participants in your study. Then, write a *reflective analysis* in which you discuss:

- What kind of interview it was (ethnographic, informant, respondent, narrative, focus group)—and why you chose this approach with this interviewee
- The interview process, including (but not limited to) the time, setting, and recording apparatus of the interview and how they influenced the interaction; the ongoing rapport between you and the interviewee; the flow of the conversation; revelatory incidents before or after the interview proper
- Aspects of the dialogue or the entire interview event that you found particularly interesting and/or worthy of further inquiry (Although it is not required, a transcription of the interview can be helpful for writing this part of the reflective analysis.)

2. As we noted in this chapter, it can be quite illuminating to read the transcription (or listen to the tape) of an interview and critique one's own performance in the interviewer role. Questions that might be useful in carrying out a critique—with the goal of improving future performance— include (but are certainly not limited to):

- How would you characterize your style? Active or passive? Affirming or skeptical? Open or guarded? And so on.
- Did you encourage the interviewee to expand on his or her ideas, stories, and accounts?
- Were there points when a follow-up question should have been asked but wasn't?
- Did you allow the interviewee a chance to finish what she or he was saying?
- How did you respond to any interest the interviewee showed in you?

7

Qualitative Analysis and Interpretation

In the previous chapters, we introduced the methods for studying communication practices and performances. Through the interplay of question asking and the practice of field method, researchers create *data*: textual, aural, and/or visual records of the object and process of research activity. After they have collected data, researchers begin to key in on a new question: What does it all mean? Or to ask it in a way that reflects what the researcher actually does: What can I make it mean? The researcher *interacts with* data on the page or the computer screen and tries to make conceptual sense of these layers upon layers of discourse and social action.

The researcher has reached the analysis and interpretation phase of the project—a phase that will extend far into the writing of the report. The sheer amount of data that must be dealt with is one challenge of this new phase, but there are other challenges at least as daunting. A second challenge is that the findings of any qualitative study can be given multiple plausible interpretations. Alter any aspect of the researcher—personality, value system, culture, or theoretical orientation—and the account of observed events will also shift prismatically (Heider, 1988). Thus, one always faces the challenge of determining how to look at data in a way that yields the most interesting and insightful view. A third challenge is that the research problem may not even be known until the data analysis is well along. Qualitative research is a journey powered by the researcher's own growth of interpretive competence, and concepts and claims usually come into focus only after a long period of study in the field. A fourth challenge is that a study must speak to (or with) two primary "audiences" before reaching its ultimate readership. The interpretation must not only be true to the localized meaning constructions of the scene under study but also engage with one or more fields of Communication. The research community—represented by its literature, theories, and styles of articulation—is always a silent partner at the table where interpretive work is done.

Finally, there is the challenge of acquiring skills in qualitative analysis. Until recently, novices had to contend with a scarcity of good sources about coding, inference, and validation. Even today, the methods sections of articles can be of little help in decoding the mystery. Authors sometimes tell us that their themes emerged after close, repeated readings of their data. But why these themes, and not others, "emerged," and how the process of emergence is started and controlled, are matters about which readers are often forced to speculate. Some authors take an individualistic, "I-did-it-my-way" stance in discussing their methods. Others may dismiss the need for a "methods section" as a positivist relic. The published narrative may be compelling on its own terms, and perhaps in some authors' view this is the best proof that the analysis was appropriate.

Admittedly, there is some truth to the image of interpretation as a self-customized and intuitive endeavor. It is true that most researchers use data in ways that are suited to their own sense of what looks and feels right. Many of them report, usually privately, that there are moments when they feel the surge of discovering the pieces finally falling into place. They suddenly are able to conceptualize something important about the notes that they have been pondering for weeks. Even if the subconscious mind is involved in these breakthrough moments, it is probably because the researcher has already done the hard, deliberate work of coding and categorizing data.

Fortunately, the last two decades have seen advances in making qualitative analysis procedures more explicit and trustworthy. This in no way negates the role of serendipidity in the process. One of the principal strengths of qualitative research remains its blend of strategy and unexpected discovery.

This chapter develops a framework for learning how to make sense of qualitative materials. The framework consists of two processes: analysis and interpretation. *Analysis* is the process of labeling and breaking down (or decontextualizing) raw data and reconstituting them into patterns, themes, concepts, and propositions. Researchers use analytic tools and procedures to manipulate data so that they will be more useful for the move into interpretation. *Interpretation* is the process of "[making] a construal"

(Spiggle, 1994, p. 492). Theory and experience come together in the writing of an interpretive claim. In reality, analysis and interpretation join together in a larger process of explicating meaning. But for the sake of clarity, we describe them as two phases that overlap between the field and the write-up. The chapter ends with an overview of methods for validating the interpretation.

Analysis

During data analysis the qualitative researcher hopes to make progress on three fronts: *data management, data reduction,* and *conceptual development.* Gaining some control over data that tend to grow rapidly is the goal of *data management.* Without tools for categorizing, sorting, and retrieving data, the job of finding one's way around these materials would be a forbidding prospect indeed. Codes enable the researcher to locate specific data, and computer software offers even greater control for organizing records, managing files, and so on.

The researcher will also recognize at some point—probably midway through the project, if not before—that not all of the material will be used. Some data will be truly critical for making sense of the research problem, whereas other data may be used to add nuance to the write-up, and the rest—maybe even the largest part of the data—may not be used at all in any direct sense. *Data reduction,* then, means that the use-value of data is prioritized according to emerging schemes of interpretation. This does not mean that data should be thrown away (one never knows when unused data will be needed for another purpose). Instead, data are "reduced" by categories and codes that put the researcher in touch with only those parts of the material that count toward his or her claims.

Finally, data analysis serves the goal of *conceptual development.* Concepts and themes grow profusely early in a project. Later, their numbers may be pruned back, but the links among them grow more dense and elaborate. Thus, analytic tools are used to shape the data in a way that is informed by theory but also grounded in a particular culture or social scene.

Early Analysis: Asides, Commentaries, and In-Process Memos

Informal data analysis starts at the very moment that fieldnotes, interview transcriptions, or document notes are created. At least one hard copy and one electronic copy of these records should be set aside as an archive. It is often helpful to periodically read the archive all the way through. This kind of reading can help the researcher review aspects of certain cases, think about strategic changes in the project, jump-start the coding process, and gain a sense of how the different narratives of the research corpus are taking shape.

In the earliest stage of analysis, the researcher reflects on the events and discourses that make up these descriptive records. This reflective thinking is channeled into "in-process analytic writing," especially the forms that Emerson and colleagues (1995) call *asides, commentaries,* and *in-process memos.* We will deal first with asides and commentaries.

Asides are "brief, reflective bits of analytic writing that succinctly clarify, explain, interpret, or raise questions about some specific happening or process described in a fieldnote" (Emerson et al., 1995, p. 101); they are usually inserted within parentheses or brackets in the fieldnote record. A *commentary* is "a more elaborate reflection on some specific event or issue; it is contained in a separate paragraph and set off with parentheses" (p. 102). A commentary, then, is simply a longer, more elaborated version of the aside. Both asides and commentaries can be inserted in interview transcriptions as well as in fieldnotes.

Asides and commentaries are composed in a relatively free-form style. They range across several areas of concern: the motives of persons depicted in the scenes; the meanings of artifacts; concepts that seem to capture what is happening in the scene; the efficacy of methods; the author's own emotions, thoughts, or understandings of his or her self and/or role in the field. In addition, researchers use these opportunities to remark on compelling incidents, sequences of action that seem to repeat in certain settings, and other details that inform the researcher's understanding. In-process writings can be of great help when it is time to code and categorize data.

Below is a sample of Stephen Haggerty's fieldnotes and embedded asides. (They are a bit too brief to be called commentaries, despite the fact they were formatted as separate paragraphs.) The scene is a training session for new car salespeople led by Skip, a professional trainer. Stephen tagged his asides with "O.C.," which means "observer's comments."

Again and again Skip made David say the words, "I want you to know that I am here to get the deal you want." He said that repetition is the key, that we have to know the script when we get on the lot, and without a script, we weren't going to sell any cars. Skip talked at length about the notion that delivering an effective question will demand an effective response. He made it crystal clear that you can't give up, that in order to sell as many cars as Steve [the owner of the dealership] wanted them to, they had to qualify the customer.

(O.C.: I found out later that the main thrust of the training session that day was on just qualifying, so they invited me back on the 16th of March for the final training session. It is interesting to note here that Skip told me later that he gets paid a lot of money for this, and that I was "lucky, because you're gettin' this for free, son.")

Skip started to role play with another person, and as he did, he again reminded the trainees (as well as myself) that repetition is the key. Another very important phrase to learn—Skip called them "word tracks," or short statements—is "I understand." Skip said you want to make sure the customer thinks he is the one who is the owner of all of the ideas in the conversation. At this point I noticed a mirror at the back of the break room with a sign above it: "Would you buy a car from this person?"

(O.C: The concept of personal responsibility to the customer and to the dealership rang clearly here as it would throughout the course of my brief interaction with Skip and the other eight people in the room.)

(Courtesy of Stephen Haggerty)

Part of the first O.C./aside refers to some information about the goals of that day's session and an invitation to attend a future training session. The other part of the first O.C./aside quotes Skip about the researcher getting this sales training for free—which says something of potential interest about Skip and the researcher's relationships with him and with the car dealer. The second O.C./aside is about what is going on in the scene at a more conceptual level and was triggered by the fieldnote passage that precedes it.

It is important to know that in-process notes are tentative and only a snapshot of what the researcher finds interesting about the current state of the research. The notions that are freeze-framed in asides may in fact be changed profoundly by later experiences in the field or further turns of analytic writing. Asides and commentaries can be computer-coded so that later they can be pulled out of their fieldnote or interview contexts. They can also be "source-tagged" so that they can be traced back to the original context.

The third kind of in-process analytic writing—the in-process memo—is not tied to any particular fieldnote or interview. Rather, in-process memos are "products of more sustained analytic writing and require a more extended time-out from actively composing fieldnotes" (Emerson et al., 1995, p. 103). Memos may be inspired by an aside or commentary, but in memos the researcher develops a much more detailed interpretation than in those other kinds of writing. In-process writing focuses on a theme or issue found in several incidents pulled together from fieldnotes and transcriptions.

Like fieldnotes, memos are meant for musing about the larger meanings of the research experience. However, the analyst "clearly envisions outside audiences and frames his [or her] thoughts and experiences in ways likely to interest them" (p. 103). Thus memos often advance claims that could hold up to the future scrutiny of others.

Coding and Categorization

The first systematic effort at data analysis usually comes with the creation of categories and a coding scheme. Researchers usually realize a need to categorize and code after a rich data set has begun to build up. A researcher might alternate a few weeks of intensive data collection with a week or two devoted to analysis—a rhythm of work that keeps the growth of data under control and keeps the analyst alert to the conceptual trajectory of the study. These time-outs, which are fully in tune with the cyclical model discussed at the beginning of Chapter 3, can be important episodes in the life of the project.

Other researchers do not engage in waves of data gathering and analysis but, instead, wait until all of the data are collected before starting to code. Or the researcher may simply prefer in-process writing as the best strategy for steering a project to completion. Either way of doing data analysis—during breaks in the fieldwork or all at once at the end—may result in a successful study.

Regardless of when they take place, categorization and coding are essential to making sense of qualitative data. *Categorization* refers to the process of characterizing the meaning of a unit of data with respect to certain generic properties. "The essence of categorization," writes Spiggle (1994, p. 493), "is identifying a chunk or unit of data (e.g., a passage of text of any length) as belonging to, representing, or being an example of some more general phenomenon." *Category*, then, is a covering term for an array of general phenomena: concepts, constructs, themes, and other types of "bins" in which to put items that are similar.

Researchers sometimes look to existing theory and research for categories and apply them to the data in deductive or *etic* fashion (see Chapter 3). The literature can be used to stimulate theoretical sensitivity to clues of meaning in the data, suggest questions that can be asked of the data, and act as a source of supplementary validation, among other things (Strauss & Corbin, 1990, pp. 50-53). For example, Steele (1999) used the four components of the Adolescents' Media Practice Model—identity work, selection, interaction, and application—to categorize her data (from focus groups, media journals, and room tours and/or interviews) about how teenagers use sexual media content in identity construction. Sass (2000), in his study of emotional labor in a nonprofit nursing home, reported, "[I] search[ed] my field notes for the types of performances that were indicated in the previous literature: task and personal rituals, and socialities of courtesy and privacy. . . . I found that episodes of courtesies and task rituals were prominent in my notes [but] personal rituals and privacy were not as useful for capturing emotional labor at Mercy" (p. 338). A priori theory can sensitize one to what *could* be important, but it should not override or overshadow the meanings that the researcher discovers in the scenes being studied.

Categories can also be derived from standard demographics (e.g., sex, race, occupation, religion, place of residence), institutional labels, and other "precoded" topics in wide public use (LeCompte & Schensul, 1999, pp. 58-62). For example, one might want to code all instances of a professional role (e.g., "manager") or an object (e.g., "cell phone"). These are low-inference categories because they denote things that are concrete and easily recognized. When dealing with these categories, we agree with Tesch's (1990) advice about paying more attention to the *topic* than the content of the text. The key question to be asked is "What is this *about?*" (p. 142).

Most often in qualitative research, a strong current of inductive thinking stimulates the development of categories; that is, a category begins to form only after the analyst has figured out a meaningful way to configure the data. These are high-inference categories, because they call for knowledge of cultural insider meanings or require the researcher to assimilate several pieces of evidence. High-inference categories are also called "fuzzy categories" due to a certain degree of ambiguity in their definition. Thus categories are seldom able to contain all of the excess (or contradictory) meanings of the incidents they are supposed to represent—although the more researchers work out the relationships between incident and category, the more likely they can reduce this ambiguity to a level that allows them to name and use the category.

In the first move of this inductive process, the analyst examines the data—usually in several sessions of close reading—and finds that several incidents (instances) in the data relate to each other in such a way that they seem to belong to a category. For example, the analyst might notice that when "manager" and "cell phone" are present in the same chunk of fieldnotes, it is usual to find that something else is going on—maybe "influence at a distance." But this is only a hunch; the analyst will need to keep looking through and thinking about the data. Organizational studies scholar Barry A. Turner (1988) explains how, in his own work, the categorization of data goes forward:

When I have accumulated several instances of a given theoretical category—from six to twelve, depending on the topic—I try to write very clear, formal theoretical definitions of the working category label which I have been using on that particular [file] card, aiming to produce a definition which would be self-explanatory to a newcomer to the research team. . . . In the process of specifying in abstract terms exactly what are the limits of the particular social category, what social phenomenon it refers to, and what it is *not*, the "sociological imagination" is stretched. (pp. 109-110)

This also happens to be a good description of how the "communication imagination" is stretched.

Codes are the linkages between the data and the categories posited by the researcher. As Charmaz (1983) puts it, "Codes . . . serve as shorthand devices to *label*, *separate*, *compile*, and *organize* data. Codes range from simple, concrete, and topical categories to more general, abstract conceptual categories for an emerging theory" (p. 111). In Charmaz's second sentence, however, we see a common confusion of category and code. Codes are not the same thing as categories. The core purpose of coding is to mark the units of text as they relate meaningfully to categories (concepts, themes, constructs).

In the very beginning of formal analysis, the analyst performs coding before he or she even knows what the final categories will be. This kind of coding—commonly known as "open coding," which will be defined and discussed below—is a creative act. Using pen, pencil, or highlighter, or computer mouse clicks, the analyst marks what seems to make cultural or theoretical sense. What that "sense" consists of may take more markings of text, more thought given to how and why they cohere as a group, and more attempts to craft a definition that "would be self-explanatory to a newcomer," as Turner put it.

In addition to their role as aids to category formation, codes carry out a more mechanical role as tools for sorting, retrieving, linking, and displaying data. Projects often end up with whole "families" of codes that help the analyst reach into diverse data sets for exactly what she or he is seeking. Although it would be an exaggeration to say that uncoded data are data that no longer exist to the analyst (out of code, out of mind?), it is more likely that the analyst will use only coded text once a project has swung into full analysis mode. Therefore, codes serve to mark the islands, archipelagos, and other land-masses of meaningful data from the surrounding sea of raw, uncoded data.

The widespread adoption of data analysis software has brought a new level of standardization to the use of codes. This development stands in sharp contrast to the days, not so long ago, when qualitative data analysis was more of a "mysterious, half-formulated art" (Miles, 1979, p. 593). Many researchers praise computer-aided coding as a symbol of the methodological progress of qualitative research, while others are wary of the constraints that the codes allegedly impose on a highly creative process. Yet, strategies for the analysis of qualitative data were being refined and widely shared even before the new software packages arrived on the scene. Researchers and students now enjoy the benefits of a plentiful literature on coding (e.g., Arnould & Wallendorf, 1994; Emerson et al., 1995; LeCompte & Schensul, 1999; Ryan & Bernard, 2000; Spiggle, 1994; Weston et al., 2001).

The growth of these sources means that researchers have more freedom than ever to choose a strategy that fits the form and assumptions of their data. Many Communication scholars seek types of analysis that will help them make sense of linguistic data such as narratives and life stories (e.g., Cortazzi, 2001; Mishler, 1986; Silverman, 2000). It has been suggested that coding stories as a first step "effectively annhilate[s] the possibility for the researcher to find out that there is such a thing as a story line or a 'narrative structure' in a life story, to be identified and perhaps later analyzed from . . . a social semiotics perspective" (Alasuutari, 1996, p. 373). Be that as it may, coding can still help analysts locate revealing moments in talk, stories, and other verbal texts. Let's look at one coding scheme for verbal exchanges—presented by H. L. Goodall, Jr. (2000, pp. 102-108)—that grows out of a cultural hermeneutics foundation.

The first move of Goodall's scheme begins with identifying a sample of talk with reference to a continuum of conversational forms, ranging from the most rule governed (phatic communication and ordinary conversation) to those that enact multiple constructions of meaning and identity (skilled conversation, personal narratives, and dialogue). The next move invokes the question of *what is going on* in the verbal exchange. Here, a series of questions is asked, using all of the resources available to the analyst. Each of the questions—*What is the frame or context? What is being said? How is it being spoken? Where are you in this scene?*—subsumes a number of specific questions. For example, nested within the question *How is it being spoken?* are these probes:

- What are the *rhythms*, the *vocal tones*, the *silences* contributing to the overall meanings? Where does the *storyline* come from? From personal history? From cultural myth? How is it gendered?
- What are the *life scripts* being invoked?
- What does it all add up to? What does it *mean*? (Goodall, 2000, p. 107)

Once the verbal text has been interrogated in this sensitive, reflexive fashion, and the results have been coded, the analyst can go on to the next move: Rendering the "*personal meanings* . . . which is a formal way of suggesting that *you* are isolating the key moments in the exchange and attributing special meaning to them" (p. 108). Among the devices that can be used to find the key moments are *rich points* (speech acts—such as jargon, slang, or ironic turns of phrase—in which cultural knowledge is expressed) and *turning points* (talk about critical decisions in an individual, a group, or an organization). The codings for a turning point (or rich point) are neither rote nor easy. Rather, analysts find that the act of making these moments sensible requires a good deal of interpretive writing (of which we will have more to say in the second half of this chapter). The earlier moves in Goodall's scheme build an analytic platform from which one can notice and explicate talk that is enriched with personal meaning.

Grounded Theory

One of the most influential models for coding qualitative data is the *grounded theory* approach, pioneered by Barney Glaser and Anselm Strauss (1967). This approach remains in wide use across all of the social sciences, including Communication. Turner (1988) even contends that "the qualitative researcher has no real alternative to pursuing something very close to grounded theory" (p. 112). Two features of grounded theory (or the *constant-comparative method*, as it is also known) are important: (1) Theory is grounded in the relationships between data and the categories into which they are coded; and (2) Codes and categories are mutable until late in the project, because the researcher is still in the field and data from new experiences continue to alter the scope and terms of his or her analytic framework.

Grounded theory has been expounded at length (see Charmaz, 2000; Glaser, 1978; Glaser & Strauss, 1967; Strauss, 1987; Strauss & Corbin, 1990), but a brief tour here should illuminate how it works in practice. We will punctuate this tour with examples from a study by Banks and colleagues (2000). These researchers set out to study the expression of identity in holiday letters—specifically, "the ways in which holiday letters manage the dialectics of contradictions between modernist sensibilities, desires, and selfhood, and the postmodern social conditions in which they are written" (p. 299). Although their study focused on documents (letters), the procedures they used do not differ much from those used in studies based on interviews or observations. We selected this article because its description of analytic steps is very clear and accessible to readers who wish to examine the process in more detail.

The first stage of the grounded theory approach involves coding as many categories as possible from the data. As we discussed earlier, some categories have their origins in the concepts and research literature that were brought into the project. But in the inductive spirit of qualitative study, much of the coding is devoted to generating categories from the researcher's own lived experiences in the scene—as these experiences were written in the research texts. One of the reasons why coding often starts so early is so that the analyst can respond with a fresh memory to the events depicted in the data. When a great deal of time passes before the coding is done, these events and their meanings may seem remote to the analyst.

Obviously this process of coding for all possible categories could go on indefinitely. What keeps the process under some control is the fact that the analyst is *comparing each incident to other incidents* in order to decide in which categories they belong. Thus when considering any new incident, the analyst compares it with incidents that have already been coded into categories. Each category's core properties are clarified by going back through the data many times. The total number of categories also begins to level out as most incidents are accounted for (although some may be uncategorizable for different reasons or simply stay uncoded due to their lack of relevance). Before long, as Glaser and Strauss (1967, p. 107) note, the analyst "starts thinking in terms of the full range of types or continua of the category, its dimensions, the conditions under which it is pronounced or minimized, its major consequences, its relations to other categories, and its other properties." As a result of this turbulent process, the analyst develops a sensibility informed by theory .

Two kinds of coding—*open coding* and *in vivo coding*—are prominent in this early stage. *Open coding* is the initial, unrestricted coding of data (Strauss, 1987, pp. 28-32). The analyst usually goes through the texts (fieldnotes, transcriptions, documents) line by line and marks those chunks of text that suggest a category. In fact, it is through the process of open coding that categories are built, are named, and have attributes ascribed to them. This stage of coding is "unrestricted" because the analyst has not yet decided the range of categories or how the categories are defined, and has also not yet unitized the coding procedure (i.e., decided what constitutes a textual unit). In other words, the analyst "categorize[s] a chunk of data on the basis of its coherent meaning—its standing on its own—not by an arbitrary designation of grammar" (Spiggle, 1994, p. 493). Thus the researcher can feel free to consider the meanings of words, phrases, sentences, and larger expressive or dialogical units on an equal basis. How the categories link to each other is also a matter that can be left for later. The goal of open coding, writes Strauss (1987), "is to *open up* the inquiry. Every interpretation at this point is tentative. . . . Whatever is wrong in interpreting those lines and words will eventually be cancelled out through later steps of the inquiry" (p. 29).

In vivo coding—terms used by the social actors themselves (recorded either from interviews or in situ conversation)—is done at the same time as open coding. Steven Haggerty's fieldnote/aside (on page 213), for example, reveals that "word tracks" is a term of persuasive discourse used in car sales circles, and "I understand" is one instance of word tracks that the student heard in the sales training setting. These instances of vivid language not only anchor conceptual categories, they also serve as category names and supply quotes for the research narrative.

At this point, a *codebook* is created. A *codebook* is "a tool for the development and evolution of a coding system and is an important means for documenting the codes and the procedures for applying them" (Weston et al., 2001, p. 395). Although a codebook can include the decision rules used by coders (alternatively, these rules can be written up in other research documents), its main purpose is to list all of the categories, the code names for each category, examples of each category, the number of incidents coded, and the location of each incident in the data records. (See LeCompte & Schensul, 1999, for variations on the design of codebooks.)

Figure 7.1 shows open coding categories 6 through 9 from the study "Constructing Personal Identities in Holiday Letters" by Banks and colleagues (2000). These categories constituted part of their codebook (codable units of meaning are called *tokens*). The authors stated that the task of labeling responded to several questions: "What appears to be the meaningfully cohesive topic unit? What does this unit of discourse describe or what is the subject described as doing? What is the underlying principle of this expression?" (p. 304). In all, they generated 80 categories through open coding from the pool of 128 holiday letters.

Often during this first stage, the analyst writes one or more *theoretical memos* that serve to flesh out the thematic qualities of the coding categories, or how their meanings shift across time, social actors, or other dimensions. The analyst may draft many memos as the analysis proceeds, and later versions may be so incisive and richly detailed that they can be used in the final write-up. Like fieldnotes, memos based on theory are closely held by the researcher, and the forms they take reflect the diverse working styles of practitioners.

The next two stages of the grounded theory approach are called *integration* and *dimensionalization*. These processes are ways of reshaping the categories and producing deeper meanings for them. The process of integrating categories starts with what is called *axial coding*—using codes that make connections between categories and thus result in the creation of either new categories or a theme that spans many categories. Axial coding tends to act on a category in several specific ways: "The [*causal*] conditions that give

Category Number and Description	Example	Tokens in Category
6. Stories of children's clever actions	"One night with a mysterious smirk On his face, he chirped, 'Hey Papa, Guess what! You're a real NERD (an effective pause) yeah, a Never-Ending-Radical-Dude.'" [#114]	3
7. Explicit statement of pride in family member	"He did an excellent job defending his thesis on December 3. I am really proud of him." [#28]	2
8. Adventures described as exciting or especially interesting	"THE GREAT ALASKA ADVENTURE" [Heading of section in letter #79]	34
9. You (reader) would be amazed by my (writer) religious experience	"My prayer every day is that each of us in every family, will choose to allow Him to demonstrate His wonderful love and power, and that He will give each a miracle or two for us to base our faith upon, if that is our need—as it was mine." [#120]	3

Source: Banks, S. P., Louie, E., & Einerson, M. (2000). Constructing personal identities in holiday letters. *Journal of Social and Personal Relationships, 17,* 299-32

Figure 7.1   Open Coding Categories From Holiday Letters

rise to it; the *context* (its specific set of properties) in which it is embedded; the action/interactional *strategies* by which it is handled, managed, carried out; and the *consequences* of those strategies" (Strauss & Corbin, 1990, p. 97). In most cases, axial coding brings previously separate categories together under a principle of integration.

In the first wave of axial coding done by Banks and colleagues (2000), the 80 categories that arose from open coding were "collapsed" into 13 broader categories of holiday letter meanings. They did this by looking at the relationships between the categories via consultation with instances of the categories and tracing new "logics of association." The 13 categories were then interrogated with the aid of probes (e.g., "What is the relation between Positive News and Bad News?"; p. 313). These axial coding interrogations resulted in six "notional categories" that captured the core themes of the holiday letters: Achievement, Adventure, Interpersonal Linkages, Moral Character, Mundane News, and Time. Thus *integration* changes the nature of categories from mere collections of incidents into theoretical constructs. Even as one pushes the categories to higher levels of abstraction, the categories are still grounded in data.

The process of dimensionalization is one of the final steps in the process of coding, categorization, and conceptual development. According to Spiggle (1994), "dimensionalization involves identifying properties of categories and constructs. . . . Once a category has been defined, the analyst may explore its attributes or characteristics along continua or dimensions" (p. 494). When we do a dimensional analysis, we examine each construct— again by constant reference to the incidents that make up the construct— and try to tease out the key variations (dimensions).

Banks and colleagues (2000) found two dimensions running through all six notional categories: "connectedness" and "distinctiveness." The two dimensions of holiday letters display the same sort of dynamics as in a dialectical view of personal relationships: "Persons are connected with others only insofar as they can otherwise express individual agency; and they achieve distinction only to the extent that their actions have evaluative grounds in commonly held standards of worth, probity, style, and so forth" (pp. 317-318). For each notional category, the authors were able to describe the content of each dimension. For the category of Adventure, for example, connectedness was indicated by "personal ties with nature & place," and the dimension of distinctiveness was indicated by "unique exotic experience; individual vigor" (p. 318).

At this stage of the grounded theory process, the category set becomes "theoretically saturated" (Glaser & Strauss, 1967, p. 110). New incidents add little new value to the concepts, and "later modifications are mainly on the order of clarifying the logic, taking out nonrelevant properties, integrating details of properties into the major outline of interrelated categories and—most importantly—reduction" (p. 110). This is about as far as the analyst can go in "explaining" the data. The next phase is the construction of interpretive claims.

In closing this section on coding and categorization, we wish to sound a word of caution. Coding schemes can become very elaborate and quite difficult to work with. There is always the danger that the more that analysts are concerned with the structures of coding, the further they drift away from the lived realities of what they study. Sometimes a simpler set of codes, designed only to navigate the data more easily, is the better way to proceed. All qualitative analysts would do well from time to time to recall that "The map is not the territory." Translation: The code (map) is not the interpretation.

Negative Case Analysis

One of the great strengths of qualitative studies is that what happens in the field can feed directly back into the process of analysis. Researchers can take advantage of new data to check the quality of categories and explanations. Negative case analysis (or analytic induction) is a well-known method for "revising hypotheses with hindsight" (Kidder, 1981, cited in Lincoln & Guba, 1985, p. 309). Here is how a negative case analysis works: As the researcher develops a theoretical explanation through a process like the grounded theory approach, more data are generated in the field. If the new data confirm the explanation, it grows stronger. But if the new data seem to refute it, then the analyst must revise the explanation and return to the cycle of using new data to test it until there are no more negative cases to account for. Ultimately negative case analysis results in a highly confident explanation of a social phenomenon—one that, in principle, approaches universal coverage.

This is a stringent procedure, and not every analyst has the time or the patience to follow through on it. Further, negative case analysis does not provide the criteria for telling when we have come to the end of the data-testing cycle (Hammersley, 1992). But negative case analysis is still an effective and widely recognized way to do in-the-field checks of an explanation.

Leaving the Field

In-the-field analysis also plays a role in researchers' deciding when to leave field settings, although these decisions are often driven just as much by practical factors. For example, major changes in the cultural scene—such as a turnover in leadership or the dissolution of the group itself—may signal that it would not be fruitful to conduct further fieldwork and that it is time for the researcher to pack up the proverbial tent. Other common reasons for field exit include fatigue, interpersonal distress, job constraints, the end of a sabbatical, the depletion of funding, the pressure to publish, or the need to finish the thesis or dissertation (see Kirk & Miller, 1986; Snow, 1980). The participants themselves can empathize with all of these reasons researchers leave, because the need to cope with work-induced stress or the deadlines of other people and organizations is nearly universal. Leaving the field can also be a temporary situation when a project goes on hiatus. The researcher may look forward to returning after a period of rest and reinvigoration, or after additional time has been found (or bought).

If the researcher is not forced to leave the field prematurely, then the internal criteria of the research—for example, indicators of data quality, redundancy, and abundance—become important factors in deciding when to leave. Snow (1980) described three tests of "information sufficiency" by which researchers can determine that their work in the field may be nearing its end. The first test, *taken-for-grantedness*, means that the researcher is no longer surprised by the participants' actions or meanings; the scene's routines can now be comprehended through the emic categories the investigator has learned. In the second test, *theoretical saturation*, the researcher reaches a point of diminished conceptual returns; that is, new data feed fewer, if any, new features into categories or explanations. In practical terms, "saturation is signaled by the continued observation of what is already known, and by repetitive field notes" (Snow, 1980, p. 103). Whereas taken-for-grantedness is a test of the researcher's ability to grasp native meanings, theoretical saturation is a test of the robustness of categories and explanations. We can see traces of each in Wellman's (1994) observations about the winding-down of his three-year participant-observation study of a longshoremen's union:

> Impatience followed fatigue. I found myself less sympathetic to stories and exchanges repeated endlessly, and my ability to record them faithfully was decreasing. I knew my job in the field was completed when I discovered the source of my impatience. I had heard the stories, witnessed the exchanges, and observed the events so many times that I knew how they would end when they began. I could predict the process as well as the outcome. . . . My research categories were saturated. To convince myself that saturation was not simply an expedient excuse for fatigue, I tried to actually predict how the process would unfold. When I succeeded, I knew the time to leave had come. (p. 582)

Finally, a third test, *heightened confidence*, tells the researcher when "the observations and findings are faithful to the empirical world under study and shed light on preexisting or emergent questions and propositions" (Snow, 1980, p. 104). Whereas theoretical saturation indicates that there are no more features to add to a conceptual framework, heightened confidence is a test of the *credibility* of each claim or concept. The researcher uses methods of validation (which we discuss near the end of this chapter) to demonstrate this credibility.

When actually disengaging from the field, researchers should reserve some time and effort to check hunches, perform member checks, run through a negative cases analysis, and do any other activities that can be done "on the ground." Researchers should also settle any moral debts with the people being studied and make plans for staying in touch later on. Friendships are often formed with participants that transcend the roles and boundaries of the project, and complicated emotions—running the gamut from affection to sorrow and mistrust—may rise up when the researcher leaves. Depending on the nature of their relationship at the time of departure, the researcher may want to "debrief" the participants on the study's findings. Failing to do this can potentially lead to misunderstandings and hurt feelings, especially if the published findings are not flattering to the community (see Ellis, 1995, for such a story). It is vital that researchers try to leave on good terms, if for no other reason than that they—and other researchers—may want to go back to this site some day.

Tools for Analysis: Manual and Computer-Assisted

In the first edition of this book, the following statement appeared: "Possibly the majority of qualitative inquirers still engage analysis as a hands-on craft." Whether or not that was true in the mid-1990s, it is probably not true now. Today, most qualitative researchers in Communication rely on computers to assist with at least some of their data analysis. Indeed, the eager embrace of data analysis software is one of the most dramatic changes in qualitative research practice. Although some investigators are happy using general purpose software like word processors and database managers, for the majority of researchers it is the software designed for higher level qualitative analysis that has the most seductive appeal. By incorporating the functions most common to qualitative data analysis—for example, text coding, retrieval, and concept building—these programs save researchers much time and effort and create a smooth digital transition from the field to the report. Even more intriguing is the idea that the programs afford new ways of thinking about—and representing—the relationships among textual, aural, and/or visual materials.

Most of this section provides a basic introduction to qualitative analysis software: the growth of computer-assisted qualitative data analysis software (CAQDAS); what the programs can do for researchers; and some concerns about the role of CAQDAS in interpretive inquiry. We do not intend to offer a comprehensive guide (see Weitzman & Miles, 1995) or endorse any particular products. We do encourage readers to become well-acquainted with their data analysis needs as well as the features of a range of programs before they decide to acquire software.

First, however, we discuss some tools and techniques of analyzing data by hand. For decades before the current era, all qualitative researchers used physical tools—paper, index cards, file folders, binders, scissors, paste—in physical spaces. The tools are simple and the effort is time-consuming, but generations of researchers have managed to get their studies done in this manner. Because methodology texts seldom described them in much detail, the techniques were passed along from mentor to apprentice (student) as in craft traditions. Some people still prefer to use manual methods, and knowledge of how they work helps researchers in learning about CAQDAS.

Manual Methods

We open this section by rejoining Alyssa Eckman, whom we met in Chapter 3 as she was starting her study of newspaper advertorial producers. Here, Alyssa faces the challenge of making sense of her data from the field:

> My field notes were kept in Microsoft Word files on disk and backed up on two different computer hard drives (home office and work office) because my biggest fear was losing all that I had accumulated. Fortunately I kept my notes in a day-to-day journal, and that linear, organized approach saved me several months later because they helped bring my memories back to life, back into focus. I also collected documents from meetings, print-outs of relevant e-mails, and even a few napkins-turned-notepads from lunch gatherings with co-workers. This accumulation of materials all landed in my home office, which is a small 10-by-12 foot loft overlooking my living room. . . . I read my notes several times and began to note recurrent terms, actions, comments, and experiences. I will confess to using the pile method of organizing the data around the six themes that I eventually developed. My small loft office proved too small, so one weekend I moved to the living room and surrounded myself with the field notes, interview transcripts, and the rest of the documents collected during the field study. Armed with scissors, a set of multi-colored markers, and post-it notes, I began to cut my notes into pieces. Each piece landed in a color-coded pile, a pile that either represented a recurrent theme or a "question mark" to be addressed later. A couple of the "question mark" collections were eventually re-designated as recurrent themes as supporting data began to grow in those piles.

Several aspects of handling data manually are notable in this scene. First, Alyssa did avail herself of a word-processing program to store, index, retrieve, and print data-texts. Very few qualitative researchers today, if any, shun the use of computers altogether. Second, manual methods of analysis engage all of the data in their original form, including Alyssa's napkins-turned-notepads. Third, the living room floor became a large canvas for Alyssa's materials. She was able to look at them from many different positions and move back and forth across the piles like an "action painter" à la Jackson Pollock. The computer screen cannot match this wide-angle view of all of the research texts. Finally, Alyssa had a tactile contact with the materials—feeling their size, color, weight, and texture, and the action of operating on them. Many researchers find this close contact with their data to be much more satisfying than gazing at pixels on a screen.

Pile sorting is one way to go about the mechanics of data analysis, but there are others. Probably the simplest way is to write the codes directly in the margins of fieldnote or transcription pages, and keep the marked-up copies in file folders or a ring binder. Tabs in the ring binder divide the project's materials into sections such as these: (1) Instruments used in the study (e.g., interview guides); (2) Codebook; (3) In-process memos and/or theoretical memos; (4) Summary information about the sample of cases (e.g., sites or people); and (5) Coded texts (which may be subdivided into sections based on type of data—fieldnotes, interview transcriptions, documents, etc.).

When one wants to retrieve all of the chunks of data that relate to a topic—let's say, all instances of "teenagers talking about the Internet"—one consults the codebook and finds the code that corresponds to the category. There is a category for teenagers' talk, TEENTALK, which contains a code for teenagers' talk about the Internet, TEENTALK-INTERNET. Next to this code is information about the location (case, record, and page number) for each chunk of text that goes with the code. Because any chunk may be coded into several categories, it helps to cross-reference the codes in the codebook.

The researcher's impetus for revising a coding scheme may be the arrival of new data, which means that the number of cases may grow and the scheme itself will probably change. It is advisable to keep all earlier versions of the codebook and coded data for validation purposes. When the analyst is ready to engage in conceptual work, the pages relevant to the categories or themes may be pulled out of the binder. Different colored pens can be used to mark the different families of codes, allowing the analyst to see at a glance the categories a page holds.

Some researchers like to work with the pages whole, whereas others cut them into chunks, as Alyssa did. The cut-up chunks can be taped or pasted to index cards. In place of pages in a binder or file folders, the cards become the carriers of coded data. (Of course, one never cuts or trims the original data. An archive of the complete data is always kept for reference and as a source for more cuttings.) Even though the card includes information about the case—date, page number, and so on—it is easy for the chunk to become decontextualized. As Miles and Huberman (1984) note, "meaninglessness of isolated chunks is the potential problem [with putting chunks of data onto cards]" (p. 66).

Conducting qualitative analysis by hand is still preferred by many people, particularly when the quantity of data is not substantial. (More instructions on how to code by manual methods can be found in Miles and Huberman, 1984, and Tesch, 1990.) According to LeCompte and Schensul (2000), it is "not worthwhile to use a computer to code fewer than 100 pages of text data because of the time required to do it" (p. 91). However, projects of even moderate complexity produce data far in excess of 100 pages, and the time-savings of specialized software is only one of its many strengths. Thus it is to computer-assisted methods that we now turn.

Computer-Assisted Qualitative Data Analysis Software (CAQDAS)

Since the late 1970s, qualitative researchers have used word-processing programs to type, edit, and store their fieldnotes, transcriptions, and other texts. The programs also allowed them to conveniently cut, paste, and copy sections of text within and between documents and to create directories of files. Later word processors built on graphical (icon based), menu-driven interfaces offer more features that aid qualitative research tasks: Key word or phrase finders; comments that can be embedded in text (for asides and commentaries); graphics created in the program or scanned-in from external sources; and linkages with other programs, such as spreadsheet and database management programs that are bundled in a "suite" (e.g., Microsoft Office). As useful as word processors are, however, they are not up to the robust tasks of qualitative analysis.

The first computer-assisted qualitative data analysis software (CAQDAS), such as The Ethnograph, QUALPRO, QUALOG, and Notebook, became available in the mid-1980s. These programs required users to "[type] in line numbers and code names at a command prompt, and there was little or no facility for memoing or other annotation or markup of text" (Weitzman, 2000, p. 804). More sophisticated programs came along in the late 1980s and the 1990s, spurred by huge increases in microcomputer power and speed, the need by analysts with large sets of data for special user applications, and the growing popularity of qualitative methods in the academy and industry. Enthusiasm with CAQDAS has also been boosted by the scientific legitimacy they seem to bestow on qualitative inquiry. As Crang, Hudson, Reimer, and Hinchliffe (1997) observe archly, "The process of interpretation can now be boxed with the software and placed in a discrete sentence in research grant application forms. Instead of difficult theoretical explanation, research proposals can say simply "field materials will be interpreted using [for instance] HyperRESEARCH software" (p. 783).

By 2001, more than 20 CAQDAS packages were available in Windows, Macintosh, and DOS formats (Fielding, 2001). Most of the newer programs were designed in close collaboration between software developers and qualitative researchers. This has ensured that the programs respond better to the needs and preferences of those who do research. Ideas for improving the design and use of CAQDAS increasingly come from the feedback of user networks and Internet discussion groups (Lewins, 1996; Miles & Weitzman, 1996, p. 213). Meanwhile, the community of users has become multinational and highly interactive on a number of fronts (Mangabeira, 1996).

Although the programs are billed as analysis tools, it is important to know that they neither "theorize" nor operate on text in any way that has not been initiated by the user. In other words, the programs only *assist* in the process of analysis. Most of the functions of CAQDAS can be categorized into three broad types of programs: Text search programs, text code-and-retrieve programs, and code-based theory builder programs. Code-based theory builders are in turn either text based or graphics based.

Text search programs—for example, ZyINDEX and the Text Collector—find words or phrases in one or several databases. They show each instance of the word or phrase in its surrounding context—that is, key word in context (KWIC)—and index the results. Simple word lists and concordances (lists of the words or phrases in their contexts) can be created, and the instances found can also be counted in a kind of content analysis procedure. In most programs, the results of these searches can be sorted into output files, which can be used in further analysis or report writing.

Text-searching programs are helpful if one already has a good idea of what to look for. They are also very fast at searching. But they do not code the text or perform any of the interesting operations with text that require coding.

Text code-and-retrieve programs—for example, Kwalitan, QUALPRO, The Ethnograph, and HyperQual2—apply codes to units of text of varying length and retrieve and display these units by mouse-clicking on the codes. For example, they not only can code for the low-inference categories (e.g., coding for "The Ethnograph" in interview data whenever respondents talk about using The Ethnograph), they also can code for a high-inference category (e.g., a concept like "computer competency") where one must decide which words, phrases, sentences, quotations, and behaviors count as instances. The initial assignment of codes to text may take almost as much time as the manual coding of paper text. But the real savings of time and effort come when the analyst retrieves groups of text tagged with a code or combination of codes. Weitzman (2000) writes that "even the weakest of these programs represents a quantum leap forward from the old scissors-and-paper approach: they're more systematic, more thorough, less likely to miss things, more flexible, and much, much faster" (p. 809).

Text code-and-retrieve programs are typically modeled after the grounded theory approach. They make it easy to revise codes and write memos that reflect the conceptual thinking that goes with the coding activity (most programs permit the memo to be attached directly to the text or a code). Some programs also allow sorting by precoded data from a "face sheet"—that is, a document that contains summary information about the respondent or the site—rather than by the contents of the fieldnote or interview transcription. By permitting a variety of ways of viewing and grouping codes, categories, and chunks of text, code-and-retrieve programs put grounded theory into motion to an unprecedented degree. Certainly they take much of the drudgery out of coding by hand and promote "a more 'playful' and insight-driven process" (Mangabeira, 1996, p. 196).

Code-based theory builders—for example, NUD*IST version 6, Atlas/ti, HyperRESEARCH, AQUAD, and N Vivo—include the functions of the other two types but go beyond them in exploring the relationships between categories. These packages "add features supporting theory-building, including extensive use of hypertext to link parts of a dataset. They help users make connections between codes, develop more abstract, formal classifications and categories, or test propositions that imply a conceptual structure which fits the data" (Fielding, 2001, p. 455). Some of these programs, like NUD*IST, are text based, while others, like N Vivo, are graphic based and can support multimedia files.

In essence, these programs help the analyst construct a visual map of the relationships among data. For example, NUD*IST allows one to develop a hierarchy out of links between "nodes" (the text points represented by codes). The links may be defined by one or more different relationships, such as causal ("leads to"), associational ("is a type of"), and Boolean ("and/or/not" relations). The entire structure of links represents theoretical propositions that can then be tested against different sets of text and subsequently revised to obtain a better fit. Theory-building software allows the analyst to attach memos to specific chunks of text and to code and categorize the memos themselves.

Hyperlinks embedded in any file enable the user to make "compound" categories of pictures, fieldnote texts, audio or video recordings, Web sites, memos, or annotations. These programs do not actually "touch" or otherwise alter one's data. Rather, they act as indexes that sit "on top of data," completely separate from it (unlike Alyssa with her scissors). If the program is unable to run video or audio files, it may include off-line codings of the video or audio in the analysis (Smith & Short, 2001). Finally, some of these programs can also interface with statistical packages like the Statistical Package for the Social Sciences (SPSS).

How one uses these programs often depends on *when* one starts using them in a project. If data analysis software is used early in the data collection process, one can employ it in a grounded theory of the growing database. Thus one can use it to actually build concepts and redefine codes. But if the software is used later in the game, to organize the emerging data, then it functions primarily as a data management tool for keeping track of data types, cases, and records. Also, at any point in the data analysis—but typically in the later stages of a project—one can use CAQDAS for powerful text searches that can save quite a bit of time, particularly for Boolean searches (for example, finding all instances of "sweat equity" with "fair" but without "men").

Concerns about the use of CAQDAS have been articulated recently and are unlikely to be resolved soon. Many observers are concerned that qualitative data analysis programs contain implicit "theories" of analysis that guide the user's thinking along certain tracks and neglect other possibilities (Mangabeira, 1996; Hinchliffe, Crang, Reimer, & Hudson, 1997). For example, the authoring of multimedia stories by multiple authors (Goldman-Segall, 1995; Mason & Dicks, 1999) may call for a new model of breaking apart and reconstructing data. This is one of the places where theory meets technology: Researchers and software developers can communicate with each other about how to design programs that theorize social relationships and narrative differently, or that open up multiple pathways of looking at data.

Some researchers have expressed concern over the CAQDAS user's alienation from the data and loss of emotional and intellectual connection with the social or cultural scene (see Fielding, 2001, p. 465; Hinchliffe et al., 1997, pp. 1112-1114; Mangabeira, 1996, p. 197). Earlier, we discussed the effect of decontextualization that coding can cause. The computer's famous ease of manipulation may push this effect much further. This is not a neo-Luddite call to return to cards, scissors, paste, and piles but, rather, a caution about the possible costs to the core values of interpretive inquiry of moving all data analysis procedures into computer hard drives and networks.

Finally, Crang and colleagues (1997) warn that CAQDAS promotes "an illusory order" in qualitative research. They are referring here to the fact that the programs come with a built-in structure for coding and building concepts. This order is illusory because it does not arise from careful study of the patterns in the data. Crang and colleagues (1997) suggest that "it encourages the researcher to collect more material rather than think more creatively with existing material" (p. 782).

In the space available here, we have briefly described some major functions and issues in the use of CAQDAS. Deeper treatments of the subject can be found in Fielding (2001), Weitzman (2000), and Weitzman and Miles (1995). As a final recommendation, we agree with Miles and Weitzman (1996) when they say that the issue of which package to buy ultimately turns on how it can "support or constrain your thinking to produce unanticipated effects" (p. 212).

Interpretation

As we have seen, analytic operations enable one to mark up (code) and retrieve the coherent units of data we have been calling "chunks." Through these operations, the researcher becomes familiar with all of the data at the micro level and begins to build a structure that interrelates the key parts of the data set. These analytic operations first *decontextualize* the incidents (i.e., coding them out of their places in fieldnotes, transcriptions, and other materials) and then *recontextualize* them into category systems by means of certain logic statements—causal, associational, typological, Boolean, and so forth. However, even a well-executed analysis does not guarantee a sensitive reading of a life, a social ritual, or a cultural scene. Left in their analytic state, the results may seem bloodless and even stillborn. There is another important step between the analysis of data and the write-up of research texts: interpretation.

Interpretation involves the translation of an object of analysis from one frame of meaning into another. For the qualitative analyst, interpretation begins with an in-depth understanding of first-order concepts: "the situationally, historically, and biographically mediated interpretations used by members . . . to account for a given descriptive property" (Van Maanen, 1979, p. 540). These emic meanings are typically explored in the open-coding phase of analysis. The analyst then constructs symbolic links—or *tropes*—that tie the first-order meanings to second-order concepts, or "notions used by the fieldworker to explain the patterning of first-order data" (p. 541). This act of translation adds tremendous value to a study by using theories or symbolic relationships to understand data and categories in a new light. Interpretations are rarely created in the linear, stepwise mode of data analysis. Instead, interpretation operates more in the mode of pattern recognition. As Spiggle (1994) writes, interpretation "occurs as a gestalt shift and represents a synthetic, holistic, and illuminating grasp of meaning, *as in deciphering a code*" (p. 497; emphasis added).

The most celebrated essay about ethnography as code cracking is anthropologist Clifford Geertz's (1973) "Thick Description: Toward an Interpretive Theory of Culture." Posing the question of what sort of distinctive knowledge comes from ethnography, Geertz introduces the example—borrowed from philosopher Gilbert Ryles—of two boys "rapidly contracting the eyelids of their right eyes" (p. 6) in each other's direction. Viewed in strictly physical terms, the boys' eyes appear to be twitching involuntarily. But interpreted in light of intersubjective and cultural knowledge, the boys are doing something else altogether. Geertz writes: "Contracting your eyelids on purpose when there exists a public code in which doing so counts as a conspiratorial signal is winking. That's all there is to it: a speck of behavior, a fleck of culture, and—voila!—a gesture" (p. 6). Of course, the boys could also be parodying someone else's wink. That would involve yet another code wrapped around the code that counts winking as a sign of conspiracy. An interpretation that succeeds—that is, an interpretation that we can depend on to both explain and enact the cultural code—is one that "sorts winks from twitches and real winks from mimicked ones" (p. 16).

When engaged in interpretation, analysts frequently take advantage of semiotic devices to decipher the codes of communication performances or practices. As Spiggle notes, "These devices (literary tropes) suggest, indicate, imply, or allude to correspondences and parallels across or within domains. The constructor of tropes uses them to expand, concretize, and emphasize meanings" (p. 498). Among the devices used "to trope" in qualitative research are the following:

• *Metaphorical*—A figurative frame of reference in which we view some aspect of the social world as if it was another, dissimilar object. For example, the shifting, animated quality of focus group members' interactions with environmental issues on television can suggest a "conversation" metaphor of public opinion (Delli Carpini & Williams, 1994).

• *Metonymic*—A relationship in which "part is taken as an emblematic representation of the whole domain" (Arnould & Wallendorf, 1994, p. 498). Countless ethnographies, from classics like Whyte's *Street Corner Society* (1943) to those of the present day, have represented a larger social system or problem through close study of a specific scene.

• *Ironic*—An expression that inverses (takes the opposite meaning of) the usual meaning of another expression. Ashcraft and Pacanowsky (1996), for example, uncovered ironic expressions of "cattiness," "female jealousy," and "pettiness" not far under the surface of a dominantly female organization.

• *Syntagmatic*—"Part of a culturally prescribed temporal or narrative sequence, such as interrupting the viewing of televised football games to eat the meal or the telling of Thanksgiving Day stories about bad times overcome, to confirm both the primacy and resiliency of family life" (Arnould & Wallendorf, 1994, p. 498).

- *Paradigmatic*—A set of attributes of a single type, usually revealing the contrasting elements of a cultural domain. In Gillespie's (1995) ethnography of the uses of television by Indian immigrants in London, the young people's accounts of how they perceive India through films was developed, in part, as a paradigmatic set of oppositions: Tradition-Modernity, Village-Rural, City-Urban, Poverty-Wealth, Communality-Individualism, and Morality-Vice (p. 82).

Also of great importance in developing interpretations and inferences are *exemplars* (Atkinson, 1990). Also called *incidents* (Spradley, 1980), *episodes* (Anderson, 1987), and *strips* (Agar, 1982), an exemplar is part—or an amalgam of parts—of a project's data that is shaped and used to advance an argument. Exemplars come from "concrete interactional events, incidents, occurrences, episodes, anecdotes, scenes, and happenings somewhere in the real world" (Lofland, 1974, p. 107). The forms they take can range from a brief excerpt (e.g., an interview segment) to a longer story that has been crafted from several sources. Gluckman (1961) has described three kinds of case materials that can be useful as exemplars: (1) an *apt illustration*, which is a description of an event that illustrates a general principle; (2) a *social situation*, which is "some restricted and limited (bounded) set of events . . . in which general principles of social organization manifest themselves in some particular specified context"; and (3) an *extended case study*, which is a sequence of events involving the same actors and settings over a long period of time that demonstrates a process in operation (cited in Mitchell, 1983, p. 193). Exemplars are also potent devices for the researcher because they usually represent rich veins of experience from the field. Or, as Mitchell (1983) puts it, "the single case becomes significant only when set against the accumulated experience and knowledge that the analyst brings to it" (p. 203).

Recall from the discussion of grounded theory that incidents from coded data are used to construct and define categories and their properties. When the researcher is ready to develop an interpretation of the results of the data analysis, these incidents—or at least the most persuasive ones—are then shaped into exemplars. As we will see in Chapter 9, exemplars are central to the rhetorical achievements of a research text. But exemplars also perform the work of—and act as the substructure for—interpretive claims. They are the best evidence that a researcher can present. Without exemplars, the claims of a qualitative study would be empty and unpersuasive.

A look at three strategies—*metaphorical, dramatistic,* and *phenomeno-logical*—suggests how exemplars are used to advance an interpretive claim. These strategies are merely illustrative of what can be accomplished; a wide array of interpretive and critical frames is reviewed in Chapter 2.

Metaphorical Strategy

Metaphors are used frequently as interpretive frames as well as the tropic device discussed earlier. A metaphor creates new meaning by fusing two concepts that are dissimilar in ordinary usage. Metaphoric comparisons also provide vivid, concise ways of suggesting complex ideas (Crider & Cirillo, 1992).

Metaphors drawn from the natural language of participants can be an effective tool for developing an interpretation. For example, in Willliam Rawlins and Cynthia Holl's (1987) study of adolescent friendship concerns, "The Communicative Achievement of Friendship During Adolescence: Predicaments of Trust and Violation," the degree of trust that can be invested in others emerged as a significant basis for the participants' evaluation of their friends. To know whether someone can be a friend, apparently one must assess the risk that secrets will be revealed. Not surprisingly, trust violation emerged as a major problematic issue in the adolescents' talk about friendship.

The most severe breach of trust mentioned by the participants was "back-stabbing." The authors noted that "the violence metaphorically implied by the phrase 'backstabbing' captures the poignancy and revulsion these adoles-cents attributed to a friend's betrayal through talk" (p. 355). Another partici-pant term, "talking behind my back," was related to backstabbing, albeit less severe. Rawlins and Holl developed their claims about the role of the backstabbing threat in a series of exemplars, as in this excerpt:

In characterizing what he valued most in a friend, one male stated:

"Um, well definitely someone whom you could talk to, whom you could trust. No one who would, um, stab you in the back or anything like that. Somebody who could, uh talk, you know, you could talk with or you could, you know, someone who you could trust."

Notice his virtual equation in friendship of someone to talk to and trust. In dis-cussing why friendships break up, a female related:

"I used to be friends with her. Pretty much she stabbed me in the back really bad. And I'm, I'm not used to that happening 'cause I choose my friends care-fully; but when she pulled that, I said forget it."

> This quotation indicates the practice and need for careful selection of friends as well as her conclusive reaction to backstabbing. (p. 355)

The meaning of the metaphor, as it relates to selecting friends and maintaining friendships, is inferred from the context of the participants' talk and from the interpretive frame developed by the authors. "Backstabbing" as a vivid emblem of treachery (the sign of the "back" as a vulnerable, unwary site of injury) is extended to similar complaints by other respondents, even when they do not use the term. Generally, metaphor making can be a creative way to thematize an interpretive claim—whether or not the metaphor originates in the participants' speech.

Dramatistic Strategy

The drama frame is well suited for studies concerned with communication as performance. Attention is focused on performance roles, the competence of those who perform, the settings and artifacts that serve as resources for performing, the cultural scripts that are evoked, and the roles of audiences who applaud, critique, or are affected by performances (Anderson, 1987, pp. 278-281). Dramas can be studied in the most mundane of scenes. In the words of Victor Turner (1957, p. 93), social drama is "a limited area of transparency on the otherwise opaque surface of regular, uneventful social life. Through it we are enabled to observe the crucial principles of social structure in their operation and their relative dominance at successive points in time."

In Nick Trujillo's (1993) "Interpreting November 22: A Critical Ethnography of an Assasination Site," Dealy Plaza in Dallas becomes the performative stage for exploring "the multiple meanings which define [the Kennedy assasination's] meaning in American culture" (p. 449). Among the themes informing Trujillo's study are the postmodern commodification of experience, the ideological struggle over the meaning of the assassination, and the fragmenting of community that followed in the wake of the traumatic event. Trujillo juxtaposes performances of different kinds and in complex ways, such as these in the section titled "The President is Shot, the Community is Shattered": a flashback of the moment of the fatal head shot; testimonies of visitors to the plaza on the 25th anniversary (which, incidentally, is the scene of the study); an elegiac commentary on the "annihilation" of the American community in the 1960s. The following is an exemplar from this narrative:

> A white woman in her fifties expresses her feelings to one reporter: "Our country took another direction after his death, an *evil* one. It's not the same world

anymore. All I can say is that with him, it would have been much better." A white male in his forties echoes similar feelings when he tells another reporter that if Kennedy had lived, "we wouldn't have had Vietnam or the situation with drugs on the streets that we have now." (p. 453)

And so it goes in the endless simulacra of Kennedy assassination tales. In Trujillo's telling, we hear and see people play their parts as ordinary citizens performing for reporters. Along with quotes from two other citizens and descriptions of strangers paying solemn respect, this exemplar expresses the author's theme of the assassination as a rupture in history and community.

Phenomenological Strategy

As we discussed in Chapter 2, phenomenology developed as a philosophical method for unpacking the essence of lived experience. It can also be put into service as a method for analyzing social routines (as in ethnomethodology) and for interpreting constructs of communicative experience. Recently, the phenomenological method has been creatively infused with concepts from other traditions, such as critical theory and cultural studies.

In "Media Consumption and Girls Who Want to Have Fun," Eric Peterson (1987, p. 41) demonstrated a phenomenological approach to audience meanings for the 1980's hit song. The interpretive strategy consisted of these steps:

1. *Description:* the discovery of "signification systems in the lived reality of everyday life"

2. *Definition:* "the reduction of the description to systematic knowledge"

3. *Interpretation:* a reflection on the previous two phases to "specify the logic and value that unite description and definition" in order to locate the "value of social existence"

Application of the strategy to 34 student essays written about the meanings of the song "Girls Just Want to Have Fun" resulted in the emergence of seven thematic clusters: danceability, fun, freedom, rebellion, performer (the persona of singer Cyndi Lauper), audience/youth, and critic. Listening to music was found to inscribe social meaning and organize pleasure for audience members through these seven themes. Further study of the themes resulted in a development of three interpretive positions: liberal individualist, liberal feminist, and teeny bopper. Thus Peterson's study explained how the song was perceived by segments of the audience (or at least by *these* audience members) in various ways—from dance tune to feminist anthem.

Theory

Theory has a critical role to play in interpretation. Theories and concepts may lay part of the groundwork for starting a project, but during the researcher's time in the field, data are collected and analyzed without being constrained by any single theory. By the time the researcher leaves the field, the need to bring theory back into the process returns. This does not mean that one must commit to a specific theory. In fact, just the opposite: "Being theoretically informed means that one is reflexive toward the deceivingly self-evident reality one faces in and through the data, able to toy with different perspectives to it, and that one is open to new insights about everyday life and society" (Alasuutari, 1996, p. 375). Thus two or more theories may be put into creative tension with each other with respect to thickly described cases created from field study. Theoretical frameworks are useful to the extent that they help researchers stretch their imaginations and create and validate claims about the data they have generated (Alasuutari, 1996; Spiggle, 1994).

Evaluating Interpretations

How can researchers be sure of the quality of their interpretations and the methods used to arrive at them? To what extent can interpretations be validated as true, correct, and dependable? These questions are as important for qualitative practitioners as they are for those in objectivist research, although the standards differ in important respects (Mishler, 1990). We begin with the traditional definitions of reliability and validity and look at problems in their application to a cultural hermeneutic epistemology. We will then turn our attention to some widely used methods of validation in qualitative research.

The question of *reliability* has to do with the consistency of observations: Whether a research instrument (e.g., questionnaire, experimental test, human observer) will yield the same results every time it is applied. If it does yield roughly the same results time after time, then it can be said that the instrument is dependable for the purpose at hand. On the other hand, if substantially different results emerge—such as two polls that report presidential job-approval ratings of 55% and 65% on national samples surveyed the same day and asked the same question—then the quality of the measuring instrument can be called into question. Reliability is a concern in social science research because a result found to be unreliable cannot be assumed to be valid (although the reverse is not true). Low reliability is vexing to researchers because there are many potential sources of the problem: The instrument may not be precise enough (for example, the questionnaire item is stated in an ambiguous way); the instrument may have been interpreted and used differently (which is the basis for using multiple coders of content or behavior); or, more precariously, the phenomenon has actually changed in terms of the attributes being measured (in which case there may be nothing wrong with the instrument itself).

Reliability is not so much of a consideration in qualitative research because, first of all, "if [a] measurement is composed of a single, nonrepeated operation, there can be no measure of reliability" (Anderson, 1987, p. 126). There are a great many single, nonrepeated operations in qualitative studies. Interviews, for example, are usually nonrepeatable because each informant is asked a particular set of questions only once, and in most types of interview research the questions will vary across participants. The more fundamental reason for the low relevance of reliability in qualitative research lies in the interpretivist assumption of multiple, changing realities. If the meanings of the social world are continually changing—and the investigator's own under-standings also change in relation to the scene under study—then replication of results via independent assessments is neither practical nor possible.

Reliability can play a role in data analysis where one has the opportunity to check the stability of category definitions by using an intercoder reliability test (for an example, see Banks et al., 2000). However, few interpretive researchers consider this to be a useful step. The categories exist in interdependent and discursive relationships to each other, and how they are defined and configured may well be unique to the study and the analyst. This is not a weakness of qualitative inquiry; it is in fact a linchpin of the process.

The question of validity has to do with the truth value of observations: whether a research instrument is accurately reporting the nature of the object of study and variations in its behavior. Validity is often characterized by its internal, conceptual, and external dimensions. In objectivist research terms, an internally valid study is one in which the instrument makes the distinctions that are intended. If the researcher is measuring reticence, for example, she or he would want to use an instrument that can in fact distinguish reticent attributes or behaviors. Potential threats to internal validity include factors in the research context (e.g., changes in the instrument, the maturation of participants, reactivity to the measures) that may result in misleading data. Conceptual validity involves measuring a phenomenon accurately according to what a theory or construct would predict. A measurement of reticence, for example, should measure "reticence," as it is defined conceptually—and not something else, such as a phobic syndrome. An externally valid study is one in which the results can be generalized to the conditions being explained. A survey study of elderly TV viewers should produce evidence of behavior that would appear regularly in the natural settings of elderly TV viewers. Potential threats to external validity occur when the testing conditions of the study differ substantially from the conditions to which the researcher wishes to generalize. Procedures that do not adequately randomize the selection of human subjects from a population may also produce data fraught with bias, severely reducing their external validity.

Applying these aspects of validity to qualitative inquiry is also difficult. In the paradigm of multiple, constructed social realities, a single representation cannot serve as the criterion for an accurate measurement. For example, the behaviors that constitute the "problem" of reticence in U.S. classroom settings may be viewed as normal and desirable in other settings or cultures. Moreover, because the qualitative researcher operates as a reflexive agent in the field—not only studying the action of others but also studying his or her own responses to others' action—it is doubtful that the conventional notion of internal validity holds much relevance for this researcher. Finally, because qualitative researchers study individual cases that are historically and culturally situated, research claims cannot readily generalize to the entire universe of similar scenes. However, thickly described data do permit readers to determine when and how the claims might "transfer" to their own situations (Lincoln & Guba, 1985).

Qualitative researchers do seek to produce and demonstrate credible data. They want to inspire confidence in readers (and themselves) that they have achieved a right interpretation. Notice that we did *not* say, *the* right interpretation. An indefinite number of interpretations could be constructed from any research experience, but usually the ones that researchers choose to develop are those that they find most plausible, insightful, and/or useful. Researchers stand a better chance of making good choices if they employ procedures for evaluating the trustworthiness and credibility of these interpretations. In qualitative inquiry, validation can be achieved by evaluating multiple forms of evidence (triangulation and disjuncture) and by cycling some of the accounts back through the participants (member validation).

Triangulation and Disjuncture

Triangulation involves the comparison of two or more forms of evidence with respect to an object of research interest. Underlying most uses of triangulation is the goal of seeking convergence of meaning from more than one direction. If data from two or more methods seem to converge on a common explanation, the biases of the individual methods are thought to "cancel out" and validation of the claim is enhanced.

There are several ways that a researcher can triangulate data. *Multiple sources* from one data gathering method can be compared, such as husband and wife reports on the Internet access that their children enjoy. Of course, each interviewee should be in a position to say something empirically meaningful about the phenomenon. Similarly, field observations can be triangulated if they occur in the same setting and in similar time frames. Fieldnotes should describe the target action in enough detail to make direct comparisons possible.

Probably the most familiar kind of triangulation is *multiple methods*. Here, the researcher looks for converging interpretations in fieldnotes, interviews, documents, artifacts, and/or other evidence, in relation to a common object of interest. Researchers can also use quantitative methods to triangulate with qualitative methods—such as using Q Methodology to sharpen understandings of participants' subjectivity (Brown, 1996) or network analysis to examine the social relationships in a setting (Lazega, 1997). Usually, somewhat more credibility is invested in data from one of the methods, with data from other methods lending complementary support to the explanation.

Multiple researchers can also be used to overcome the styles, biases, or shortcomings of a lone investigator working in the field (Douglas, 1976, pp. 189-226; Olesen, Droes, Hatton, Chico, & Schatzman, 1994). This kind of triangulation assumes different forms depending on the design and phase of the project: Several observers can be deployed in the same field setting; two interviewers can operate as moderators in focus group interviews; analysts can work as a team on coding and categorization of data. Rather than aim for perfectly aligned observations, researchers who work in teams usually try to take advantage of their distinct, but overlapping, competencies.

In triangulation, multiple sources, methods, or researchers are used to dispel doubts about the reality of a finding. For example, the stories that one informant tells about a pattern of ritual insults in the office may be subjected to the usual questions about the observer's motive, perspective, and accuracy of observation. But similar stories told by two or three other informants can go far toward settling the factual basis of the events. And when one writes theoretic claims about data, the presence of exemplars of different types that converge on a set of interpretations can be quite persuasive.

Some methodologists, however, warn against using triangulation uncritically as a validation exercise. Bloor (1997) asserts that "all research findings are shaped by circumstances of their production, so findings collected by different methods will differ in their form and specificity to a degree that will make their direct comparison problematic" (p. 39). Similarly, Arnould and Wallendorf (1994) argue that multiple methods produce data that articulate different realities. They use the term *disjunctures* to refer to the differences in perspective produced by various data sources and methods. Verbal data, for example, can take the form of "overgeneralizations," such as statements of a cultural ideal, that may not be confirmed in ethnographic observations. Drawing on their study of Thanksgiving family consumption rituals, they note that

> examining multiple sources of data about Thanksgiving reveals a disjuncture between informants' recurring verbal reports that they "always" do the same thing each year, and observation of them negotiating about what should be done and who should do it as the ritual unfolds. . . . Disjunctures between observational and verbal report data provide an opening for etic interpretation building that goes beyond mere summaries of emic perspectives. (p. 495)

Instances of nonconvergence (disjuncture) often reveal the frequent contradictions between what people say they do and what they do.

This discussion, therefore, suggests a dual role for multiple data sources, methods, and researchers: They can serve the purpose of validating a claim on the basis of source-method-researcher agreement, which is triangulation in the classic sense, or they can validate a claim of disjuncture. The former role is probably best-suited for the task of *descriptive validity* (Maxwell, 1992), which is the factual accuracy of reportage about events, although *interpretive validity*—testing the validity of one's account of the actors' own meanings and constructions—can sometimes be conducted as well through triangulation. Alternatively, multiple sources and methods can help validate a claim of disjuncture. Differences in the meanings of data— between methods or between sources—may prompt the researcher to account for a more complex social reality than was first imagined.

Member Validation

Traditionally, social-scientific knowledge has been considered superior to the limited perspectives of lay people; however, interpretive social science has promoted the view of culture members as highly knowledgeable about their social worlds (Emerson & Pollner, 1988). Presumably, culture members are also capable of assessing the descriptions that others write of their practices, routines, and beliefs. This is the logic of member validation. *Member validation*—also known as *member checks* (Lincoln & Guba, 1985), *member tests of validity* (Douglas, 1976), and *host verification* (Schatzman & Strauss, 1973)—means taking findings back to the field and determining whether the participants recognize them as true or accurate.

Several techniques are included under the term *member validation*—for example, the researcher trying to "pass" as a member or using a taxonomy to predict members' descriptions (Bloor, 1997)—but the primary method involves the researcher sitting down with one or more participants and asking what they think of a description, an interpretation, or an explanation. Typical questions that researchers ask are: "Is there anything you particularly like about this? What did I get wrong? Did you recognize anyone? Have I been fair?" (St.Pierre, 1999, p. 275). Participants may be given an excerpt from the research write-up that pertains only to an area in which they are highly skilled or knowledgeable. Sometimes the whole text—article, dissertation, or book—is provided. In that case, the participants have the chance to comment on everything that was written about their scene.

These meetings usually come near the end of the project, because researchers want to be sure about the truth value of their accounts before putting them in print. But member validations can also happen at many points during the process of collecting data (e.g., St.Pierre, 1999). Here is an excerpt from Novek's (1995) description of the member validation of her ethnography of African American youth culture:

> Nearly a year after conducting the research, I took a draft of the ethnography to the high school and asked several former class members to review it. Kahn wrote, "This is an excellent paper. It covers all points on how young black youth survive and strive in [West Urbania]. You excellently used phrases that showed the pain of some of the students, as well as their happiness." . . . Duck said, "You need to talk more about the good stuff." (I have since responded to these and other critiques with revisions.) Richard said he had "understood everything, because most of the situations the author focused on, either I myself have experienced some of the hardship and I have a lot of friends who experience the downfalls of everyday struggles. . . . The author did nothing more than spoke the truth." (p. 184)

As this passage shows, there was some mild dissent about her account, which Novek took seriously enough to revise her work, but for the most part, the participants seemed to think she had gotten it right. It is also not uncommon for the researcher to learn new information from a member validation, which then can be used to revise the findings.

Member validation, we hasten to note, is not innocent of participants' biases or the residual effects of the researcher's relationships with them. Researchers often go back to the people whom they most respect or those who were the best informants. The participants' remarks may reflect their fondness for the researcher (St.Pierre, 1999) or bespeak a "strategically modulated expression of deeper reservations" if they disagree with the account

(Emerson & Pollner, 1988, p. 193). As a result of such predispositions, participants may not be completely candid or forthcoming. Also, as Bloor (1997) notes, participants might focus their remarks on aspects of the account that the researcher considers to be secondary to the "main point." A member validation, he concludes, "is not a scientific test but a social event, constrained . . . by the social dictates of polite conversation and shaped by the biographies and circumstances of the discussants" (p. 47). This may well be true, but how is it different from any other encounter in the field? All information given by participants is influenced by social context and the history of their relationship with the researcher. Member validations can be valuable exercises if the researcher comes to them self-aware of the possible influences on what is said by the participant.

Recently, another role for cultural memberships in validation has been suggested in which interpretive claims—and the research process itself—"catalyze" participants to realize the structural sources of their lived experience and to mobilize effectively for change (Denzin, 1997, pp. 9-14; Lather, 1986). Rather than being acted upon, the cultural members *act toward* a claim that catalyzes their political consciousness. The research claim itself becomes part of the participants' social struggle. This perspective on validation arises out of explicitly values-based research in sociology and education, but it is worth consideration for qualitative research conducted in Communication.

Conclusion

We began this chapter by noting the challenges of qualitative analysis and interpretation. Some challenges, such as the need to decide among multiple (possibly competing) interpretations, are central to the enterprise. The task of understanding what actions or discourses "mean" resists shortcuts and technical solutions. Other challenges have been faced and reduced to some degree by recent advancements in the field. For example, enough progress has been made in codifying qualitative data analysis procedures that novices no longer have to feel they are entering a zone of mystery when they begin to code, categorize, and interpret their data. Yet researchers still find ways of making their own adaptations of these methods. These adaptations—which are sometimes reported in journals like *The Journal of Contemporary Ethnography* and *Qualitative Inquiry*—are often aimed at getting more "performance" out of the "factory-produced" models of analysis (i.e., books like ours). As long as researchers do not manipulate data in ways that distort the local contexts they studied, there is nothing wrong with doing this. In fact, the satisfaction that researchers feel at the end of a study can be much greater when they have found their own solutions to problems of analysis.

The development of computer technologies and software has also met certain challenges of data analysis head-on. As we noted in this chapter, computer-assisted qualitative data analysis software (CAQDAS) reduces the time spent doing data analysis and—in the view of its ardent users—increases the precision and thoroughness of analytic operations. It may also help qualitative researchers in their quest for funding and higher professional standing among their peers in the social sciences. But whether CAQDAS markedly improves the quality of interpretations—or the theoretical contributions of qualitative studies—is still a hotly debated issue. There is concern among some researchers about whether the software somehow diminishes the intimate, creative relationship that many analysts have with their data.

We will revisit analysis and interpretation in the next two chapters. In Chapter 8, we observe the ways in which qualitative researchers have been studying communication in cyberspace. Common procedures—such as member validation—assume different forms and meanings when they are conducted with "disembodied," dispersed participants. In Chapter 9, we will see glimpses of the role played by analysis and interpretation in writing qualitative research reports. You will learn that interpretive strategies are as closely integrated with the act and products of writing as they are with fieldwork.

Exercises

1. Categorization and coding can be done with almost any narrative or discursive text. Many of these texts are in the public domain. For example: Talk show transcriptions (e.g., CNN and PBS programs) can be found by searching LEXIS-NEXUS; newspaper letters-to-the-editor on a particular topic can be collected; cyberspace discussions can be downloaded. As an exercise in learning to code, take a group of such texts and code them with a partner.

• Did you and your partner tend to see the same categories in the same way? What were the areas of disagreement or uncertainty?

• How many times did you revise the codes until you were satisfied that they covered all of the meaningful incidents?

• Did the coding help you think about how to interpret the themes or concepts of these texts?

2. As we mentioned in this chapter, published qualitative studies in Communication exhibit very little standardization in their reporting of data analysis procedures and decisions. Whether or not this is a "problem" for readers is a subject of some debate among scholars in the discipline. Choose two Communication journal articles that use qualitative field methods. Compare and contrast the articles' specification of data analysis and interpretation procedures. Some elements to look for include: mention of a model of analysis (e.g., grounded theory); coding and categorization procedures and decisions; coding tools and operations (e.g., manually or with a software package); interpretation strategies; validation methods.

- In what respects do these articles differ?

- In your view, is the data analysis reporting of each article appropriate to its goals, findings, and overall style? Do you think that certain key information was left out (error of omission) or was described inadequately (error of commission)?

Would you advocate a minimum standard for reporting data analysis in Communication journal articles? If so, what would constitute that standard? If not, why not?

8

Qualitative Research and Computer-Mediated Communication

Outlining the Field of Computer-Mediated Communication

This chapter looks at a rapidly growing field of qualitative research—the study of computer-mediated communication (CMC). Because this field is relatively new, and may be unfamiliar to some readers, this discussion is formatted a little differently from those in previous chapters. Rather than focusing only on methodological issues, we instead first review what CMC is and why qualitative researchers would want to study it. We then discuss three central areas of CMC research to date. Next, we review key methodological dimensions of qualitative research in CMC. Here, we focus on five topics that mirror some of those covered earlier in this volume: design, observing and participating, interviewing, data collection and analysis, and ethics. We conclude by considering the image of *qualitative cyborgs*—a term that captures the implications of CMC as both a topic and a medium of future research.

Because technology can be a confusing and controversial topic, we should make clear at the outset which perspective we are using to discuss CMC. Specifically, we adopt a *social constructionist* position (Bijker, Hughes, & Pinch, 1987) that emphasizes the role of both human and nonhuman agents in technological systems. In this view, these agents interact to create combinations of material forms and symbolic meanings. Those combinations are understood and acted toward by humans *as* "technology." When applied to CMC, this perspective emphasizes organized—yet also dynamic—relationships between the following elements:

- *Tools*: specific, concrete artifacts (such as monitors and modems) that extend human senses and allow experience to be symbolized as "information"

- *Programs*: sets of instructions encoded in tools for generating, exchanging, and storing information

- *Media*: historical forms of communication (e.g., writing) that have influenced the development of human consciousness and society

Media differ in their means of generating, exchanging, and storing information. Significantly, evolving media do not replace each other. Instead, "residues" of old media interact with emerging media to form hybrid, dynamic forms (Bolter & Grusin, 2000). Different forms of CMC contain different residual mixtures of orality, writing, and electronic media.

- *Culture*: the shared norms, values, and beliefs that define a group's identity, and the symbolic practices by which its members reproduce and transform those elements

Media and culture interact to mutually define the nature of human experience (Chesebro & Bertelsen, 1996).

- *Producers*: persons and groups who fund, invent, design, manufacture, and distribute tools and programs

- *Users*: consumers of and audiences for tools, media, and programs

- *Regulators*: individuals and groups with formal and legal responsibility for monitoring and controlling the activities of producers and users

- *Discourse*: the rhetoric of producers, consumers, and regulators that expresses their social, political, and economic interests

It does this by constructing preferred images of CMC systems (e.g., as "inevitable"). Discourses circulate in culture as various "texts" (e.g., television commercials) that "articulate" technologies with particular values and forms of feeling (e.g., optimism and anxiety). CMC discourses are often polarized and contend with each other for legitimacy and authority as "common (technological) sense." They shape popular understandings of what CMC is, how it operates, and what it means to participate in it

(Brummett, 1999; Marvin, 1988; Slack, 1989). One example of this involves the dominant characterization of online "chat" that uses connotations (e.g., of idle or frivolous small talk) associated with its corresponding genre of face-to-face (FTF) communication (Meakins & Rintel, 2000).

We define CMC, then, as the process through which humans create, maintain, and transform meaning by interacting as users of computerized systems of communication. These systems are historically quite recent. They are the result of a collaboration between producers and users that succeeded in reframing computers—technologies that were originally designed for large-scale, institutional purposes such as calculation and manufacturing—as tools for exchanging information in domestic and organizational settings (Reed, 2000; Williams, 1988). Central to this adaptation has been the integration of computers with telecommunication networks (e.g., for telephone, satellite, and cable television transmission). In the past three decades, the use of computers for communication has become increasingly common. Their rate of adoption has been fueled by continuous improvements in their speed, memory, functionality, transparency, autonomy, and interactivity.

Although CMC involves a variety of different systems (as discussed below), it displays a number of distinguishing qualities. The following list is partly based on the arguments of Newhagen and Rafaeli (1996):

- *Digitization*: the standardization of diverse forms of information (e.g., text, audio, and video) as binary computer "bits"

- *Packet switching*: the ability of transmission systems to disassemble digitized messages, route their components along various paths to maximize efficiency, and reassemble them at their destination

- *Synchronicity:* the relative capacity for simultaneous (versus delayed) interaction

- *Interactivity*: the capacity of systems to generate an experience of relatively synchronous and responsive communication between users (Downes & McMillan, 2000)

- *Hypertextuality*: the systematic linkage of information in nonlinear, weblike fashion

This quality allows users to navigate connections within and between texts in autonomous, unpredictable ways (Cali, 2000; Mitra & Cohen, 1999, pp. 182-188). Hypertextuality is widely celebrated, but Jackson (1997) notes that constraints imposed by commercial and security interests ensure that its reality falls short of its ideal, in which *all* documents are fully and accessibly linked. Provocatively, Barbatsis, Fegan, and Hansen (1999) argue that "cyberspace" is an ideational artifact of hypertextual rhetoric. That is, CMC users imagine it to possess volume (i.e., as "outside" and "elsewhere") because hyperlinks signify (and promise to overcome) textual "gaps."

- *Multimedia*: the growing capability of "broadband" systems to simultaneously transmit various forms of information, creating rich, three-dimensional simulations of interaction

This characteristic is especially significant because most studies of CMC to date have focused on text-based—and thus, in the increasingly rapid cycles of "Internet time," *historical*—systems (Soukup, 2000).

- *Convergence*: the interpenetration of "old" and "new" media at the levels of form and content.

Baym's (2000) groundbreaking study of CMC among viewers of television soap operas, for example, indicates that researchers wishing to study broadcast media audiences can find significant evidence of their activity on the Internet (see also Scodari & Felder, 2000). In addition, systems such as Web TV create a structural interface between cable television and Internet content. Convergence also occurs among "new" CMC systems. One example of this involves the embedding of addresses for a Web page within the content of messages on advanced e-mail systems. When users click on that URL, they activate their personal computer (PC) web browser and direct it to download that page.

Forms of Computer-Mediated Communication

CMC research has focused to date on five principal systems. In this section, we briefly review their distinguishing characteristics.

E-Mail

In e-mail, users send messages to each other for reading, storing, and printing. Although this exchange is frequently interpersonal, the "list-serv" format allows individuals to post messages to a central address that distributes them to all other "subscribers" (distribution is automatic on "unmoderated" list-servs; messages posted to "moderated" list-servs are first scrutinized for appropriateness). E-mail messages are traditionally textual. Their significant elements include addresses, signatures (and other forms of user identification), and attached files. Interaction via e-mail is relatively asynchronous, but it satisfies many users as a convenient and timely medium. E-mail provides the opportunity to craft and reflect on messages, although users are also prone to impulsiveness. E-mail is a hybrid medium that combines the informality and responsiveness of orality with the abstraction and linearity of writing (Wood & Smith, 2001, p. 9). Its use is pervasive in organizational and domestic settings, particularly following the mainstreaming of Internet Service Providers (ISPs) such as America Online (AOL). E-mail is the primary use of the Internet.

Bulletin Board Systems (BBS)

Users of BBS connect to computers serving as hubs for particular, special interest conferencing or "newsgroups." Users then post messages to a single address, and read and respond to messages posted by others. Messages are archived, and are produced and displayed in a "threaded" format corresponding to their topicality. Exchanges are asynchronous. This interaction occurs in the *Usenet* portion of the Internet.

Internet Relay Chat (IRC)

Chat users employ special software to access dedicated servers that allow multiple, synchronous, text-based conversations to be conducted in select, thematically organized channels (or "rooms"). For users, the experience is analogous to entering a large party and choosing to join a specific conversation group in progress. If they wish, users can retire from public channels to conduct more intimate conversations in "private" chat rooms. IRC has been conventionalized in formats such as Instant Messaging, in which users send multimedia content over dedicated channels to appear in the displays of recipients' "smart" devices (e.g., cell phones). IRC is considered to be more synchronous than e-mail. Messages are not stored. Instead, they are displayed on scrolling screens in the order they are received by servers (which, due to different connection speeds, is not necessarily the order in which they are produced by users). Additionally, messages are not displayed in emergent form; they appear after they are prepared and sent by the user. For these reasons, competent participation in chat requires users to type rapidly, to decode unconventional uses of spelling and grammar (Waskul, Douglass, & Edgley, 2000), to connect nonadjacent (and otherwise incoherent) turns (Herring, 1999), to interpret delayed responses (e.g., as artifacts of either system lag or users pausing for reflection), and to track multiple conversations occurring within and between channels. Multitasking teens, for example, simultaneously monitor—in addition to other media sources—up to 10 open "windows" of IRC (Hafner, 2001).

Multiple User Domains (MUDs)

One of the oldest forms of CMC, MUDs (the "D" also stands for "Dungeons" and "Dimensions") predate the development of the Internet. They possess several variants, known as MOO (MUDs, object oriented), MUSH (multiple user shared hallucination), and MUCK (multiple user character kingdom). All of these forms involve synchronous, text-based programs that allow users to enter and navigate simulated environments. Originally, these primitive virtual realities involved fantasy and adventure oriented role-play (e.g., Dungeons and Dragons). They have since evolved to become more diverse, sophisticated, and multifunctional (e.g., allowing users to e-mail, "page," and "whisper" to each other in relative privacy or to post messages to public discussion boards). In these elaborately atmospheric environments, users create and perform characters, interact with other characters and objects, and negotiate programmed plots (e.g., quests) by executing complex keyboard commands. MUDs differ in their dedicated purposes (e.g., task versus play), their levels of formality, and the balance they strike between user agency and programmed constraints.

World Wide Web (Web Pages)

The Internet is a vast and rapidly growing infrastructure that links various government, corporate, and educational computer networks. It allows users of PCs and other "smart" devices to exchange multimedia content (e.g., animation, streaming audio, etc.). The *World Wide Web* is a portion of the Internet devoted to posting, navigating, and interacting with multimedia texts known as *Web pages*. Users perform these activities through Web "browsers" that typically provide a "graphical user interface" (i.e., point-and-click modality). This interface connects their local tools to ISPs and to specific computer servers on which Web pages are stored. Easy access to and navigation among these hypertextual pages is facilitated by a number of elements. These include hardware, such as routers and fiber-optic cable, and software protocols for posting content and for locating and moving between servers (e.g., HTML, URL, DNS, and HTTP).

Why Study CMC?

There are a variety of compelling reasons for communication researchers to study CMC (Newhagen & Rafaeli, 1996). One reason involves its dramatic impact on contemporary society, which is felt across many different communication contexts. These contexts range from globally dispersed families holding "Internet reunions" to the recent economic rise and fall of Internet start-up companies attempting to realize the promise of "e-commerce." In this way, we don't need the hyperbole of industry promotion to acknowledge that CMC is changing the ways we work, shop, play, and love. Further, the *rate* of these changes is growing steadily. Although we should not assume that this growth rate is sustainable, or leads inevitably to universal access (Sterne, 1999, p. 279), it is nonetheless dramatic.

Propelling this growth in users is rapid innovation in the various tools and programs associated with CMC, and a more gradual (and unevenly distributed) "wiring" (or fiber-optic "cabling") of global cultures. In theory, these developments provide users with increased opportunities to acquire needed and timely information, to enjoy entertainment programming, to maintain relational connections, and to participate in community affairs.

The realities, of course, are more complex, and qualitative researchers are poised to help users, producers, and regulators understand and respond to this complexity. This help may be especially important *because* there is already a cacophony of "advice" coming from—and directed at—these groups. Unfortunately, these "pontifications" (Couch, 1995, p. 242) often reflect the motives and logics of the elite professional groups (e.g., engineers and marketers) who produce CMC systems. Because it is pervasive and often unquestioned, this rhetoric can infect researchers. Sterne (1999) cautions that

> Internet scholars have a tendency to . . . grossly overestimat[e] the impact, magnitude, accessibility and universality of their object of study. Basic claims . . . do not withstand even superficial scrutiny. Many writers have made wildly exaggerated claims about ease of access to the medium, its relative importance to the shape of modern politics, the Internet as a public sphere, and the Internet's rate of growth. (p. 278)

This is a worthwhile caution, as is the observation that CMC research may be recapitulating the history of broadcast media audience research. In that history, researchers have affiliated either with a dominant "administrative" concern for measuring ratings or with an upstart interpretivism committed to understanding audience practices for their own sake (Mitra & Cohen, 1999, pp. 180-181). Frequently, "administrative" interests are more concerned with revenues than with the complexities of how people actually *use* and *experience* CMC systems.

Qualitative research, then, is especially useful for providing fine-grained data about an often-mystified social phenomenon. This research is valuable *because* its findings contradict conventional wisdom (e.g., regarding egalitarian, "raceless" communication on the Internet; Kolko, Nakamura, & Rodman, 2000). Invoking an analogy, Newhagen and Rafaeli (1996) argue that good research can help communication scholars move from the passive role of "judging" CMC—as if it were a sporting event—to the more active (and satisfying) role of "coaching" the "athletes." One paradigm that unites producers and researchers in this enterprise is that of "user-focused" (or "user-centered") design. Here, qualitative researchers examine the use of communication technology in context (e.g., how hair stylists use the telephone to schedule appointments while they are working on their clients), and feed those data back into the design process (e.g., by having designers role-play customers using the technology) (Burns, Dishman, Johnson, & Verplank, 1995). Potentially, such work reconfigures existing relationships between users, tools, and producers.

Researchers can also engage CMC as an opportunity to refine and strengthen the claims of existing communication theory (e.g., the adequacy of classification schemes for communication systems; Caplan, 2001). Hine (2000, p. 8) identifies four theoretical issues that are uniquely suited for qualitative CMC research: (1) How do users interpret the potential relevance and significance of CMC systems? How do they realize this potential in practice? (2) How does CMC affect the organization of social relationships in time and space? (3) What are the implications of CMC for the perceived authenticity and authority of communicative performances? and (4) How are online and offline realities symbolically constructed, and how is the relationship between them configured?

Let us focus now more closely on the consequences of adopting CMC as a topic and/or methodology of qualitative research. Mann and Stewart (2000, pp. 17-38) list several advantages stemming from this adoption. They include expanded access to hard to reach populations (e.g., the homebound elderly) and sites (e.g., those that are remote or dangerous); reduced savings in time (e.g., for travel) and cost (e.g., of renting focus-group venues); the convenience of automatically generated transcription (e.g., in archived logs of Newsgroup postings); the preformatting of data for analysis (e.g., in programmed sorting of e-mail messages as they are received); and the capacity for CMC to provide participants with a safe, informal, and collaborative context for participation. These advantages can be quite compelling: As Hine (2000) notes, "the popularity of the ethnographic approach to online phenomena probably owes something to the accessibility of the field site to increasingly desk-bound academics. In the current academic climate, time for prolonged immersion in a . . . [physically remote] site is hard to come by" (p. 22).

Mann and Stewart (2000) also note, however, corresponding *dis*advantages posed by CMC for qualitative research. These include the necessity of developing basic technological skills as well as advanced communication competence on specific CMC systems of locating, compiling, and managing a database of contact information for participants (e.g., there are no universal "phonebooks" of e-mail addresses); of enticing the participation of techno-phobic or busy subjects; of ensuring that all participants have compatible equipment and the necessary access and skill; and of sustaining subjects' participation over the length of projects.

To understand CMC research, it helps to know its early (and enduring) lines of study. One principal research program was developed among organi-zational communication scholars (see Culnan & Markus, 1987; Fulk & Steinfield, 1990; Zuboff, 1988). These researchers were concerned with dis-covering the effects of new technologies (such as teleconferencing) on organi-zational structures and on employees' performance of interdependent tasks (such as group decision making). This research established that employees used CMC for both task and relational purposes, and that its adoption pro-duced dramatic consequences. These consequences varied widely, however, because of the ambiguous potential of unique CMC systems and the differing contexts in which they were implemented. Generally, CMC offers organi-zational users increased abilities to produce, store, retrieve, process, and exchange information. As a result, CMC can flatten hierarchies and promote desirable outcomes such as increased efficiency, flexibility, participation, col-laboration, and innovation. In other organizational contexts, however, the introduction of CMC has produced disorientation (e.g., by increasing the rate and volume of information flow) and reinforced *un*desirable tendencies toward surveillance, isolation, conflict, and alienation.

Consequently, a great deal of research has been devoted to exploring the contexts of design and implementation that produce these differences (Heaton, 1998). In this process, researchers have established that many users—organizational and otherwise—experience "narrowband" CMC sys-tems as impersonal because of their inability to convey nonverbal cues and provide immediate feedback. As a result, users develop unconventional prac-tices that manipulate available resources (e.g., the characters of the QWERTY keyboard) to compensate for these limitations and to meet their socioemotional needs. These practices constitute a sophisticated "electronic paralanguage" involving codes of abbreviation, acronyms, underlining, punctuation, spelling, and—most famously—"emoticons" that graphically represent users' affect. Although the material traces of these practices may be small, their significance for users is not. Hine (2000), for example, notes that

> in newsgroups, the use of the > symbol to denote a piece of text quoted from a previous posting performs a number of different things, including: a set of expectations about what the audience should or should not be able to remember from previous postings; moral statements about the ownership and attribution of words; and conversationality, operationalized as turn-taking. (p. 94)

Initial research also established that, for some users, the anonymity of CMC reduces inhibition and encourages impulsiveness (e.g., in angry "flaming" of other users). Communities of users, as a result, develop and enforce norms (e.g., "netiquette") for effective and appropriate participation (Reid, 1995).

These findings are particularly interesting because they signal conditions faced by qualitative researchers who use CMC to study these very phenomena. These conditions saturate efforts to negotiate entries to virtual sites and to wring warmth, richness, and sensitivity out of otherwise cold and impersonal media (Lindlof & Shatzer, 1998).

Although groundbreaking, early programs of CMC research were subject to a number of critiques. Research on organizational CMC, for example, displayed a narrow focus on managerial concerns, an objectivist conceptualization of technology, and a positivist focus on measuring "effects." Researchers in other settings (such as MUDs) acknowledged that their research was in a formative stage of description. The higher level work of theorizing would need to unfold. These (self-) critiques have created an opening for qualitative researchers to leverage their strengths in depicting the social construction of CMC.

Central Areas of CMC Research

In this section, we focus on three topics that have generated the greatest interest among qualitative researchers of CMC: identity, relationships, and community. We briefly review the central themes and issues in the study of each area.

Identity

Traditionally, the topic of identity involves cultural modes of understanding and performing the self. It represents the intersection of multiple perceptions and actions associated with the relationship between self and other. These elements include who we think we are, how we wish others to perceive us, how we present ourselves, how others actually perceive us, and how others perform those perceptions (Wood & Smith, 2001, p. 47). Identity has been an enduring topic of scholarly inquiry and has generated competing theories about its nature and production. Qualitative research has made a central contribution to understanding identity and CMC. Centrally, that research has focused on the expressive opportunities provided by CMC, and their consequence for conventional ways of knowing and doing identity. Here, the work of MIT researcher Sherry Turkle (1984, 1995) has been groundbreaking. Her studies of the subcultures of "hackers" (i.e., mischievous and unauthorized users) and MUDs have influenced a generation of scholarship (see Donath, 1999; Wood & Smith, 2001, pp. 47-69). The central themes of this work include:

- Computer users identify strongly with their tools and programs. Over time, this identification collapses the conceptual distinction between user and system. Users attribute human qualities to their technologies, and technological qualities to social phenomena (e.g., in metaphors of mind as "computer" and of communication as "transmission" or "conduit").
- "Inside" CMC systems, users find vivid, alternative worlds characterized by logic and order. In navigating and mastering these worlds, they experience new levels of pleasure, safety, and creativity. Their communication becomes more playful and stylized.
- The dominant computing culture displays a masculine preference for disembodied, hyperrational, and controlling interaction. This worldview potentially inhibits the development of traits associated with communication competence (e.g., empathy).
- The anonymity and reduced cues associated with many CMC systems encourage users to experiment with the expression of elements of their identity (e.g., gender and sexual orientation). Users adopt and perform new identities by crafting "avatars" (i.e., condensed signifiers of identity, such as a MUD character name) from system resources. In this process, they selectively disguise their undesirable aspects and symbolically adopt more desirable aspects. Users deploy their avatars in interaction with each other (and frequently inquire about the relationship between an avatar and the user identity that it signifies). Over time, users attribute forms of reputation and status (i.e., *personae*) to each other's avatars (e.g., as friendly, argumentative, intelligent, etc.).
- The practical separation by CMC systems of users' *bodies* (as material containers of identity) from their *expressions* (as symbolic performances of identity) resonates deeply with postmodern theories. Generally, these theories reject models of identity emphasizing its singularity, depth, essence, stability, and originality. Alternately, they favor models emphasizing its multiplicity, diversity, simultaneity, fluidity, surface, and relational production.
- These implications of CMC have created controversy about the ethics and politics of identity. Although many users (e.g., the disabled) experience online activity as liberation from the constraints of their embodied, offline existence, others exploit the opportunity to perform deception. Some critics reject the casual assumption and shedding of alternate identities by CMC users, arguing that this practice minimizes the integrity of minority groups' struggle for dignity and voice. As a result, users, producers, and regulators are continuously engaged in a spirited debate about the nature and consequences of online deception. In this debate, issues of identity overlap with those of community as users attempt to define norms and enforce appropriate sanctions.

Relationships

Research on the creation, maintenance, and transformation of relationships in CMC has been dominated by three competing explanations (Walther, 1996; see also Wood & Smith, 2001, pp. 70-91). As noted above, early research established that because CMC stripped nonverbal cues and afforded easy exit from interaction, users experienced it as shallow, ambiguous, stark, and impersonal. This "cues filtered out" effect was recorded in experiments conducted in laboratory settings. These experiments used "zero history" groups whose members performed artificial tasks with no anticipation of further interaction. When researchers altered these conditions, they discovered that if users were given adequate opportunities for personal interaction over time, they could develop satisfying relationships. This is known as the "social information processing" perspective. Another explanation, the "hyper-personal" perspective, holds that CMC users exploit features such as narrow bandwidth and asynchrony to create preferred images of self (i.e., in carefully composing a newsgroup posting). This strategic self-presentation encourages message recipients to project idealized traits onto ambiguous and incomplete texts of others' identities. As a result, CMC potentially accelerates the development of intimacy between participants.

These competing explanations indicate that researchers should take into account contextual features such as users' histories and a setting's official purpose. In studying CMC, qualitative researchers are poised to help resolve a number of connected issues: How do CMC users import and manage expectations generated in their offline relationships in online interaction? How does the reverse occur (e.g., the management of impressions formed online among users who subsequently meet FTF; Jacobson, 1999)? How do the features of different CMC systems affect the development of relationships (Rintel, Mulholland, & Pittam, 2001)? Because most research has focused on the conduct of relationships developed online, we need to ask: How do *offline* partners conduct their relationships online (Campbell & Wickman, 2000)? In turn, how do these users import their online interaction back into their offline relationships? Also, because most research has focused on newly established online relationships, we need to find out: How do long-term online partners interact? And finally, what are the long-term consequences of using CMC as a medium for relationships? A recent national study, for example, reported that even average users experience a greater incidence of loneliness and depression than nonusers and are more likely than nonusers to neglect their relationships with friends and family members.

Community

As their etymological similarity indicates, the phenomena of *community* and *communication* are intimately related. Communication is commonly viewed as the lifeblood of community; community is a principal context in which the communication is viewed as a sacred human activity. In recent years, the creation of "virtual communities" on CMC systems has generated heated debates among scholars, government officials, citizen groups, and commentators about the relationship of such communities to "traditional" communities (Fernback, 1999; Wood & Smith, 2001, pp. 109-125).

Like the debates involving CMC and identity, these debates often suffer from the fallacies of objectification and nostalgia. As the prominent Internet scholar Steven Jones (1995, 1997, 1998) notes, popular definitions of community are shaped in a tension between the residual values of oral culture (e.g., those privileging "neighborly" association) and traumatic developments in postwar society (e.g., the commercialization of public space that eliminates "great good place[s]" of civic association outside home and work). As a result, critics of CMC often adopt standards for defining community (e.g., common inhabitation of a locale, self-sufficiency from the external world, interdependence, common identity, and binding ritual) that are "imaginary" (i.e., ideological) and ethnocentric (Kollock & Smith, 1999, p. 16). This condition does not render those criteria illegitimate, however—only contingent. Additionally, it does not invalidate concerns that CMC potentially fragments users, encouraging them to withdraw and avoid the hard work of "real" citizenship in favor of consuming services and simulations. Furthermore, as James Carey (1989) argues, popular understanding of the relationship between community and communication has historically been shaped by the development of technologies such as the railroad and the telegraph. Carey argues that, because of their practical benefits for dominant political and economic groups, these technologies have been promoted in ways that encourage us to view communication as instrumental "transmission," and not as communal "ritual."

CMC, however, functions precisely to restore the ontological link between community and communication. Thus it establishes that communication is a necessary *and* sufficient condition for CMC users to *act as if they are* members of a community (Rheingold, 1993). Through communication, groups of CMC users can create and maintain "settlements" that distinguish them from transient online gatherings. Quentin Jones (1997) argues that this phenomenon occurs when CMC satisfies the following conditions: (1) a minimum level of interaction (e.g., users exchange messages in sufficient quantities and rates); (2) a variety of communicators (e.g., sufficient to engender differences of opinion); (3) a common public space (i.e., an identifiable place for inhabitation and interaction); and (4) a minimum level of sustained membership (i.e., as opposed to single, or only intermittent, interactions). "The existence of a virtual settlement," Jones concludes, "is proof of the existence of a related virtual community." Liu (1999), however, notes a number of challenges posed to these criteria by actual CMC features, including resident "robot" programs that simulate users' presence, rapid shifts in user nicknames, and the discontinuous termination and revival of IRC channels by their users.

Qualitative researchers have been instrumental in documenting how users of text-based CMC systems (e.g., BBS, MUDs, and IRCs) develop, maintain, and transform elements that are analogous to those of offline communities (Jones, 1995, 1998; Kollock & Smith, 1999). These elements include charters of purpose; categories of membership (e.g., "lurkers" who observe activity but do not interact with other users); norms for interaction (e.g., prohibitions against the "spamming" of unwanted messages to an entire user population); procedures for allocating resources, adjudicating disputes, and punishing transgression (Correll, 1995; Dibbell, 1994); and binding rituals of initiation, passage, and degradation. Researchers here have focused on how users—who are often highly skilled and creative—evoke implicit, contextual material that defines their commonality and develop "strong ties" through the use of jargon and vernacular (Fernback, 1999; Marvin, 1995). They have noted that CMC allows users to compensate for the perceived shortcomings of their offline communities (e.g., isolation, prejudice, downward mobility, and crime). Many researchers are interested in the potential of CMC to *strengthen* existing communities (e.g., through the development of local systems that encourage citizen dialogue and counteract the negative impacts of globalization). Some, laudably, have applied their expertise to developing these systems (Harrison & Stephen, 1999).

Methodological Issues in Qualitative Research of CMC

Design: Conceptualizing the Field and Site of CMC

A central issue for qualitative researchers involves defining both online and offline worlds, and the relationships that exist among and between them (Lindlof & Shatzer, 1998; Lyman & Wakeford, 1999, pp. 361-363; Mann & Stewart, 2000, pp. 203-207; Sterne, 1999, pp. 269-270). These definitions have significant implications for "where" researchers view themselves as operating and how they should account for their findings. This issue arises partly because the field of cyberspace is produced in the interaction between multiple layers of phenomena, including *metaphors* and *discourses* (e.g., from "cyberpunk" science fiction), *artifacts* (e.g., wireless pagers), *actors* (e.g., hackers), *infrastructure* (e.g., the historical ARPANET) (Star, 1999), and *experiences* (e.g., of so-called Internet addiction) (Gourgey & Smith, 1996;

Kendall, 1999; Strate, 1999). This complexity requires researchers to specify *which type* of phenomena they view CMC as evidence of. The issue also arises because CMC demonstrates that elements of postmodern society have transformed traditional assumptions about the nature of fieldwork (Green, 1999). Specifically, CMC is a globalizing force that has undermined the presumed isolation, stability, and "uniqueness" of "local" cultures that motivated generations of anthropologists to study them. This development has forced researchers to acknowledge that their fields are increasingly multisited, partial, dispersed, and mediated. As opposed to singular, self-contained "locations," these fields are "spaces of flow" organized around "connections" between people, practices, events, and objects (Hine, 2000, p. 61). One implication of this development is that traditional criteria for valid qualitative research—such as physical "travel" by researchers to remote sites and extended, immediate interaction with cultural members there—are no longer universal or appropriate (Lyman & Wakeford, 1999).

Hine (2000) notes that these conditions have given rise to at least two dominant paradigms for studying CMC. One paradigm is to treat CMC as a "place" where online cultures are performed (e.g., as "play" on IRC; Ruedenberg, Danet, & Rosenbaum-Tamari, 1995). A second, more materialist approach treats CMC as a cultural artifact: "a technology that was produced by particular people with contextually situated goals and priorities" (Hine, 2000, p. 9). In this view, as Lyman and Wakeford (1999) note, "the importance of . . . artifacts is not that they signify discrete, intrinsically meaningful entities, but rather that the ways they are used introduce new repertoires of practice" (p. 367). Hine's point is that each approach suggests a different view of the research site. The first approach emphasizes how CMC displays stylistic conventions and communal ideology (such as norms, values, and beliefs). The second approach focuses on the production and interpretation of CMC as a contingent activity. It emphasizes that forms of CMC that we take for granted might have been otherwise—that they have been shaped by the constraints of infrastructure and by the contextual discourses of marketing, formal instruction, and peer-evaluation. Hine's (2000) study of Web pages surrounding a controversial legal case demonstrates this approach by showing how they emerged through "social processes of negotiation between different interest groups who view the advantages and disadvantages of the technology differently" (p. 33).

In addressing this issue, some researchers treat CMC as relatively continuous with "real life" (RL). In this view, CMC is a medium in which users report activities and experiences associated with their offline existence. In this process, users draw on their offline knowledge (e.g., of how to assess race, class, and gender identities and of other users' "real" characteristics) to perform and interpret CMC. Kendall (1998, 1999) argues that this condition significantly constrains the overrated potential for users to revise their identities online. In this view, online and offline practices (and their consequences) are *connected*, *similar*, or *equivalent* (e.g., the orgasms produced by cybersex). So-called LAN parties, in which computer game players converge at a venue both to compete online *and to* flirt with, taunt, and encourage each other FTF, would be an example of a hybrid site appropriate for this perspective. By extension, in this logic, there are "universal" practices of qualitative research that link the two spheres, such as the need to monitor informant deception (Fernback, 1999, p. 216).

Other researchers, however, treat CMC as a relatively distinct and self-contained phenomenon. In this view, CMC may form a supplement to the "real" data generated in FTF fieldwork (e.g., Workman, 1995). A related approach views CMC as evidence (only) of how users interact on particular systems or create "pocket universes" in which they contest the dominant meanings of media texts (Scodari & Felder, 2000). This perspective may emerge as a solution to encountered problems: In their study of cybersex among IRC users, Waskul and colleagues (2000) quickly found that participants rejected their attempts to gather personal information. As a result, these researchers discontinued those attempts and qualified their site as "the online environment in which individuals create a context for the experience of cybersex" (p. 381). They argued that this decision formed an acceptable trade-off between the ethical and logistical problems associated with gathering such information and the inevitable bias associated with self-selection by respondents to such requests. Although this view privileges online over offline activity, it does not necessarily view CMC as a static site. Rintel, Mulholland, and Pittam (2001), for example, note that IRC users move unpredictably between accessible "public" channels and secure "private" channels. This means that tracking the relationship *among* users' multiple identities within a CMC system may be as challenging as attempting to match them to an offline corollary (Lyman & Wakeford, 1999, p. 363).

Finally, other researchers adopt hybrid positions to strengthen the richness and validity of their claims. In her studies of online identity, for example, Turkle (1995) only reported data about users she had also interviewed offline. Although she did not do this to prove that her subjects were more "real" in one context than another, it helped to refine her conceptual distinction between online deception and creative self-construction.

Overshadowing this decision point is popular wisdom emphasizing a *disjuncture* between the two contexts—for example, in sensational media coverage of predatory online deception. This distinction is based on a persistent cultural embrace of FTF as a normalized "gold standard" against which other media are evaluated (Chesebro & Bertelsen, 1996, pp. 83-107; Rintel et al., 2001). This unreflective embrace, however, is dubious. It clouds the fact that FTF is itself mediated by elaborate conventions (e.g., surrounding flirtation) that communicators have historically developed to coordinate their actions and achieve consensus. Additionally, as Caplan (2001) notes, "interpersonal" communication is frequently mediated (e.g., in telephone conversation).

An obvious decision point here involves studying the online versus offline activities of subjects. Many CMC researchers focus exclusively on online activity, but the limitations of this choice are increasingly clear. It evokes the same criticism faced by audience studies that only observe television viewers in the act of viewing: Such studies fail to depict how CMC is integrated into users' larger life experience and activity (e.g., their use of other media; Scodari & Felder, 2000). Other researchers take a more holistic perspective. In their portrait of Trinidadian use of the Internet, for example, Miller and Slater (2000) analyze specific settings (e.g., cyber-cafés) and practices to show that that "virtuality" is a social accomplishment, not an inherent feature or direct effect of technology. Nardi and O'Day (1999), similarly, conceptualize CMC as a type of "information ecology." In this view, CMC is "a system of people, practices, values, and technologies [configured] in a particular local environment" (p. 49). Researchers focus on the unique and dynamic relationships that exist between different "species" of users in CMC contexts (e.g., between students, faculty, and reference librarians in university libraries). Users are believed to alternately collaborate and compete in defining technologies, establishing their relationships, and managing their use. One example of this involves college dormitories in which residents establish "quiet hours" favoring computer usage over stereo music and roommates negotiate rules for sharing online access.

Researchers may also reject a hard distinction between online and offline activity in cases where users' *personae* are relatively consistent across those realms and where there is no consensus among users about *what the difference is* between them. Instead of presuming the prior existence of online and offline worlds, researchers can investigate their construction by users as they invoke local norms, values, and beliefs. In this perspective, online and offline "realities" are not objective contexts but the topics and products of evolving communication. Researchers focus on understanding and documenting the various ways in which these realms may be conceptualized and configured (Kendall, 1998; Markham, 1998). In their analysis of game playing on IRC, for example, Ruedenberg and colleagues (1995) argued that "real life" is just one among multiple frames evoked by users to contextualize their interaction. In her study of a MUD, however, Cherny (1995) argued that its members treated CMC "as an extension of real life, rather than an escape from it." Once researchers have resolved this conceptual issue, they may move to more practical ones associated with identifying potential sites and subjects. Our concern here is with how researchers justify their decisions. Thanks to the relatively "low search costs" associated with CMC (Kozinets, 2001), researchers may easily identify a starting point for inquiry, such as the formal location of a virtual community. Within that site, they can begin to characterize its internal zones (e.g., by studying an available "site map") and membership categories. Contextualizing that site, however, may prove more difficult. The hypertextuality of Web pages, for example, requires researchers to define those that are "central" to a study (e.g., based on their rate of citation by other pages) and to characterize their relationships (for example, by charting dominant paths of user navigation; Hine, 2000). The issue here, note Mitra and Cohen (1999, p. 194), involves deciding "how deep into hypertext one needs to go in the process of analyzing the interconnected text"—where to stop, in other words, because one *must* stop somewhere. Otherwise, the volume of data quickly becomes unmanageable.

Researchers may need to identify and contact gatekeepers (such as listserv moderators or MUD "wizards") to negotiate entry to the site and access to user data (which is often protected as confidential). Researchers should also monitor a bias toward studying accessible "public" sites of CMC; activity in more private and secure channels remains understudied, and its absence affects the validity of claims about community practice (Kendall, 1999, p. 70). The anonymity associated with many CMC systems can also prevent researchers from gathering preliminary data on user qualities. While researchers may choose to incorporate surveys in their research design (Zurawski, 1999), they must also face various barriers to verifying the responses. Additionally, inequities of technological access and skill create a condition in which Internet communities (despite their increasing diversity) are hardly representative of global populations (Mann & Stewart, 2000, pp. 31-37).

The choices made around these issues should lead researchers to qualify their claims regarding CMC users and their related activities. For example, in published findings some researchers depict users as social actors who "self-present" *as* a particular age, race, or gender. This qualification alerts readers that they are *not* reading an account of a verified performance *by* a member of those groups. Similarly, researchers may or may not choose to contextualize their data as drawn from (variously) representative samples of a known population of users.

Observing and Participating

At one level, CMC is a dream come true for qualitative researchers: It clarifies the textual dimensions of communication and allows easy recording of those data. Researchers of textual CMC systems (such as e-mail) can readily observe language in action, as well as some limited nonverbal and metacommunicative practices. Emerging multimedia systems expand these opportunities by depicting codes such as proxemics (e.g., on-screen spatial relations between graphical avatars) (Krikorian, Lee, & Chock, 2000) and paralinguistics (e.g., the vocal intonation of teleconference participants). Participant observation is uniquely suited to exploring the production by users of different types of social meaning. These include meanings associated with using a particular CMC system, with membership in a virtual community, and with practices that define online identities and relationships and express community values (Mann & Stewart, 2000, p. 88).

Different camps of qualitative researchers, however, orient differently to CMC's ambiguous gifts. Here, we recall our earlier discussions of key differences between discourse analysts and ethnographers. Discourse analysts generally favor an observational role for researchers, the systematic analysis of transcribed data, and the avoidance of "talk-extrinsic" context in that analysis. Ethnographers favor participation as a means of reflexively generating knowledge about membership, construct data in descriptive and narrative fieldnotes, and readily invoke cultural context in data analysis.

These differences affect researchers' orientations to participating in CMC. One view, most closely aligned with discourse analysis, favors creating logs or accessing archives of interaction, and analyzing them for exemplars of communicative practice. If participation is necessary to record data, the limited role of "lurking" is preferred, so as to minimize the impact on "naturally occurring" interaction. Denzin's (1999) study of Newsgroup postings by recovering codependents, and Rintel and colleagues' (2001) study of conversational openings among IRC users exemplify this approach. The benefits of this approach include isolation, formalization, and rigorous consideration of data.

Ethnographers, however, note several drawbacks to this approach. First, lurking is a consequential performance. Although lurkers may be relatively invisible on systems such as a list-serv, that is not the case in IRCs or MUDs, which automatically announce the presence of arriving users to others present in the channel. In this way, lurkers may not be active participants, but this does not mean that others do not orient to them (i.e., in the way that residents of a rumored haunted house orient to its ghosts). Kendall (1999, pp. 70-71), for example, argues that researchers who adopt anonymity in studying sites are likely to elicit suspicion—and anonymity in kind—from other users. This artifact of their strategy may lead them to misrepresent the prevalence of its use in CMC. Users, then, may address lurkers implicitly or explicitly, and specifically or generally (e.g., in direct appeals by members of sleepy list-servs for greater participation).

Second, many archiving systems (such as logs of IRC, even when turns are time stamped) do not capture the dynamic experience of unfolding communication (e.g., rates of turn-taking). Third, logs cannot capture the material contexts in which CMC is produced. One example of this involves the textured collapse of online and offline worlds that users produce around their interface: the glow of monitor light on skin deprived of sunlight, strewn containers of cold, half-eaten food, frantic tacking between user manuals and on-screen data, and painful protest from atrophied bodies (Markham, 1998). Finally, Reid (1995) notes that CMC discourse is typically addressed to others who are directly involved in interaction; as a result, a pure observational stance may fail to capture the experience of membership evoked in the moment of that address.

While these sketches of discourse-analytic and ethnographic approaches are not exhaustive of the ways that qualitative researchers conceptualize participation and observation online, they usefully punctuate the alternatives. Many studies tend toward one extreme or the other, or reference these values in negotiating hybrid positions (Smyres, 1999).

The invisibility of CMC systems creates opportunities and challenges for participant observers. Although we have noted above some problems associated with the extended use of lurking, it offers curious researchers an easy way to case a scene before they assert a more active participant role (Kozinets, 2001). Additionally, CMC's decoupling of bodies from expression means that material signifiers of identity (such as age or race) that might otherwise facilitate rapport with subjects must be renegotiated through CMC. Here, researchers may choose to provide subjects with a link to images (or other texts of identity) that help them to resolve their uncertainty about a researcher's attributes (although they should remember to disable such links after they have left the field, or face the consequences of "lingering telepresence"; Kozinets, 2001). An alternative is to perform the researcher role through one's avatar (for example, by incorporating a virtual tape recorder into the description associated with a MUD character). In addition, researchers who might normally be excluded from a group because of a detectable trait may utilize CMC to shape its disclosure (by deferring its discussion or by minimizing or reframing its connotations).

The line between these strategies and unethical deception is razor thin. We sympathize with the argument that online deception can facilitate the critical goals of disrupting oppressive power relationships (e.g., female researchers can reduce harassment and patronizing by male users) and exposing hegemonic practices to greater scrutiny. At the least, then, researchers considering these strategies should rigorously interrogate their motives, formalize their rationale, anticipate the potential consequences, and account for the impact of deception on data collection and analysis. Generally, we recommend that researchers *not* misrepresent their research purposes in their online personae. At the very least, researchers should follow ethical norms developed by relevant online communities for the expression of those purposes.

Interviewing

As we discussed in Chapter 6, qualitative interviewing involves striking a balance between the researcher's agenda and subjects' capacities for sense-making and expression. In this light, researchers generally agree that synchronous forms of CMC (e.g., IRC) are best suited for nonstandardized (e.g., ethnographic) interviewing (Mann & Stewart, 2000, p. 76). The immediacy of real-time interaction in these forms allows participants to ask and answer questions efficiently, and contributes to a climate of intimacy in which understandings can be carefully developed and explored. Although they may serve in a pinch, asynchronous forms of CMC such as e-mail discourage this quality of relationship. Researchers using asynchronous CMC must decide how much of the interview guide to send in a single turn. In text-based formats, sending an entire list of questions effectively transforms the interview into a survey. The alternative—parceling out a question at a time—presents the challenge of managing small bits of sequentially received data. Additionally, it increases the possibility that bored or distracted interviewees will invest their time and attention elsewhere before completing the interview.

In some areas, CMC interviewers face challenges similar to those encountered in offline research. Subjects must be recruited and oriented through appropriate media. Real-time interviews with multiple participants (such as focus groups) involve additional orientation concerning protocols for turn-taking and topic-shifting. Distracting "noise" is another universal concern: Interviews are likely to be unsuccessful if conducted in channels that may be interrupted by others (or where interviewees may be cautious about the presence of lurkers).

Other concerns, however, are unique to CMC. The global reach of the Internet means that participants may be interviewing "from" vastly different time zones. A researcher's mid-afternoon task may be an interviewee's cure for insomnia. Such differences in the body's circadian rhythms affect participants' concentration, speed of response, and endurance (Lyman & Wakeford, 1999, p. 365). If interviewers adopt text-based formats, they must adapt to the lack of nonverbal cues (posture, facial expression, tone of voice, etc.) that would otherwise guide them in interpreting responses and in designing subsequent turns (e.g., follow-up probes). Although this challenge is real, it is not insurmountable. Qualitative interviewing, you will recall, is performed in the context of an evolving relationship. As we discussed above, researchers have discovered that, given sufficient time, CMC users can create adequate context for interpreting ambiguous events and can develop rapport.

To achieve this goal, however, CMC interviewers must do considerable work. They must use limited information in moment-to-moment decisions about the significance (and implications) of message form and content. Among IRC and MUD users, for example, it is common to divide the content of an otherwise extended turn into a series of messages: a single posted message does not, therefore, necessarily represent a complete a response to a question. Relatedly, definitions of significant delay in response differ both among and between users of different CMC systems. Some users of e-mail check their in-box once a day (and may prioritize received messages for immediate versus deferred response); other users check it every hour. IRC users (who are infamous for multitasking) may leave an interviewer hanging for any number of reasons: They may be considering the question, be composing a lengthy response, be attending to another conversation, or have temporarily left their interface. Generally, then, interview participants must negotiate procedures for managing several contingencies. These include: demonstrating their continued presence and availability to each other; re-establishing contact if a channel is disrupted or terminated; managing turn-taking; resolving the ambiguity of statements (Hamman, 1997); and determining when an interview is completed. Here, the virtues of patience and sensitivity and the generous provision of reassurance are all recommended. Interviewers and interviewees may explicitly coach each other on how to use a CMC system for this type of dialogue. In the process, they may turn the interview into a reflexive performance of the research topic (Markham, 1998).

Collecting and Analyzing Data

In Chapter 7 we discussed the use of computer software programs for qualitative data analysis; we focus here on the unique issues arising from the use of computers to collect and analyze CMC data.

The development of CMC has stimulated debate within and between qualitative research camps about the effects of "new" technologies on collecting and analyzing data (Mann & Stewart, 2000, pp. 181-194). Implicitly, these debates concede that some form of technology *always* mediates qualitative research. Traditionalists alarmed by the implications of new technologies appear to have forgotten (or naturalized) the role played by their own preferred tools (e.g., ink pens and notebooks) in producing data.

More central to these discussions, however, is the sense of what is won and lost in the apparent "shortcut" to data offered by CMC (Mann & Stewart, 2000, pp. 181-194). As we discussed above, this shortcut involves the automatic logging of interaction and the bypassing of transcription (but not fieldnote) chores. Also, as noted, qualitative researchers orient differently to this opportunity depending on their preferences for the researcher role, forms of data, and the admission of context to data analysis. Additionally, researchers differ in the value they place on the "hybrid inheritance" (Mann & Stewart, 2000, p. 184) of speech and writing that characterizes CMC's textual data. Systems such as IRC, for example, favor the ephemeral and superficial qualities of speech and may be viewed as inappropriately informal and disjointed for some research purposes. Alternatively, some researchers may view the option of careful composition in e-mail as a deterrent to studying spontaneous and improvisational communication. Others may view the loss of nonverbal (and other contextual) cues in CMC data to be unacceptable for studying complex processes.

For better and worse, however, nearly all forms of CMC may be textualized as data (see Liu, 1999, for an extended review of systems for logging IRC). The issue is whether researchers will supplement those data with other documents (e.g., downloaded Web pages) and narratives (e.g., fieldnotes) or analyze them directly for evidence of particular social practices (or creatively combine these approaches). Again, these practices follow from the premises of membership in a particular research community. Reed and Ashmore (2000) note that traditional conversation analysts may disdain the formatted posting of Newsgroups because those data have not been manually transcribed. This disdain is ironic, however, because successful transcriptions efface their own construction and create an illusion of transparency as windows onto naturally occurring conversation. As a result, Reed and Ashmore (2000) argue that discourse analysts should treat Newsgroup postings as no less "naturally occurring" than offline interaction. Their records are simply produced by a *different* technology.

The issue of automation is not limited to discourse analysts. Angrosino and Mays de Peréz (2000) note that this technology has confronted ethnographers with resurgent objectivism. Even as interpretive and critical epistemology emphasizes the values of contingency, reflexivity, and embodiment in qualitative research, technologies for "capturing" data increasingly privilege its record "at the expense of the lived experience as the ethnographer has personally known it" (p. 696). In this sense, ethnographers are fighting an uphill battle against cultural myths about "transparent" CMC systems (such as Virtual Reality) that immerse users in simulations of interaction (Bolter & Grusin, 2000). One solution to this dilemma is for ethnographers to play to their strengths: situate the evidence of online interaction in reflective and descriptive narratives of its collaborative production. Kozinets (2001) describes this focus as involving the "subtexts, pretexts, conditions and personal emotions that occur during . . . participant observation." An example of this is Markham's (1998) study of online chat, in which she does all this and then goes a step further to exploit the codes of ethnographic representation. Her published account juxtaposes excerpts from logged chat and fieldnotes, uses different typefaces to signal a narrative shift between reportage and reflection, and creatively alters the appearance of online data (e.g., to conform to the genre of novelistic dialogue) to simulate for readers its associated experience. In a related example, Waskul and colleagues (2000) edited the appearance of logged IRC data in their published study to eliminate misleading conventions (e.g., ellipses employed by users to denote pauses) and to filter out unrelated messages so as to clarify the evolution of a single discussion thread.

The uses of CMC in data analysis can range from the simple and peripheral to the central and complex. The practice of obtaining member checks forms one example. An increasing number of researchers, for example, use CMC (e.g., in file attachments to e-mail messages) as a means of communicating with subjects about evolving interpretations of data (Ceglowski, 2000). Rosson (1999), however, went a step further in her study of users' stories about CMC by employing a Web site *as a means of collecting them* (see http://miso.cs.vt.edu/story). This reflexive research design forms an interesting case. Early in her study, Rosson posted the themes generated by her initial analysis of those stories (e.g., "Getting Started" and "Cyber-Relationships") on the Web site. Subsequent visitors (the site is still operative) have been invited to review and respond to the stories posted under these headings and to post their own stories. The site interface also provides users with a default option of "miscellaneous" for categorizing their submissions. After examining the actual Web site, however, we argue that this design is an innovative but contradictory use of CMC for qualitative research. Specifically, in creating this design, Rosson both solicits stories from users and—potentially—allows them to comment on her evolving analysis. The problem, however, is that the site blurs the functions of data collection and analysis. It structurally reifies Rosson's initial categories by imposing them as options for submission; that is, users are encouraged to conform to the existing scheme in the act of posting their stories. The interface does not appear to provide users with the option of constructing new or alternate themes, and it does not encourage feedback on the adequacy of the existing themes. In technologically submitting their stories to the site, users must also "submit" to the researcher's categories. Thus, the interpretive validity of these categories declines—not grows—over time. Their accumulated content does not reflect a scheme that has been validated by analytic induction (in which the *researcher* bears the responsibility for ensuring the mutual transformation of data and interpretive categories). Here, through questionable use of CMC, an initially inductive study appears to have reverted midstream to deduction.

Ethics

Ethical issues associated with studying CMC have been extensively debated (Cavanagh, 1999; Mann & Stewart, 2000, pp. 39-64; Thomas, 1996). In general, these debates note the dilemmas posed by conducting research in a dynamic context that currently lacks universal regulation. This condition, in which barriers to access and norms of conduct vary locally, is ethically ambiguous. On the one hand, it offers researchers some freedom to collaboratively improvise solutions with affected subjects, and with their Institutional Review Boards. On the other hand, a lack of effective sanctions for unethical behavior may encourage irresponsible research. For example, Sharf (1999) notes that calculated "harvesting" of CMC by online groups without obtaining their consent or risking personal participation "is doable and ostensibly legal, yet flies in the face of what thousands, maybe millions, of Internet group members feel is permissible and ethical" (pp. 251-252).

In recent years, the tenor of these debates has shifted. An initial laissez-faire tolerance of textual harvesting (rationalized by an analogy drawn between CMC and "exempt" forms of public interaction, such as that occurring in shopping malls) has been replaced by a deeper sense of responsibility for researcher participation in CMC as *interaction*. This shift has included distinctions between widely accessible, "public" sites of CMC that carry less obligation for obtaining informed consent and other sites in which participants have—by virtue of restrictions to membership or the nature of disclosures—a "reasonable expectation of privacy," and thus entitlement to greater consideration. Liu (1999) notes, however, that these distinctions are not objective or stable: "public" channels with relatively few participants encourage an experience of "private" interaction, and vice versa. Because many virtual communities have already been "studied" by journalists and scholars (with varying agendas and consequences), researchers interested in a site should check (e.g., in the FAQ archive) to see if the potential site has developed either formal policies or informal norms regulating research activities. Gajjala (1999) presents an interesting case in this regard: After several reports of studies in progress (some of them hoaxes), members of the virtual community she was studying passed a resolution that prohibited unauthorized representations of their group position. Because of the ambiguous scope and force of this resolution (e.g., researchers were permitted to solicit individual members for permission to publish their statements), and because of other ethical restrictions adopted in her research design, Gajjala decided to continue her research nonetheless.

Participants in these debates have identified several ethical issues associated with CMC research. We present them below, along with some recommended solutions.

The computerized collection of data creates unprecedented issues involving its storage and circulation. Because those data are potentially revealing, commercially profitable, and easily copied, researchers should identify for subjects the purposes to which data will be put and how it will be publicized. They should also consider providing subjects with reasonable access to (and eventual retention of) data in which personal identification has been preserved. Researchers should carefully protect subjects (e.g., by constructing network "firewalls") against risks posed by unauthorized access, modification, disclosure, or loss of data. Data should not be circulated outside of preapproved and researcher-secured channels without the consent of subjects (Mann & Stewart, 2000, pp. 40-44).

Although online environments (e.g., public chat channels) pose formidable challenges to obtaining informed consent, researchers should make reasonable efforts to notify subjects of their presence and activities. Kozinets (2001) labels such efforts "strategies of high visibility." Depending on the particular features of CMC systems and the phase of the study, these efforts may take a variety of forms. Researchers may, for example, construct a Web site that provides information about the study traditionally required for obtaining consent (e.g., potential risks of participation, options for withdrawal, etc.). They may then provide subjects with links to this site in brief, repeated messages (e.g., solicitations and updates). Alternatively, researchers may choose not to widely disclose their presence and purpose in a "public" CMC site, but they may seek consent from particular participants after data collection to include their expressions in published accounts. At a minimum, researchers should ensure that interviewees "complete" consent forms before participating in CMC interviews. Again, this goal may be accomplished by a variety of means tailored to situational needs: incremental presentation of elements in the evolving turns of IRC and MUD dialogue (Markham, 1998); exchange of e-mail messages; and downloading for completion by subjects of consent forms from Web sites, followed by their return as e-mail attachments. Sophisticated Web site designers may even create an interactive form for online completion.

As a topic and a means of conducting research, CMC erodes traditional structures of anonymity and confidentiality for subjects. Traditionally, subjects' identities and activities have been buffered from exposure by virtue of their occurrence in "offline" venues. In these venues, researchers may document activities, but they are also local affairs that are otherwise ephemeral. However, CMC research often draws its data from the archives of BBS and list-servs. Unless these sites are secured by administrators, their archives are increasingly networked with other sites. The development of powerful search engines (such as Google.com) ensures that, even when researchers disguise online identities and locations, sufficiently motivated persons can locate and expose actual events (e.g., by searching for a unique passages of text presented as data) (Gergen & Gergen, 2000, p. 1040). Potentially, this condition also presents researchers with a dilemma of validity: they may need to alter identifying characteristics of messages when those characteristics are the very topic of CMC (e.g., when MUD users comment on each other's character names) and the focus of research (e.g., online performances of identity).

Conclusion: Qualitative Cyborgs: Futures of CMC Research

We invoke the term *cyborg* here to organize several reflections about the possible futures of CMC and qualitative research. This term has been famously developed by the feminist philosopher Donna Haraway (1991) as a metaphor that organizes popular ambivalence about the increasing integration of organic and technological materials (e.g., through implants and prosthetics). Among other things, this fusion has produced a situation in which various types of professionals (e.g., air traffic controllers and real estate agents) are tethered to communication technologies that regulate and enhance their performance. Qualitative researchers are no different, and it is entertaining to imagine how they will innovate technologies to keep up with "real life" (RL).

Pruitt and Barrett's (1991) discussion of the "personal virtual workspace" offers one scenario. Here we can imagine, say, a futuristic organizational ethnographer beginning her workday by entering her customized "virtual research space." After donning her data gloves and head-mounted display, she immerses herself in multimedia data, collected by interfacing with an organization's communication and surveillance systems, and orally composes fieldnotes through a voice-computer interface. She seamlessly accesses connections to online materials for her literature review (some of which, she notes with ambivalence, have been "authored" by nonhuman intelligence). Once downloaded, these materials are holographically displayed as floating books with self-turning pages. She also notes the impending release of virtual reality systems that will allow her to immerse her audiences in 3-D multimedia simulations of organizational events. After lunch, our ethnographer continues her day with a number of activities: "interviewing" a senior artificial intelligence program responsible for organizational strategy, resolving an ethical dilemma about hacking into a desired but restricted database, monitoring the interaction between her data collection programs and the organization's "Sentient Resources" database, and real-time triangulation of data with her distant research team members. The next time she pauses, she notices that the day is nearly over.

This scenario is of course tongue-in-cheek; some of its elements are familiar, and some are speculative. We hope that it makes the desired point: It remains to be seen how our research tools and practices will evolve in relation to the technological features of our chosen sites.

As a result, it is clear that researchers need increased dialogue about the methodological consequences posed for qualitative research by CMC. An obvious concern derived from this scenario is human researchers' abdication of their interpretive agency to machines. Another concern involves the growing *digital divide* between researchers and elite sites. This term is typically used to describe the inequities of access and skill that exist between global users of CMC. It is relevant here because the expense associated with purchasing, programming, and updating CMC systems is significant. Although funding bodies increasingly value the missions of technological education and research, public funding for higher education is generally on the decline. In this climate of scarcity, qualitative research of CMC potentially becomes the domain of the management-approved, grant-supported, or independently wealthy. It is worth considering how this trend will influence which research topics and questions are actively pursued, and by whom.

Gergen and Gergen (2000, pp. 1039-1041) note additional challenges posed by the "technorevolution" of CMC. These include the problems of "vanishing subject matter," in which CMC contributes to an increasing acceleration of—but not critical thinking about—human activity. In part, this means that CMC researchers are subject to the tyranny of "faster" (Gleick, 1999), in which scholarship lags behind the evolution of systems. This acceleration affects traditional goals and strategies of inquiry. The need for reflection is corroded by urgent deadlines; the effort expended to describe stable patterns is frustrated by rapid fluctuations in membership and performance (thus requiring an extended period of sampling) (Liu, 1999); and the relevance of findings fades amid short-lived contexts of value. "How are we to justify studying various cultures," the Gergens ask, ". . . when the very conception of culture as a group of people who share an enduring pattern of meaning and action is being eroded?" (2000, p. 1040).

This question is certainly provocative, but qualitative researchers should not feel hopeless. As we have discussed, logging programs help to combat the impermanency of the CMC text, and this condition may itself become the focus of research (e.g., What rates of updating do Web designers believe are necessary to keep their sites "current"?) (Mitra & Cohen, 1999, p. 198). More to the point, however, CMC poses fundamental questions for communication research that endure across particular product life cycles. These questions form the proverbial ball on which we should keep our eye, even as industry obsesses with exploiting the "new new thing" (Lewis, 2000). Further, adopting the position of novice is still an effective strategy for participant observers, and many virtual communities have established identities (e.g., "newbie") and rituals (e.g., posting and reading FAQs) for socializing newcomers. Qualitative researchers concerned with relevance may choose to align their mission more closely with that of independent journalism: "contributing to the cultural dialogues on the here and now as opposed to the there and then" (Gergen & Gergen, 2000, p. 1040). In addition, as noted above, researchers can use CMC itself as a means of building communities of interest around particular research areas (e.g., by using Web sites to post research reports and invite stakeholder feedback). This solution poses its own dilemma, however. Unless researchers encourage the participation of diverse stakeholders, their efforts will contribute to the antidemocratic trend of atomization, in which small groups of like-minded users interact primarily to refine their common interests.

For scholars, a related matter involves the traditional advisor-advisee relationship. Advisors have commonly presumed authority over the theory (and often practice) associated with a particular research project. However, because rapid technological evolution creates subcultures in which age is inversely correlated with expertise (Lewis, 2001), older advisors may need to yield some of this authority to younger, more technologically fluent students. Markham (1998) depicts a successful resolution of this dilemma in which she and her advisor *educated each other* about the interrelated technical and social dimensions of CMC. In these conversations, advisor and advisee respected each other's relative expertise (e.g., in MUD navigation and interview methodology). In some ways, this interaction preserves a tradition in which advisors encourage advisees to reflect about their fieldwork, but the cultural fetish of technology (which privileges the expertise of producers and users) can make this process awkward.

Another practical challenge, posed by the increasing multimedia status of CMC, involves embracing theories and methods for analyzing *visual*—as well as verbal—texts (Gay, 2000). We discussed some of these methods in Chapter 7. Here, we note that speech communication scholars (who are used to studying verbal symbols) may have more ground to make up than their cousins in media studies. At the same time, it is worth remembering that hybrid residues can have long cultural half-lives; that is, the study of text-based systems may persist as long as there are groups of users who find their features advantageous (Mateas & Lewis, 1996; Paccagnella, 1997)—and nostalgic subcultures devoted to preserving "dead media" are themselves worthy of study.

These issues indicate that, as a field of qualitative research, CMC is far from monolithic. There appear to be abundant opportunities for researchers to engage significant—even compelling—topics, no matter what their level of technological expertise. As a result, we hope we have stimulated some of you who would otherwise never study CMC to seriously consider doing so. We believe, in other words, that CMC is one field where your research can speak to the real needs of technological stakeholders and influence the evolution of related systems. For these reasons, we view developments in this field with anticipation and cautious optimism.

Exercises

1. We have argued in this chapter that qualitative researchers need to define the relationship between online and offline phenomena in their studies of CMC. To show how this can be done, here is a brief example performed in the spirit of discourse analysis. The example uses a representative anecdote from an imaginary study of "talk about e-mail" to develop the claim that communicators negotiate—in their online and offline performances—how their associated identities will be related. In some performances, they may be opposed; in others, they may be connected. Imagine, then, a face-to-face setting in which one speaker asks another (the "addressee") the following question: "Did you see my e-mail?" Although seemingly straightforward, this question contains several assumptions about the relationship between online and offline identities:

- That the addressee has successfully *received* the speaker's message on his or her e-mail system
- That the addressee has *read* the message
- That the addressee has sufficiently *understood* the implications of that message so as to formulate a meaningful response

- That the addressee is willing and able to *recall* the content and implications of this message in the present FTF setting
- That the addressee recognizes the speaker's utterance as both (a) a request to verify his or her receipt of the message, and (b) a pre-sequence to a *second* request *to perform his or her response to the message in the current FTF setting*
- That the addressee is willing and able to *perform* that response

Our point is that the addressee's response may or may not validate these assumptions. He or she may, for example, comply with its implicit demand by restating the content of the online response: "Yes, I did. I think you've got an interesting research question, but you'll need to find more scholarly sources to support your argument." Alternatively, the addressee might respond by saying, "Yes, I did. Did you see my reply?" Note how this second response *disconfirms* the speaker's implicit request to blend online and offline identities and maintains them as separate. Interestingly, the final question posed by the addressee in this response both cements this rejection and continues the cycle. It poses a question whose answer is obvious—if the first speaker had seen the reply, he or she would never have asked the question. This question appears to offer the first speaker the same choice of blending or opposing online and offline identities (but really, it's a veiled instruction for that speaker to go read his or her e-mail).

Now, choose a representative anecdote from a potential or actual site of CMC research. Discuss how it expresses user understandings about online and offline phenomena and the relationships between them.

2. Mann and Stewart (2000, pp. 128-159) argue that qualitative researchers who are preparing to conduct online interviews can usefully adapt Baym's (1998b) list of factors affecting CMC. These factors, and their associated issues, include:

- *The purpose of the interaction:* How might it encourage or discourage participation?
- *The temporal context of the study:* Are synchronous or asynchronous systems being used? Are participants involved in a single interaction or a series of actions?
- *The CMC system in use:* How does it alternately facilitate and constrain interaction? How can particular features of the system be used to facilitate a successful interview?
- *The characteristics of the participants:* What is the number of participants, and how many groups do they represent? Do the participants reflect relative diversity or similarity in their attributes and attitudes? Do they have an existing relationship, or will this be their first interaction? What is their level of technological expertise? What is their general communication competence?
- *The external research context:* How do larger social, political, and economic issues affect the form and content of the interview?

Use this list to prepare a reflective memo about a planned or hypothetical online interview. In this memo, discuss how these factors affect how you design and conduct the interview. How do the specifics of your case either confirm or revise the recommendations made in this chapter?

3. One of the most innovative collaborations between CMC producers and qualitative researchers exists at the Intel Architecture Labs. The Intel Corporation is a famous manufacturer of computer chips, but it is also broadly interested in research and development of CMC systems. As a result, Intel employs qualitative researchers to study user behavior in various public and private settings. Their findings (e.g., concerning the impact of digital technology on the creation and display of personal media collections) are presented to Intel designers, who then incorporate them into their own work. After following this link to the IAL homepage, http://developer.intel.com/ial/about/index.ht, explore the contents of this site. Read the rationale that is presented for conducting this type of research and the various summaries of completed projects. Does this profile stimulate you to imagine similar collaborations with industries or agencies that are affected by your research? How does the methodology presented (e.g., "deep hanging out") compare and contrast with the discussion presented in this volume? What might you gain and lose as a qualitative researcher if you joined a corporate lab?

9

Authoring and Writing

[It appears as if an] object is ready-made, the linguistic means for its depiction are ready-made, the artist himself is ready-made, and his world view is ready-made. And here with ready-made means in light of a ready-made world view, the ready-made poet reflects a ready-made object. But in fact, the object is created in the process of creativity, as are the poet himself, his world view, and his means of expression.

— Bakhtin (1986, p. 120)

I know your secrets. I have tasted their fruit.

— Brooke (2001)

Going Public

This chapter focuses on the moment when researchers decide to "go public" with their work. This moment can arrive immediately after the completion of fieldwork or many months later. The goal may be to produce a comprehensive account or the first of many works that selectively treat various aspects of a project. The audience may be familiar, small, and rigorous (such as a thesis committee) or a largely unknown mass with unpredictable tastes (e.g., the buyers of a published volume). Whatever their situation, however, qualitative writers usually experience both anticipation and anxiety about "bringing it home."

Below, we examine several aspects of this moment, beginning with recent paradigm shifts that have transformed conventional understandings of what research writing is and how it should be conducted. We then review three concepts that have shaped the reception of this shift in Communication. Next, we discuss a variety of practices that constitute "alternative" and "experimental" writing. Current controversy surrounding these practices has led us to include a brief discussion of the professional politics associated with writing and publishing qualitative research. We then shift to a discussion of concrete strategies for organizing the research report. As illustrations, we look at two very different published works that show how these strategies can be enacted. Finally, we conclude the chapter and this volume with some reflections about writing and the state(s) of qualitative communication research.

In a recent essay, Tom (Lindlof, 2001) provides a useful entry to this material: "The main purpose of qualitative texts is to explicate the action and discourse observed in the field, and to invite readers to understand what it means to live in the scene under study" (p. 78). What exactly does this mean? One answer to this question is that researchers quickly discover that writing activates the various memberships they have assumed in completing their studies. That is, through writing, researchers experience commitments both to their participants and to the communities that evaluate their research as a professional activity. As a result, such writing is shot through with multiple, simultaneous, and competing social realities (Clifford, 1988, pp. 21-54). In writing, researchers embody the borders and boundaries between these realities. "The completed work," notes Smith (1983), "is thus . . . a temporary truce among contending forces" (p. 24). In negotiating this truce, writers rediscover two key premises of interpretivism: that knowledge does not exist prior to its creation by speakers and that, as a result, qualitative knowledge claims are talk about talk. In this sense, researchers return from one type of dialogue in the field only to begin a new type by writing for their audiences.

The Crisis of Representation

For over two decades, qualitative researchers have been working in the aftermath of a controversy that erupted in sociology and anthropology during the 1970s and 1980s. This controversy, commonly known as *the crisis of representation*, was developed in volumes by Brown (1977), Clifford and

Marcus (1986), Marcus and Fischer (1986), and Ruby (1982), and has been summarized by others (Van Maanen, 1995a). Reflecting on the tainted legacy of colonialism in cultural anthropology, and the implications of postmodernism for academic discourse, the key figures in this controversy produced manifestos that "made research and writing more reflexive, and called into question the . . . [influences] of gender, class, and race" on the research process (Clifford & Marcus, 1986, p. 10). The crisis of representation problematized the very nature of authorship and led qualitative researchers to confront the autobiographical and political dimensions of their writing.

The confrontation with autobiography involved renouncing the positivist fiction of the objective observer. Reflective narratives produced by fieldworkers gradually exposed the way in which this fiction arbitrarily suppressed their vivid and messy—but no less significant—experiences and repressed their personal issues in favor of professional credibility. Because these issues "returned" nonetheless (e.g., in relationships between fieldworkers and participants), this critique questioned how personal and professional interests have been defined and configured in qualitative research.

In their confrontation with politics, researchers addressed the relations of power that suffuse all practices of qualitative research. Here, they elaborated its historical complicity with oppressive imperial and corporate interests (e.g., in "understanding" cultural members so as to discipline and commodify them). They also challenged the practices by which researchers enter scenes, use their participants, and claim authority over their interpretation.

These two critiques intersected in a commitment to reverse the colonial gaze that ethnographers have traditionally trained on cultures and that has produced—not reflected—their status as primitive and exotic. In this "reverse cutting" (Clough, 1995, p. 528) the ethnographic gaze was turned back upon its own body, agency, and ways of seeing, and also the taken-for-granted practices of "writing it up." In this process, ethnography expanded its boundaries to accommodate the critical narratives of postcolonial and indigenous writers (Brettell, 1993).

The role of writing in securing professional ideologies (as well as distorted images of cultural others) was central to this critique. Significantly, it did not argue for the objective "truth" of one representation over another. Instead, it focused on the often-invisible influences of literary and rhetorical elements such as narrative (Brodkey, 1987b; E. M. Bruner, 1987; Richardson, 1995), genres, metaphors, tropes, and humor (Fine & Martin, 1995; see Rosaldo, 1987). These elements complement the more mundane practices through which writers relate with their readers, such as using inclusive pronouns, posing questions, and referring to shared knowledge (Hyland, 2001). Armed with the resources of criticism, the "new" ethnographers interrogated research texts about their relationships to fieldwork and to larger political, economic, and social structures. At issue were the significance and consequence of particular representations. These scholars also sought new strategies for resisting the influence of dominant ideologies on their writing (see, for example, Conquergood, 1985). Horwitz (1993) summarizes this agenda in a series of questions: "If ethnographic stories are really to be worth telling and hearing, what kinds of stories, whose story, should be told? Who decides? How, in short, should ethnography be authored?" (p. 131).

After the Fall: Reading and Writing Qualitative Research

The crisis of representation produced a number of consequences for qualitative research. Most directly, it led researchers to explore postmodern critical theories—particularly feminism (Gordon, 1988) and postcolonialism (Said, 1989)—as resources for transforming their work. Simultaneously, researchers turned to other types of writing (such as creative nonfiction; Agar, 1995) for provocative models. And as noted in Chapter 8, the crisis undermined traditional assumptions about the isolation, stability, and uniqueness of "local" cultures in the context of globalization (Marcus, 1998, pp. 79-104). As a result, research fields were revised to emphasize their multisited, partial, dispersed, and mediated qualities. It quickly became apparent that new strategies were required to engage the sites and scenes associated with these fields.

We are concerned here with writing, but the aforementioned consequences implicate all dimensions of qualitative research. As Marcus (1998) observes, "ethnographers would no longer be able to define sites and objects of study that had not already been written about and represented, and they could no longer constitute [those] objects . . . without explicit strategies of engaging other, often competing modes of [their] representation" (p. 16).

In this way, qualitative writing was understood to be *polyvocal, heteroglossic, dialogic,* and *intertextual.* It was constructed from the utterances of multiple speakers. It embodied a variety of dialect, jargon, and vernacular performed by those speakers, and that encoded their group interests. It established its significance by responding to prior discourses (most notably of law, politics, and media) and by anticipating the responses of its audience. And rather than having a pure, original, or unique identity, it was thoroughly saturated and interrupted by other discourses (Gottschalk, 1998). These conditions encouraged researchers to reflect on—and even celebrate—the communicative dimensions of their work.

In this process, they adopted a number of concepts from literary and rhetorical theory. We focus here on three that are central to reading and writing qualitative research: *voice, narrative presence,* and the *genre-audience nexus.*

Voice

This term refers to the ethical and emotional modes of expression that writers use to influence how audiences will understand a text (Goodall, 2000, pp. 131-151; Lindlof, 2001, p. 93). Voice emerges out of choices made by researchers in response to competing influences: the relationships they desire to construct with their readers; the documented relationships they have constructed with participants; and their use of language to depict persons, objects, and events. Depending on these choices, voices can vary widely between the evocative and the analytic (Charmaz & Mitchell, 1996). Commenting on a series of published essays, Strine (1997) observes that voice is central as both a topic and a condition of academic writing. In the first case, scholars examine how voices "mediate human consciousness, linking utterances to particular points of view, value orientations, and conceptual horizons" (p. 448). In the second case, experimental writing "critically interrogate[s] the authorizing assumptions, conventions, and discursive practices whereby voices have come to represent (and stand for) pregiven, unitary identities in the production of communication scholarship" (p. 449). By depicting "unsettled relationships between voice and identity formation," Strine concludes, innovative writers "suggest ways for more subtle, contextually nuanced thinking about voice in the communication process" (p. 449).

Narrative Presence

Three concepts from narrative theory (Chatman, 1978) help us to understand the multiple layers of voice that can be produced in a qualitative study. First, the term *author* refers to an actual human who produces a finished research text. In this usage, we have not forgotten the lessons of the crisis of representation. "Authorship" is increasingly invoked to signal the collaborative production of qualitative data. And "authors" does not include only researchers: in rare cases, participants may become so involved in fieldwork that they remain on to formally write the text. Nonetheless—and as postmodern anthropology confirms—someone eventually assumes the power to represent others in (and as) the text.

The second concept is *personae.* Over time in their work, "real" authors often depict themselves in consistent and distinctively stylized fashion. As a result, they develop *personae*—or mediated impressions of their "actual" identities. Many communication scholars, for example, are familiar with Goodall's (1989, 1991, 1996) "organizational detective" sifting mundane clues to solve spiritual mysteries, Ronai's (1995, 1996) courageous survivor of horrifying childhood abuse, and Bochner and Ellis's (1992) performance of their overlapping personal and professional relationships. The point is that authors' texts inevitably stand between their own existence and our understanding of—and encounters with—that existence (e.g., in hotel lobbies at professional conferences). A classic morality tale in Western culture involves authors (and their audiences) who lose the ability to distinguish between "real" identities and celebrity *personae*, with often tragic consequences. Qualitative writers sometimes wrestle with this tendency, "taking it personally" when reviewers criticize their textual *personae*.

Finally, authors may deploy *narrators* in their texts. Narrators are agents or "characters" depicted as responsible for the immediate selection and interpretation of events. They are a constructed intelligence that filters the relationships between authors, depicted events, and readers. Qualitative authors frequently do double duty as narrators of a descriptive scene, and they are almost always the narrators of analysis. In this process, however, authors may reflect on the difference between their current identities displayed as authors of a finished report (e.g., sadder but wiser) and their own narrative voices (e.g., naïve and enthusiastic) recorded in earlier data. Additionally, qualitative authors may choose to focus the reader's experience of a scene through the point of view of a particular participant (or character; see Brown & McMillan, 1991). Narrators can vary tremendously in their transparency, continuity, reliability, scope of knowledge, and temporal vantage point.

There are two implications of distinguishing between these dimensions of narrative presence. The first implication is that there is no necessary connection between the author, *persona*, or narrator of a qualitative research text. These connections are wholly symbolic and are produced by stylistic conventions that alternately connect and oppose these entities. Strine and Pacanowsky (1985) have conceptualized this process in proposing three dimensions of narrative presence in research texts. *Authorial stance* is the closeness of the researcher to the subjects' world and can range from full involvement to detachment. *Authorial status* refers to the researcher's presence within the discourse and can range from a voice that speaks intimately at the center of the work to a virtual absence from the subjects' world. *Contact* refers to the "writer-reader relationship that the researcher's stance and status enables" (pp. 288-289); such relationships may range from didactic instruction to poignant confession. The second implication here is that writers and readers may succeed or fail in making useful distinctions among different modes of voice. For example, a recent controversy in speech communication surrounding a published essay (Corey & Nakayama, 1997) pivoted on the authors' deliberately ambiguous use of a first-person narrator who spoke like an ethnographer engaged in fieldwork. As a result, the narrator's discourse appeared to some readers as a thinly veiled memoir of "real" events performed by the authors themselves. For others, it was not necessary that the events depicted had actually happened to produce indignation.

The Genre-Audience Nexus

As a professional activity, qualitative research is constrained by codes that dictate the form and content of writing. These codes are similar to literary genres that form "contracts" between authors and audiences (Atkinson, 1992; Rabinow, 1986). These contracts specify reader expectations for what will appear in qualitative reports and how it will appear. Genres standardize the types of characters and plots that will appear in those reports, and their general tone and style. Researchers internalize generic conventions in the course of their professional socialization. They subsequently perform them in writing as strategies for hailing audiences and for convincing them of the credibility of a particular account. In this process, that account is understood to be an exemplar *of* a particular genre. These contracts are flexible and evolving because writers and audiences are continually finessing them. For their part, readers invoke genre as a frame that helps to reduce their uncertainty about the quality of a narrative and the type of experience it will generate. In this way, there are pleasures to reading "classic" studies that richly fulfill the expectations aroused by their generic cues (e.g., the citation of a particular theoretical tradition). At the same time, readers also seek novelty. As a result, narratives that evoke *and* innovate tradition create a different kind of pleasure—as do, in some cases, complete frame breakers. In turn, writers understand this condition, and they wrestle with the tension between the impulse to create something original and the need to "market" their work within established categories.

In this process, qualitative writers shape their work to appeal to particular, imagined audiences. The use of genre to standardize writing corresponds to the use of categories that define audience needs and interests. These categories thus form an imperfect intersection between the mystery of "real" audiences and professional stereotypes about them (see Ang, 1991). Marcus and Cushman (1982) and Van Maanen (1988) distinguish five types of audiences that illustrate how this process operates. The first type of audience is what Van Maanen calls *area specialists*. This category designates readers presumed to be most knowledgeable about the specific research topic, associated theory, and general conventions for reading a qualitative study. The members of these groups—which roughly correspond to disciplinary subfields such as those described in Chapter 1—converse with each other in various outlets by means of technical discourse (or jargon) that maintains the boundaries of their specialty (e.g., group communication). This discourse articulates the standards of quality by which specialists judge new contributions to a research genre. Adherents in these traditions will look to their specialty journals for exemplars or converge around particular publications in journals with wide appeal.

General disciplinary readers, alternately, are "most concerned with the overall arrangement of a work and with the way theory is brought to bear upon the facts under consideration" (Marcus & Cushman, 1982, p. 51). Compared with area specialists, general disciplinary readers are presumed to be minimally interested in the specific knowledge a work offers. Rather, they attend to the elegance, strength, and scope of its theoretical contribution and the innovative ways in which the narrative is used. For example, readers across the subfields of interpersonal and organizational communication and media studies have historically recognized Janice Radway's *Reading the Romance* (1984) and Donal Carbaugh's *Talking American* (1988b) for their unifying contributions to common concerns. The contributions made by these two works to understanding more specific concerns (gendered media consumption and television talk shows, respectively) are probably of more interest to area specialists.

Social science readers are located outside of qualitative traditions, and often outside the particular discipline in which a study is completed. They "wish only to be informed about certain facts the fieldworker has unearthed. . . . Ordinarily [they] take only the raw empirical material of an ethnography and ignore the arguments that surround and give meaning to the facts" (Van Maanen, 1988, p. 30). Often, these readers are not interested in the epistemological, fieldwork, or hermeneutical problems pursued in a study, and therefore they may not be a primary audience for the author. Instead, they read through these (for them) "details" to mine relevant factual or value claims for their own teaching or research. Occasionally, however, interdisciplinary coalitions will emerge whose members recognize themselves to be engaged in a common enterprise. These coalitions satisfy the criteria for inclusion in this category, but their reading and appropriation of each other's work is more subtle and informed. Thus this category would perhaps be more accurately labeled *human science readers* to accommodate the diversity of these constituencies.

A fourth group, *action-oriented readers,* consists of administrators, government officials, research staffers, and cultural workers who seek "information which can be directly translated into practical policies and procedures" (Marcus & Cushman, 1982, p. 52). Qualitative reports typically interest these readers when they downplay theory, instead emphasizing problem-specific or site-specific descriptions and options for action. Qualitative researchers in health and organizational communication (Kreps & Herndon, 2001) are perhaps most likely to craft this appeal in their work, although authors of cultural studies (Bennett, 1992) increasingly seek to influence policy.

Finally, *general (popular) readers* "[look] to ethnography for its message or truth in a culturally familiar framework and [demand] readability with only enough jargon to legitimize the expertise of the account" (Marcus & Cushman, 1982, p. 52). For ordinary folk, ethnographies of exotic or deviant worlds can provide a safe and entertaining way to confront ethnocentric beliefs (Van Maanen, 1988, pp. 31-33). These readers want a user-friendly text largely devoid of theory. Although such texts are often regarded by academics as suspect scholarship, popular ethnography sometimes presents plausible, insightful accounts of topics that are not fit for "serious ethnography." On rare occasions, a work can find audiences in both popular and scholarly realms. Kidder's (1981) study of driven computer engineers, for example, has become a classic in both high-technology industry and organizational studies because it vividly captures the core, enduring elements of that industrial culture (Ratliff, 2000).

Genre and audience categories facilitate appropriate encounters between texts and audiences. Sometimes, however, the alignment of texts and audiences can become a goal in itself. When writers and readers focus excessively on this goal, they create inward-looking, self-serving cliques. The vitality of intellectual conversation may suffer as the members of these cliques concern themselves with "correct" usage of concepts and methods. Fortunately, the discipline of Communication is far from a closed system. There are multiple audiences for qualitative research, both inside and outside the discipline. This activity helps to prevent atrophy, although all the limbs of the collective body occasionally grow stiff. When this happens, stretching can be (at least temporarily) painful. It is this theme to which we turn next.

Alternative Writing Formats: Innovation and Controversy

In general, the crisis of representation produced a rich critique of modernist research narratives. This critique rejected the conventional elements of these narratives, including neutrality, detachment, monologue, disembodiment, coherence, totality, closure, and abstraction—generally, anything that promoted invisible or unaccountable authority (Brodkey, 1987a). Van Maanen (1988) has described these narratives as *realist tales*. We use this term with some caution, because the narratives in this category are diverse and variously reflect generic characteristics. Also, as we will explore in the examples below, a particular research narrative can reflect elements and tendencies associated with multiple genres. That said, we submit that exemplary realist tales are characterized by several features: the suppression of authorial experience in favor of objective reporting about "others"; a documentary focus on mundane details of member practices; explanations that render the "native's point of view" on those practices; and "interpretive omnipotence" whereby researchers imply (or directly assert) that their claims are plausible and avoid questions about alternative strategies for collecting, analyzing, and depicting data.

The permission to experiment granted by this critique of modern research narratives has been taken up by numerous scholars in the human sciences. Some of the earliest experiments in Communication include a reflective confessional tale by Benson (1981) and fiction by Pacanowsky (1983, 1988b). This type of work is conducted under *many* different names. Ellis and Bochner (2000, p. 739), for example, identify 36 variants of a single term— *autoethnography*—and six larger genres claiming that term as a variant. In any event, *autoethnography* (Ellis & Bochner, 2000; Crawford, 1996), *performative writing* (Pelias, 1999; Pollock, 1998), and *postmodern* or *new ethnography* (Bochner & Ellis, 1996; Goodall, 2000) are the most familiar descriptors in Communication. Each of these terms connotes a unique interdisciplinary heritage and set of writing practices. Generally, however, they are consistent in valuing the following qualities of research narratives: dialogue, accountability, partiality, fragmentation, embodiment, vulnerability, and ambiguity (Presnell, 1994). Tyler (1986) elliptically summarizes the goal of this work: "a cooperatively evolved text consisting of fragments of discourse intended to evoke in the minds of both reader and writer an emergent fantasy of a possible world of commonsense reality, and thus to provoke an aesthetic integration that will have a therapeutic effect" (p. 125). Novices wondering how to apply such definitions may take heart in Gottschalk's (1998) assessment: "I believe that writing a postmodern ethnography is more or *differently* demanding [than traditional ethnography] . . . because, in addition to [standard requirements for data collection and analysis, it] also requires its author to remain constantly and critically attentive to issues such as subjectivity, rhetorical moves, problems of voice, power, textual politics, limits to authority, truth claims, unconscious desires, and so on (p. 207). Throw in the lack of clear guidelines for conducting this kind of research, Gottschalk concludes, "and it seems reasonable to suggest that the work ... has not simply increased, but has become remarkably more complex" (p. 207).

Van Maanen's (1988) typology identifies three genres in which these qualities may appear:

- *Confessional tales* are traditionally supplements to the realist text (e.g., appendices) that foreground the contingencies of fieldwork. They are characterized by a focus on fieldworkers' "trials and tribulations" (Van Maanen, 1995b, p. 8) and shift the narrative focus from the studied culture to sensemaking processes. The crisis in representation, however, has justified the production of these as self-sufficient, stand-alone narratives.

- *Impressionist tales* are provocative narratives that undermine realist conventions by evoking fieldwork as a sensuous and mysterious experience about which only fragmentary knowledge is possible. This effect is supported by the development of richly detailed characters (see Lindlof, 1995, pp. 263-267). Ideally, the actions of these characters contribute to a distinguishable plot line (i.e., characterized by tension, rising action, climax, and denouement). This plot is constructed so as to possess interest, coherence, and relevance for the reader.

- *Critical tales* are morally concerned with depicting social structure from the perspective of disadvantaged groups and with addressing inequalities in the interest of achieving greater social, political, and economic justice (see Denzin, 2000, for a more explicitly politicized account of this genre).

These three genres suggest—but by no means exhaust—the possibilities for alternative writing. Currently, qualitative research is abuzz with experimentation (see, for example, Bochner & Ellis, 1996; Ellis & Bochner, 1996). Researchers are self-consciously using allegory (Goodall, 2000), poetry (Eisenberg, 1998; Richardson, 1994), personal narrative, fiction (Banks, 1998; Frank, 2000), photo-collage (Smith, 1998), theatrical and cinematic scripts (Madison, 1999; Miller, 1998), and bricolage that creatively combines different media, genres, forms, and styles (J. Jones, 1997; S. H. Jones, 1998; Miller, Creswell, & Olander, 1998; Richardson, 1997). Almost all of these works document the complex experience of living in postmodern culture. Almost all struggle against the rational and linear conventions of writing and print. Many focus on the unexpectedly emotional experiences associated with understanding and depicting other people's lives and the role of past personal trauma in shaping that work (Ellingson, 1998). Some works—particularly in autoethnography—focus directly on the experience of the researcher in order to unpack their significance for social and political theory. A few works boldly engage the grinding apparatus of academic professionalism in its current state of crisis (Bochner, 1997; Geist, 1999; Richardson, 1996; Shelton, 1995). Charmaz and Mitchell (1996, p. 300) neatly characterize the spirit of this work: "We need all our words to tell the whole story."

Although enthusiasm for alternative writing is spreading, such enthusiasm is not universal, and several opponents have emerged to express concerns. These expressions vary widely in their tone and utility. Often, they reflect the "skepticism, doubt, and even hostility" (Ellis & Bochner, 2000, p. 745) of groups whose traditions and privilege have been called into question. These voices seek to discredit and suppress alternatives because they believe that the alternatives appear illegitimate and unprofessional. In published and electronic formats (Gans, 1999; Kellett & Goodall, 1999; Shields, 2000) critics have variously accused alternative formats of being naïve, bizarre, treasonous, faddish, solipsistic, romantic, melodramatic, formulaic, sensational, anarchist, banal, narcissistic, doomed to failure, and obscene. Aptly, Gray (1997) describes these performances as "calling the cops."

We can trace at least three lessons from these controversies. The first lesson is that general disciplinary readers sometimes assume broad license to pronounce judgment, even when that task might better be left to area specialists. Everyone is entitled to his or her opinion, of course, and academic knowledge is by definition community property. Thus we are not advocating the stifling of dissent—only the moderation of its mean-spirited and underinformed varieties. A second lesson is that the ideology of individualism (in which "the personal" appears to be distinct from "the social" or "the political") endures as an orthodox frame for (mis-) reading experimental writing. A final lesson is that academics—at least in Communication— seem most likely to tolerate sexuality in their journals if its depictions are muted, heteronormative, and moralized (e.g., with clearly identified villains and victims). Narratives that vex this code by celebrating bodily pleasure, by exposing the complicity of participants in sexualized encounters (e.g., during fieldwork; Nelson, 1998), or by using desire to interrogate knowledge and power (Corey & Nakayama, 1997) risk provoking controversy (see also Fox, 1996). That reaction, of course, may prove the value of alternative writing, but it is a bumpy ride transporting this standard from the world of art to the human sciences.

Other critics (including the experimenters themselves) have raised issues that seem more useful. These issues include the potential for alternative writing to inhibit the performance of fieldwork (i.e., the triumph of *auto-* over *ethno-*) (Gans, 1999), the responsibility of authors to clarify oblique meaning (Baym, 1998a), the resistance of experiments to classification by subfield schema (Delaney, 2000), the influence of commercial media culture on confessional narratives of trauma and victimization (Altheide, 1995), and the challenge of training ethnographers to become critics (Van Maanen, 1995b, pp. 65-66). These critics are open to accommodating alternative writing based on its demonstrated utility for engaging professional concerns—assuming that those concerns are always open to scrutiny and revision. We note, for example, that autoethnography is especially useful for gaining access to private scenes of social action (e.g., the practices of bingeing, purging, concealment, and denial among bulimics and their families; Tillman-Healy, 1996) that would likely not be documented otherwise by fieldworkers.

Perhaps the greatest value of this controversy is its generation of issues that qualitative researchers may take into account when they are reading and writing in alternative formats. The following list, adapted from Bochner and Ellis (1997), suggests the scope of current debate:

- What are the politics of disclosure and confession? When and how does a narrative construct the writer as a narcissist, and the reader as a voyeur? How can writers usefully render personal experience without inappropriately soliciting the validation of epiphany?
- How can writers cultivate and sustain a reader's interest in the relationship between personal experience and cultural truths?
- How do writers construct relationships between their narrators, readers, and the trauma or mystery under consideration?
- How is theory invoked and deployed? Different relationships between data and theory are suggested, for example, by the phrases "writing *from* theory" (i.e., in a deductive and deterministic manner) and "writing *to* theory" (i.e., in a selective, reflective, and mutually transforming manner).
- How should readers evaluate the validity of events recalled by narrators?

The fact that these issues are not yet resolved should not suggest that this enterprise is flying blind. Indeed, there is an emerging consensus around the appropriateness of using the following criteria to evaluate experimental research narratives (Bochner & Ellis, 1997; Denzin, 1997; Goodall, 2000; Richardson, 2000):

- Narratives must be written well (i.e., lyrically). They must engage the reader emotionally and intellectually by evoking shared experiences, interests, and frames of reference.
- Narratives should effectively address multiple audiences.
- Stories presented in the narratives should be credible and interesting.
- Narrators should reflect on their role in producing the data they interpret.
- Narrators should be ethically and politically accountable.
- Narratives should productively negotiate the tension between resolution and open-endedness.
- Narratives should invite readers to become active participants in their interpretation.

- Narratives should alternate foci between "personal" and "social" realms.
- Narratives should be substantive in contributing to our understanding of social life.
- Narratives should be generalizable. That is, they should detail a particular form or scene of social life so as to implicate—or "transfer" it to—a more general form or scene.

Academic Politics and the Production of Qualitative Research

As this discussion indicates, qualitative research is thoroughly enmeshed "in the ideological practices of the academy" (West, 1993, p. 216); that is, it is a *disciplined* activity subject to the power relations through which professionals maintain their communities. As a recent and growing interest, qualitative research has confronted several barriers that constrain its forms and circulation.

These barriers are institutional, and they emerge around the practices of writing and publication (Taylor & Trujillo, 2001). Historically, they include journals that are preformatted (i.e., in limits on the page length of submissions) to favor positivist research; editorial protocols requiring the deductive and linear presentation of content; the devaluation of subjectivity per se as a topic or narrative style; preferentiality among funding institutions for "traditional" topics and methods, and among promotion committees for high numbers of rapidly produced articles. To these, we can add other, mundane forms of violence in academic life: "how-to" discourses that commodify the product of writing without problematizing the conditions of its production (Bach, Blair, Nothstine, & Pym, 1996); the assassination of legitimate innovation by journal editors and reviewers (Blair, Brown, & Baxter 1994); the public ambush of job candidates with hostile and inappropriate questions; constant competition and criticism (Goodall, 2000, pp. 25-29); and the staffing of graduate methods seminars with instructors who are unfamiliar with or unsympathetic to the range of issues in qualitative research (Krizek, 1998). The lingering—and periodically resurgent—force of these barriers can discourage scholars from investing time and labor in qualitative research (particularly as that investment competes with women's traditionally assigned responsibilities for childbearing and child rearing).

We do not recount these barriers to discourage you. As we discussed in Chapter 1, their status in Communication is clearly changing. Anderson (2001), for example, is blasé in his assessment: "It seems [currently] as though nearly anything can be published and nearly everything will be rejected *somewhere*" (p. 98). Our goal is to clarify the challenges that qualitative researchers *potentially* face in publishing their work and in using publication as a means to achieve their professional goals. Forewarned, we believe, is forearmed (and writers can arm themselves further by carefully assessing the potential for success in submitting to particular publication outlets; Lindlof, 2001, pp. 79-81). Our own experiences indicate that for every constraint detailed above, there is usually a sustaining counterpart: the generous colleague, the risk-taking editor, or the unexpected letter of support.

However, if the current enthusiasm for qualitative research is to endure, the material practices of academic discipline must be transformed. Professional associations must appoint journal editors (and editors must appoint editorial boards) who are competent to evaluate both traditional and innovative research. Editors must—as appropriate to their journal's mission—invite, review, and publish a wide range of research (and authors should remember that editors can only work with the submissions and revisions they *actually* receive). Reviewers—and other institutional gatekeepers— must apply appropriate criteria in their evaluations (e.g., of interdisciplinary publications in tenure decisions). If these conditions cannot be sustained, arguments for new publication outlets and evaluation criteria should be made vigorously. Further, criticism of innovative work should appropriately account for its theoretical and methodological contexts. That criticism—like the work itself—should produce more precise disagreements and edifying conversations regarding the purposes and legitimate forms of qualitative research (Bochner & Ellis, 1996). And finally, we can each show our support for laudable research by reading, discussing, teaching, citing, and generally *responding* to it.

Ironically, though, framing this discussion around issues of writing and publication perpetuates the marginalization of *nondiscursive* representation. As Conquergood (1991) has noted:

> It is one thing to talk about performance as a model for cultural process . . . as long as that performance-sensitive talk eventually gets "written down." . . . The hegemony of inscribed texts is never challenged by fieldwork because, after all is said and done, the final word is on paper. . . . It is interesting to note that even the most radical deconstructions still take place on the page. (p. 190)

Conquergood's point is that qualitative researchers should consider using performance formats (e.g., theatrical staging) to present their findings (see Welker & Goodall, 1997). He has modeled this advice in making two documentaries on his Chicago-based fieldwork with Hmong shamans (Siegel & Conquergood, 1985) and multicultural youth gangs (Siegel & Conquergood, 1990). Similarly, Mara Adelman (Adelman & Schultz, 1997) produced a documentary related to her study (conducted with Larry Frey) of "fragile community" among the staff and residents of a group home for people with AIDS.

While we support Conquergood's call, we believe that these two examples suggest some important considerations for those who heed it. The first consideration is that Conquergood is a leading scholar of performance studies, and his work is subject to the evaluative standards of that subfield. Although the production of documentary film is potentially legitimate within that subfield, other subfields may not accord it similar status. Additionally, the researchers mentioned above have also published written accounts of their studies (Adelman & Frey, 1997; Conquergood, 1992, 1994). These examples suggest that qualitative researchers can and should attempt to reach multiple audiences through different forms of representation. In this process, those concerned about evaluation can hedge their bets.

We believe that qualitative researchers should carefully consider the consequences of using experimental formats for their unique situations. Some institutions, for example, value "creative work" as an alternative to traditional publication. Also, tenured scholars can experiment with less risk than can those who are not tenured (e.g., in conducting "second projects" following the dissertation and promotion; Marcus, 1998, pp. 233-236). Within the current climate of controversy, however, we believe that students who are attracted to alternatives should seek wise counsel concerning their most effective use and their role in developing a career path. In theory (or at least in professional mythology), excellence is its own guarantee of success. Some entrepreneurial paths, however, are riskier than others. One pitfall among students who prematurely embrace alternatives, we have noticed, is their failure to adequately learn the traditions that those alternatives critique. Two reasonable suggestions, then, would be (where appropriate): leveraging alternative writing to establish one's affiliation with a particular subfield and building a body of work that combines both traditional and alternative formats to demonstrate the full range of one's abilities and interests.

The Craft of Writing: Strategies and Tactics

Let us turn now to some concrete issues in qualitative writing. Lindlof (2001) likens the traditional format of the qualitative essay (e.g., the journal article) to a four-act play. This allegory is less valid for experimental, hypertextual (see Mason & Dicks, 1999), and book-length formats, but it indicates key functions that may be fulfilled by alternate means in those formats (e.g., by devoting entire chapters to particular acts). We develop this allegory below, incorporating suggestions made by other commentators on the craft of qualitative writing (Goodall, 2000; Richardson, 2000; Wolcott, 2001).

Act One

In opening a study, authors pursue three goals. They develop a theoretical rationale for the study, unfold its guiding research problem, and introduce its chosen scene. This first goal involves the infamous "review of the literature" and requires authors to demonstrate their familiarity with relevant concepts and theories and with previously published studies. Here, Lindlof (2001, pp. 81-86) suggests that writers *not* follow the model of quantitative studies, which involves tracking incremental advances in knowledge for the purposes of greater predictive power. Rather, authors should cite a mixture of conceptual discussions and empirical studies that indicate the diversity of related performances in particular social worlds. Literature reviews, additionally, should be focused, displaying "incisive usage of key works" (p. 83) as opposed to a mass of glossed citations. This review, ultimately, is strategic: it should "show the reader why *this* world of scholarship we commonly inhabit would be changed for the better by an empirical exploration of *this* problem" (p. 84). Finally, good descriptions of the research scene efficiently convey its "organization, history, routines . . . key social actors, and . . . the flavor of the quotidian life there" (p. 85).

Act Two

In the second act of a study, writers report on their methods and analytic procedures. This account reviews the logic of the study's design, including the selection of the site, strategies for gaining access and inclusion, the use of particular methods (such as interviewing), and procedures for recording and analyzing data. It should also include relevant information about the conditions under which the study was conducted (e.g., during a period of organizational decline). Including specific detail—the total number of contact hours, patterns of reactions by participants to the researcher's fieldwork persona, numbers and average length of interviews conducted, numbers of pages of documents reviewed, and so on—will help the reader to evaluate the researcher's credibility as an analyst of the scene. Writers may wish to provide some of this information (i.e., interview protocols) in separate appendices at the back of a manuscript. Reports on data analysis should emphasize why particular strategies were selected and how they were used. Emphasis should be placed on the outcomes of analysis (e.g., triangulation, theoretical saturation) that enhance the credibility of data. However, writers should not fear documenting the actual history of improvisation and revision in their strategies. Rather than displaying "error," this information contributes to an impression of appropriate responsiveness to the unpredictable character of the fieldwork experience.

Act Three

In this—often the longest—act, writers construct and present their interpretations of the research experience. Rhetorical skill here is paramount: "It is no exaggeration to say that [success] . . . depends on your ability to represent a cultural world with authenticity, completeness, and subtlety" (Lindlof, 2001, p. 88). Here, writers present selected fragments of data to illustrate features of the scene and advance their argument.

We can understand the work of this act by focusing on three particular issues. In the first, writers often wrestle with the question, *What evidence should I select for presentation*? Researchers who are ready to write have by definition passed through the crucible of analysis. Ideally, their data have been validated by the reflective practices of coding and categorization. Nonetheless, writers are usually faced with numerous candidates (e.g., quotes from interview transcripts) auditioning for inclusion in a final report. What principles should the writer use to thin this field? First, researchers should take a moment to congratulate themselves on their exertions during fieldwork. It's better to have too many choices at this point than too few. (As we noted in Chapter 7, data not included in a final report are not "lost" or "wasted." They have served the crucial functions of verifying and elaborating the researcher's categories.) Next, writers should select data that clearly reflect the nature and scope of their claim; that is, data should embody the phenomenon that forms the object of the claim (and not some other phenomenon). Data should also reflect the diversity of times, places, events, and actors that is organized within the claim (e.g., that some groups, but not others, engaged in an activity, or that the activity was performed at some locations—but not all). As further criteria, Katz (2001) suggests the following:

- Data characterized by *enigma, paradox,* and *absurdity* are useful for introducing problems that form the object of explanation
- *Rich* and *varied* data help to confirm explanations by qualifying them and by suggesting—and ruling out—alternate explanations
- *Revealing* data "show how forces shaping social life are routinely overlooked, purposively hidden, or ontologically invisible"
- *Vivid* and *colorful* data indicate how social action is creatively crafted amid contextual constraints
- *Poignant* data "capture people humbled by transcending concerns that structure persistent patterns in their lives" (p. 447)

In a second issue, writers wrestle with the question, *How should I present evidence?* Generally, the data selected should lend themselves to clear and concise depiction. The process of converting analyzed data to finished text involves both *editing existing material* (e.g., for factual accuracy, thematic continuity, stylistic effectiveness, and aesthetic formatting) and *adding new material* (e.g., additional interpretation or citations) (Goodall, 2000, pp. 165-168). Anderson (2001) notes that writers presenting qualitative data have at least two responsibilities. One responsibility involves establishing the *authenticity* of that presentation. This effect occurs when authors demonstrate that they have been "inside" a scene and its performances, have been affected by them, and yet were conscientious recorders of their experience. The other responsibility involves demonstrating "sufficient complexity" in the data so that they can bear the weight of higher order analysis (e.g., they are not transparent). This complexity also should be inherently interesting to the reader.

One format that accomplishes these purposes is *the exemplar.* This term describes self-contained depictions of events that are vivid, fine-grained, and dense with significance. Exemplars endow data with the quality of "eventful-ness" (Lindlof, 1995, pp. 267-270). At one level, exemplars satisfy the need (discussed above) to focus the relevance of data as evidence for a particular claim. In this way, exemplars possess *metonymic* and *enthymematic* quali-ties. They are fragments that "stand for" a larger phenomenon by demon-strating its practical dimensions. Because they are evocative, exemplars also stimulate readers to consider *what* is being demonstrated and thus antici-pate the writer's impending interpretation. To illustrate this process, here is an exemplar from Bryan's study of a Salt Lake City bookstore (Taylor, 1999). This organization was owned by the LDS (Mormon) Church and, for the most part, employed members of that church.

Kate, the display specialist for the store, is stacking some brightly-colored, cardboard savings banks for children on a table located on the Church Floor. Like their more-subdued plastic counterparts sold downstairs, these banks are divided into three equal sections. One section is labeled *Tithing.* A second is entitled *Mission.* A third is marked *Savings.*

This particular bank, Kate explains, has the virtue of being fully-sealed between its partitions. "With the other banks," she says mock-seriously, "the problem is that *tithing* [deposits] keep on slipping, falling, *jumping* [shakes the bank vigorously] over into *savings,* and later on, you can't figure out how it got there."

"Just all by itself," I reply, mirroring her ironic tone. "Can't figure it out, huh?"

"Exactly," she nods. "You've got it."

"I can see how that could happen."

"Uh-huh."(p. 77)

Although one of us authored this exemplar and we are not completely objective, we believe that it reflects some desirable qualities of exemplars. By opening with an activity in process, it suggests to the reader that this activity will become significant. It provides detail about the features of an artifact that is central to this activity (its construction and location) and proceeds to reveal how those features are significant for the actors in the scene. The author (who is also a narrator of and character in the scene) animates these actors by suggesting the affect (muted irony, collegial affection) underlying their performances. He provides details of nonverbal communication (e.g., mock agitation) to show that these performances are embodied and intertextual (i.e., Kate is "quoting" an allegedly common cultural practice). In the context of the larger report, this exemplar succeeds if it demonstrates the claim it was designed to service: that performances (such as highly coded banter) surrounding the interpretation of products in this setting allowed employees to simultaneously perform their corporate and religious identities. In this process, they revealed a range of reactions (e.g., ambivalence) to this confluence of organization in their lives.

The presentation of data is followed by the discourse of *interpretation*, in which authors reconstruct the experience of participants depicted in scenes, decipher operant cultural codes, or construct patterns that connect the significance of data to other scenes, sites, and fields. Anderson (2001, p. 102) argues that writers in this stage must have already demonstrated thorough knowledge of how local practices are performed and "deep knowledge of the cultural themes that are in play" (p. 102).

Because this work is so crucial to the success of a qualitative report, we focus here on six strategies commonly used by writers to organize their presentation of analysis and interpretation. The first strategy, and one of the most common, is to present the *themes and topics* that emerged from data analysis. This process involves making classes (categories) out of the range of materials and experiences noted in the field. The themes or topics an author uses may already be available from previous theory, as in the "notes and queries" model developed in mid-20th-century anthropology (Atkinson, 1992, pp. 32-35). If so, writers use incidents to illustrate, elaborate, or recast the concepts for the case under study (see, for example, Katriel, 1987). The strategy of using an available theme or topic brings order to a wide range of phenomena and builds theory by comparing studies using the same framework. But "it does have the potential drawback of leading one towards orthodox or obvious themes" (Hammersley & Atkinson, 1983, p. 224). It may also impose categories that have little relevance for a particular culture or research problem. The researcher can deal with this difficulty by building categories from the ground up—that is, from participants' own folk (or first-order) terms and categories of social action.

In a second strategy, called *narrowing and expanding the focus* (Hammersley & Atkinson, 1983, pp. 220-221), the author moves the reader through different levels of analysis by introducing a subject, exploring it contextually, and finally arriving at a general explanation—and repeating this for any number of themes. Authors may nest each cycle within others, so that they finally reach a superordinate explanation of the entire phenomenon. This effect can be pictured as a zoom lens, focusing closer in on or further away from a subject. The narrowing and expanding may go on consecutively, resulting in a sort of edited "montage" understanding (see, for example, Lindlof, 1992).

The *puzzle-explication* strategy starts with an event or performance that is mystifying and requires understanding. The puzzle is then gradually fleshed out, usually as a story, and sometimes including the author as a witnessing actor. The analysis pulls the puzzle apart and puts it back together again, using one or more theories to reconfigure it. Often the conclusion is a more satisfying understanding of the event, but occasionally the inadequacy of the theoretical strategy itself is revealed (Bateson, 1936). Geertz's (1973) analysis of a Balinese cockfight is a famous example of this approach in cultural anthropology. Rosen's (1985) analysis of domination at a corporate power-breakfast is a classic in organizational studies.

Similar to puzzle explication, a strategy that *separates narration and analysis* provides the reader with two perspectives: one that experiences through the eyes (and other senses) of the author and one that tries to critique through the disciplinary knowledge of the author. The objective here, according to Hammersley and Atkinson (1983), is to solve the problem—commonly present in ethnographies—of conflating description and evaluation. The separation of the ethnographic narrative from the analysis allows the reader to assess theoretic claims apart from descriptive claims. In the "narration" portion, authors write a full descriptive treatment of a culture; they sometimes appear in the first person. This narrative is not burdened with technical language, but it is also not totally free of the author's decisions about what to select and how to show it. The reader receives an accessible and informative account "from the inside" of a culture, before being exposed to higher level interpretations. Short of making all the data available, this may be the best way for authors to show how they moved from description to theory.

Although this strategy has much to recommend it, it is unclear to what extent a narrative can ever claim to be preanalytic (Hammersley & Atkinson, 1983, p. 222). Also, in some writings using this style, an analytic frame may seem to be simply "tacked on" to the ethnography. Authors therefore need to establish clearly the relationship between the two (Lofland, 1974, p. 109).

Two final strategies, the *chronology* and the *natural history* (Hammersley & Atkinson, 1983, pp. 215-220), are explicitly based in the conventions of narrative. A *chronology* models the text after the phenomenon itself—its phases, stages, or sequences. It is an effective way to express change as a function of the passage of time, and the constraints, institutional and personal, that go with and influence such change. In sociology, for example, classic symbolic interactionist studies have documented the "careers" of such social types as medical students, prison inmates, and marijuana users. Typically, the career trajectory begins with an interest (or diagnosis or incarceration or some other precondition), followed by entry into a setting, socialization to its norms and routines, adaptation of the individual's identity to others, and so on.

Finally, the *natural history* also takes a "career" path, but it is the career of the researcher entering and adapting to the cultural scene that organizes the text. We get an account of authors' discoveries and hardships as they experienced their unique learning curve. This approach has the interesting potential of showing the reader the very process of doing qualitative research. Hammersley and Atkinson (1983, pp. 215-216) caution, however, that the natural history is difficult to sustain for very long in a text. More seriously, they claim that the natural history cannot really replicate the fieldwork and analysis experience, because the researcher's view of the entire project changes retrospectively. Past events are interpreted through the more sophisticated sensibility of the present. Hammersley and Atkinson assert that the natural history works best as transitional material within the larger text, such as when a confessional tale is called for.

A third and final issue faced by writers in Act Three is: *How should I construct the relationship between data and theory?* This process has already commenced in the literature review completed in Act One. Here, the process must continue by joining the analysis of data to concepts and theories in order to produce "higher-level inferences" (Lindlof, 2001, p. 88) about their significance. The analytic dimensions of this process were discussed in Chapter 7. Here, the task is to rhetorically connect the presentations of data and theory so that the reader is convinced that their connections are reasonable and effective. In this process of *analytic synthesis* (Lindlof, 2001, p. 90), writers return to the research problems guiding the study to establish its grand level of significance. Lindlof notes that managing voices becomes tricky at this point: Writers can disrupt a good read by continually (or prematurely) interrupting their interpretation with theorizing, or by failing to distinguish between interpretation and theorizing.

Act Four

In this final act, writers conclude the study by reminding readers why they began reading it in the first place (the research problem) and by summarizing the implications of the study for further engagement with that problem. An example would include recommendations that apply the relevance of findings to policies developed by (or for) the group studied.

Getting Down to Cases

It is time now to look at some examples of published research to see how elements such as voice, narrative presence, the genre-audience nexus, and textual organization are actually used. The two articles we have selected exhibit high levels of skill in their conceptualization, design, and execution. They also create a useful contrast between traditional and experimental approaches. They are not (yet) classics, but this too is for the best. Because they are overexposed, classics can sometimes inspire formulaic imitation. We note, finally, that space does not permit full elaboration of these works. Interested readers should consult the originals.

Speaking of the Border

Sheryl Lindsley's (1999) study "Communication and 'The Mexican Way'" describes and analyzes "core cultural symbols" used by Mexican managers of *maquiladoras* (U.S. American-owned assembly plants located in Mexico) and by residents of the communities surrounding those facilities. Its central claim is that Mexicans perceive "stability" and "trust" as constructs that organize identities and relationships in *maquiladoras* and that generally contribute to effective communication. The policy implications of the study are foreshadowed in its abstract by the claim that Mexicans evaluate the communication of U.S. Americans as eroding these core ideals.

Act One is organized in a funnel-sequence that begins with a broad discussion of the article's major concept (core cultural symbols). Through the use of citations, Lindsley gradually narrows its scope. First, she reviews the concept's significance for researchers in intercultural communication and the ethnography of communication (EOC). She then develops its relevance for the study of organizational communication and culture. She concludes this act with the following claim: "The study of core cultural symbols can be particularly useful in organizational contexts in which communication and/or cultural identity is problematic" (p. 2).

This claim provides a segue to Act Two, a discussion of the research field. Lindsley provides detailed information about the economic, industrial, and cultural contexts of *maquiladoras*. By citing a variety of associated problems, she signals that there is conflict and misunderstanding ahead. She indicates that *maquiladoras* are an empirical example of the theoretical "borderlands" that currently interest cultural and critical scholars. In such sites, "we are likely to find culture in process, emergent, and socially negotiated in everyday intercultural interaction" (p. 3). Invoking a classic rationale for qualitative research, Lindsley notes that previous analyses of these sites have focused on social structure (e.g., patronage systems). This focus creates the need for "analysis of [actual] communicative practices of the people who live in the borderlands and work in maquiladora contexts" (p. 4). Her research questions propel the reader through this opening: "What (if any) core symbols function as the organizing principles which guide the enactment of Mexican cultural identity in maquiladora relationships? What insights does the use of such core symbols provide into Mexican cultural norms for communication in maquiladora contexts?"

In this act, Lindsley also reviews the site and scenes of the study. She details how her methods (interviewing, participant observation, and document analysis) were refined to engage their social action. The site—the Sonoran capital of Hermosillo—is singular, but its scenes (including "restaurants, managers' offices, and homes"; p. 4) are multiple. This account focuses on numbers and types of relevant phenomena. It details the period and duration of Lindsley's resident fieldwork, documents that she studied, and interviews she conducted. Implicitly, it depicts emergent opportunities and constraints. Lindsley was restricted, for example, to observation inside the *maquiladoras* (e.g., as a tour member). She compensated, however, by actively developing "extensive personal relationships" with fellow residents. She concludes this act by describing her generally inductive approach to data analysis and the specific use of procedures developed by EOC researcher Donal Carbaugh. "What emerged" from this analysis, she reports (p. 7), were two key cultural symbols: "stability" and "trust." Acts One and Two are relatively brief, accounting for a little over one-quarter of the article's length.

Act Three systematically explores these symbols. It is the longest of the acts, accounting for nearly 60% of the article's length. It is organized into two sections, one for each symbol. Lindsley introduces each section by discussing the symbol's relevance for identities and relationships in the *maquiladoras*. These introductions develop the integrity of the symbol as an analytic construct. They provide the reader with a basis for evaluating evidence of their semantic dimensions.

This evidence is presented in the form of themes. These themes form a substructure of the two larger sections. Each theme is discussed separately. Each section has a heading, taken from Lindsley's data, which signals the content of its theme. For example, the analysis of "stability" is organized around a discussion of five themes: "Families Give Us Stability"; They're "Missing Families"; The Wives Need to "Cross the Border"; Men, Women, and "The Natural Balance"; and Employees are "Just Heads." Internal summaries are used when the discussion of themes is exceptionally long or complex (e.g., p. 22) and also to conclude the discussion of each symbol (pp. 18, 24). The discussion of trust differs from that of stability by continuing to develop three dimensions that "differentiate the characteristics of interactions which adhere to norms of trust from characteristics of interactions which violate these norms" (p. 24). These dimensions are labeled using antonymic pairs (e.g., close/distant). Sharp readers will recall that the dispreferred items in each pair (e.g., distant) were previously associated in Lindsley's narrative with negative perceptions by Mexicans of U.S. American communication style. This discussion closes Act Three.

Act Four is brief, accounting for 8% of the article's length. It begins by summarizing the interpretation that has just been performed. It clarifies the contrast between Mexicans' perceptions of the importance of these core symbols and of U.S. Americans' communication. The analysis is justified as providing "a clearer understanding of what it means to live in this cultural, political, and economic borderland between two worlds" (p. 26). Lindsley then provides a series of practical recommendations directed at would-be managers of *maquiladoras* (presumably U.S. Americans). These recommendations are organized as implications of the analysis of each core symbol (e.g., "use indirect forms of communication to protect, self, other, and relational identities in face-threatening situations"; p. 27). Because her data suggest that Hermosillans believe these practices will increase their job satisfaction and motivation, Lindsley argues that managers adopting these practices "may very well enhance organizational communication, productivity, and bottom-line profits" (p. 27). She also summarizes the practices' benefits for the Communication discipline (e.g., enhanced understanding of identity performances in multicultural organizations). The limits of the study (e.g., the absence of line-worker data) and its potential generalizability (maybe to other Mexican, Central, or Latin American organizations) are also discussed.

This is a skillful performance of the traditional format. It displays conventional strategies in almost all of the areas we have discussed. For example, Lindsley uses citations in Act One to hail the members of particular subfields as her "area specialist" audiences and links their agendas in the transition between Acts One and Two.

The article subsequently satisfies the expectations of those readers. Specifically, it fulfills traditional requirements for an EOC study. It systematically details features of a cultural system and their significance for the members of that culture. It does so by using a "themes and topics" scheme for presenting analysis and interpretation. The reader takes pleasure in the author's careful unfolding of this system. The validity of the analysis is grounded in its steady accumulation of evidence. The smallest building blocks here are the exemplars contained in the theme sections. Because these are sound, the themes are sound. Because the themes are sound, the core values are sound.

Lindsley's voice is primarily subdued. She speaks in a rational and measured tone about these phenomena. Her voice reflects the residue of a constraint historically imposed on EOC narrators. This constraint arises from EOC's founding commitment to counter abstract linguistic theory with empirical data about communication. However, the anthropological linguistics that influences EOC harbors a latent objectivism. This objectivism positions its writers as detached analysts, inventorying the communicative components of cultural systems (Brodkey, 1987b, p. 33). Although Lindsley (1999) justifies the study as a rare portrait of social practice (p. 9), much of her evidence is taken from accounts provided by interviewees. These accounts emphasize the "what" of the communication system over the "how" of its associated performances. Even when they are taken from fieldnotes, the exemplars are primarily of quoted, reflective speech, not scenes of action (e.g., factory work) performed together by the researcher and her participants. Although these accounts are offered as reports of social practice, they are not validated by observation of that practice.

Despite this constraint, Lindsley's persona displays skill, ingenuity, thoroughness, and credibility. She casually remarks, for example, that she is bilingual (a crucial requirement for Anglo researchers in Mexico). She exploits unexpected opportunities by turning casual conversations into informal interviews. Implicitly addressing the issue of ethnic politics, she provides quotes from her participants indicating their trust of her intentions and endorsement of her goals. She reports her segregation of dubious data and the use of member checks to validate them. She reinforces her claims about core symbols by providing evidence of talk about their semantic *opposites*.

Furthermore, the influence of tradition on this article is not total. Lindsley occasionally resists the prescribed narrative voice. She reflects about the potential influence of her ethnicity on her data (p. 6), recounts her role in soliciting and developing accounts (p. 16), and provides a near-confessional tale about an informant's stereotyping of her gender (p. 10). Significantly, however, these last two accounts are used as evidence for themes associated with the core values. We are only allowed brief flashes of the author's personhood. She avoids explicit doubt and extended reflexivity in favor of confident declaration.

Running With the Wrong Crowd

Readers of Michael Bowman's "Killing Dillinger: A Mystory" (2000) will immediately recognize they are no longer in the Kansas of the traditional format. If they are reading in sequence, their first clue is the subtitle, whose wordplay evokes the intersection of mystery and autoethnography. Their second clue is the article's abstract, which consists of a single-sentence invitation: "*I want to show you some pictures and tell you some stories. . . .*" (p. 342). If they miss these clues, conventional readers will certainly notice the author's immediate, first-person, direct address. Provocatively, this address *discourages* (selectively) its potential audience. "If you are associated with the FBI or CRTNET, let me encourage you *not* to read my piece. . . . You won't like it. . . . Trust me" (p. 342).

Following an italicized reflection concerning the relationship between writing and performance, Bowman directs a second challenge to the reader: "Do you like it soft? Or do you like it hard?" (p. 342). The question, however, is not only sexual innuendo. It also refers to phonetic variants of a particular name: that of the infamous "criminal," John *Dillinger*. Briefly, Bowman recounts how discrimination surrounding World War I led the Indiana state legislature to outlaw bilingual education accommodating its German "ancestors . . . relatives . . . [and] neighbors" (p. 343). Dillinger's "people," Bowman notes, "were Germans" (p. 342).

This observation is followed by an inset photograph of a crowd, faces cropped, gathered on a paved street around a mark formed by tape or paint. The caption above the photograph states: "Writing toward disappearance." Below the photograph is poetry, set in smaller type. In rough vernacular, it interprets the depicted scene. "Yep, this is where it happened / 'X' marks the spot / Look at those assholes there / Next to where Johnnie got shot."

These opening pages establish the dominant forms of voice in this narrative. They are shortly joined by one more. This voice involves Bowman's memoir of his personal connection to the Dillinger mythology. As a resident of Indiana, Bowman grew up in a regional culture whose members indirectly drew on the Dillinger icon to construct (sometimes cruelly) class and gender identities. These identities distinguished insiders from outsiders and connected that culture to the larger structures of nationalism and capitalism (pp. 351-354). Speaking in this voice, Bowman alternates between different periods of his life. He juxtaposes, for example, his youthful re-enactment of gangster films (with his brother and their friends) with his later return to Indiana as an adult, and a moment of recognition involving his brother's son: "Jesse and most of his friends like to dress like gangsters, too. . . ." (p. 348). The more things change, the narrative suggests, the more they remain the same (Although some changes are irreversible. A final photo and dedication suggest that, through this article, Bowman is mourning a recent death—perhaps his brother's).

The subversive form of this article reinforces the themes of its content. Its opening pages display several complex operations. The abstract, for example, is a self-conscious transgression of professional norms: The form of address in abstracts is typically passive, indirect, and third-person. The opening reference to CRTNET readers, and the sexual puns, are inside jokes. They invoke recent controversy associated with publication in the same journal of a piece of alternative writing (see Kellett & Goodall, 1999). As such, they signify the solidarity of area specialists (in performance studies) against the tyranny of general disciplinary readers. They warn, but also dare the reader to keep reading. They invite readers to reflect on what types of readers they are—or wish to be. As such, these dares are nearly irresistible.

The initial references to discrimination connect the object of Dillinger with Bowman's persona. Without making a simple or direct comparison, Bowman suggests the symbolic affinities that exist between Dillinger and the performative writer. Both are cultural "outlaws" who transgress norms and suffer the wrath of traditionalists. The "careers" of Dillinger and Bowman are linked, in that the former provides a resource for the latter to understand the challenges associated with his professional identity. Their connection is allegorical, not literal.

> By way of analogy or conceit, I would like to say that doing performance research and writing are akin to the activities of a legendary outlaw since, in both, the idiomatic (one's personal or private discourse) joins with the institutional (the recognized "grammar" of one's discipline) in order to rewrite (or, in Brecht's terms, refunction) an object of study. For the famous outlaw, this means projecting one's inimitable style or signature onto the grammar of law-breaking (e.g., robbing a bank) in order to recompose . . . our standard attitudes toward "law and order. (Bowman, 2000, p. 362)

Bowman's goal is thus not to perpetuate the conventional demonization or counter-cultural martyrdom of Dillinger. Instead, he seeks to historicize the potent (and irrational) mixture of fascination and horror that animates the disciplining of deviance, ranging from shoot-outs to academic politics. This analysis intervenes in culture by avoiding the overworked scenes of representation and by recovering what they suppress.

> The other thirty years [prior to Dillinger's brief criminal career] find no place in the iconography of Depression-era outlaws . . . and they are not to be found in the [contemporary] landscape . . . of [texts about] mobsters, mass murderers, forensic science, FBI stories, bad-boys-bad-boys-whatcha-gonna-do, and so on. (p. 355)

To focus on this absence is to remember the mundane—and seemingly intractable—conditions that inspire an outlaw's career (such as poverty, discrimination, and ignorance). The spectacle, Bowman implies, is inevitably a distraction from engaging these issues.

The first photograph and poem in this piece establish the themes of commodification and voyeurism that saturate the Dillinger mythology. In both life and death, these texts suggest, Dillinger was a symbol appropriated by various producers and audiences to meet their (often base) needs. They also suggest the role of signs in endlessly deferring the "truth" of events. These signs form a "macabre" (p. 369) economy of talismans evoking cultural ambivalence about bodies, gender (e.g., a trick postmortem photo of Dillinger's manly "endowment"; p. 369), and law: "Some folks brought him flowers / Others came for blood / Dipped their hankies and their hems / In that crimson flood" (p. 343).

This use of multimedia forms a complex bricolage. This code stimulates the reader to move back and forth between nonlinear fragments. Images from dreams, commercial media, archives (e.g., of Dillinger's letters and FBI forensics), and the author's present life swirl, recur, and commingle (pp. 359-360). These fragments interrupt and comment on each other. Collectively, they form a pulsing reflection on the Dillinger myth and its significance for various audiences. As such, they mimic the vivid, evolving—and potentially disconcerting—qualities associated with performance itself. This is indeed writing about—and as—performance. In this process, Bowman layers multiple voices: direct authorial address; a professional academic narrator (e.g., addressing the role of memory in performance and the relationship between methods and violence; pp. 349-350, 361); a Beatlike poet evoking the crackling rhythms and textures of modern American life (p. 350); a reflective, autobiographical subject; and an implicit author of the photo captions. Collectively these voices testify that Dillinger is both unknown and unknowable, but that these conditions do not impede cultural mythologizing. Indeed, because of Dillinger's utility as a cultural symbol, they compel it. As such, this piece exemplifies the forms and purposes of "experimental" writing.

Some Final Thoughts on Writing

If this discussion of strategies and examples has not yet proven sufficient, we conclude by passing along some maxims about writing. This list represents the best wisdom that we have read, heard, and lived. It's not a long list. After all, if we haven't established our credibility as writers by this point, why should you believe us now? We encourage you to argue with and add to these items, and generally to make your own list.

- Regrettably, most academic disciplines view training in writing as an informal, secondary, and occasional practice. As a result, we encourage you to seek out courses, conversations, and relationships dedicated to improving your writing. When you find these resources, be grateful for the help and pass it along.
- The best writers are also dedicated *readers*. They read published scholarship, as well as fiction, journalism, essays, poetry, and autobiography. They continuously seek models of good writing that deepen their appreciation, wisdom, and inspiration concerning communication and the human condition.
- You are more likely to write if you do so frequently and engage in forms that allow you to feel creative, safe, and joyful. Writing can be a form of devotion.
- It's been remarked that successful writing on one day is no guarantee of success on the next day. As a result, enjoy your streaks while they last. When they end, be tolerant of your inconsistency and imperfection. The muse eventually returns.
- No one else can write for you. Sometimes, what appears to be procrastination is really the ferment of prewriting. If it persists, you may need to change your routine (and ask for help). Some of the things you need to change your writing may be out of your control—but not all of them.
- Writing is, as they say, rewriting. This means that what first appears on the screen or the page is already a reworking of something you have previously thought, said, or heard. It also means that no word and no sentence are necessarily finished. See if you can make them better.
- The mechanism of editorial review is imperfect but necessary. It works best when participants treat it as a dialogue designed to ensure the quality of writing. As clichéd as it sounds, the golden rule goes a long way here.
- Writing always takes longer than you think. When setting goals and deadlines, try to factor in time for the unexpected (a sick family member) and the necessary (a night at the movies to clear your head).
- Always keep your audience in mind. It's true that, in some ultimate sense, we write for ourselves. But our efforts are wasted if our actual audience finds that work obscure, tedious, or precious. Regarding the use and abuse of theoretical jargon, we believe the

stylistic pendulum is swinging back toward accessibility and clarity. These values are not to be confused with anti-intellectualism. Instead, we invoke them to encourage writing that speaks *to* or *with* its audience, not *at* or *down* to them.

This Way to Exit

When Tom was concluding the first edition of this volume, he meditated on the paradox of that task. Methods texts, he noted, are inherently conservative. They round up exemplars of best practices and prescribe their imitation. Like ghosts (or some types of angels), they float above the ecstasy and the wreckage, speaking a discourse of moderation and detachment. And then suddenly at the end, they touch down and point to the horizon. They declare the future to be filled with promise. "The reader," Tom noted, "should be suspicious of last minute enthusiasm from a source of that kind" (Lindlof, 1995, p. 279).

This paradox has not gone away, but at least now there are two of us to mull it over. While mulling, we thank you for investing your time and energy in reading this volume. We hope it stimulates and improves your work. It was (trust us) as much of a journey to write as it probably has been to read. And perhaps that is the best place to begin to conclude.

In completing this volume, we developed some working hypotheses about the state of qualitative research in Communication. This felt like a large responsibility. One of those claims (repeated often) was that "qualitative communication research" is no longer—if it ever was—a singular, clearly identifiable phenomenon. Instead, our (reflexively) interpretive approach to this task—one sensitive to differentiated realities—found just that: multiple and partial—but not unconnected—stories of what qualitative methods are and how they should be used.

This statement is not meant to confirm your fears about the unfalsifiability of interpretive claims. Instead, it signals that, for better and worse, qualitative communication research is becoming a local and centrifugal matter. That is, while there are rare moments of disciplinary communion to honor or vilify qualitative research (Kellett & Goodall, 1999), and bold exceptions addressed to the general readership (Crawford, 1996), the day-to-day reality seems to be one of researchers using qualitative methods to pursue the agendas of their affiliated subfields. Witnessed from the angels' roost, this collective enterprise sounds like diverse dialects, not a standardized language. These subfields have drawn differently on the eclectic resources of qualitative research to fashion solutions to their specific problems. This means that there is much variation in what counts as "good" use of these methods. This standard is always filtered through the code of subfield histories.

We are not leading to a simple judgment here. Instead, we are describing the state of our discipline. Here, we are tempted to think of either complete order or chaos as the solution to this condition. But we reject both options—we are not necessarily describing a *problem*. Instead, our solution is encoded in this volume. Its coauthorship and wide scope (however imperfectly realized) reflect our belief that researchers should notice how their colleagues in other subfields are using qualitative methods. This is particularly rewarding when those uses are innovative and exciting. Additionally, we believe that students should be exposed to a full range of theoretical and methodological options in order to make informed and accountable choices about pursuing projects. While this advice—if taken—may complicate our personal agendas, who can say what might be produced in the ensuing dialogues? At least things would be different, and for some, that is enough (see Geist, 1999).

This appearance of localism is also, we believe, partly misleading. This is because the use of qualitative methods in some subfields has contributed to the formation of networks linking their members with researchers in other disciplines (or metadisciplines). These researchers use similar (if not identical) methods to examine similar (if not identical) problems. Qualitative methods, in other words, are a principal medium of interdisciplinarity. As such, the title of this volume is somewhat incomplete. A more accurate version might be *Qualitative Methods Used By Researchers Who Affiliate With the Discipline of Communication, and By Researchers Who Belong to Other Disciplines Yet Gravitate to Questions Asked By Qualitative Communication Researchers (or Who Ask Questions to Which These Researchers Gravitate)*. Needless to say, this title will never grace an actual book cover, but we hope it makes our point. As the discipline diversifies, some of its stems and flowers grow outward. This does not mean, however, that their roots also leave the discipline—only that "the state of the field" is an arbitrary punctuation of multiple conversations that are alternately expanding and contracting in their scope.

Let us shift to a more direct conclusion: It is getting harder for academics to conduct fieldwork. Here, we agree with Gans (1999) that participant observation

> is very labor intensive and time consuming; and when the subject is a community or a major institution, it and the book in which the work is reported require a number of years of individual or team work. As a result, it is expensive, both in time and salaries, and is virtually impossible to do between meeting one's classes. (p. 544)

Although we have not analyzed the appropriate indicators (e.g., published articles reflecting expansive vs. limited use of qualitative methods), we believe that the barriers described in this passage (and earlier in this chapter) are influencing qualitative researchers as they design and conduct their studies. In this way, powerful forces currently seeking to industrialize and commercialize the university (e.g., by eradicating tenure, developing online educational markets, and increasing teaching loads; Bromell, 2002) will inevitably affect who conducts qualitative research, which problems it engages, and how it engages those problems. As a result, we believe a critical perspective on academic institutions will be increasingly necessary to meet the goals of this volume.

Finally, we pose some questions for you to ponder (Lindlof, 2001, pp. 93-94): What difference do qualitative studies make, not only in the academy but also in the public sphere and the everyday lives of people? In what sense are they worth the enormous effort and risk that they involve?

Answering these questions is perhaps the most important challenge of qualitative research. In our view, qualitative research addresses enduring needs for knowing how culture is reproduced, how value and power are constituted, how people experience their selves in relation to the larger cultural order, and how communication within and across cultural identities and systems can be accomplished. Out of these broad needs come many of the specific problems studied by communication scholars, such as the ways in which power and resistance are actually performed. Scholars are one of the few groups in society that can engage these problems with only the public as the beneficiary of their work.

However, as both apologists for and critics of qualitative communication research, we continue to want more. Each project of communication research changes the world it seeks to study. Yet we seldom think very carefully about what these interventions really mean. We seldom think about how insular the audiences for the vast bulk of our work really are. We don't often consider how our experiences from the field *could* come into contact with experiences of the larger world. Our challenges for the future, then, will include expanding the formats and outlets in which we write, while trying to understand how our work can make a greater—and new kinds of—social and ethical difference.

We all have a stake in that future. And each of us, no matter what our particular commitments, can contribute.

Exercises

1. In this chapter, we have analyzed examples of "traditional" and "experimental" writing formats. Find a published study that seems interesting and relevant to your own research. Examine how elements such as voice,

narrative presence, the genre-audience nexus, and textual organization are displayed and managed by its author (or authors). Begin by describing the structure and content of this research narrative. Then comment on the significance of its operations. How, for example, does it evoke and satisfy reader expectations? (Bonus question: Imagine how this example would appear if written in its opposite format—for example, an experimental format rewritten as a traditional format.)

2. Select a handful of journals that are relevant to your primary subfield (e.g., interpersonal communication). Scan recent volumes of these journals, looking for examples of qualitative research. How has the crisis of representation been reflected—if at all—in the style, form, and content of those articles? What do your findings suggest about the politics of publishing qualitative research in this subfield?

3. Review the discussion of "exemplars" in this chapter. Construct an exemplar from data collected in your own qualitative research. Share this exemplar (only) with other colleagues (e.g., classmates). Request their feedback on its demonstrated "eventfulness." Ask them to anticipate what interpretive claim it is intended to service. Incorporate their feedback into further writing.

References

Abu-Lughod, L. (1997). The interpretation of culture(s) after television. *Representations, 59*, 109-130.

Adams, L. (1999). The mascot researcher: Identity, power, and knowledge in fieldwork. *Journal of Contemporary Ethnography, 28*, 331-363.

Adelman, M. B., & Frey, L. R. (1996). *The fragile community: Living together with AIDS*. Mahwah, NJ: Lawrence Erlbaum.

Adelman, M. B. (Producer), & Schultz, P. (Director). (1997). *The pilgrim must embark: Living in community* [Videotape]. Chicago: Terra Nova Films.

Adler, P. A., & Adler, P. (1987). *Membership roles in field research*. Newbury Park, CA: Sage.

Advanced Practices Council. (2001). *Eleventh request for proposals for applied research on IT management*. Retrieved May 17, 2001 from http://faculty-staff.ou.edu/Z/Robert.W.Zmud-1/APC/

Agar, M. (1982). Toward an ethnographic language. *American Anthropologist, 84*, 779-795.

Agar, M. (1995). Literary journalism as ethnography. In J. Van Maanen (Ed.), *Representation in ethnography* (pp. 112-129). Thousand Oaks, CA: Sage.

Agar, M. (1996). *The professional stranger* (2nd ed.). San Diego, CA: Academic Press.

Agar, M., & MacDonald, J. (1995). Focus groups and ethnography. *Human Organization, 54*, 78-86.

Alasuutari, P. (1996). Theorizing in qualitative research: A cultural studies perspective. *Qualitative Inquiry, 2*, 371-384.

Allen, C. (1997, November). Spies like us: When sociologists deceive their subjects. *Lingua Franca*, pp. 30-39.

Altheide, D. L. (1995). Horsing around with literary loops, or why postmodernism is fun. *Symbolic Interaction, 18*, 519-526.

Altheide, D. L., & Snow, R. P. (1988). Toward a theory of mediation. In J. A. Anderson (Ed.), *Communication yearbook 11* (pp. 194-223). Newbury Park, CA: Sage.

Alvesson, M., & Deetz, S. (1996). Critical theory and postmodernism: Approaches to organizational studies. In S. R. Clegg, C. Hardy, & W. R. Nord (Eds.), *Handbook of organization studies* (pp. 191-216). Thousand Oaks, CA: Sage.

Alvesson, M., & Willmott, H. (1992). On the idea of emancipation in management and organization studies. *Academy of Management Review, 17*, 432-464.

Ammerman, N. T. (1982). Dilemmas in establishing a research identity. *New England Sociologist, 4*, 21-27.

Anderson, J. A. (1987). *Communication research: Issues and methods*. New York: McGraw-Hill.

Anderson, J. A. (1991). The social action of organizing: Knowledge, practice, and morality. *Australian Journal of Communication, 18*(3), 1-18.

Anderson, J. A. (1996a). *Communication theory: Epistemological foundations*. New York: Guilford.

Anderson, J. A. (1996b). Thinking qualitatively: Hermeneutics in science. In M. B. Salwen & D. W. Stacks (Eds.), *An integrated approach to communication theory and research* (pp. 45-59). Mahwah, NJ: Lawrence Erlbaum.

Anderson, J. A. (2001). The challenge of writing the interpretive inquiry. In A. Alexander & W. J. Potter (Eds.), *How to publish your communication research: An insider's guide* (pp. 97-112). Thousand Oaks, CA: Sage.

Anderson, J. A., & Meyer, T. P. (1988). *Mediated communication: A social action perspective*. Newbury Park, CA: Sage.

Ang, I. (1991). *Desperately seeking the audience*. New York: Routledge.

Angrosino, M. V., & Mays de Peréz, K. A. (2000). Rethinking observation: From method to context. In N. K. Denzin & Y. S. Lincoln (Eds.), *Handbook of qualitative research* (2nd ed., pp. 673-702). Thousand Oaks, CA: Sage.

Arcury, T. A., & Quandt, S. A. (1999). Participant recruitment for qualitative research: A site-based approach to community research in complex societies. *Human Organization, 58,* 128-133.

Arendell, T. (1997). Reflections on the researcher-researched relationship: A woman interviewing men. *Qualitative Sociology, 20,* 341-368.

Arnold, L. B. (1995). Through the narrow pass: Experiencing same-sex friendship in heterosexual(ist) settings. *Communication Studies, 46*(3-4), 234-244.

Arnould, E. J., & Wallendorf, M. (1994). Market-oriented ethnography: Interpretation building and marketing strategy formulation. *Journal of Marketing Research, 31,* 484-504.

Ashcraft, K. L. (2000). Empowering "professional" relationships: Organizational communication meets feminist practice. *Management Communication Quarterly, 13,* 347-392.

Ashcraft, K. L., & Pacanowsky, M. E. (1996). "A woman's worst enemy": Reflections on a narrative of organizational life and female identity. *Journal of Applied Communication Research, 24,* 217-239.

Atkinson, P. A. (1988). Ethnomethodology: A critical review. *Annual Review of Sociology, 14,* 441-465.

Atkinson, P. A. (1990). *The ethnographic imagination.* London: Routledge.

Atkinson, P. A. (1992). *Understanding ethnographic texts.* Newbury Park, CA: Sage.

Baba, M. L. (1998, May 8). Anthropologists in corporate America: Knowledge management and ethical angst. *Chronicle of Higher Education, 44*(35), B4-B5.

Bach, T. E., Blair, C., Nothstine, W. L., & Pym, A. L. (1996). How to read "How to Get Published." *Communication Quarterly, 44,* 399-422.

Bailey, B. (2000). Communicative behavior and conflict between African-American customers and Korean immigrant retailers in Los Angeles. *Discourse & Society, 11*(1), 86-108.

Bakalaki, A. (1997). Students, natives, colleagues: Encounters in academia and in the field. *Cultural Anthropology, 12,* 502-526.

Bakhtin, M. M. (1986). *Speech genres and other late essays.* Minneapolis: University of Minnesota Press.

Ball, M. (1998). Remarks on visual competence as an integral part of ethnographic fieldwork practice: The visual availability of culture. In J. Prosser (Ed.), *Image-based research: A source book for qualitative researchers* (pp. 131-147). London: Falmer.

Banks, S. (1998). The Tioga tapes. In A. Banks & S. Banks (Eds.), *Fiction and social research: By ice or fire* (pp. 255-262). Walnut Creek, CA: AltaMira.

Banks, S. P. (1994). Performing flight announcements: The case of flight attendants' work discourse. *Text and Performance Quarterly, 14,* 253-267.

Banks, S. P., Louie, E., & Einerson, M. (2000). Constructing personal identities in holiday letters. *Journal of Social and Personal Relationships, 17,* 299-327.

Bantz, C. R. (1993). *Understanding organizations: Interpreting organizational communication cultures.* Columbia: University of South Carolina Press.

Bantz, C. R. (2001). Ethnographic analysis of organizational cultures. In S. L. Herndon & G. Kreps (Eds.), *Qualitative research: Applications in organizational life* (2nd ed., pp. 171-184). Cresskill, NJ: Hampton.

Barbatsis, G., Fegan, M., & Hansen, K. (1999). The performance of cyberspace: An exploration into computer-mediated reality. *Journal of Computer-Mediated Communication, 5.* Retrieved December 16, 2001, from http://www.ascusc.org/jcmc/vol5/issue1/barbatsis.html

Barker, C. (2000). *Cultural studies: Theory and practice.* Thousand Oaks, CA: Sage.

Barker, J. R., & Cheney, G. (1994). The concept and the practices of discipline in contemporary organizational life. *Communication Monographs, 61,* 19-43.

Barnes, D. B., Taylor-Brown, S., & Wiener, L. (1997). "I didn't leave y'all on purpose": HIV-infected mothers' videotaped legacies for their children. *Qualitative Sociology, 20,* 7-31.

Barthes, R. (1957/1972). *Mythologies* (A. Lavers, Trans.). New York: Hill & Wang.

Bastien, D. T., & Hostager, T. J. (1988). Jazz as a process of organizational innovation. *Communication Research, 15,* 582-602.

Bateson, G. (1936). *Naven.* Stanford, CA: Stanford University Press.

Bateson, G. (1972). *Steps to an ecology of mind.* New York: Ballantine.

Bauman, R. (1986). *Story, performance, and event.* New York: Cambridge University Press.

Bauman, R., & Sherzer, J. (1975). The ethnography of speaking. *Annual Review of Anthropology, 4*, 95-119.

Baumeister, R. F., & Newman, L. S. (1994). How stories make sense of personal experiences: Motives that shape autobiographical narratives. *Personality and Social Psychology Bulletin, 20*, 676-690.

Baxter, Leslie A. (1993). "Talking things through" and "putting it in writing": Two codes of communication in an academic institution. *Journal of Applied Communication, 21*, 313-326.

Baym, N. K. (1998a). [Review of the book *Composing ethnography*]. *Quarterly Journal of Speech, 84*, 120-121.

Baym, N. K. (1998b). The emergence of on-line community. In S. G. Jones (Ed.), *Cybersociety 2.0* (pp. 35-68). Thousand Oaks, CA: Sage.

Baym, N. K. (2000). *Tune in, log on: Soaps, fandom, and online community.* Thousand Oaks, CA: Sage.

Beach, W. A. (1996). *Conversations about illness: Family preoccupations with bulimia.* Mahwah, NJ: Lawrence Erlbaum.

Beck, C. S. (1995). You make the call: The co-creation of media text through interaction in an interpretive community of "Giants" fans. *Electronic Journal of Communication, 5*(1). Retrieved December 8, 1998, from http://www.cios.org/getfile\Beck_V5N195

Becker, H. S. (1964). Problems in the publication of field studies. In A. Vidich, J. Bensman, & M. Stein (Eds.), *Reflections on community studies* (pp. 267-284). New York: John Wiley.

Becker, H. S. (1970). Problems of inference and proof in participant observation. In H. S. Becker, *Sociological work: Method and substance* (pp. 25-38). Chicago: Aldine.

Becker, H. S. (1986). *Doing things together.* Evanston, IL: Northwestern University Press.

Becker, H. S., & McCall, M. M. (Eds.). (1990). *Symbolic interaction and cultural studies.* Chicago: University of Chicago Press.

Bell, E., & Forbes, L.C. (1994). Office folklore in the academic paperwork empire: The interstitial space of gendered (con)texts. *Text and Performance Quarterly, 14*, 181-196.

Bennett, T. (1992). Putting policy into cultural studies. In L. Grossberg, C. Nelson, & P. Treichler (Eds.), *Cultural studies* (pp. 23-37). New York: Routledge.

Bennett, T., & Wollacott, J. (1988). *Bond and beyond: The political career of a popular hero.* London: Macmillan.

Benney, M., & Hughes, E. C. (1970). Of sociology and the interview. In N. K. Denzin (Ed.), *Sociological methods* (pp. 190-198). Chicago: Aldine.

Benson, T. W. (1981). Another shooting in Cowtown. *Quarterly Journal of Speech, 67*, 347-406.

Benson, T. W. (Ed.). (1985). *Speech communication in the 20th century.* Carbondale: Southern Illinois University Press.

Berger, B. (1998). *Where have all the horses gone? An ethnography of gamblers and simulcast racing.* Unpublished manuscript, University of Kentucky, Lexington.

Berger, P. L., & Luckmann, T. (1967). *The social construction of reality.* Garden City, NY: Doubleday.

Berman, M. (1982). *All that is solid melts into air: The experience of modernity.* New York: Simon & Schuster.

Bernard, R. H., Killworth, P., Kronenfeld, D., & Sailer, L. (1984). The problem of informant accuracy. *Annual Review of Anthropology, 13*, 495-517.

Bernstein, R. J. (1978). *The restructuring of social and political theory.* Philadelphia: University of Pennsylvania Press.

Betteridge, J. (1997). Answering back: The telephone, modernity and everyday life. *Media, Culture & Society, 19*, 585-603.

Biernacki, P., & Waldorf, D. (1981). Snowball sampling: Problems and techniques of chain referral sampling. *Sociological Methods & Research, 10*(2), 141-163.

Bijker, W. E., Hughes, T. P., & Pinch, T. J. (Eds.). (1987). *The social construction of technological systems: New directions in the sociology and history of technology.* Cambridge: MIT Press.

Bingham, W. V. D., & Moore, B. V. (1959). *How to interview* (4th ed.). New York: Harper & Row.

Bird, S. E. (1992). Travels in nowhere land: Ethnography and the "impossible" audience. *Critical Studies in Mass Communication, 9*, 250-260.

Bird, S. E. (1995). Understanding the ethnographic encounter: The need for flexibility in feminist reception studies. *Women and Language, 18*(2), 22-26.

Birdwhistell, R. L. (1970). *Kinesics and context.* Philadelphia: University of Pennsylvania Press.

Blair, C., Brown, J. R., & Baxter, L. A. (1994). Disciplining the feminine. *Quarterly Journal of Speech, 80*(4), 383-409.

Blair, C., & Michel, N. (1999). Commemorating the theme park zone: Reading the Astronauts' Memorial. In T. Rosteck (Ed.), *At the intersection: Cultural studies and rhetorical studies* (pp. 29-83). New York: Guilford.

Blee, K. M. (1998). White-knuckle research: Emotional dynamics in fieldwork with racist activists. *Qualitative Sociology, 21*, 381-399.

Bloor, M. (1997). Techniques of validation in qualitative research: A critical commentary. In G. Miller & R. Dingwall (Eds.), *Context and method in qualitative research* (pp. 37-50). Thousand Oaks, CA: Sage.

Blumer, H. (1969). *Symbolic interactionism: Perspective and method*. Englewood Cliffs, NJ: Prentice Hall.

Bochner, A. P. (1985). Perspectives on inquiry: Representation, conversation, and reflection. In M. L. Knapp & G. R. Miller (Eds.), *Handbook of interpersonal communication* (pp. 27-58). Beverly Hills, CA: Sage.

Bochner, A. P. (1997). It's about time: Narrative and the divided self. *Qualitative Inquiry, 3*, 418-438.

Bochner, A. P., & Eisenberg, E. M. (1985). Legitimizing speech communication: An examination of coherence and cohesion in the development of the discipline. In T. W. Benson (Ed.), *Speech communication in the 20th century* (pp. 299-321). Carbondale: Southern Illinois University Press.

Bochner, A. P., & Ellis, C. (1992). Personal narrative as a social approach to interpersonal communication. *Communication Theory, 2*, 165-172.

Bochner, A. P., & Ellis, C. (Eds.). (1996). Taking ethnography into the twenty-first century. *Journal of Contemporary Ethnography, 25*, 3-5.

Bochner, A. P., & Ellis, C. (1997, November 19). *Interpretive and narrative ethnography*. Seminar at the National Communication Association conference, Chicago.

Bogdan, R. C., & Biklen, S. K. (1982). Qualitative research for education: An introduction to theory and methods. Boston: Allyn & Bacon.

Boje, D. M. (1991). The storytelling organization: A study of story performance in an office-supply firm. *Administrative Science Quarterly, 36*, 106-126.

Boje, D. M. (1995). Stories of the storytelling organization: A postmodern analysis of Disney as "Tamara-Land." *Academy of Management Journal, 38*, 997-1035.

Bolter, J. D., & Grusin, R. (2000). *Remediation: Understanding new media*. Cambridge: MIT Press.

Borman, K. M., LeCompte, M. D., & Goetz, J. P. (1986). Ethnographic and qualitative research design and why it doesn't work. *American Behavioral Scientist, 30*, 42-57.

Bourgault, L. M. (1992). Talking to people in the oral tradition: Ethnographic research for development communication. *International Communication Bulletin, 27*(3-4), 19-24.

Bowman, M. S. (2000). Killing Dillinger: A mystory. *Text and Performance Quarterly, 20*, 342-374.

Boyce, M. E. (1995). Collective centering and collective sense-making in the stories and storytelling of one organization. *Organization Studies, 16*, 107-137.

Bradford, L., Meyers, R., & Kane, K. (1999). Latino expectations of communicative competence: A focus group interview study. *Communication Quarterly, 47*(1), 98-117.

Braithwaite, C. (1990). Communicative silence: A cross-cultural study of Basso's hypothesis. In D. Carbaugh (Ed.), *Cultural communication and intercultural contact* (pp. 321-327). Hillsdale, NJ: Lawrence Erlbaum.

Braithwaite, C. (1997). Were you there?: A ritual of legitimacy among Vietnam veterans. *Western Journal of Communication, 61*, 423-447.

Braithwaite, D. O., Dollar, N., Fitch, K., & Geist, P. (1996). Case studies for ethics in qualitative research. Panel materials developed for the Western States Communication Association conference, Pasadena, CA.

Brenner, M. (1978). Interviewing: The social phenomenology of a research instrument. In M. Brenner, P. Marsh, & M. Brenner (Eds.), *The social contexts of method* (pp. 122-139). New York: St. Martin's.

Brenner, M. (1985). Intensive interviewing. In M. Brenner, J. Brown, & D. Canter (Eds.), *The research interview* (pp. 147-162). London: Academic Press.

Brettell, C. B. (1993). Introduction: Fieldwork, text, and audience. In C. B. Brettell (Ed.), *When they read what we write: The politics of ethnography* (pp. 1-24). Westport, CT: Bergin & Garvey.

Briggs, C. L. (1986). *Learning how to ask: A sociolinguistic appraisal of the role of the interview in social science research.* Cambridge, UK: Cambridge University Press.

Brodkey, L. (1987a). Writing critical ethnographic narratives. *Anthropology & Education Quarterly, 18,* 67-76.

Brodkey, L. (1987b). Writing ethnographic narratives. *Written Communication, 4,* 25-50.

Bromell, N. (2002, February). *Summa cum avaritia:* Plucking a profit from the groves of academe. *Harper's Magazine,* pp. 71-76.

Brooke, J. (2001). Room in my heart. On *Steady pull* [CD]. Malibu, CA: Bad Dog Records.

Brown, M. H., & McMillan, J. (1991). Culture as text: The development of an organizational narrative. *Southern Communication Journal, 57,* 49-60.

Brown, R. H. (1977). *A poetic for sociology.* Cambridge, UK: Cambridge University Press.

Brown, S. R. (1996). Q methodology and qualitative research. *Qualitative Health Research, 6,* 561-568.

Bruder, K. A., & Ucok, O. (2000). Interactive art interpretation: How viewers make sense of paintings in conversation. *Symbolic Interaction, 23,* 337-358.

Bruess, C. J. S., & Pearson, J. C. (1997). Interpersonal rituals in marriage and adult friendship. *Communication Monographs, 64*(1), 25-46.

Brummett, B. (1999). *Rhetoric of machine aesthetics.* Westport, CT: Praeger.

Bruner, E. M. (1987). Ethnography as narrative. In V.W. Turner & E. M. Bruner (Eds.), *The anthropology of experience* (pp. 139-155). Urbana: University of Illinois Press.

Bruner, J. (1987). Life as narrative. *Social Research, 54,* 11-32.

Bull, M. (2001). The world according to sound: Investigating the world of Walkman users. *New Media & Society, 3,* 179-197.

Burgess, R. G. (1984). *In the field.* London: Allen & Unwin.

Burns, C., Dishman, E., Johnson, B., & Verplank, B. (1995, August 8). *"Informance": Min(d)ing future contexts for scenario-based interaction design.* Performance at the Interval Research Corporation, Palo Alto, CA.

Buttny, R. (1997). Reported speech in talking race on campus. *Human Communication Research, 23,* 477-506.

Caldarola, V. J. (1985). Visual contexts: A photographic research method in anthropology. *Studies in Visual Communication, 11,* 33-53.

Cali, D. D. (2000). The logic of the link: The associative paradigm in communication criticism. *Critical Studies in Media Communication, 17,* 397-408.

Cameron, D. (2001). *Working with spoken discourse.* Thousand Oaks, CA: Sage.

Campbell, C., & Wickman, S. A. (2000). Familiars in a strange land: A case study of friends chatting online. *M/C: A Journal of Media and Culture, 3.* Retrieved December 18, 2001, from http://www.media-culture.org.au/0008/friends.txt

Caplan, S. E. (2001). Challenging the mass-interpersonal communication dichotomy: Are we witnessing the emergence of an entirely new communication system? *Electronic Journal of Communication, 11.* Retrieved December 16, 2001, from http://www.cios.org/getfile/Caplan_v11n101

Carbaugh, D. (1988a). Cultural terms and tensions in the speech at a television station. *Western Journal of Speech Communication, 52,* 216-237.

Carbaugh, D. (1988b). *Talking American: Cultural discourses on Donahue.* Norwood, NJ: Ablex.

Carbaugh, D. (1991). Communication and cultural interpretation. *Quarterly Journal of Speech, 77,* 336-342.

Carbaugh, D. (1993). "Soul" and "self": Soviet and American cultures in conversation. *Quarterly Journal of Speech, 79,* 182-200.

Carbaugh, D. (1995). The ethnographic communication theory of Philipsen and associates. In D. P. Cushman & B. Kovacic (Eds.), *Watershed research traditions in human communication theory* (pp. 269-297). Albany: State University of New York Press.

Carbaugh, D., & Hastings, S. O. (1992). A role for communication theory in ethnography and cultural analysis. *Communication Theory, 2,* 156-164.

Carey, J. W. (1975). Communication and culture. *Communication Research, 2,* 173-191.

Carey, J. W. (1989). *Communication as culture: Essays on media and society.* Boston: Unwin Hyman.

Carey, M. A. (1994). The group effect in focus groups: Planning, implementing and interpreting focus group research. In J. Morse (Ed.), *Critical issues in qualitative research methods* (pp. 225-241). Thousand Oaks, CA: Sage.

Carlson, R. G., Wang, J., Siegal, H. A., Falck, R. S., & Guo, J. (1994). An ethnographic approach to targeted sampling: Problems and solutions in AIDS prevention research among injection drug and crack-cocaine users. *Human Organization, 53,* 279-286.

Carter, K., & Presnell, M. (Eds.). (1994). *Interpretive approaches to interpersonal communication.* Albany: State University of New York Press.

Cavanagh, A. (1999). Behaviour in public? Ethics in online ethnography. *Cybersociology, 6.* Retrieved December 16, 2001, from http://www.socio.demon.co.uk/magazine/6/cavanagh.html

Ceglowski, D. (2000). Research as relationship. *Qualitative Inquiry, 6,* 88-103.

Chambon, A. S. (1995). Life history as dialogical activity: "If you ask me the right questions, I could tell you." *Current Sociology, 43*(2-3), 125-135.

Chang, B. G. (1996). *Deconstructing communication: Representation, subject, and economies of exchange.* Minneapolis: University of Minnesota Press.

Charmaz, K. (1983). The grounded theory method: An explication and interpretation. In R. M. Emerson (Ed.), *Contemporary field research* (pp. 109-126). Boston: Little, Brown.

Charmaz, K. (1995). Between positivism and postmodernism: Implications for methods. *Studies in Symbolic Interaction, 17,* 43-72.

Charmaz, K. (2000). Grounded theory: Objectivist and constructivist methods. In N. K. Denzin & Y. S. Lincoln (Eds.), *Handbook of qualitative research* (2nd ed., pp. 509-536). Thousand Oaks, CA: Sage.

Charmaz, K., & Mitchell, R. G. (1996). The myth of silent authorship: Self, substance, and style in ethnographic writing. *Symbolic Interaction, 19,* 285-302.

Chatham-Carpenter, A., & De Francisco, V. (1997). Pulling yourself up again: Women's choices and strategies for recovering and maintaining self-esteem. *Western Journal of Communication, 61,* 164-187.

Chatman, S. (1978). *Story and discourse: Narrative structure in fiction and film.* Ithaca, NY: Cornell University Press.

Cheney, G. (1999). *Values at work: Employee participation meets market pressure at Mondragón.* Ithaca, NY: Cornell University Press.

Cheney, G. (2000). Interpreting interpretive research: Toward perspectivism without relativism. In S. R. Corman & M. S. Poole (Eds.), *Perspectives on organizational communication: Finding common ground* (pp. 17-45). New York: Guilford.

Cherny, L. (1995). The modal complexity of speech events in a social MUD. *Electronic Journal of Communication, 5.* Retrieved December 16, 2001, from http://www.cios.org/getfile/ Cherny_V5N495

Chesebro, J. W., & Bertelsen, D. A. (1996). *Analyzing media: Communication technologies as symbolic and cognitive systems.* New York: Guilford.

Cicourel, A. (1974). *Cognitive sociology.* New York: Free Press.

Cicourel, A. (1980). Three models of discourse analysis: The role of social structure. *Discourse Processes, 3,* 101-132.

Clair, R. P. (1998). *Organizing silence: A world of possibilities.* Albany: State University of New York Press.

Clifford, J. (1988). *The predicament of culture: Twentieth-century ethnography, literature, and art.* Cambridge, MA: Harvard University Press.

Clifford, J., & Marcus, G. E. (Eds.). (1986). *Writing culture: The poetics and politics of ethnography.* Berkeley: University of California Press.

Clough, P. (1995). Beginning again at the end(s) of ethnography: Response to "The man at the end of the machine." *Symbolic Interaction, 18,* 527-534.

Collier, M. J. (1998). Researching cultural identity: Reconciling interpretive and postcolonial perspectives. In D. V. Tanno & A. Gonzalez (Eds.), *Communication and identity across cultures: International and intercultural communication annual* (Vol. 21, pp. 122-147). Thousand Oaks, CA: Sage.

Collier, M. J. (2000). Current research themes of politics, perspectives, and problematics. In M. J. Collier (Ed.), *Constituting cultural difference through discourse: International and Intercultural communication annual* (Vol. 21, pp. 1-25). Thousand Oaks, CA: Sage.

COMST 298. (1997). Fragments of self at the postmodern bar. *Journal of Contemporary Ethnography, 26,* 251-292.

Conquergood, C. (1985). Performing as a moral act: Ethical dimensions of the ethnography of performance. *Literature in Performance, 5,* 1-13.

Conquergood, D. (1991). Rethinking ethnography: Towards a critical cultural politics. *Communication Monographs, 58,* 179-194.

Conquergood, D. (1992). Performance theory, Hmong shamans, and cultural politics. In J. Reinelt & J. Roach (Eds.), *Critical theory and performance* (pp. 41-64). Lansing: University of Michigan Press.

Conquergood, D. (1994). Homeboys and hoods: Gang communication and cultural space. In L. R. Frey (Ed.), *Group communication in context: Studies of natural groups* (pp. 23-55). Hillsdale, NJ: Lawrence Erlbaum.

Corey, F. C. (1996). Personal narratives and young men in prison: Labeling the outside inside. *Western Journal of Communication, 60,* 57-75.

Corey, F. C., & Nakayama, T. K. (1997). Sextext. *Text and Performance Quarterly, 17,* 58-68.

Corner, J. (1999). *Critical ideas in television studies.* New York: Oxford University Press.

Correll, S. (1995). The ethnography of an electronic bar. *Journal of Contemporary Ethnography, 24,* 270-298.

Cortazzi, M. (2001). Narrative analysis in ethnography. In P. Atkinson, A. Coffey, S. Delamont, J. Lofland, & L. Lofland (Eds.), *Handbook of ethnography* (pp. 384-394). Thousand Oaks, CA: Sage.

Cottle, T. J. (1973). The life study: On mutual recognition and the subjective inquiry. *Urban Life, 2,* 344-360.

Couch, C. J. (1995). Oh, what webs these phantoms spin. *Symbolic Interaction, 18,* 229-245.

Craig, R. T. (1989). Communication as a practical discipline. In B. Dervin, L. Grossberg, B. J. O'Keefe, & E. Wartella (Eds.), *Rethinking communication: Vol. 1. Paradigm issues* (pp. 97-122). Newbury Park, CA: Sage.

Craig, R. T. (1999). Communication theory as a field. *Communication Theory, 9,* 119-161.

Crang, M. A., Hudson, A. C., Reimer, S. M., & Hinchliffe, S. J. (1997). Software for qualitative research: 1. Prospectus and overview. *Environment and Planning A, 29,* 771-787.

Crawford, L. (1996). Personal ethnography. *Communication Monographs, 63,* 158-170.

Crider, C., & Cirillo, L. (1992). Systems of interpretation and the function of metaphor. *Journal for the Theory of Social Behaviour, 21,* 171-195.

Croft, S. E. (1999). Creating locales through storytelling: An ethnography of a group home for men with mental retardation. *Western Journal of Communication, 63*(3), 329-347.

Cronkhite, G. (1986). On the focus, scope, and coherence of the study of human symbolic activity. *Quarterly Journal of Speech, 72*(3), 231-246.

Culnan, M. J., & Markus, M. L. (1987). Information technologies. In F. M. Jablin, L. L. Putnam, K. H. Roberts, & L. W. Porter (Eds.), *Handbook of organizational communication: An interdisciplinary perspective* (pp. 420-444). Beverly Hills, CA: Sage.

Curry, T. J. (1986). A visual method of studying sports: The photo-elicitation interview. *Sociology of Sport Journal, 3,* 204-216.

Cushman, D. P. (1977). The rules perspective as a theoretical basis for the study of human communication. *Communication Quarterly, 25,* 30-45.

Cushman, D. P., & Whiting, G. (1972). An approach to communication theory: Toward consensus on rules. *Journal of Communication, 22,* 217-238.

Davis, S. (1997). *Spectacular nature: Corporate culture and the Sea World experience.* Berkeley: University of California Press.

De Andrade, L. L. (2000). Negotiating from the inside: Constructing racial and ethnic identity in qualitative research. *Journal of Contemporary Ethnography, 29*, 268-290.

Deetz, S. (1998). Discursive formation, strategized subordination, and self-surveillance. In A. McKinlay & K. Starken (Eds.), *Foucault, management, and organization theory* (pp. 151-172). London: Sage.

Deetz, S., & Putnam, L. (2000). Thinking about the future of communication studies. In W. Gudykunst (Ed.), *Communication Yearbook 24* (pp. 2-15). Thousand Oaks, CA: Sage.

Delaney, S. (2000, June). [Review of the book *Kaleidoscope Notes*]. *Forum: Qualitative Social Research.* Retrieved January 10, 2002, from http://qualitative-research.net/fqs-texte/2-00/-2-00review-delaney-e.htm

Delia, J. G. (1977). Constructivism and the study of human communication. *Quarterly Journal of Speech, 63*, 66-83.

Delia, J. G. (1987). Communication research: A history. In C. R. Berger & S. H. Chaffee (Eds.), *Handbook of communication science* (pp. 20-97). Newbury Park, CA: Sage.

Delia, J. G., & O'Keefe, B. J. (1979). Constructivism: The development of communication in children. In E. Wartella (Ed.), *Children communicating* (pp.157-185). Beverly Hills, CA: Sage.

Della-Piana, C. K., & Anderson, J. A. (1995). Performing community: Community service as cultural conversation. *Communication Studies, 46*, 187-200.

Delli Carpini, M. X., & Williams, B. A. (1994). Methods, metaphors, and media research: The uses of television in political conversation. *Communication Research, 21*, 782-812.

Denzin, N. K. (1969). Symbolic interactionism and ethnomethodology: A proposed synthesis. *American Sociological Review, 34*, 922-934.

Denzin, N. K. (1977). *Childhood socialization.* San Francisco: Jossey-Bass.

Denzin, N. K. (1978). *The research act* (2nd ed.). New York: McGraw-Hill.

Denzin, N. K. (1997). *Interpretive ethnography: Ethnographic practices for the 21st century.* Thousand Oaks, CA: Sage.

Denzin, N. K. (1999). Cybertalk and the method of instances. In S. Jones (Ed.), *Doing Internet research* (pp. 107-126). Thousand Oaks, CA: Sage.

Denzin, N. K. (2000). Aesthetics and the practices of qualitative inquiry. *Qualitative Inquiry, 6*, 256-265.

Denzin, N. K., & Lincoln, Y. S. (2000). Introduction. In N. K. Denzin & Y. S. Lincoln (Eds.), *Handbook of qualitative research* (2nd ed., pp. 1 - 28). Thousand Oaks, CA: Sage.

Dervin, B., & Clark, K. D. (1999). Exemplars of the use of the sense-making methodology (meta-theory and method): In-depth introduction to the sensemaking issues of the *Electronic Journal of Communication. Electronic Journal of Communication, 9*(2-4). Retrieved July 13, 2001, from http://www.cios.org/getfile/Dervin1_V9N23499

Dervin, B., Grossberg, L., O'Keefe, B. J., & Wartella, E. (Eds.). (1989). *Rethinking communication: Vol. 1. Paradigm issues.* Newbury Park, CA: Sage.

DeVault, M. L. (1990). Talking and listening from women's standpoint: Feminist strategies for interviewing and analysis. *Social Problems, 37*, 96-116.

Dewey, J. (1954). *The public and its problems.* New York: Henry Holt. (Original work published 1927)

Dewey, J. (1958). *Experience and nature.* New York: Dover. (Original work published 1929)

Dibbell, J. (1994). A rape in cyberspace. In M. Dery (Ed.), *Flame wars: The discourse of cyberculture* (pp. 237-261). Durham, NC: Duke University Press.

Dilthey, W. (1974). On the special character of the human sciences. In M. Truzzi (Ed.), *Verstehen: Subjective understanding in the social sciences* (pp. 8-17). Reading, MA: Addison-Wesley. (Reprinted from *Wilhelm Dilthey: An introduction*, pp. 110-113, 120-124, 128-131, 133, 141-143, by H. A. Hodges, 1944, London: Routledge & Kegan Paul)

Dollar, N. J., & Merrigan, G. M. (2001). Ethnographic practices in group communication research. In L. R. Frey (Ed.), *New directions in group communication* (pp. 59-78). Thousand Oaks, CA: Sage.

Donath, J. (1999). Identity and deception in the virtual community. In M. A. Smith & P. Kollock (Eds.), *Communities in cyberspace* (pp. 29-59). London: Routledge.

Douglas, J. D. (1976). *Investigative social research.* Beverly Hills, CA: Sage.

Downes, E. J., & McMillan, S. J. (2000). Defining interactivity: A qualitative identification of key dimensions. *New Media and Society, 2*, 157-179.

Drew, P., & Heritage, J. (Eds.). (1992). *Talk at work: Interaction in institutional settings.* Cambridge, UK: Cambridge University Press.

Duncan, H. D. (1962). *Communication and social order.* Oxford, UK: Oxford University Press.

Eastland, L. S. (1993). The dialectical nature of ethnography: Liminality, reflexivity, and understanding. In S. L Herndon & G. L. Kreps (Eds.), *Qualitative research: Applications in organizational communication* (pp. 121-138). Cresskill, NJ: Hampton.

Eckman, A. (2001). *Negotiating the gray lines: An ethnographic study of the occupational roles and practices of advertorial producers at a medium market American newspaper.* Unpublished doctoral dissertation, University of Kentucky, Lexington.

Eichler, M. (1997). Feminist methodology. *Current Sociology, 45,* 9-36.

Eisenberg, E. M. (1990). Jamming: Transcendence through organizing. *Communication Research, 17,* 139-164.

Eisenberg, E. M. (1998). From anxiety to possibility: Poems, 1987-1997. In A. Banks & S. Banks (Eds.), *Fiction and social research: By ice or fire* (pp. 195-202). Walnut Creek, CA: AltaMira.

Eisenberg, E. M., Murphy, A., & Andrews, L. (1998). Openness and decision-making in the search of a university provost. *Communication Monographs, 65,* 1-23.

Eisenhardt, K. M. (1989). Building theories from case study research. *Academy of Management Review, 14,* 532-550.

Ellen, R. F. (1984). *Ethnographic research: A guide to general conduct.* London: Academic Press.

Ellingson, L. L. (1998). "Then you know how I feel": Empathy, identification, and reflexivity in fieldwork. *Qualitative Inquiry, 4,* 492-514.

Ellingson, L. L., & Buzzanell, P. M. (1999). Listening to women's narratives of breast cancer treatment: A feminist approach to patient satisfaction with physician-patient communication. *Health Communication, 11*(2), 153-183.

Ellis, C. (1995). Emotional and ethical quagmires in returning to the field. *Journal of Contemporary Ethnography, 24,* 68-98.

Ellis, C., & Bochner, A. P. (Eds.). (1996). *Composing ethnography: Alternative forms of qualitative writing.* Walnut Creek, CA: AltaMira.

Ellis, C., & Bochner, A. P. (2000). Autoethnography, personal narrative, reflexivity: Researcher as subject. In N. K. Denzin & Y. S. Lincoln (Eds.), *Handbook of qualitative research* (2nd ed., pp. 733-768). Thousand Oaks, CA: Sage.

Ellis, C., Kiesinger, C. E., & Tillmann-Healy, L. M. (1997). Interactive interviewing: Talking about emotional experience. In. R. Hertz (Ed.), *Reflexivity and voice* (pp. 119-149). Thousand Oaks, CA: Sage.

Ellis, D. G. (1980). Ethnographic considerations in initial interaction. *Western Journal of Speech Communication, 44,* 104-107.

Ely, J., Anzul, M., Friedman, T., Garner, D., & Steinmetz, A. M. (1991). *Doing qualitative research: Circles within circles.* London: Falmer.

Emerson, R. M., Fretz, R. I., & Shaw, L. L. (1995). *Writing ethnographic fieldnotes.* Chicago: University of Chicago Press.

Emerson, R. M., & Pollner, M. (1988). On the uses of members' responses to researchers' accounts. *Human Organization, 47,* 189-198.

Espiritu, Y. L. (2001). "We don't sleep around like white girls do": Family, culture, and gender in Filipina American lives. *Signs, 26,* 415-440.

Facio, E. (1993). Ethnography as a personal experience. In J. H. Stanfield, II & R. M. Dennis (Eds.), *Race and ethnicity in research methods* (pp. 75-91). Newbury Park, CA: Sage.

Faules, D. F., & Alexander, D. C. (1978). *Communication and social behavior: A symbolic interaction perspective.* Reading, MA: Addison-Wesley.

Ferguson, M., & Golding, P. (Eds.). (1997). *Cultural studies in question.* London: Sage.

Fernback, J. (1999). There is a there there: Notes toward a definition of cybercommunity. In S. Jones (Ed.), *Doing Internet research* (pp. 203-220). Thousand Oaks, CA: Sage.

Ferris, K. O. (2001). Through a glass, darkly: The dynamics of fan-celebrity encounters. *Symbolic Interaction, 24,* 25-47.

322   Qualitative Communication Research Methods

Fielding, N. (2001). Computer applications in qualitative research. In P. Atkinson, A. Coffey, S. Delamont, J. Lofland, & L. Lofland (Eds.), *Handbook of ethnography* (pp. 453-467). Thousand Oaks, CA: Sage.

Finch, J. (1984). "It's great to have someone to talk to": The ethics and politics of interviewing women. In C. Bell & H. Roberts (Eds.), *Social researching: Politics, problems, practice* (pp. 70-87). London: Routledge & Kegan Paul.

Fine, G. A., & Martin, D. D. (1995). Humor in ethnographic writing: Sarcasm, satire, and irony as voices in Erving Goffman's *Asylums*. In J. Van Maanen (Ed.), *Representation in ethnography* (pp. 165-197). Thousand Oaks, CA: Sage.

Fine, G. A., & Sandstrom, K. L. (1988). *Knowing children: Participant observation with minors*. Newbury Park, CA: Sage.

Fine, G. F. (1993). Ten lies of ethnography: Moral dilemmas of field research. *Journal of Contemporary Ethnography, 22*, 267-294.

Fine, M. G. (1993). New voices in organizational communication: A feminist commentary and critique. In S. P. Bowen & N. Wyatt (Eds.), *Transforming visions: Feminist critiques in communication studies* (pp. 125-166). Cresskill, NJ: Hampton.

Fiske, J. (1991a). For cultural interpretation: A study of the culture of homelessness. *Critical Studies in Mass Communication, 8*, 455-474.

Fiske, J. (1991b). Writing ethnographies: Contribution to a dialogue. *Quarterly Journal of Speech, 77*, 330-335.

Fitch, K. L (1991). The interplay of linguistic universals and cultural knowledge in personal address: Colombian *madre* terms. *Communication Monographs, 58*, 254-272.

Fitch, K. L. (1994a). A cross-cultural study of directive sequences and some implications for compliance-gaining research. *Communication Monographs, 61*, 185-209.

Fitch, K. L. (1994b). Culture, ideology and interpersonal communication research. In S. Deetz (Ed.), *Communication yearbook 17* (pp. 104-135). Newbury Park, CA: Sage.

Fluehr-Lobban, C. (1994). Informed consent in anthropological research: We are not exempt. *Human Organization, 53*, 1-10.

Forester, J. (1992). Critical ethnography: On fieldwork in a Habermasian way. In M. Alvesson & H. Wilmott (Eds.), *Critical management studies* (pp. 46-65). Newbury Park, CA: Sage.

Foster, H. (Ed.). (1983). *The anti-aesthetic: Essays on postmodern culture*. Port Townsend, WA: Bay.

Fox, K. V. (1996). Silent voices: A subversive reading of child sexual abuse. In C. Ellis & A. P. Bochner (Eds.), *Composing ethnography: Alternative forms of qualitative writing* (pp. 330-356). Walnut Creek, CA: AltaMira.

Frank, K. (2000). "The management of hunger": Using fiction in writing anthropology. *Qualitative Inquiry, 6*, 474-488.

Frazer, C. F., & Reid, L. N. (1979). Children's interactions with commercials. *Symbolic Interaction, 2*(2), 79-96.

Freeman, L. C., Romney, A. K., & Freeman, S. C. (1987). Cognitive structure and informant accuracy. *American Anthropologist, 89*, 310-325.

Frey, J. H., & Fontana, A. (1991). The group interview in social research. *Social Science Journal, 28*, 175-187.

Frey. L. R. (1994a). Call and response: The challenge of conducting research on natural group communication. In L. R. Frey (Ed.), *Group communication in context: Studies of natural groups* (pp. 293-304). Hillsdale, NJ: Lawrence Erlbaum.

Frey, L. R. (Ed.). (1994b). *Group communication in context: Studies of natural groups*. Hillsdale, NJ: Lawrence Erlbaum.

Frey, L. R. (1994c). The naturalistic paradigm: Studying small groups in the postmodern era. *Small Group Research, 25*, 551-577.

Frey, L. R., Anderson, S., & Friedman, P. G. (1998). The status of instruction in qualitative communication research methods. *Communication Education, 47*(3), 246-260.

Frey, L. R., O'Hair, D., & Kreps, G. L. (1990). Applied communication methology. In D. O'Hair & G. L. Kreps (Eds.), *Applied communication theory and research* (pp. 23-56). Hillsdale, NJ: Lawrence Erlbaum.

Frow, J., & Morris, M. (2000). Cultural studies. In N. K. Denzin & Y. S. Lincoln (Eds.), *Handbook of qualitative research* (pp. 315-346). Thousand Oaks, CA: Sage.

Fulk, J., & Steinfield, C. (Eds.). (1990). *Organizations and communication technology.* Newbury Park, CA: Sage.

Gajjala, R. (1999). Cyborg diaspora and virtual imagined community: Studying SAWNET. *Cybersociology, 6.* Retrieved December 16, 2001, from http://www.cyberdiva.org/erniestuff/sanov.html

Gans, H. J. (1982). The participant observer as a human being: Observations on the personal aspects of fieldwork. In R. G. Burgess (Ed.), *Field research: A source book and field manual* (pp. 53-61). London: George Allen & Unwin.

Gans, H. J. (1999). Participant observation in the era of "ethnography." *Journal of Contemporary Ethnography, 28,* 540-548.

Gareis, E. (1995). *Intercultural friendship: A qualitative study.* Lanham, MD: University Press of America.

Garfinkel, H. (1967). *Studies in ethnomethodology.* Englewood Cliffs, NJ: Prentice Hall.

Garfinkel, H., Lynch, M., & Livingston, E. (1981). The work of discovering science construed with materials from the optically discovered pulsar. *Philosophy of Social Science, 11,* 131-158.

Gay, G. (2000). Editor's introduction: Computer-mediated visual communication. *Journal of Computer-Mediated Communication, 5.* Retrieved December 16, 2001, from http://www.ascusc.org/jcmc/vol5/issue4/gay.html

Geertz, C. (1973). *The interpretation of cultures: Selected essays.* New York: Basic Books.

Geiser-Getz, G. (1998). *Cops* and the comic frame. In L. R. Vande Berg, L.A. Wenner, & B. E. Gronbeck (Eds.), *Critical approaches to television* (pp. 200-213). Boston: Houghton Mifflin.

Geist, P. (Ed.). (1999). Disenchantment and renewal in the academy [Special issue]. *Communication Theory, 9*(4).

Geist, P., & Gates, L. (1996). The poetics and politics of re-covering identities in health communication. *Communication Studies, 47*(3), 218-228.

Geraghty, C. (1998). Audiences and ethnography: Questions of practice. In C. Geraghty & D. Lusted (Eds.), *The television studies book* (pp.141 -157). New York: Arnold.

Gerbner, G. (Ed). (1983). Ferment in the field [Special issue]. *Journal of Communication, 33*(3).

Gergen, M. M. (1988). Toward a feminist metatheory and methodology in the social sciences. In M. M. Gergen (Ed.), *Feminist thought and the structure of knowledge* (pp. 87-104). New York: New York University Press.

Gergen, M. M., & Gergen, K. J. (2000). Qualitative inquiry: Tensions and transformations. In N. K. Denzin & Y. S. Lincoln (Eds.), *Handbook of qualitative research* (2nd ed., pp. 1025-1046). Thousand Oaks, CA: Sage.

Gibson, J. (1994). *Warrior dreams: Violence and manhood in post-Vietnam America.* New York: Hill & Wang.

Gillespie, M. (1995). *Television, ethnicity and cultural change.* London: Routledge.

Gillespie, S. (2001). The politics of breathing: Asthmatic Medicaid patients under managed care. *Journal of Applied Communication, 29,* 97-116.

Ginsburg, F. (1995). Mediating culture: Indigenous media, ethnographic film, and the production of identity. In L. Devereaux & R. Hillman (Eds.), *Fields of vision* (pp. 256-291). Berkeley: University of California Press.

Ginsburg, F. D. (1989). *Contested lives: The abortion debate in an American community.* Berkeley: University of California Press.

Gitlin, T. (1979). Prime time ideology: The hegemonic process in television entertainment. *Social Problems, 26,* 251-266.

Gitlin, T. (1983). *Inside prime time.* New York: Pantheon.

Glaser, B. G. (1978). *Theoretical sensitivity.* Mill Valley, CA: Sociology Press.

Glaser, B. G., & Strauss, A. L. (1967). *The discovery of grounded theory: Strategies for qualitative research.* Chicago: Aldine.

Glaser, J. M. (1996). The challenge of campaign watching: Seven lessons of participant-observation research. *PS, Political Science & Politics, 29,* 533-537.

Gleick, J. (1999). *Faster: The acceleration of just about everything.* New York: Pantheon.

Gluckman, M. (1961). Ethnographic data in British social anthropology. *Sociological Review, 9,* 5-17.

Goffman, E. (1959). *The presentation of self in everyday life.* Garden City, NY: Doubleday.

Goffman, E. (1961). *Asylums.* Garden City, NY: Doubleday.

Goffman, E. (1967). *Interaction ritual: Essays on face-to-face behavior.* Garden City, NY: Anchor.

Gold, R. L. (1958). Roles in sociological field observations. *Social Forces, 36,* 217-223.

Goldman-Segall, R. (1995). Configurational validity: A proposal for analyzing ethnographic multi-media narratives. *Journal for Educational Multimedia and Hypermedia, 4*(2), 163-182. Retrieved October 15, 2001 from http://www.merlin.ubc.ca/publications/references/configurational.html

Goldsmith, D. J., & Fitch, K. (1997). The normative context of advice as social support. *Human Communication Research, 23,* 454-476.

Goodall, H. L., Jr. (1989). *Casing a promised land: The autobiography of an organizational detective.* Carbondale: Southern Illinois University Press.

Goodall, H. L., Jr. (1991). *Living in the rock-n-roll mystery: Reading context, self, and others as clues.* Carbondale: Southern Illinois University Press.

Goodall, H. L., Jr. (1996). *Divine signs: Connecting spirit to community.* Carbondale: Southern Illinois University Press.

Goodall, H. L., Jr. (2000). *Writing the new ethnography.* Walnut Creek, CA: AltaMira.

Goodall, H. L., Jr. (2001). Writing the American ineffable, or the mystery and practice of feng shui in everyday life. *Qualitative Inquiry, 7,* 3-20.

Gorden, R. L. (1969). *Interviewing: Strategies, techniques and tactics:* Homewood, IL: Dorsey.

Gordon, D. (1988). Writing culture, writing feminism: The poetics and politics of experimental ethnography. *Inscriptions, 3/4,* 7-24.

Gordon, D. P. (1983). Hospital slang for patients: Crocks, gomers, gorks, and others. *Language in Society, 12,* 173-185.

Gottschalk, S. (1998). Postmodern sensibilities and ethnographic possibilities. In A. Banks & S. Banks (Eds.), *Fiction and social research: By ice or fire* (pp. 205-234). Walnut Creek, CA: AltaMira.

Gourgey, H., & Smith, E. B. (1996). "Consensual hallucination": Cyberspace and the creation of an interpretive community. *Text and Performance Quarterly, 16,* 233-247.

Gray, P. H. (1997, November). *Calling the cops.* Paper presented at the National Communication Association conference, Chicago.

Green, G., Barbour, R. S., Barnard, M., & Kitzinger, J. (1993). "Who wears the trousers?" Sexual harassment in research settings. *Women's Studies International Forum, 16,* 627-637.

Green, N. (1999). Disrupting the field: Virtual reality technologies and "multisited" ethnographic methods. *American Behavioral Scientist, 43,* 409-421.

Grodin, D. (1991). The interpreting audience: The therapeutics of self-help reading. *Critical Studies in Mass Communication, 8,* 404-420.

Grossberg, L. (1997). *Dancing in spite of myself: Essays on popular culture.* Durham, NC: Duke University Press.

Guba, E. G., & Lincoln, Y. S. (1994). Competing paradigms in qualitative research. In N. K. Denzin & Y. S. Lincoln (Eds.), *Handbook of qualitative research* (pp. 105-117). Thousand Oaks, CA: Sage.

Gubrium, J. F., & Holstein, J. A. (2000). Analyzing interpretive practice. In N. K. Denzin & Y. G. Lincoln (Eds.), *Handbook of qualitative research* (pp.487-508). Thousand Oaks, CA: Sage.

Guidelines for the conduct of research involving subjects at the National Institutes of Health. (1995, March 2). Retrieved May 28, 2001, from http://ohsr.od.nih.gov/guidelines.php3

Gupta, A., & Ferguson, J. (Eds.). (1997). *Anthropological locations: Boundaries and grounds of a field science.* Berkeley: University of California Press.

Hafner, K. (2001, April 12). Teenage overload, or digital dexterity? Retrieved April 15, 2001, from http://www.nytimes.com/2001/04/12/technology/12Teen.html

Hall, E. T. (1959). *The silent language.* Garden City, NY: Doubleday.

Hall, S. (1993). Encoding/decoding. In S. During (Ed.), *The cultural studies reader* (pp. 90-103). New York: Routledge.

Hall, S. (1982). The rediscovery of ideology: Return of the repressed in media studies. In M. Gurevitch, T. Bennett, J. Curran, & J. Woollacott (Eds.), *Culture, society and the media* (pp. 56-90). New York: Methuen.

Hall, S. (1985). Signification, representation, ideology: Althusser and the post-structuralist debates. *Critical Studies in Mass Communication, 2*, 91-114.

Hallstein, D. L. O. (1999). A postmodern caring: Feminist standpoint theories, revisioned caring, and communication ethics. *Western Journal of Communication, 63*, 32-56.

Hamman, R. (1997). The application of ethnographic methodology in the study of cybersex. *Cybersociology, 1*. Retrieved December 16, 2001, from http://www.socio.demon.co.uk/magazine/plummer.html

Hammersley, M. (1992). *What's wrong with ethnography? Methodological explorations.* London: Routledge.

Hammersley, M., & Atkinson, P. (1983). *Ethnography: Principles in practice.* London: Tavistock.

Haraway, D. (1991). *Simians, cyborgs, and women: The reinvention of nature.* New York: Routledge.

Harper, D. (2000). Reimagining visual methods: Galileo to Neuromancer. In N. K. Denzin & Y. S. Lincoln (Eds.), *Handbook of qualitative research* (2nd ed., pp. 717-732). Thousand Oaks, CA: Sage.

Harper, R. H. R. (1998). *Inside the IMF: An ethnography of documents, technology and organizational action.* San Diego, CA: Academic Press.

Harrison, T. M., & Stephen, T. (1999). Researching and creating community networks. In S. Jones (Ed.), *Doing Internet research* (pp. 221-242). Thousand Oaks, CA: Sage.

Hawes, L. C. (1983). Epilogue. In L. L. Putnam & M. E. Pacanowsky (Eds.), *Communication and organization: An interpretive approach* (pp. 257-259). Beverly Hills, CA: Sage.

Hawes, L. C. (1998). Becoming other-wise: Conversational performance and the politics of experience. *Text and Performance Quarterly, 18*, 273-299.

Heap, J. L., & Roth, P. A. (1973). On phenomenological sociology. *American Sociological Review, 38*, 354-367.

Heaton, L. (1998). Preserving communication context: Virtual workspace and interpersonal space in Japanese CSCW. *Electronic Journal of Communication, 8*. Retrieved December 16, 2001, from http://www.cios.org./getfile/Heaton_V8N398

Hegde, R. S. (1998). A view from elsewhere: Locating difference and the politics of representation from a transnational feminist perspective. *Communication Theory, 8*, 271-297.

Heider, K. G. (1988). The Rashomon effect: When ethnographers disagree. *American Anthropologist, 90*, 73-81.

Helmericks, S. G., Nelsen, R. L., & Unnithan, N. P. (1991). The researcher, the topic, and the literature: A procedure for systematizing literature searches. *Journal of Applied Behavioral Science, 27*, 285-294.

Heritage, J. (1984). *Garfinkel and ethnomethodology.* Cambridge, MA: Polity.

Herring, S. (1999). Interactional coherence in CMC. *Journal of Computer-Mediated Communication, 4*. Retrieved December 1, 2001, from http://www.ascusc.org/jcmc/vol4/issue4/herring.html

Hertz, R., & Imber, J. B. (1995). Introduction. In R. Hertz & J.B. Imber (Eds.), *Studying elites using qualitative methods* (pp. vii-xi). Thousand Oaks, CA: Sage.

Heyl, B. S. (2001). Ethnographic interviewing. In P. Atkinson, A. Coffey, S. Delamont, J. Lofland, & L. Lofland (Eds.), *Handbook of ethnography* (pp. 369-383). Thousand Oaks, CA: Sage.

Hickey, J. V., Thompson, W. E., & Foster, D. L. (1998) Becoming the Easter bunny: Socialization into a fantasy role. *Journal of Contemporary Ethnography, 17*, 67-95.

Hinchliffe, S. J., Crang, M. A., Reimer, S. M., & Hudson, A. C. (1997). Software for qualitative research: 2. Some thoughts on "aiding" analysis. *Environment and Planning A, 29*, 1109-1124.

Hine, C. (2000). *Virtual ethnography.* London: Sage.

Hirschmann, K. (1999). Blood, vomit, and communication: The days and nights of an intern on call. *Health Communication, 11*(1), 35-57.

Holmer-Nadesan, M. (1996). Organizational identity and space of action. *Organization Studies, 7*(1), 49-81.

Hopper, R. (1992). *Telephone conversation.* Bloomington: Indiana University Press.

Hopper, R., Koch, S., & Mandelbaum, J. (1986). Conversation analysis methods. In D. G. Ellis & W. A. Donahue (Eds.), *Contemporary issues in language and discourse processes* (pp. 169-186). Hillsdale, NJ: Lawrence Erlbaum.

Horowitz, R. (1986). Remaining an outsider: Membership as a threat to research support. *Urban Life, 14*, 409-430.

Horwitz, R. P. (1993). Just stories of ethnographic authority. In C. B. Brettell (Ed.), *When they read what we write: The politics of ethnography* (pp. 131-144). Westport, CT: Bergin & Garvey.

Huesca, R. (1995). Subject-authored theories of media practice: The case of Bolivian Tin Miner's Radio. *Communication Studies, 46(3-4)*, 149-168.

Hunt, J., & Manning, P. K. (1991). The social context of police lying. *Symbolic Interaction, 14*, 51-70.

Huspek, M., & Kendall, K. (1991). On withholding political voice: An analysis of the political vocabulary of a non-political speech community. *Quarterly Journal of Speech, 77*, 1-19.

Husserl, E. (1931). *Ideas: General introduction to pure phenomenology* (W. R. B. Gibson, Trans.). New York: Macmillan.

Hyland, K. (2001). Bringing in the reader: Addressee features in academic articles. *Written Communication, 18*, 549-574.

Hymes, D. (1962). The ethnography of speaking. In T. Gladwin & W. C. Sturtevant (Eds.), *Anthropology and human behavior* (pp. 13-53). Washington, DC: Anthropology Society of Washington.

Jackson, J. E. (1990). "I am a fieldnote": Fieldnotes as a symbol of professional identity. In R. Sanjek (Ed.), *Fieldnotes: The makings of anthropology* (pp. 3-33). Ithaca, NY: Cornell University Press.

Jackson, M. J. (1997). Assessing the structure of communication on the World Wide Web. *Journal of Computer-Mediated Communication, 3*. Retrieved January 9, 2002, from http://www.ascusc.org/jcmc/vol3/issue1/jackson.html

Jacobson, D. (1999). Impression formation in cyberspace: Online expectations and offline experiences in text-based virtual communities. *Journal of Computer-Mediated Communication, 5*. Retrieved December 16, 2001, from http://www.ascusc.org/jcmc/vol5/issue1/jacobson.html

Jameson, F. (1977). Ideology, narrative analysis and popular culture. *Theory and Society, 4*, 543-559.

Janesick, V. J. (1999). A journal about journal writing as a qualitative research technique: History, issues, and reflections. *Qualitative Inquiry, 5*, 505-524.

Jarmon, L. (1996). Performance as a resource in the practice of conversation analysis. *Text and Performance Quarterly, 16*, 336-355.

Jenkins, H. (1988). Star Trek rerun, reread, rewritten: Fan writing as textual poaching. *Critical Studies in Mass Communication, 5*, 85-107.

Jenkins, H. (1992). *Textual poachers: Television fans and participatory culture.* New York: Routledge.

Jenkins, H. (1996, June). Fandom, the new identity politics. *Harper's Magazine*, pp. 23-24.

Jenkins, H. (1999). Professor Jenkins goes to Washington. Retrieved August 10, 2001, from http://web.mit.edu/21fms/www/faculty/henry3/profjenkins.html

Jensen, K. B. (1991). When is meaning? Communication theory, pragmatism, and mass media reception. In J. A. Anderson (Ed.), *Communication yearbook 14* (pp. 3-32). Newbury Park, CA: Sage.

Johnson, F. G., & Kaplan, C. D. (1980). Talk-in-the-work: Aspects of social organization of work in a computer center. *Journal of Pragmatics, 4*, 351-365.

Johnson, R. (1986-1987). What is cultural studies anyway? *Social Text, 16*, 38-80.

Jones, J. L. (1996). The self as other: Creating the role of Joni the ethnographer for *Broken Circles. Text and Performance Quarterly, 16*, 131-145.

Jones, J. L. (1997). Performing Osun without bodies: Documenting the Osun festival in print. *Text and Performance Quarterly, 17*, 69-93.

Jones, Q. (1997). Virtual-communities, virtual settlements & cyber-archaeology: A theoretical outline. *Journal of Computer-Mediated Communication, 3*. Retrieved December 16, 2001, from http://www.ascusc.org/jcmc/vol3/issue3/jones.html

Jones, R. A. (1994). The ethics of research in cyberspace. *Internet Research, 4(3)*, 30-35.

Jones, S. G. (1995). Understanding community in the information age. In S. G. Jones, *Cybersociety: Computer-mediated communication and community* (pp. 10-35). Thousand Oaks, CA: Sage.

Jones, S. G. (1997). The Internet and its social landscape. In S. G. Jones (Ed.), *Virtual culture: Identity and communication in cybersociety* (pp. 7-35). London: Sage.

Jones, S. G. (1998). Information, Internet, and community: Notes toward an understanding of community in the information age. In S. G. Jones (Ed.), *Cybersociety 2.0* (pp.1-34). Thousand Oaks, CA: Sage.

Jones, S. G. (Ed.). (1999). *Doing Internet research.* Thousand Oaks, CA: Sage.

Jones, S. H. (1999). Women, music, bodies, and texts: The gesture of women's music. *Text and Performance Quarterly, 19*, 217-235.

Jones, S. H. (1998). Kaleidoscope notes: Writing women's music and organizational culture. *Qualitative Inquiry, 4*, 148-177.

Jorgenson, J. (1989). Where is the "family" in family communication? Exploring families' self-definitions. *Journal of Applied Communication Research, 17*, 27-41.

Jorgenson, J. (1992). Communication, rapport, and the interview: A social perspective. *Communication Theory, 2*, 148-156.

Kahn, R., & Mann, F. (1969). Developing research partnerships. In G. J. McCall & J. L. Simmons (Eds.), *Issues in participant observation* (pp. 45-51). Reading, MA: Addison-Wesley.

Kant, I. (1929). *The critique of pure reason* (N. K. Smith, Trans.). London: Macmillan.

Katriel, T. (1987). "Bexibudim!" Ritualized sharing among Israeli children. *Language in Society, 16*, 305-320.

Katriel, T. (1990). "Griping" as a verbal ritual in some Israeli discourse. In D. Carbaugh (Ed.), *Cultural communication and intercultural contact* (pp. 99-113). Hillsdale, NJ: Lawrence Erlbaum.

Katriel, T. (1993). "Our future is where our past is": Studying heritage museums as ideological and performative arenas. *Communication Monographs, 48*, 301-317.

Katriel, T., & Farrell, T. (1991). Scrapbooks as cultural texts: An American art of memory. *Text and Performance Quarterly, 11*, 1-17.

Katriel, T., & Philipsen, G. (1981). "What we need is communication": "Communication" as a cultural category in some American speech. *Communication Monographs, 48*, 302-317.

Katz, J. (2001). From how to why: On luminous description and causal inference in ethnography (Part 1). *Ethnography, 2*, 443-473.

Kauffman, B. J. (1992). Feminist facts: Interview strategies and political subjects in ethnography. *Communication Theory, 2*, 187-206.

Kellett, P. M., & Goodall, H. L. (1999). The death of discourse in our own chatroom: "Sextext," skillful discussion, and virtual communities. In D. Slayden & R. K. Whillock (Eds.), *Soundbite culture: The death of discourse in a wired world* (pp. 155-190). Thousand Oaks, CA: Sage.

Kellner, D. (1993). *Communications vs. cultural studies: Overcoming the divide.* Retrieved October 4, 2001, from http://www.uta.edu/huma/illuminations/kell4.htm

Kelly, J. W. (1985). Storytelling in high tech organizations: A medium for sharing culture. *Journal of Applied Communication Research, 13*, 45-58.

Kendall, L. (1998). Meaning and identity in "cyberspace": The performance of gender, class, and race online. *Symbolic Interaction, 21*, 129-153.

Kendall, L. (1999). Recontextualizing "cyberspace": Methodological considerations for on-line research. In S. Jones (Ed.), *Doing Internet research* (pp. 57-74). Thousand Oaks, CA: Sage.

Kidder, T. (1981). *The soul of a new machine.* Boston: Little, Brown.

Kinchloe, J. L., & McLaren, P. (2000). Rethinking critical theory and qualitative research. In N. K. Denzin & Y. S. Lincoln (Eds.), *Handbook of qualitative research* (pp. 279-314). Thousand Oaks, CA: Sage.

Kirk, J., & Miller, M. L. (1986). *Reliability and validity in qualitative research.* Beverly Hills, CA: Sage.

Kitzinger, J. (1994). The methodology of focus groups: The importance of interaction between research participants. *Sociology of Health & Illness, 16*, 103-121.

Kleinman, S., Stenross, B., & McMahon, M. (1994). Privileging fieldwork over interviews: Consequences for identity and practice. *Symbolic Interaction, 17*, 37-50.

Knuf, J. (1989-1990). Where cultures meet: Ritual code and organizational boundary management. *Research on Language and Social Interaction, 23*, 109-138.

Knuf, J. (1992). "Spit first and then say what you want!": Concerning the use of language and ancillary codes in ritualized communication. *Quarterly Journal of Speech, 78*, 466-482.

Kockelmans, J. J. (1967). *Edmund Husserl's phenomenological psychology: A historico-critical study* (B. Jager, Trans.). Pittsburgh, PA: Duquesne University Press.

Kolko, B., Nakamura, L., & Rodman, G. (Eds.). (2000). *Race in cyberspace.* New York: Routledge.

Kollock, P., & Smith, M. A. (1999). Communities in cyberspace. In M. A. Smith & P. Kollock (Eds.), *Communities in cyberspace* (pp. 3-25). London: Routledge.

Kozinets, R. V. (2001). *The field behind the screen: Using the method of Netnography to research market-oriented virtual communities.* Retrieved May 23, 2001, from http://www.kellogg.nwu.edu/faculty/Kozinets/htm/Research/Virtual/field_behind_the_screen.htm

Kraidy, M. M. (1999). The global, the local, and the hybrid: A native ethnography of glocalization. *Critical Studies in Mass Communication, 16*, 456-476.

Kreps, G. L., & Herndon, S. L. (2001). Introduction: The power of qualitative research to address organizational issues. In S. L. Herndon & G. L. Kreps (Eds.), *Qualitative research: Applications in organizational communication* (pp. 1-9). Cresskill, NJ: Hampton.

Krikorian, D. H., Lee, J., & Chock, T. M. (2000). Isn't that spatial? Distance and communication in a 2-D virtual environment. *Journal of Computer-Mediated Communication, 5.* Retrieved December 16, 2001 from the World Wide Web: http://www.ascusc.org/jcmc/vol5/issue4/krikorian.html

Krizek, R. L. (1998). Lessons: What the hell are we teaching the next generation anyway? In A. Banks & S. Banks (Eds.), *Fiction and social research: By ice or fire* (pp. 89-114). Walnut Creek, CA: AltaMira.

Krotz, F., & Eastman, S. T. (1999). Orientations toward television outside the home. *Journal of Communication, 49*(1), 5-27.

Kurtz, L. R. (1984). *Evaluating Chicago sociology.* Chicago: University of Chicago Press.

Lang, K., & Lang, G. (1953). The unique perspective of television and its effect: A pilot study. *American Sociological Review, 18*, 3-12.

Langellier, K. M. (1989). Personal narratives: Perspectives on theory and research. *Text and Performance Quarterly, 9*, 243-276.

Langness, L. L., & Frank, G. (1981). *Lives: An anthropological approach to biography.* Novato, CA: Chandler & Sharp.

Lannamann, J. W. (1991). Interpersonal communication research as ideological practice. *Communication Theory, 1*, 179-203.

LaRossa, R., Bennett, L. A., & Gelles, R. J. (1981). Ethical dilemmas in qualitative family research. *Journal of Marriage and the Family, 43*, 303-313.

Lather, P. (1986). Issues of validity in openly ideological research: Between a rock and a soft place. *Interchange, 17*(4), 63-84.

Lazarsfeld, P. F. (1944). The controversy over detailed interviews. *Public Opinion Quarterly, 8*, 38-60.

Lazega, E. (1997). Network analysis and qualitative research: A method of contextualization. In G. Miller & R. Dingwall (Eds.), *Context and method in qualitative research* (pp. 119-138). Thousand Oaks, CA: Sage.

LeBaron, C., & Streeck, J. (1997). Space, surveillance and the interactional framing of experience during a murder interrogation. *Human Studies, 20*, 1-25.

LeCompte, M. D., & Schensul, J. J. (1999). *Analyzing and interpreting ethnographic data.* (Ethnographer's toolkit, vol. 5). Walnut Creek, CA: AltaMira.

Leeds-Hurwitz, W. (1984). On the relationship of the "ethnography of speaking" to the "ethnography of communication." *Papers in Linguistics, 17*, 7-32.

Leeds-Hurwitz, W. (1989). *Communication in everyday life: A social interpretation.* Norwood, NJ: Ablex.

Leeds-Hurwitz, W. (1992). Forum introduction: Social approaches to interpersonal communication. *Communication Theory, 2*(2), 131-139.

Lemish, D. (1982). Television viewing in public places. *Journal of Broadcasting, 26*, 757-782.

Lesch, C. L. (1994). Observing theory in practice: Sustaining consciousness in a coven. In L. R. Frey (Ed.), *Group communication in context: Studies of natural groups* (pp. 57-84). Hillsdale, NJ: Lawrence Erlbaum.

Lester, M. (1980). Generating newsworthiness: The interpretive construction of public events. *American Sociological Review, 45,* 984-994.

Levine, E. (2001). Toward a paradigm for media production research: Behind the scenes at *General Hospital. Critical Studies in Media Communication, 18*(1), 66-82.

Lévi-Strauss, C. (1974). *Tristes tropiques.* New York: Atheneum. (Original work published 1955)

Lewins, A. (1996). The CAQDAS networking project: Multilevel support for the qualitative research community. *Qualitative Health Research, 6,* 298-304.

Lewis, M. (2000). *The new new thing: A Silicon Valley story.* New York: Norton.

Lewis, M. (2001). *Next: The future just happened.* New York: Norton.

Lewis, O. (1961). *The children of Sanchez.* New York: Random House.

Liberman, K. (1999). From walkabout to meditation: Craft and ethics in field inquiry. *Qualitative Inquiry, 5,* 47-63.

Liebow, E. (1967). *Tally's corner: A study of Negro street corner men.* Boston: Little, Brown.

Lincoln, Y. S., & Guba, E. G. (1985). *Naturalistic inquiry.* Beverly Hills, CA: Sage.

Lindlof, T. R. (1987). Ideology and pragmatics of media access in prison. In T. R. Lindlof (Ed.), *Natural audiences: Qualitative research of media uses and effects* (pp. 175-197). Norwood, NJ: Ablex.

Lindlof, T. R. (1988). Media audiences as interpretive communities. In J. A. Anderson (Ed.), *Communication yearbook 11* (pp. 81-107). Newbury Park, CA: Sage.

Lindlof, T. R. (1991). The qualitative study of media audiences. *Journal of Broadcasting & Electronic Media, 35,* 23-42.

Lindlof, T. R. (1992). Computing tales: Parents' discourse about technology and family. *Social Science Computer Review, 10,* 291-309.

Lindlof, T. R. (1995). *Qualitative communication research methods.* Thousand Oaks, CA: Sage.

Lindlof, T. R. (2001). The challenge of writing the qualitative study. In A. Alexander & W. J. Potter (Eds.), *How to publish your communication research: An insider's guide* (pp. 77-96). Thousand Oaks, CA: Sage.

Lindlof, T. R., & Grubb-Swetnam, A. (1996). Seeking a path of greatest resistance: The self becoming method. In T. R. Lindlof & D. Grodin (Eds.), *Constructing the self in a mediated world* (pp. 179-205). Thousand Oaks, CA: Sage.

Lindlof, T. R., & Shatzer, M. J. (1998). Media ethnography in virtual space: Strategies, limits, and possibilities. *Journal of Broadcasting & Electronic Media, 41,* 18-37.

Lindsley, S. L. (1999). Communication and "the Mexican way": Stability and trust as core symbols in Maquiladoras. *Western Journal of Communication, 66*(1), 1-31.

Ling, R., Nilsen, S., & Granhaug, S. (1999). The domestication of video-on-demand. Folk understanding of a new technology. *New Media & Society, 1*(1), 83-100.

Liu, G. Z. (1999). Virtual community presence in Internet Relay Chatting. *Journal of Computer-Mediated Communication, 5.* Retrieved December 16, 2001, from http://www.ascusc.org/jcmc/vol5/issue1/liu.html

Lofland, J. (1971). *Analyzing social settings.* Belmont, CA: Wadsworth.

Lofland, J. (1974). Styles of reporting qualitative field research. *American Sociologist, 9,* 101-111.

Lotz, A. D. (2000). Assessing qualitative television audience research: Incorporating feminist and anthropological theoretical innovation. *Communication Theory, 10,* 447-467.

Lull, J. (1985). Ethnographic studies of broadcast media audiences: Notes on method. In J. Dominick & J. Fletcher (Eds.), *Broadcasting research methods* (pp. 80-88). Boston: Allyn & Bacon.

Lull, J. (1987). Thrashing in the pit: An ethnography of San Francisco punk subculture. In T. R. Lindlof (Ed.), *Natural audiences: Qualitative research of media uses and effects* (pp. 225-252). Norwood, NJ: Ablex.

Lunt, P., & Livingstone, S. (1996). Rethinking the focus group in media and communication research. *Journal of Communication, 46*(2), 79-98.

Lyman, P., & Wakeford, N. (1999). Introduction: Going into the virtual field. *American Behavioral Scientist, 43,* 359-376.

Lynch, M., Livingston, E., & Garfinkel, H. (1983). Temporal order in laboratory work. In K. Knorr-Cetina & M. Mulkay (Eds.), *Science observed: Perspectives on the social study of science* (pp. 205-238). Beverly Hills, CA: Sage.

MacGregor, B., & Morrison, D. E. (1995). From focus groups to editing groups: A new method of reception analysis. *Media, Culture & Society, 17*, 141-150.

Madison, D. S. (1999). Performing theory/embodied writing. *Text and Performance Quarterly, 19*, 107-124.

Malinowski, B. (1967). *A diary in the strict sense of the term.* New York: Harcourt.

Mangabeira, W. C. (1996). CAQDAS and its diffusion across four countries: National specifities and common themes. *Current Sociology, 44*(3), 191-205.

Mann, C., & Stewart, F. (2000). *Internet communication and qualitative research.* London: Sage.

Manning, P. (1995). The challenges of postmodernism. In J. Van Maanen (Ed.), *Representation in Ethnography* (pp. 245-272). Thousand Oaks, CA: Sage.

Marcus, G. E. (1995). Ethnography in/of the world system: The emergence of multi-sited ethnography. *Annual Review of Anthropology, 24*, 95-117.

Marcus, G. E. (1998). *Ethnography through thick and thin.* Princeton, NJ: Princeton University Press.

Marcus, G. E., & Cushman, D. (1982). Ethnographies as texts. *Annual Review of Anthropology, 11*, 25-69.

Marcus, G. E., & Fischer, M. M. J. (1986). *Anthropology as cultural critique.* Chicago: University of Chicago Press.

Markham, A. (1998). *Life online: Researching real experience in virtual space.* Walnut Creek, CA: AltaMira.

Markowitz, L. (2001). Finding the field: Notes on the ethnography of NGOs. *Human Organization, 60*, 40-46.

Marshall, J. (1993). Viewing organizational communication from a feminist perspective: A critique and some offerings. In S. A. Deetz (Ed.), *Communication yearbook 16* (pp. 122-143). Newbury Park, CA: Sage.

Martin, J., & Nakayama, T. (1999). Thinking dialectically about culture and communication. *Communication Theory, 9*(1), 1-25.

Martin, P. Y. (1989). The moral politics of organizations: Reflections of an unlikely feminist. *Journal of Applied Behavioral Science, 25*(4), 451-470.

Martindale, D. (1968). Verstehen. In *International encyclopedia of the social sciences* (pp. 308-312). New York: Macmillan.

Marvin, C. (1988). *When old technologies were new: Thinking about electric communication in the late nineteenth century.* New York: Oxford University Press.

Marvin, L. (1995). Spoof, spam, lurk and lag: The aesthetics of text-based virtual realities. *Journal of Computer-Mediated Communication, 1.* Retrieved December 9, 1997, from http://jcmc.huji.ac.il/vol1/issue2/marvin.html

Marx, G. T. (1999). What's in a name? Some reflections on the sociology of anonymity. *The Information Society, 15*, 99-112.

Mason, B., & Dicks, B. (1999). The digital ethnographer. *Cybersociology, 6.* Retrieved December 16, 2001, from http://www.socio.demon.co.uk/magazine/6/dicksmason.html

Mason, J. (1994). Linking qualitative and quantitative data analysis. In A. Bryman & R. G. Burgess (Eds.), *Analyzing qualitative data* (pp. 89-110). New York: Routledge.

Mateas, M., & Lewis, S. (1997). A MOO-based virtual training environment. *Journal of Computer-Mediated Communication, 2* Retrieved December 9, 1997, from http://jcmc.huji.ac.il/vol2/issue3/

Maxwell, J. A. (1992). Understanding and validity in qualitative research. *Harvard Educational Review, 62*, 279-300.

Maynard, D. W., & Klayman, S. E. (1991). The diversity of ethnomethodology. *Annual Review of Sociolinguistics, 17*, 385-418.

Mayrl, W. W. (1973). Ethnomethodology: Sociology without society? *Catalyst, 7*, 15-28.

McCall, G. J. (1984). Systematic field observation. *Annual Review of Sociology, 10*, 263-282.

McGirr, L. (2001). *Suburban warriors: The origins of the new American right.* Princeton, NJ: Princeton University Press.

McKinney, J. P., & McKinney, K. G. (1999). Prayer in the lives of late adolescents. *Journal of Adolescence, 22*, 279-290.

McQuail, D. (1994). *Mass communication theory* (2nd ed.). Thousand Oaks, CA: Sage.

Mead, G. H. (1934). *Mind, self and society.* Chicago: University of Chicago Press.

Meakins, G., & Rintel, S. (2000). Editorial: "Chat." *M/C: A Journal of Media and Culture, 3*. Retrieved May 15, 2002, from http://www.mediaculture.org.au/0008/edit.html

Mehan, H. (1979). *Learning lessons.* Cambridge, MA: Harvard University Press.

Mellinger, W. M. (1994). Negotiated orders: The negotiation of directives in paramedic-nurse interaction. *Symbolic Interaction, 17*, 165-185.

Meyer, T. P., Traudt, P. J., & Anderson, J. A. (1980). Non-traditional mass communication research methods: Observational case studies of media use in natural settings. In D. Nimmo (Ed.), *Communication yearbook 4* (pp. 261-275). New Brunswick, NJ: Transaction.

Mies, M. (1981). Towards a methodology for feminist research. In G. Bowles & R. Duelli-Klein (Eds.), *Theories of women's studies, II* (pp. 25-46). Berkeley: University of California, Women's Studies Department.

Miles, M. B. (1979). Qualitative data as an attractive nuisance: The problem of analysis. *Administrative Science Quarterly, 24*, 590-601.

Miles, M. B., & Huberman, A. M. (1984). *Qualitative data analysis: A sourcebook of new methods.* Beverly Hills, CA: Sage.

Miles, M. B., & Weitzman, E. A. (1996). The state of qualitative data analysis software: What do we need? *Current Sociology, 44*(3), 206-225.

Miller, D., & Slater, D. (2000). *The Internet: An ethnographic approach.* Oxford, UK: Berg.

Miller, D. L., Creswell, J. W., & Olander, L. S. (1998). Writing and retelling multiple ethnographic tales of a soup kitchen for the homeless. *Qualitative Inquiry, 4*, 469-491.

Miller, G. (1994). Toward ethnographies of institutional discourse: Proposal and suggestions. *Journal of Contemporary Ethnography, 23*, 280-306.

Miller, G. (1997). Contextualizing texts: Studying organizational texts. In G. Miller & R. Dingwall (Eds.), *Context and method in qualitative research* (pp. 77-91). Thousand Oaks, CA: Sage.

Miller, K. (2002). *Communication theories: Perspectives, processes, and contexts.* Boston: McGraw-Hill.

Miller, M. (1998). (Re)presenting voices in dramatically scripted research. In A. Banks & S. Banks (Eds.), *Fiction and social research: By ice or fire* (pp. 67-78). Walnut Creek, CA: AltaMira.

Mishler, E. G. (1986). *Research interviewing: Context and narrative.* Cambridge, MA: Harvard University Press.

Mishler, E. G. (1990). Validation in inquiry-guided research: The role of exemplars in narrative studies. *Harvard Educational Review, 60*, 415-442.

Mitchell, J. C. (1983). Case and situation analysis. *Sociological Review, 31*, 187-211.

Mitra, A., & Cohen, E. (1999). Analyzing the Web: Directions and challenges. In S. Jones (Ed.), *Doing Internet research* (pp. 179-202). Thousand Oaks, CA: Sage.

Moore, L. F. (1991). Inside Aunt Virginia's kitchen. In P. J. Frost, L. F. Moore, M. R. Louis, C. C. Lundberg, & J. Martin (Eds.), *Reframing organizational culture* (pp. 366-372). Newbury Park, CA: Sage.

Morgan, D. L. (1988). *Focus groups as qualitative research.* Newbury Park, CA: Sage.

Morgan, D. L. (1996). Focus groups. *Annual Review of Sociology, 22*, 129-153.

Morley, D. (1992). *Television, audiences, and cultural studies.* New York: Routledge.

Morley, D. (1997). Theoretical orthodoxies: Textualism, constructivism and the "new ethnography" in cultural studies. In M. Ferguson & P. Golding (Eds.), *Cultural studies in question* (pp. 121-137). Thousand Oaks, CA: Sage.

Morrill. C., & Snow, D. A. (2003). Introduction. In C. Morrill, D. A. Snow, & C. H. White (Eds.), *Relational ethnography: Personal relationships in public contexts.* Berkeley: University of California Press.

Morris, G. H., & Hopper, R. (1987). Symbolic action as alignment: A synthesis of rules approaches. *Research on Language and Social Interaction, 21*, 1-29.

Morris, M. B. (1977). *An excursion into creative sociology.* New York: Columbia University Press.

Morrison, D. E. (1998). *The search for a method: Focus groups and the development of mass communication research.* Luton, Bedfordshire, UK: University of Luton Press.

Mumby, D. (1997). Modernism, postmodernism, and communication studies: A rereading of an ongoing debate. *Communication Theory, 7*, 1-28.

Mumby, D. (1998). The problem of hegemony: Rereading Gramsci for organizational communication studies. *Western Journal of Communication, 61*, 343-375.

Murphy, P. D. (1999a). Doing audience ethnography: A narrative account of establishing ethnographic identity and locating interpretive communities in fieldwork. *Qualitative Inquiry, 5,* 479-504.

Murphy, P. D. (1999b). Media cultural studies' uncomfortable embrace of ethnography. *Journal of Communication Inquiry, 23*(3), 205-221.

Musello, C. (1980). Studying the home mode: An exploration of family photography and visual communication. *Studies in Visual Communication, 6*(1), 23-42.

Myerhoff, B. (1978). *Number our days.* New York: Penguin.

Myerhoff, B., & Ruby, J. (1982). Introduction. In B. Myerhoff & J. Ruby (Eds.), *A crack in the mirror* (pp. 1-35). Philadelphia: University of Pennsylvania Press.

Nakayama, T. K., & Krizek, R. L. (1995). Whiteness: A strategic rhetoric. *Quarterly Journal of Speech, 81,* 291-309.

Nardi, B. A., & O'Day, V. L. (1999). *Information ecologies: Using technology with heart.* Cambridge: MIT Press.

Natanson, M. (1968). Alfred Schutz on social reality and social science. *Social Research, 35,* 217-244.

Nelson, C., Treichler, P. A., & Grossberg, L. (1992). Cultural studies: An introduction. In L. Grossberg, C. Nelson, & P. A. Treichler (Eds.), *Cultural studies* (pp. 1-16). New York: Routledge.

Nelson, C. K. (1994). Ethnomethodological positions on the use of ethnographic data in conversation analytic research. *Journal of Contemporary Ethnography, 23,* 307-329.

Nelson, S. (1998). Intersections of eros and ethnography. *Text and Performance Quarterly, 18,* 1-21.

Neumann, M. (1993). Living on tortoise time: Alternative travel as the pursuit of lifestyle. *Symbolic Interaction, 16,* 201-235.

Neumann, M. (1994). The contested spaces of cultural dialogue. In S. Deetz (Ed.), *Communication Yearbook 17* (pp. 148-158). Newbury Park, CA: Sage.

Neumann, M., & Simpson, T. A. (1997). Smuggled sound: Bootleg recording and the pursuit of popular memory. *Symbolic Interaction, 20,* 319-341.

Newhagen, J. E., & Rafaeli, S. (1996). Why communication researchers should study the Internet: A dialogue. *Journal of Computer-Mediated Communication, 1.* Retrieved December 18, 2001, from http://www.ascusc.org/jcmc/vol1/issue4/rafaeli.html

Novek, E. M. (1995). West Urbania: An ethnographic study of communication practices in inner-city youth culture. *Communication Studies, 46,* 169-186.

O'Keefe, D. J. (1980). Ethnomethodology. *Journal for the Theory of Social Behaviour, 9,* 187-219.

Olesen, V. (2000). Feminisms and qualitative research at and into the millennium. In N. K. Denzin & Y. S. Lincoln (Eds.), *Handbook of qualitative research* (pp. 215-256). Thousand Oaks, CA: Sage.

Olesen, V., Droes, N., Hatton, D., Chico, N., & Schatzman, L. (1994). Analyzing together: Recollections of a team approach. In A. Bryman & R. G. Burgess (Eds.), *Analyzing qualitative data* (pp. 111-128). London and New York: Routledge.

Olesen, V., & Whittaker, E. W. (1967). Role-making in participant observation: Processes in the researcher-actor relationship. *Human Organization, 26,* 273-281.

Ollenburger, J. C., & Moore, H. A. (1992). *A sociology of women: The intersection of patriarchy, capitalism and colonization.* Englewood Cliffs, NJ: Prentice Hall.

Orbe, M. P., & King, G. (2000). Negotiating the tension between policy and reality: Exploring nurses' communication about organizational wrongdoing. *Health Communication, 12*(1), 41-61.

Ortner, S. B. (1997). Introduction [Special Issue on Clifford Geertz]. *Representations, 59,* 1-13.

Osborne, L. (2002, January 13). Consuming rituals of the suburban tribe. *The New York Times Magazine,* pp. 28-31.

Otnes, C., Kim, K., & Kim, Y. C. (1994). Yes, Virginia, there is a gender difference: Analyzing children's requests to Santa Claus. *Journal of Popular Culture, 28,* 17-29.

Pacanowsky, M. E. (1983). A small-town cop: Communication in, out, and about a crisis. In L. L. Putnam & M. E. Pacanowsky (Eds.), *Communication and organizations* (pp. 261-282). Beverly Hills, CA: Sage.

Pacanowsky, M. E. (1988a). Communication in the empowering organization. In J. A. Anderson (Ed.), *Communication yearbook 11* (pp. 356-379). Newbury Park, CA: Sage.

Pacanowsky, M. E. (1988b). Slouching towards Chicago. *Quarterly Journal of Speech, 74,* 453-467.

Pacanowsky, M. E., & O'Donnell-Trujillo, N. (1982). Communication and organizational cultures. *Western Journal of Speech Communication, 46,* 115-130.

Pacanowsky, M. E., & O'Donnell-Trujillo, N. (1983). Organizational communication as cultural performances. *Communication Monographs, 50,* 126-147.

Paccagnella, L. (1997). Getting the seats of your pants dirty: Strategies for ethnographic research on virtual communities. *Journal of Computer-Mediated Communication, 3.* Retrieved May 19, 1999, from http://www.ascusc.org/jcmc/vol3/issue1/paccagnella.html

Paget, M. A. (1983). Experience and knowledge. *Human Studies, 6,* 67-90.

Palmer, R. E. (1969). *Hermeneutics: Interpretation theory in Schleiermacher, Dilthey, Heidegger and Gadamer.* Evanston, IL: Northwestern University Press.

Pardun, C. J. (1999). Theory into practice: An analysis of qualitative research in the *Journal of Broadcasting and Electronic Media,* 1978-1998. *Journal of Broadcasting and Electronic Media, 44*(3), 529-534.

Patton, M. Q. (1990). *Qualitative evaluation and research methods* (2nd ed.). Newbury Park, CA: Sage.

Pearce, W. B. (1985). Scientific research methods in communication studies and their implications for theory and research. In T. W. Benson (Ed.), *Speech communication in the 20th century* (pp. 255-281). Carbondale: Southern Illinois University Press.

Pearce, W. B., & Cronen, V. E. (1980). *Communication, action and meaning: The creation of social realities.* New York: Praeger.

Pearce, W. B., & Pearce, K. (2000). Extending the theory of the coordinated management of meaning (CMM) through a community dialogue process. *Communication Theory, 10,* 405-423.

Pelias, R. J. (1999). *Writing performance: Poeticizing the researcher's body.* Carbondale: Southern Illinois University Press.

Pelto, P. J., & Pelto, G. H. (1978). *Anthropological research: The structure of inquiry* (2nd ed.). Cambridge, UK: Cambridge University Press.

Peters, J. D. (1986). Institutional sources of intellectual poverty in communication research. *Communication Research, 13,* 527-559.

Peterson, E. E. (1987). Media consumption and girls who want to have fun. *Critical Studies in Mass Communication, 4,* 37-50.

Peterson, E. E., & Langellier, K. M. (1997). The politics of personal narrative methodology. *Text and Performance Quarterly, 17,* 135-152.

Petronio, S., & Bourhis, J. (1987). Identifying family collectivities in public places: An instructional exercise. *Communication Education, 36,* 46-51.

Philipsen, G. (1975). Speaking "like a man" in Teamsterville: Culture patterns of role enactment in an urban neighborhood. *Quarterly Journal of Speech, 61,* 13-22.

Philipsen, G. (1976). Places for speaking in Teamsterville. *Quarterly Journal of Speech, 62,* 15-25.

Philipsen, G. (1986). Mayor Daley's council speech: A cultural analysis. *Quarterly Journal of Speech, 72,* 247-260.

Philipsen, G. (1989). An ethnographic approach to communication studies. In B. Dervin, L. Grossberg, B. J. O'Keefe, & E. Wartella (Eds.), *Rethinking communication: Vol. 1. Paradigm issues* (pp. 258-268). Newbury Park, CA: Sage.

Philipsen, G., & Carbaugh, D. (1986). A bibliography of fieldwork in the ethnography of communication. *Language in Society, 15,* 387-397.

Pierce, J. L. (1995). Reflections on fieldwork in a complex organization: Lawyers, ethnographic authority, and lethal weapons. In R. Hertz & J. B. Imber (Eds.), *Studying elites using qualitative methods* (pp. 94-109). Thousand Oaks, CA: Sage.

Podsakoff, P. M., & Dalton, D. R. (1987). Research methodology in organizational studies. *Journal of Management, 13,* 419-441.

Pollock, D. (1998). Performing writing. In P. Phelan & J. Lane (Eds.), *The ends of performance* (pp. 73-103). New York: New York University Press.

Poole, S., & McPhee, R. (1994). Methodology in interpersonal communication research. In M. L. Knapp & G. R. Miller (Eds.), *Handbook of interpersonal communication* (2nd ed., pp. 42-100). Thousand Oaks, CA: Sage.

Potter, W. J. (1996). *An analysis of thinking and research about qualitative methods.* Mahwah, NJ: Lawrence Erlbaum.

Presnell, M. (1994). Postmodern ethnography: From representing the other to co-producing a text. In K. Carter & M. Presnell (Eds.), *Interpretive approaches to interpersonal communication* (pp. 11-43). Albany: State University of New York Press.

Press, A. L. (1989, May). *Toward a qualitative methodology of audience study: Using ethnography to study the popular culture audience.* Paper presented at the annual meeting of the International Communication Association, San Francisco.

Press, A. L., & Cole, E. R. (1995). Reconciling faith and fact: Pro-life women discuss media, science and the abortion debate. *Critical Studies in Mass Communication, 12,* 380-402.

Prosser, J., & Schwartz, D. (1998). Photographs within the sociological research process. In J. Prosser (Ed.), *Image-based research: A source book for qualitative researchers* (pp. 115-130). London: Falmer.

Pruitt, S., & Barrett, T. (1991). Corporate virtual workspace. In M. Benedikt (Ed.), *Cyberspace: First steps* (pp. 383-409). Cambridge: MIT Press.

Punch, M. (1986). *The politics and ethics of fieldwork.* Beverly Hills, CA: Sage.

Putnam, L. L., Bantz, C., Deetz, S., Mumby, D., & Van Maanen, J. (1993). Ethnography versus critical theory: Debating organizational research. *Journal of Management Inquiry, 2,* 221-235.

Putnam, L. L., & Pacanowsky, M. E. (Eds.). (1983). *Communication and organizations.* Beverly Hills, CA: Sage.

Putnam, L. L., & Stohl, C. (1990). Bona fide groups: A reconceptualization of groups in context. *Communication Studies, 41,* 248-265.

Putnis, P. (1993). National preoccupations and international perspectives in communication studies in Australia. *Electronic Journal of Communication, 3*(3-4). Retrieved June 19, 2001, from http://www.cios.org/getfile/Putnis_v3n393

Rabinow, P. (1986). Representations are social facts: Modernity and post-modernity in anthropology. In J. Clifford & G. E. Marcus (Eds.), *Writing culture: The poetics and politics of ethnography* (pp. 234-261). Berkeley: University of California Press.

Rabinow, P., & Sullivan, W. M. (1987). The interpretive turn: A second look. In P. Rabinow & W. M. Sullivan (Eds.), *Interpretive social science: A second look* (pp. 1-30). Berkeley: University of California Press.

Radway, J. (1984). *Reading the romance: Feminism and the representation of women in popular culture.* Chapel Hill: University of North Carolina Press.

Ratliff, E. (2000, December). O, Engineers! *Wired,* pp. 357-367.

Rawlins, W. K. (1983). Openness as problematic in ongoing friendships: Two conversational dilemmas. *Communication Monographs, 50,* 1-13.

Rawlins, W. K. (1989). A dialectical analysis of the tensions, functions, and strategic challenges of communication in young adult friendships. In J. A. Anderson (Ed.), *Communication Yearbook 12* (pp. 157-189). Newbury Park, CA: Sage.

Rawlins, W. K., & Holl, M. (1987). The communicative achievement of friendship during adolescence: Predicaments of trust and violation. *Western Journal of Speech Communication, 51,* 345-363.

Ray, G. B. (1987). An ethnography of nonverbal communication in an Appalachian community. *Research on Language and Social Interaction, 21,* 171-188.

Reed, D., & Ashmore, M. (2000). The naturally-occurring chat machine. *M/C: A Journal of Media and Culture, 3.* Retrieved December 18, 2001, from http://www.mediaculture.org.au/0008/machine.txt

Reed, L. (2000). Domesticating the personal computer: The mainstreaming of a new technology and the cultural management of a widespread technophobia, 1964-. *Critical Studies in Media Communication, 17,* 159-185.

Reid, E. (1995). Virtual worlds: Culture and imagination. In S. G. Jones (Ed.), *Cybersociety: Computer-mediated communication and community* (pp. 164-183). Thousand Oaks, CA: Sage.

Reid, E. (1996). Informed consent in the study of on-line communities: A reflection on the effects of computed-mediated social research. *The Information Society, 12,* 169-174.

Rheingold, H. (1993). *The virtual community: Homesteading on the electronic frontier.* New York: HarperCollins.

Richardson, L. (1992). The consequences of poetic representation: Writing the other, rewriting the self. In C. Ellis & M. G. Flaherty (Eds.), *Investigating subjectivity: Research on lived experience* (pp. 125-140). Newbury Park, CA: Sage.

Richardson, L. (1994). Nine poems: Marriage and the family. *Journal of Contemporary Ethnography, 23*, 3-13.

Richardson, L. (1995). Narrative and sociology. In J. Van Maanen (Ed.), *Representation in ethnography* (pp. 198-221). Thousand Oaks, CA: Sage.

Richardson, L. (1996). Educational birds. *Journal of Contemporary Ethnography, 25*, 6-15.

Richardson, L. (1997). *Fields of play: Constructing an academic life.* New Brunswick, NJ: Rutgers University Press.

Richardson, L. (2000). Writing: A method of inquiry. In N. K. Denzin & Y. S. Lincoln (Eds.), *Handbook of qualitative research* (2nd ed., pp. 923-948). Thousand Oaks, CA: Sage.

Ricoeur, P. (1977). The model of the text: Meaningful action considered as a text. In F. R. Dallmayr & T. A. McCarthy (Eds.), *Understanding and social inquiry* (pp. 316-334). Notre Dame, IN: University of Notre Dame Press.

Rintel, E. S., Mulholland, J., & Pittam, J. (2001). First things first: Internet Relay Chat openings. *Journal of Computer-Mediated Communication, 6.* Retrieved December 16, 2001, from http://www.ascusc.org/jcmc/vol6/issue3/rintel.html

Robbins, T., Anthony, D., & Curtis, T. E. (1973). The limits of symbolic realism: Problems of empathic field observation in a sectarian context. *Journal for the Scientific Study of Religion, 12*, 259-271.

Rock, P. (1979). *The making of symbolic interactionism.* Totowa, NJ: Rowman & Littlefield.

Rockler, N. (1999). From magic bullets to shooting blanks: Reality criticism and *Beverly Hills, 90210. Western Journal of Communication, 63*, 72-94.

Rodriguez, A. (1996). Objectivity and ethnicity in the production of *Noticiero Univision. Critical Studies in Mass Communication, 13*, 59-81.

Ronai, C. R. (1992). The reflexive self through narrative: A night in the life of an erotic dancer/researcher. In C. Ellis & M. G. Flaherty (Eds.), *Investigating subjectivity: Research on lived experience* (pp. 102-124). Newbury Park, CA: Sage.

Ronai, C. R. (1995). Multiple reflections of child sexual abuse: An argument for a layered account. *Journal of Contemporary Ethnography, 23*, 395-426.

Ronai, C. R. (1996). My mother is mentally retarded. In C. Ellis & A. P. Bochner (Eds.), *Composing ethnography: Alternative forms of qualitative writing* (pp. 109-131). Walnut Creek, CA: AltaMira.

Rosaldo, R. (1987). Where objectivity lies: The rhetoric of anthropology. In J. S. Nelson, A. Megill, & D. McCloskey (Eds.), *The rhetoric of the human sciences: Language and argument in scholarship and public affairs* (pp. 87-110). Madison: University of Wisconsin Press.

Rose, D. (1987). *Black American street life: South Philadelphia 1969-1971.* Philadelphia: University of Pennsylvania Press.

Rosen, M. (1985). Breakfast at Spiro's: Dramaturgy and dominance. *Journal of Management, 11*, 31-48.

Rosson, M. B. (1999). I get by with a little help with my cyber-friends: Sharing stories of good and bad times on the Web. *Journal of Computer-Mediated Communication, 4.* Retrieved December 16, 2001, from http://www.ascusc.org/jcmc/vol4/issue4/rosson.html

Rosteck, T. (1999). Introduction. In T. Rosteck (Ed.), *At the intersection: Cultural studies and rhetorical studies* (pp. 1-23). New York: Guilford.

Rubin, R. B., Rubin, A. M., & Piele, L. J. (1999). *Communication research: Strategies and sources* (5th ed.). Belmont, CA: Wadsworth.

Ruby, J. (Ed.). (1982). *A crack in the mirror: Reflexive perspectives in anthropology.* Philadelphia: University of Pennsylvania Press.

Ruedenberg, L., Danet, B., & Rosenbaum-Tamari, Y. (1995). Virtual virtuosos: Play and performance at the computer keyboard. *Electronic Journal of Communication, 5.* Retrieved December 16, 2001, from http://www.cios.org/getfile/Rueden_V5N495

Ruhleder, K., & Jordan, B. (1997, January 6). *Capturing complex, distributed activities: Video-based interaction analysis as a component of workplace ethnography.* Paper presented at the 1997 IFIP

WG 8.2 Working Conference. Retrieved June 13, 2002, from http://alexia.lis.uiuc.edu/~ruh-leder/publications/97.IFIPWG82.html

Rusted, B. (1995, November 17). *Setting the cat among the pigeons.* Written panel response presented at the Speech Communication Association conference, San Antonio, TX.

Ruud, G. (2000). The symphony: Organizational discourse and the symbolic tensions between artistic and business ideologies. *Journal of Applied Communication Research, 28*(2), 117-143.

Ryan, G. W., & Bernard, H. R. (2000). Data management and analysis methods. In N. K. Denzin & Y. S. Lincoln (Eds.), *Handbook of qualitative research* (2nd ed., pp. 769-802). Thousand Oaks, CA: Sage.

Sabourin, T. C., and Stamp, G. H. (1995). Communication and the experience of dialectical tensions in family life: An examination of abusive and nonabusive families. *Communication Monographs, 62*(3), 213-242.

Sacks, H. (1963). Sociological description. *Berkeley Journal of Sociology, 8,* 1-16.

Sacks, H., Schegloff, E., & Jefferson, G. (1974). A simplest systematics for the organization of turn-taking for conversation. *Language, 50,* 696-735.

Saenz, M. (1997). The deployment of culture. *Journal of Communication Inquiry, 21,* 6-22.

Saferstein, B. (1991, August). *Constructing and constraining television violence.* Paper presented at the annual meeting of the American Sociological Association, Cincinnati, OH.

Saferstein, B. (1995). *Focusing opinions: Conversation, authority, and the (re)construction of knowledge.* Paper presented at the annual meeting of the American Sociological Association, Washington, DC.

Said, E. W. (1989). Representing the colonized: Anthropology's interlocutors. *Critical Inquiry, 15,* 205-225.

Sanday, P. R. (1983). The ethnographic paradigm(s). In J. Van Maanen (Ed.), *Qualitative methodology* (pp. 19-36). Beverly Hills, CA: Sage.

Sanjek, R. (Ed.). (1990a). *Fieldnotes: The makings of anthropology.* Ithaca, NY: Cornell University Press.

Sanjek, R. (1990b). A vocabulary for fieldnotes. In R. Sanjek (Ed.), *Fieldnotes: The makings of anthropology* (pp. 92-121). Ithaca, NY: Cornell University Press.

Sass, J. S. (2000). Emotional labor as cultural performance: The communication of caregiving in a nonprofit nursing home. *Western Journal of Communication, 64,* 330-358.

Schatzman, L., & Strauss, A. L. (1973). *Field research: Strategies for a natural sociology.* Englewood Cliffs, NJ: Prentice Hall.

Schegloff, E. (1968). Sequencing in conversational openings. *American Anthropologist, 70,* 1075-1095.

Scheibel, D. (1992). Faking identity in clubland: The communicative performance of "fake ID." *Text and Performance Quarterly, 12,* 160-175.

Scheibel, D. (1994). Graffiti and "film school" culture: Displaying alienation. *Communication Monographs, 61,* 1-18.

Schely-Newman, E. (1995). Sweeter than honey: Discourse of reproduction among North-African Israeli women. *Text and Performance Quarterly, 15,* 175-188.

Schutz, A. (1944). The stranger: An essay in social psychology. *American Journal of Sociology, 49,* 499-507.

Schutz, A. (1962). On multiple realities. In M. Natanson (Ed.), *Collected papers I: The problem of social reality* (pp. 207-259). The Hague, The Netherlands: Martinus Nijhoff.

Schutz, A. (1967). *The phenomenology of the social world.* Evanston, IL: Northwestern University Press.

Schwandt, T. A. (1989). Solutions to the paradigm conflict: Coping with uncertainty. *Journal of Contemporary Ethnography, 17,* 379-407.

Schwandt, T. A. (1997). *Qualitative inquiry: A dictionary of terms.* Thousand Oaks, CA: Sage.

Schwandt, T. A. (2000). Three epistemological stances for qualitative inquiry: Interpretivism, hermeneutics, and social constructionism. In N. K. Denzin & Y. S. Lincoln (Eds.), *Handbook of qualitative research* (pp. 189-214). Thousand Oaks, CA: Sage.

Schwartz, M. S., & Schwartz, C. G. (1955). Problems in participant observation. *American Journal of Sociology, 60,* 343-354.

Schwartzman, H. (1993). *Ethnography in organizations.* Newbury Park, CA: Sage.

Scodari, C., & Felder, J. L. (2000). Creating a pocket universe: "Shippers," fan fiction, and *The X-Files* online. *Communication Studies, 51,* 238-257.

Scott, M. B., & Lyman, S. M. (1968). Accounts. *American Sociological Review, 33*, 46-62.

Seibold, D. (1995). *Theoria* and *praxis*: Means and ends in applied communication research. In K. N. Cissna (Ed.), *Applied communication in the 21st century* (pp. 23-38). Mahwah, NJ: Lawrence Erlbaum.

Shalin, D. N. (1986). Pragmatism and social interactionism. *American Sociological Review, 51*, 9-29.

Shapiro, M. J. (1988). *The politics of representation: Writing practices in biography, photography, and policy analysis.* Madison: University of Wisconsin Press.

Sharf, B. F. (1999). Beyond netiquette: The ethics of doing naturalistic discourse research on the Internet. In S. Jones (Ed.), *Doing Internet research* (pp. 243-256). Thousand Oaks, CA: Sage.

Sharf, B. F., & Street, R. L. (1997). The patient as a central construct: Shifting the emphasis. *Health Communication, 9*(1), 1-11.

Shelton, A. (1995). The man at the end of the machine. *Symbolic Interaction, 18*, 505-518.

Sheriff, R. E. (2000). Exposing silence as cultural censorship: A Brazilian case. *American Anthropologist, 102*(1), 114-132.

Shields, D. C. (2000). Symbolic convergence and special communication theories: Sensing and examining dis/enchantment with the theoretical robustness of critical autoethnography. *Communication Monographs, 67*, 392-421.

Shields, V. R., & Dervin, B. (1993). Sense-making in feminist social science research: A call to enlarge the methodological options of feminist studies. *Women's Studies International Forum, 16*, 65-81.

Shimanoff, S. (1980). *Communication rules.* Beverly Hills, CA: Sage.

Sholle, D. J. (1988). Critical studies: From the theory of ideology to power/knowledge. *Critical Studies in Mass Communication, 5*, 16-41.

Shome, R. (1996). Postcolonialist interventions in the rhetorical canon: An "other" view. *Communication Theory, 6*, 40-59.

Shue, L. L., & Beck, C. S. (2001). Stepping out of bounds: Performing feminist pedagogy within a dance education community. *Communication Education, 50*, 125-143.

Shulman, D. (1994). Dirty data and investigative methods: Some lessons from private detective work. *Journal of Contemporary Ethnography, 23*, 214-253.

Siegel, T. (Co-Producer and Director), & Conquergood, D. (Co-Producer). (1985). *Between two worlds: The Hmong shaman in America* [Film]. (Available from Filmmakers Library, 124 East 40th Street, New York, NY 10016; 212-808-4980.)

Siegel, T. (Co-Producer), & Conquergood, D. (Co-Producer). (1990). *Hearts broken in half: Chicago's street gangs* [Film]. (Available from FilmmakersLibrary, 124 East 40th Street, New York, NY 10016; 212-808-4980.)

Sigman, S. J. (1980). On communication rules from a social perspective. *Human Communication Research, 7*, 37-51.

Sigman, S. J. (1986). Adjustment to the nursing home as a social interaction accomplishment. *Journal of Applied Communication Research, 14*, 37-58.

Sigman, S. J. (1987). *A perspective on social communication.* Lexington, MA: Lexington.

Silverman, D. (1985). *Qualitative methodology and sociology.* London: Gower.

Silverman, D. (2000). Analyzing text and talk. In N. K. Denzin & Y. S. Lincoln (Eds.), *Handbook of qualitative research* (2nd ed., pp. 821-834). Thousand Oaks, CA: Sage.

Slack, J. D. (1989). Contextualizing technology. In B. Dervin, L. Grossberg, B. O'Keefe, & E. Wartella (Eds.), *Rethinking communication: Vol. 2. Paradigm exemplars* (pp. 329-345). Newbury Park, CA: Sage.

Slack, J. D., & Semati, M. M. (1997). Intellectual and political hygiene: The "Sokal affair". *Critical Studies in Mass Communication, 14*, 201-227.

Smircich, L., & Calas, M. (1987). Organizational culture: A critical assessment. In F. Jablin (Ed.), *Handbook of organizational communication* (pp. 228-263). Newbury Park, CA: Sage.

Smith, B. H. (1983). Contingencies of value. *Critical Inquiry, 10*, 1-35.

Smith, C., & Short, P. M. (2001). Integrating technology to improve the efficiency of qualitative data analysis—A note on methods. *Qualitative Sociology, 24*, 401-407.

Smith, S. M. (1998). On the pleasures of ruined pictures. In A. Banks & S. Banks (Eds.), *Fiction and social research: By ice or fire* (pp. 179-194). Walnut Creek, CA: AltaMira.

Smyres, K. M. (1999). Virtual corporeality: Adolescent girls and their bodies in cyberspace. *Cybersociology, 6*. Retrieved December 16, 2001, from http://www.socio.demon.co.uk/magazine/6/smyres.html

Snow, D. A. (1980). The disengagement process: A neglected problem in participant-observation research. *Qualitative Sociology, 3,* 100-122.

Snow, D. A., Benford, R. D., & Anderson, L. (1986). Fieldwork roles and informational yield. *Urban Life, 14,* 377-408.

Soukup, C. (2000). Building a theory of multi-media CMC. *New Media & Society, 2,* 407-425.

Speier, M. (1973). *How to observe face-to-face communication: A sociological introduction.* Pacific Palisades, CA: Goodyear.

Spencer, J. W. (1994). Mutual relevance of ethnography and discourse. *Journal of Contemporary Ethnography, 23,* 267-279.

Spiggle, S. (1994). Analysis and interpretation of qualitative data in consumer research. *Journal of Consumer Research, 21,* 491-503.

Spradley, J. P. (1979). *The ethnographic interview.* New York: Holt, Rinehart & Winston.

Spradley, J. P. (1980). *Participant observation.* New York: Holt, Rinehart & Winston.

Spradley, J. P., & McCurdy, D. W. (1972). *The cultural experience: Ethnography in complex society.* Chicago: Science Research Associates.

St.Pierre, E. A. (1999). The work of response in ethnography. *Journal of Contemporary Ethnography, 28,* 266-287.

Stacey, J. (1988). Can there be a feminist ethnography? *Women's Studies International Forum, 11,* 21-27.

Stamp, G. H. (1999). A qualitatively constructed interpersonal communication model: A grounded theory analysis. *Human Communication Research, 4,* 531-547.

Star, S. L. (1999). The ethnography of infrastructure. *American Behavioral Scientist, 43,* 377-391.

Starosta, W. J., & Hannon, S. W. (1997). The multilexicality of the Mohawk incident in Oka, Quebec as reflected in the recounted narratives of members of different receiving communities. In A. Gonzalez & D. V. Tanno (Eds.), *Politics, communication, and culture: International and intercultural communication annual* (Vol. 20, pp. 141-165). Thousand Oaks, CA: Sage.

Steele, J. (1999). Teenage sexuality and media practice: Factoring in the influences of family, friends, and school. *Journal of Sex Research, 36,* 331-341.

Sterne, J. (1999). Thinking the Internet: Cultural studies versus the millennium. In S. Jones (Ed.), *Doing Internet research* (pp. 257-288). Thousand Oaks, CA: Sage.

Stewart, J., & Philipsen, G. (1984). Communication as situated accomplishment: The cases of hermeneutics and ethnography. In B. Dervin & M. J. Voigt (Eds.), *Progress in communication sciences* (Vol. 5, pp. 179-217). Norwood, NJ: Ablex.

Stoller, P. (1989). *The taste of ethnographic things.* Philadelphia: University of Pennsylvania Press.

Strate, L. (1999). The varieties of cyberspace: Problems in definition and delimitation. *Western Journal of Communication, 63,* 382-412.

Strauss, A. L., & Corbin, J. (1990). *Basics of qualitative research.* Newbury Park, CA: Sage.

Strauss, A. L. (1987). *Qualitative analysis for social scientists.* Cambridge, UK: Cambridge University Press.

Strinati, D. (1995). *An introduction to theories of popular culture.* London: Routledge.

Strine, M. S. (1991). Critical theory and "organic" intellectuals: Reframing the work of cultural critique. *Communication Monographs, 58,* 195-201.

Strine, M. S. (1997). Deconstructing identity in/and difference: Voices "under erasure." *Western Journal of Communication, 61,* 448-459.

Strine, M. S., & Pacanowsky, M. E. (1985). How to read interpretive accounts of organizational life: Narrative bases of textual authority. *Southern Speech Communication Journal, 50,* 283-297.

Stromer-Galley, J., & Schiappa, E. (1998). The argumentative burdens of audience conjectures: Audience research in popular culture criticism. *Communication Theory, 8*(1), 27-62.

Sunderland, P. L. (1999). Fieldwork and the phone. *Anthropology Quarterly, 72*(3), 105-117.

Taylor, B. C. (1997). Home zero: Images of home and field in nuclear-critical studies. *Western Journal of Communication, 61,* 209-234.

Taylor, B. C. (1999). Browsing the culture: Membership and intertextuality at a Mormon bookstore. *Studies in Cultures, Organizations, and Societies, 5,* 61-95.

Taylor, B. C., & Trujillo, N. (2001). Issues in qualitative research. In F. Jablin and L. Putnam (Eds.), *The new handbook of organizational communication* (pp. 161-194). Thousand Oaks, CA: Sage.

Taylor, C. (1977). Interpretation and the sciences of man. In F. R. Dallmayr & T. A. McCarthy (Eds.), *Understanding and social inquiry* (pp. 101-131). Notre Dame, IN: University of Notre Dame Press.

Tedlock, B. (1991). From participant observation to the observation of participation: The emergence of narrative ethnography. *Journal of Anthropological Research, 47,* 69-94.

Tesch, R. (1990). *Qualitative research: Analysis types and software tools.* New York: Falmer.

Thomas, J. (1993). *Doing critical ethnography.* Newbury Park, CA: Sage.

Thomas, J. (1996). Introduction: A debate about the ethics of fair practices for collecting social science data in cyberspace. *The Information Society, 12,* 107-118.

Thompson, J. B. (1990). *Ideology and modern culture.* Stanford, CA: Stanford University Press.

Thornton, A., Freedman, D. S., & Camburn, D. (1982). Obtaining respondent cooperation in family panel studies. *Sociological Methods & Research, 11,* 33-51.

Thornton, S. (1999). An academic Alice in adland: Ethnography and the commercial world. *Critical Quarterly, 41,* 54-68.

Tillman-Healy, L. M. (1996). A secret life in a culture of thinness: Reflections on body, food, and bulimia. In C. Ellis & A. P. Bochner (Eds.), *Composing ethnography: Alternative forms of qualitative writing* (pp. 76-108). Walnut Creek, CA: AltaMira.

Titscher, S., Meyer, M., Wodak, R., & Vetter, E. (2000). *Methods of text and discourse analysis.* Thousand Oaks, CA: Sage.

Tong, T. (1989). *Feminist thought: A comprehensive introduction.* Boulder, CO: Westview.

Townsley, N. C., & Geist, P. (2000). The discursive enactment of hegemony: Sexual harassment and academic organizing. *Western Journal of Communication, 64,* 190-217.

Tracy, K. (2001). Discourse analysis in Communication. In D. Schiffrin, D. Tannen, & H. Hamilton (Eds.), *Handbook of discourse analysis* (pp. 725-749). Malden, MA: Blackwell.

Tracy, K., & Baratz, S. (1993). Intellectual discussion in the academy as situated discourse. *Communication Monographs, 60,* 300-320.

Tracy, K., & Gallois, C. (Eds.). (1997). Qualitative contributions to empirical research [Special issue]. *Human Communication Research, 23*(4), 451-615.

Tracy, S. J., & Tracy, K. (1998). Emotion labor at 911: A case study and theoretical critique. *Journal of Applied Communication Research, 26,* 390-411.

Tripp, D. H. (1983). Co-authorship and negotiation: The interview as an act of creation. *Interchange, 14*(3), 32-45.

Trost, J. E. (1986). Statistically nonrepresentative stratified sampling: A sampling technique for qualitative studies. *Qualitative Sociology, 9,* 54-57.

Trujillo, N. (1993). Interpreting November 22: A critical ethnography of an assasination site. *Quarterly Journal of Speech, 79,* 447-466.

Trujillo, N., & Dionisopoulos, G. (1987). Cop talk, police stories, and the social construction of organizational drama. *Central States Speech Journal, 38,* 196-209.

Tuchman, G. (1991). Qualitative methods in the study of news. In K. B. Jensen & N. W. Jankowski (Eds.), *A handbook of qualitative methodologies for mass communication research* (pp. 79-92). London: Routledge.

Tudor, A. (1999). *Decoding culture.* Thousand Oaks, CA: Sage.

Turkle, S. (1984). *The second self: Computers and the human spirit.* London: Granada.

Turkle, S. (1995). *Life on the screen: Identity in the age of the Internet.* New York: Simon & Schuster.

Turner, B. A. (1988). Connoisseurship in the study of organizational cultures. In A. Bryman (Ed.), *Doing research in organizations* (pp. 108-122). London: Routledge.

Turner, V. (1957). *Schism and continuity in an African society.* Manchester, UK: University of Manchester Press.

Tyler, S. (1986). Post-modern ethnography: From document of the occult to occult document. In J. Clifford & G. E. Marcus (Eds.), *Writing culture: The poetics and politics of ethnography* (pp. 122-140). Berkeley: University of California Press.

Valentine, K. B., & Matsumoto, G. (2001). Cultural performance analysis spheres: An integrated ethnographic methodology. *Field Methods, 13*(1), 68-87.

Van Maanen, J. (1979). The fact of fiction in organizational ethnography. *Administrative Science Quarterly, 24,* 535-550.

Van Maanen, J. (1983). Reclaiming qualitative methods for organizational research: A preface. In J. Van Maanen (Ed.), *Qualitative methodology* (pp. 9-18). Beverly Hills, CA: Sage.

Van Maanen, J. (1988). *Tales of the field: On writing ethnography.* Chicago: University of Chicago Press.

Van Maanen, J. (1995a). An end to innocence: The ethnography of ethnography. In J. Van Maanen (Ed.), *Representation in ethnography* (pp. 1-35). Thousand Oaks, CA: Sage.

Van Maanen, J. (1995b). Trade secrets: On writing ethnography. In R. H. Brown (Ed.), *Postmodern representations: Truth, power, and mimesis in the human sciences and public culture* (pp. 60-79). Urbana: University of Illinois Press.

Vanderford, M., Jenks, E., & Sharf, B. (1997). Exploring patients' experiences as a primary source of meaning. *Health Communication, 9*(1), 13-26.

Vidich, A. J., & Lyman, S. M. (2000). Qualitative methods: Their history in sociology and anthropology. In N. K. Denzin & Y. S. Lincoln (Eds.), *Handbook of qualitative research* (2nd ed., pp. 37-84). Thousand Oaks, CA: Sage.

Walther, J. (1996). Computer-mediated communication: Impersonal, interpersonal, and hyperpersonal interaction. *Communication Research, 23,* 3-43.

Warren, C. A. B. (1988). *Gender issues in field research.* Newbury Park, CA: Sage.

Warren, J. T. (2001). Doing whiteness: On the performative dimensions of race in the classroom. *Communication Education, 50,* 91-108.

Wartella, E. (1987). Commentary on qualitative research and children's mediated communication. In T. R. Lindlof (Ed.), *Natural audiences: Qualitative research of media uses and effects* (pp. 109-118). Norwood, NJ: Ablex.

Waskul, D., Douglass, M., & Edgley, C. (2000). Cybersex: Outercourse and the enselfment of the body. *Symbolic Interaction, 23,* 375-397.

Wax, M. L. (1972). Tenting with Malinowski. *American Sociological Review, 37,* 1-13.

Wax, R. H. (1971). *Doing fieldwork: Warnings and advice.* Chicago: University of Chicago Press.

Webb, E. J., Campbell, D. T., Schwartz, R. D., & Sechrest, L. (1966). *Unobtrusive measures: Nonreactive research in the social sciences.* Chicago: Rand McNally.

Weber, L. R., Miracle, A., & Skehan, T. (1994). Interviewing early adolescents: Some methodological considerations. *Human Organization, 53,* 42-47.

Weber, M. (1968). *Economy and society.* New York: Bedminster.

Weick, D. E., & Roberts, K. H. (1993). Collective mind in organizations: Heedful interrelating on flight decks. *Administrative Science Quarterly, 38,* 357-381.

Weick, K. (1985). Systematic observation methods. In G. Lindzey & E. Aronson (Eds.), *Handbook of social psychology: Vol 1. Theory and method* (3rd ed., pp. 567-634). New York: Random House.

Weil, M. (1989). Research on vulnerable populations. *Journal of Applied Behavioral Science, 25,* 419-437.

Weiss, R. S. (1994). *Learning from strangers: The art and method of qualitative interview studies.* New York: Free Press.

Weitzman, E. A. (2000). Software and qualitative research. In N. K. Denzin & Y. S. Lincoln (Eds.), *Handbook of qualitative research* (2nd ed., pp. 803-820). Thousand Oaks, CA: Sage.

Weitzman, E. A., & Miles, M. B. (1995). *Computer programs for qualitative data analysis.* Thousand Oaks, CA: Sage.

Welker, L. S., & Goodall, H. L. (1997). Representation, interpretation, and performance: Opening the text of *Casing a Promised Land. Text and Performance Quarterly, 17,* 109-122.

Wellman, D. (1994). Constituting ethnographic authority: The work process of field research. *Cultural Studies, 8,* 569-583.

Wendt, R. F. (1995). Women in positions of service: The politicized body. *Communication Studies, 46* (3-4), 276-296.

Wendt, R. F. (2001). *The paradox of empowerment: Suspended power and the possibility of resistance.* Westport, CT: Praeger.

West, J. T. (1993). Ethnography and ideology: The politics of cultural representation. *Western Journal of Communication, 57,* 209-220.

Weston, C., Gandell, T., Beauchamp, J., McAlpine, L., Wiseman, C., & Beauchamp, C. (2001). Analyzing interview data: The development and evolution of a coding system. *Qualitative Sociology, 24,* 381-400.

White, G. E., & Thomson, A. N. (1995). Anonymized focus groups as a research tool for health professionals. *Qualitative Health Research, 5,* 256-262.

Whitten, P., Sypher, B. D., & Patterson, J. D. (2000). Transcending the technology of telemedicine: An analysis of telemedicine in North Carolina. *Health Communication, 12*(2), 109-135.

Whyte, W. F. (1943). *Street corner society.* Chicago: University of Chicago Press.

Whyte. W. F. (1982). Interviewing in field research. In R. G. Burgess (Ed.), *Field research: A source book and field manual* (pp. 111-122). London: George Allen & Unwin.

Williams, D. E. (1988). Rhetorically acculturating the computer as a given of society. *American Behavioral Scientist, 32,* 208-222.

Willis, P. (1977). *Learning to labour: How working class kids get working class jobs.* London: Saxon House.

Winch, P. (1958). *The idea of a social science and its relation to philosophy.* London: Routledge & Kegan Paul.

Wolcott, H. F. (1999). *Ethnography: A way of seeing.* Walnut Creek, CA: AltaMira.

Wolcott, H. F. (2001). *Writing up qualitative research.* Thousand Oaks, CA: Sage.

Wood, A. F., & Smith, M. J. (2001). *Online communication: Linking technology, identity, and culture.* Mahwah, NJ: Lawrence Erlbaum.

Workman, J. P. (1995). Using electronic media to support fieldwork in a corporate setting. In R. Hertz & J. B. Imber (Eds.), *Studying elites using qualitative methods* (pp. 65-71). Thousand Oaks, CA: Sage.

Yount, K. R. (1991). Ladies, flirts, and tomboys: Strategies for managing sexual harrassment in an underground coal mine. *Journal of Contemporary Ethnography, 19,* 396-422.

Zelditch., M., Jr. (1962). Some methodological problems of field studies. In G. J. McCall & J. L. Simmons (Eds.), *Issues in participant observation* (pp. 5-19). Reading, MA: Addison-Wesley.

Zimmerman, D. H., & Wieder, L. (1977). The diary: Diary-interview method. *Urban Life, 5,* 479-498.

Zuboff, S. (1988). *In the age of the smart machine: The future of work and power.* New York: Basic Books.

Zurawski, N. (1999). Among the Internauts: Notes from the cyberfield. *Cybersociology, 6.* Retrieved December 16, 2001, from http://www.socio.demon.co.uk/magazine/6/zurawski.html

Name Index

Subject Index

About the Authors

Thomas R. Lindlof is a Professor in the School of Journalism and Telecommunications at the University of Kentucky in Lexington. He specializes in the cultural analysis of mediated communication, audience theory and research, social uses of communication technologies, and interpretive research methods. His research has been published in many communication journals and edited volumes. He edited the books *Natural Audiences* and *Constructing The Self in a Mediated World,* and is the author of the first edition of *Qualitative Communication Research Methods.* He received his B.A. from the University of Florida, and his M.A. and Ph.D. from the University of Texas at Austin. His current research involves studies of the cultural politics of transgressive media and the organizational practices and producers of reality simulations. During 2001 to 2004, he is the editor of the *Journal of Broadcasting & Electronic Media.*

Bryan C. Taylor is an Associate Professor at the University of Colorado–Boulder who specializes in qualitative methods and cultural, organizational, and technology studies. His qualitative research has been published in *Communication Research;* the *Journal of Applied Communication Research;* the *Journal of Contemporary Ethnography;* the *Journal of Organizational Change Management; Studies in Cultures, Organizations, and Societies;* and the *Western Journal of Communication.* He received his B.A. from the University of Massachusetts–Amherst, and his M.A. and Ph.D. from the University of Utah. Prior to joining the University of Colorado–Boulder faculty he served on the faculty at Texas A&M University. His principal research program involves studies of nuclear and (post-) Cold War communication.